# Children's Psychological Testing

This book is printed on recycled paper.

# Children's Psychological Testing
## A Guide for Nonpsychologists
### *Third Edition*

by

**David L. Wodrich, Ph.D.**

**Phoenix Children's Hospital**
**Phoenix, Arizona**

Baltimore • London • Toronto • Sydney

**Paul H. Brookes Publishing Co.**
Post Office Box 10624
Baltimore, Maryland 21285-0624

www.brookespublishing.com



Typeset by PRO-Image Corporation, York, Pennsylvania.
Manufactured in the United States of America by
The Maple Press Company, York, Pennsylvania.

First printing, February 1997.
Second printing, July 1999.

**Library of Congress Cataloging-in-Publication Data**

Wodrich, David L., 1948–
Children's psychological testing : a guide for nonpsychologists / by David L. Wodrich.—3rd ed.
p. cm.
Includes bibliographical references (p. ) and index.
ISBN 1-55766-277-0 (pbk.)
1. Psychological tests for children. I. Title.
BF722.W63 1997
155.4'028'7—dc20 96-38720
CIP

British Library Cataloguing in Publication data are available from the British Library.

# Contents

# List of Tables

# List of Figures

# About the Author

David L. Wodrich, Ph.D., ABPP, is Clinical Director of Child Psychology at Phoenix Children's Hospital. He has been a regular user of psychological tests for children for more than 20 years, including using standardized instruments to address learning and developmental problems, emotional adjustment, and personality factors, and, after completing training in neuropsychology, to determine the neuropsychological status of children with brain impairments. He has worked in school, clinic, and hospital settings through which he has developed an appreciation of not only the characteristics of various psychological tests but also their limitations and how to use them best to help children.

Dr. Wodrich is a diplomate of the American Board of Professional Psychology; fellow of the American Academy of School Psychology; past president of the Arizona Psychological Association; and recipient of a 1992 award for "Distinguished Contribution to the Practice of Psychology" from the Arizona Psychological Association. In addition to being a member of the teaching faculty at Phoenix Children's Hospital, he is an adjunct faculty member in the Department of Education in Psychology at Arizona State University. He is a frequent presenter to professional groups on the topic of psychological assessment of children.

# Preface

The third edition of this book was prompted by changes not only in the array of test instruments that recently have become available but also by the changes in the culture and context in which the process of testing occurs. Schools have undergone rapid changes in the past few years—there has been significant downsizing in some places, some services have been curtailed, and teachers and administrators find their roles in flux. Revisions have broadened the Individuals with Disabilities Education Act (IDEA)—the special education law—to mandate new categories of exceptionalities: autism and traumatic brain injury. The number of children diagnosed with attention-deficit/hyperactivity disorder has expanded exponentially during the 1990s, and parents and teachers have become concerned about the proper identification of such students and how to help them once they are identified. These events occurred simultaneously with intensified efforts to include students with disabilities in general classrooms and to diminish practices that exclude and stigmatize. All of these factors have accentuated the already substantial need for good psychological and psychoeducational testing to help both psychologists and nonpsychologists understand the strengths and weaknesses of children and adolescents in schools. As the decision-making process becomes more widely shared among educational professionals, it is increasingly incumbent on administrators, teachers, and allied educational professionals to comprehend the uses, advantages, and limitations of children's psychological testing.

Changes are just as widespread in the health care and social services venues. More and more babies are born without the benefits of adequate prenatal care and nourishment. In some areas, hospitals are overrun with babies born with the effects of exposure to addictive and pernicious substances such as cocaine. Likewise, increasing numbers of children are deemed to be at risk for learning and developmental problems based on the impoverished circumstances in which they are born and are reared. If the needs of these children are to be understood—and correspondingly, their lives improved—it is essential that accurate and thorough measurement be made of their overall status and of their unique patterns and abilities. It is equally important that those who are in a position to help them—parents, health care providers, early childhood educators, social services personnel—understand the uses of psychological testing.

The 1990s have been termed the Decade of the Brain, a designation prompted in part by the explosion in knowledge about the brain's and central nervous system's functioning. Reports appear almost daily in the popular press describing what has been learned about various anatomical brain structures, about the role on learning or behavior of this or that neurotransmitter, or about how an ever-lengthening list of diseases affects the brain and the psychological functions it performs. Although many of these advances are at the biological level, it is at the crucial human performance level that scientists must invariably turn to quantified measures of mental functioning. That is, scientists must turn to psychological tests if the practical, real-world manifestations of findings about the brain's functions are to be understood.

In this third edition of *Children's Psychological Testing: A Guide for Nonpsychologists,* broad consideration has been given to the use of neuropsychological testing and to the use of psychological and educational tests related to the new categories under IDEA, as well as to the most topical diagnostic entity of the 1990s: attention-deficit/hyperactivity disorder. Furthermore, the reader will find coverage of tests—especially tests of memory and executive function—that were either not yet developed at the time of the previous editions or lacked a sufficient theoretical basis to make their discussion meaningful to the consumer of test information.

Similar to the first and second editions, the third is designed to provide nonpsychologists with an overview of children's psychological testing. The book encompasses changes in the uses of psychological tests with children, just as it includes descriptions of the individual tests themselves. In this regard, the third edition mirrors the first two; it emphasizes the testing process rather than the tests alone. Therefore, the emphasis is placed on understanding the circumstances under which tests can be used, comprehending how tests help to answer practical questions, learning tests' advantages and limitations, and—most important—understanding how tests can be used to help children. The book is foremost designed to help readers become informed consumers of psychological testing. It is arranged to provide a general overview of measurement principles in Chapter 1 and to allow each chapter to stand alone, requiring no foundation from previous chapters.

As before, this edition is not a scholarly review of the literature nor is it a "how-to guide" for performing psychological testing of children, and it is not an exhaustive cataloging of all the psychological tests that the consumer may encounter. Instead, an effort has been made to sample the most commonly used tests and to give a flavor of the types of tests that currently are used. This fact should make the volume useful even if a specific title of interest is not included. Many tests not discussed in the body of the text are summarized in the Appendix. New to this edition is a Glossary of frequently used terms. Every effort has been made to minimize the jargon that so frequently accompanies the use of psychological testing and to include practical examples so that the text is useful for professionals from a variety of disciplines. Readers should note that the histories and descriptions of children in the case illustrations included throughout the book are fictitious. These illustrations have been designed to illuminate important points about children's learning, development, and emotional adjustment. Some actual test responses, however, have been used within these studies.

# Acknowledgments

I want specifically to thank three individuals who helped broaden my horizons by teaching me about neuropsychology: neuropsychologists Dr. H. Daniel Blackwood and Dr. Marc S. Walter and neurologist Dr. Allen M. Kaplan. Each helped to guide me during my neuropsychology training at Phoenix Children's Hospital; their patience and generosity of time is greatly appreciated. To the extent that ideas related to neuropsychology in this book are clear and cogent, they should be credited. I also want to thank my colleagues at Phoenix Children's Hospital with whom I work each day, especially my friends in psychology, psychiatry, and neurology: Dr. Thomas DiBartolomeo; Dr. Karlsson Roth; Dr. Saunder Bernes, who again helped by reading chapter drafts of this book; Dr. Ronald Hadden; Dr. Eric Benjamin; and Dr. Randall Ricardi.

The finest of Tempe Elementary School District also reviewed portions of this book: my psychology colleague and friend Dr. Ronald Davis of the Psychology Department; and my dear wife, Susan Wodrich, of the Special Education Department. There is no way they could say no to me.

*This book is dedicated to my children:*

*Matthew Davisson Wodrich and Jill Anne Wodrich*

## CHAPTER ONE

# Principles of Psychological Testing

Mental measurement, or psychological testing, is an area filled with unique terms and concepts; some examples include *T-scores* and *z-scores, reliability coefficients,* and *concurrent validity.* Tests themselves often have fancy names and make impressive claims to measure traits. Test findings are laced with numbers and are sometimes summarized in a manner similar to "This subtest was 8, that subtest was 11, the Full Scale IQ was 83, and the percentile rank was 13." Using these test scores, psychologists seem to claim access to information unavailable to most people. How do these tests work?

This chapter attempts to help you understand how the tests work by revealing some of the logic behind and principles of psychological testing. The uniqueness of mental measurement, or psychological tests, is based on several key concepts and principles. Among these are uniform administration and objective scoring, quantification of results, the use of norm referencing and derived scores, and two concepts called *reliability* and *validity.* Although some of these concepts can be complex, for the purposes of this book an effort has been made to simplify them and to keep discussion brief. By developing an understanding of these concepts, readers will greatly enhance their understanding of how psychological tests can be used.

## UNIFORMITY AND OBJECTIVITY

Most psychological tests have uniform administration and objective scoring; most informal procedures do not. (Some authorities, such as Cronbach, 1984, refer to this uniformity and objectivity as standardization.) Standardized IQ (intelligence quotient) tests are examples of psychological tests; they require exacting item presentation and careful adherence to objective scoring criteria. One of these IQ tests, the Wechsler Intelligence Scale for Children–III (Wechsler, 1991), is so refined that its test manual specifies how much clarification is permitted when subjects give hazy answers to verbal questions and how to score even minor errors made by children on block construction tasks. Proficiency in administering and scoring the Wechsler scales requires a semester-long graduate course.

Such uniformity and objectivity contrast sharply with the informal procedures nonpsychologists frequently use to measure development. For instance, a pediatrician may utilize what he or she views as a fairly standard office procedure for assessing the development of children who have potential delays. All children may be asked to explain what some words mean, to identify some colors, and to draw some simple shapes. The pediatrician may have developed a personal and subjective "feel" for "average" performance at various ages. While trying to maintain consistency, the pediatrician may ask one child what "dog," "cat," and "donkey" are but ask a second child about "doggy," "kitty," and "donkey." A reluctant child may be encouraged to respond with, "You know, a doggy—bow-wow." One child may be asked to point out things in the room that are "red," "blue," "green," and "yellow," but another child may arrive on a day when no blue objects are available and so may be asked to identify an orange object instead. Other minor inconsistencies may occur on drawing tasks. Assuming that through practice the pediatrician had developed a reasonable set of age standards for development, then his or her procedures would probably be adequate to pick out most gross developmental delays, but many mild delays might be missed. In contrast, a more uniform, objective procedure would potentially have the advantage of identifying almost all gross delays and most mild delays as well.

The pediatrician's informal method described above has limitations because subtle delays cannot be detected with informal procedures. The informal diagnostician cannot know whether small observed differences are the result of variations in administration and scoring or of real differences in a child's development. Perhaps the extra encouragement ("bow-wow") given to the reluctant child represents an important advantage for that child and a disadvantage for another child. In contrast, the psychologist using formal testing with virtually identical administration and scoring can be fairly confident that even small observed differences reflect variations in subjects' development. In psychometric terms, informal techniques contain much greater measurement "error" than do formal, standardized techniques.

## QUANTIFIABILITY

Psychological tests are generally *quantifiable;* that is, they yield numerical scores. Measurement has been defined as the systematic assignment of numbers to individuals using controlled, prescribed, and repeatable procedures (Allen & Yen, 1979). At the simplest level, this may be the tabulation of the number of items correct, which simply is called the *raw score.* Such tabulation is easy when tests consist of objective pass–fail items, but psychologists go further and strive to quantify what appear to be inherently nonquantifiable tests. An example is the Bender Visual Motor Gestalt Test (Bender, 1946) seen in Figure 1.1. If any test seems nonquantifiable, the Bender Gestalt test does. The test consists of nine geometric designs that are copied by a child onto a blank page. The intent is to measure visual fine-motor maturity. Traditionally, without a quantifiable scoring system available, psychologists evaluated drawings subjectively for the general quality of the reproductions. A major advance occurred when psychologist Elizabeth Koppitz (1963) developed a quantifiable system that allowed each protocol to be scored quantitatively (and objectively) for 27 possible errors. Why is quantification such an advantage? There are two reasons. First, numbers provide a more precise description than verbal statements, which leads to better communication. A description of a Bender Gestalt protocol with eight errors tells the trained diagnostician more about the appearance of that protocol than simply saying that the Bender drawings were rotated, fragmented, and poorly drawn. Second, and more important, numerical scores can be manipulated arithmetically to allow even better communication, as seen below.

To the casual observer, objectivity and quantification are the only differences between formal psychological testing and informal assessment. Certainly it is easy to see that the psychologist rigidly administers each item in exactly the same fashion and ends up with numbers, whereas the informal diagnostician does not. Objectivity and quantification are, however, merely the most obvious, rather than the most important, advantages of psychological testing. The real power of psychological testing comes from comparison with a norm group.

## NORMATIVE COMPARISON AND DERIVED SCORES

Standardized psychological tests undergo a research and development phase before they are released for clinical use. As part of this phase, a prospective test is administered to many children. The scores from

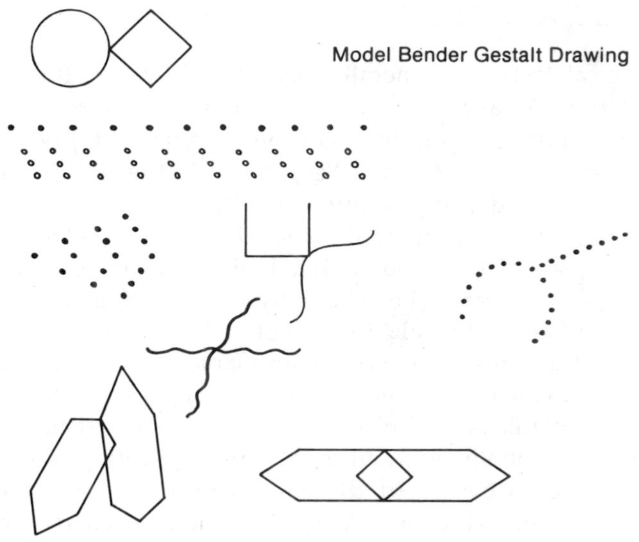


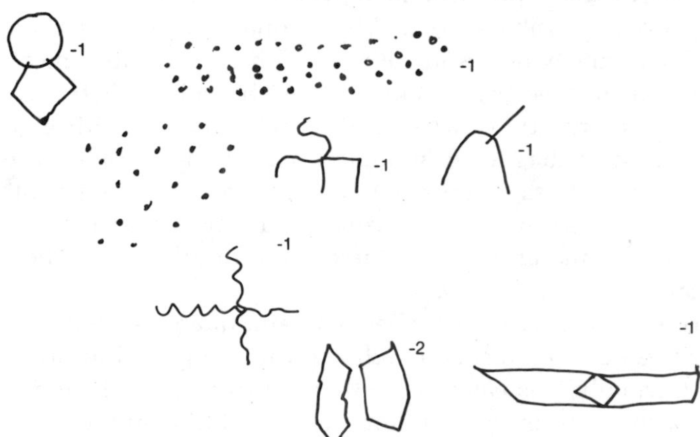


Figure 1.1. Model Bender Gestalt drawing and child's reproduction with eight Koppitz errors. (Reprinted, with permission, from *A Visual Motor Gestalt Test and Its Clinical Use* by Loretta Bender, Copyright and distributed by the American Orthopsychiatric Association, Inc.)

these children form a *norm group* (Aiken, 1994), which is also frequently referred to as a *standardization sample.* Creation of a norm group is a key distinguishing characteristic of standardized psychological tests. The norm group helps psychologists keep tabs on what really is normal. When a test is released for general use, each child's score can be compared with the norm group to determine his or her standing in relation to peers. Later in this chapter this principle of normative comparison is further discussed in the section entitled "Selection of a Representative Sample."

The ability to make normative comparisons is an enormous advantage for formal psychological testing. Without a norm group, the diagnostician must rely on a subjective impression and on a personal estimation of what a "typical" child's performance may be like. With a norm group, psychologists do not need to estimate whether an individual's performance was average; they simply compare the performance with the norm group and see how it stacks up.

The full impact of normative comparing is evident when derived scores are used. A *derived score* is a single score that shows how a child's performance compares to the norm group, which provides a way of summarizing performance. Derived scores are arrived at by first calculating a raw score. The raw score is usually simply the number of items correct. The next step is to refer to tables that tell how the norm group did. These tables allow psychologists to produce a derived score, such as an age equivalent, a percentile rank, or a standard score. In this sense, all of these scores are derived by comparing an individual's performance with those of a peer group. The purpose of derived scores is to convert an otherwise meaningless raw score into a score that makes sense (Helmstadter, 1964). Most scores with which readers are familiar from taking admissions tests (College Board Scholastic Aptitude Test [SAT], Law School Admission Test [LSAT], Medical College Admission Test [MCAT]) are derived scores.

## Age and Grade Equivalents

*Equivalent scores* are used to describe traits that develop as a child grows older (e.g., reading skills, perceptual maturity). Equivalent scores tell what level of growth or development a child has reached by indicating what age or grade the child's performance was equal to or "equivalent" with. For example, a seventh-grade reading equivalent means that a child's raw score (number of reading items correct) was the same as the mean (average) raw score for other seventh graders. In actual practice, age and grade equivalents are broken down into fractions of years. Hence, an age equivalent of 7-11 indicates that an individual's performance was identical to the mean performance of all children age 7 years, 11 months in the norm group (see Table 1.1). Similarly, a grade equivalent of 3.2 in reading indicates that the child's reading score was identical to the mean score earned by norm group children in the second month of the third grade. Equivalent scores of all types are popular in educational settings and among nonpsychologist diagnosticians.

Table 1.1. Sample conversion tables

| Raw score | Age equivalents (years/months) | Percentile ranks for 8-year-olds |
|---|---|---|
| 17 | 10–0 | 99 |
| 16 | 9–6 | 98 |
| 15 | 9–0 | 96 |
| 14 | 8–6 | 91 |
| 13 | 8–5 | 84 |
| 12 | 8–2 | 75 |
| 11 | 8–1 | 63 |
| 10 | 8–0 | 50 |
| 9 | 7–6 | 37 |
| 8 | 7–3 | 25 |
| 7 | 7–1 | 16 |
| 6 | 7–0 | 8 |
| 5 | 6–8 | 5 |
| 4 | 6–2 | 2 |
| 3 | 6–0 | 1 |
| 2 | 5–11 | 1 |
| 1 | 5–5 | 1 |

## Percentile Ranks

Percentile ranks are as straightforward as equivalent scores. *Percentile ranks* tell what percentage of the norm group was exceeded by an individual's score. Thus, a percentile rank of 23rd indicates that this individual's score exceeded 23 out of every 100 people in the norm group; the 75th percentile rank indicates that 75 out of 100 norm group members' scores were exceeded, and so forth. As with age and grade equivalents, these scores offer a means to explain a given individual's performance compared with those of peers. An additional, more refined method of measuring performance is using standard scores.

## Standard Scores

*Standard scores* are derived scores that offer a precise method of pinpointing an individual's performance compared to a defined peer group. This task is accomplished by specifying the number of standard units above or below the mean a score is. To clarify, let's examine some background concepts and terms. First, many physical and psychological traits are distributed in a bell-shaped frequency polygon, with most scores clustering around the mean and then tapering off on both sides of the mean (Cronbach, 1984). This describes the familiar *bell-shaped curve,* or normal distribution. The mean of this bell-shaped curve is easy to calculate by averaging all the scores in the norm group. Second, a "yardstick" is needed to index how far an individual's score might depart from the mean. The standard deviation is such a yardstick. *Standard deviation* is a statistic that measures a dis-

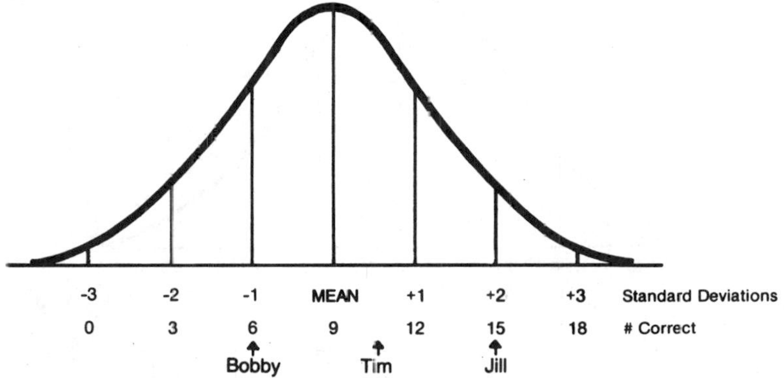


Figure 1.2. Score distribution of a 20-word vocabulary test.

tribution's amount of dispersion and is calculated from the scores of the norm group just as the mean can be calculated.[1] By knowing the mean and standard deviation for the norm group, psychologists can find exactly where an individual score falls in the bell-shaped frequency polygon. An example explains: Assume a psychologist administers a 20-word vocabulary test to all 8-year-old school children in Tempe, Arizona. The mean is calculated to be 9 correct responses, and the standard deviation to be 3 correct responses (see Figure 1.2). With this information, any subsequent score can be located in terms of relative position from the mean. Bobby got 6 correct, so he is 1 standard deviation below the mean. Jill got 15 correct, so she is 2 standard deviations above the mean. Tim got 10 correct, so he is 0.33 standard deviations above the mean. All standard score systems, of which there are a variety, explain an individual's performance by describing how many standard deviations above or below the mean an individual's score is.

The standard deviation is a useful way to show how far an individual's score differs from the mean. For example, a normal distribution, or bell-shaped frequency polygon, shows a symmetrical distribution of scores, such that approximately 68% of scores fall within ±1 standard deviation, 95% of scores fall within ±2 standard deviations, and 99% of all scores fall within ±3 standard deviations (see Figure 1.3).

---

[1]The formula for standard deviation is as follows:

$$\text{s.d.} = \sqrt{\frac{\Sigma(X - \overline{X})^2}{N - 1}}$$

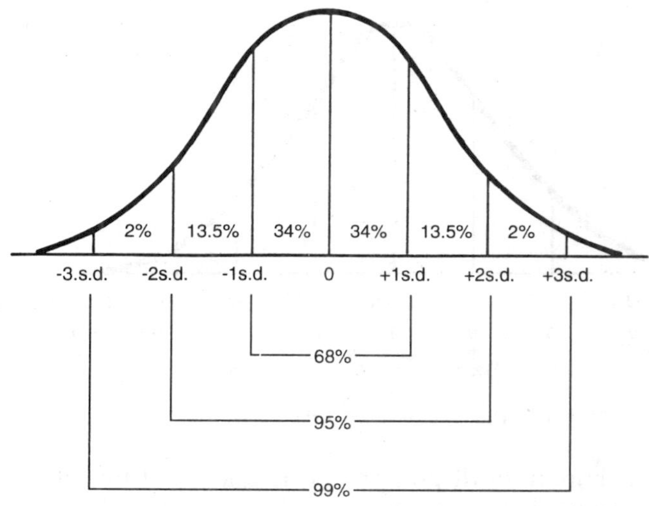


Figure 1.3. Distribution of scores by percentage in a normal distribution or bell-shaped frequency polygon.

***Z-Scores, T-Scores, and IQ Scores*** Long ago, psychologists recognized that it would be helpful to describe an individual's location in a bell-shaped frequency polygon with a single score, known as the "z" distribution. (The designation "z" is arbitrary; the distribution could have easily been called "y" or "x.") By convention, it was decided to call all scores that are at the mean zero, all scores 1 standard deviation above the mean +1, all scores 2 standard deviations above the mean +2, all scores 1 standard deviation below the mean −1, and so forth (see Figure 1.4). Other statisticians developed alternative scoring systems that can also be seen in Figure 1.4. It is unclear why so many different number systems were developed. Another system, the T-score system, calls all scores at the mean 50; scores 1 standard deviation above the mean 60, 2 standard deviations above the mean 70, and so forth. The Minnesota Multiphasic Personality Inventory (MMPI) (Hathaway & McKinley, 1967), the McCarthy Scales of Children's Abilities (McCarthy, 1972), and the Children's Category Test (Boll, 1993) have scores that are reported as T-scores. Some group achievement tests also report scores as T-scores. Wechsler IQ scores are reported as standard scores with a mean of 100 and standard deviation of 15. This means that scores 1 standard deviation above the mean equal 115, and scores 1 standard deviation below the mean equal 85. Stanford-Binet IQ scores also have a mean of 100, but have a standard deviation of 16 (Thorndike, Hagen, & Sattler, 1986).

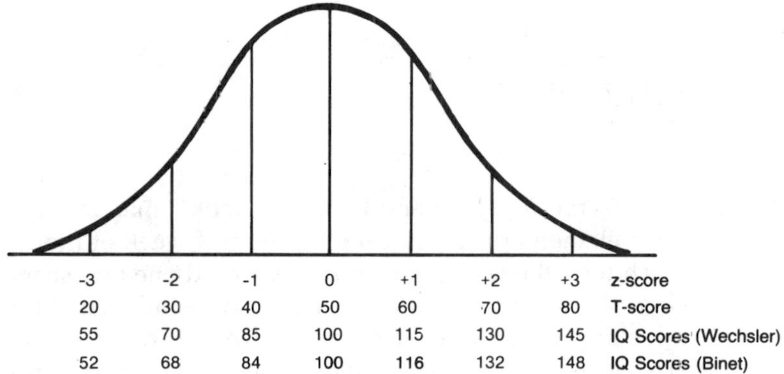


Figure 1.4. Standard score distributions.

***Advantages of Standard Scores*** Standard scores are consistently preferred over percentile ranks and age-equivalent scores by psychologists and others who work regularly with tests. But why are standard scores preferred? Percentile ranks and age equivalents are *ordinal,* not *interval-level data.* With ordinal data such as percentile ranks, there is no specification of the distance between ranks. We only know that one person, say percentile rank 14, scored better than another person, say percentile rank 13. There is no way to know how much better. Because most individuals score near the mean, most percentile ranks are clustered near the mean. Near the mean, the addition of only a few raw score points to someone's score would increase his or her percentile rank substantially. Similarly, subtracting only a few raw score points from someone near the mean would cause an appreciable reduction in his or her percentile rank. Conversely, at the outer bound of the distribution, where only a few people score, the change of a few raw score points would result in only a movement of a few or, in some cases, no percentile ranks. In this sense, percentile ranks are not uniform across the distribution. Illustration 1.1 provides a more concrete example of the limitations of percentile ranks.

## SELECTION OF A REPRESENTATIVE SAMPLE

Derived scores (percentile ranks or z-scores) are excellent for determining where a child stands when compared to a norm group. But who makes up this norm group? Can we merely keep track of the scores of those we test in our offices? Can we compile the scores of those who show up for evaluation at the offices of many psychologists across the United States, and then use these individuals as a norm

## Illustration 1.1

Assume two children, John and Pam, each took a manual dexterity test for elementary school children. After a week of motor training, each took the test again, and each scored one raw score point higher. We would expect the derived score for each child to reflect this improved performance by showing some increase. But the size of this increase depends on whether scores are reported as percentile ranks or standard scores (e.g., z-scores) and where each child stands compared to average. John, who scored near the mean, looks at his percentile rank increase and believes that his dexterity has improved greatly. Meanwhile, Pam, who scored way above the mean, looks at her percentile rank and believes she has hardly improved. If John and Pam were to focus on their z-scores (examples of standard scores) instead, each would recognize more accurately the amount of improvement he or she had made. Similar advantages for standard scores over percentile ranks exist when children are compared with others or when one aspect of their own performance is compared with another aspect (e.g., math with reading).

| | Raw score | Z-score | Percentile rank | |
|---|---|---|---|---|
| John | 10 | 0.33 | 63 | Initial score |
| (near mean) | 11 | 0.66 | 75 | Subsequent score |
| | 1 | 0.33 | 12 | Change |
| Pam | 15 | 2.00 | 98 | Initial score |
| (distant from mean) | 16 | 2.33 | 99 | Subsequent score |
| | 1 | 0.33 | 1 | Change |

group? Such procedures would certainly be unacceptable because those who arrive for such testing are likely to be different in some key ways from a random group of children. Such a system would be analogous to recording the temperatures of all patients who arrive in a pediatrician's office and using this as the basis for determining what are normal and abnormal temperatures for children (half of the children who arrive in such offices may have a fever). What is needed is a representative, or typical, group with which to compare. An adequate *representative norm group* must meet two criteria: 1) randomness, or representativeness; and 2) size. The patients whose temperatures are recorded in the pediatrician's office above are neither a random nor a representative sample. Rather than compiling available test scores that are potentially unrepresentative and simply using them as a norm group, test constructors must develop some method of selecting individuals who are representative. Without a representative sample, averages may be inaccurate, and the clinician may attribute normalcy to scores that are deviant compared to *all* children of a particular age or may attribute deviancy to scores that are really normal. Using representative samples when selecting a norm group ensures accuracy when individual children's scores collected in clinical practice are compared to the norm group. In practice it is rarely possible for clinicians to collect a representative sample of scores in their own geographic area. Therefore, clinicians rely on published tests with representative national samples. See Illustration 1.2 for an example of how an adequate national norm group is selected.

The norm group must not only be random, but it must also be sufficiently large. If a norm group consists of only three 8-year-olds, it is possible that the three children selected are way above or way below average, thus producing a biased view of what really is average. If fifty 8-year-olds were randomly selected, then the chance of having such bad luck in selection would be reduced enormously. Some published tests, as seen in subsequent chapters, have norm groups that are unacceptably small or unrepresentative. These deficiencies severely limit these tests' clinical utility.

For those who may question the practical relevance of collecting a representative and contemporary standardization sample, the point raised by Flynn (1984) that the American population is growing brighter over time provides reason to reflect. Flynn suggested that IQ gains over time averaged approximately 0.3 points per year. Some have come to call these gains the "Flynn effect" (Neisser et al., 1996), and it has obvious implications, as seen below. Even the most carefully standardized instruments, the Wechsler intelligence scales, are restandardized only every 18–25 years. As might be suspected, restandardizing the test produces scores that would be 5–8 points lower. That is, if the immediately released version of the Wechsler scale were used rather than the version that had just been retired, then an individual would score 5–8 points lower. These differences are highly meaningful at the extremes of the IQ distribution where identification decisions, which may affect school placement, are made. For example, using a recently standardized test would move many individuals who would have previously scored in the 70–74 IQ range into the 65–69 IQ range, where their chances of being identified as having mental retardation

## Illustration 1.2

### SELECTING A NATIONAL SAMPLE

Often it is logistically impossible to select randomly from all children across the entire United States in order to construct a completely random norm group. A powerful alternative is to stratify the population on key variables and then select quotas. For instance, the Wechsler Intelligence Scale for Children–III (Wechsler, 1991), a well-normed instrument, drew a norm group of children that approximates U.S. Census data (see Figure 1.5) on the following characteristics:

1. Gender (percentage of boys and girls)
2. Ethnicity (percentage of Caucasian, African American, and Hispanic children)

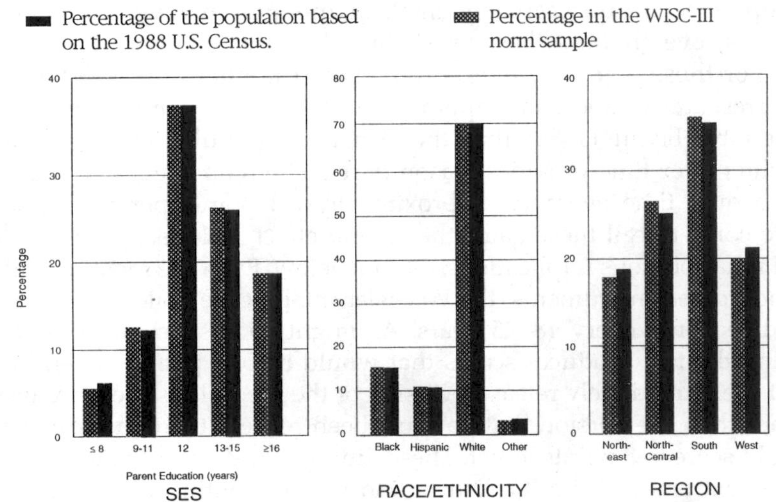

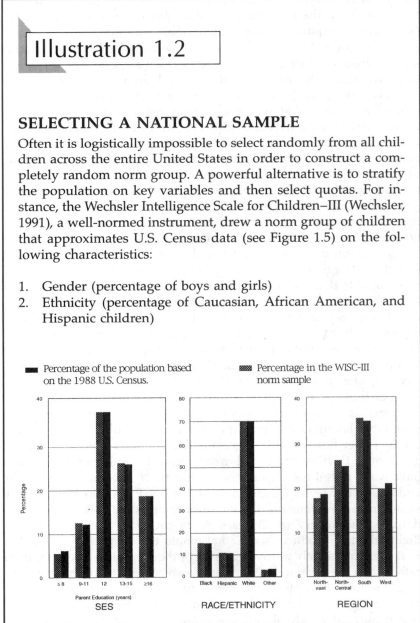

Figure 1.5. Demographic characteristic of the standardization sample compared with those of the U.S. population. (Item from the Wechsler Intelligence Scale for Children–Third Edition. Copyright © 1990 by the Psychological Corporation. Reproduced by permission. All rights reserved.)

*(continued)*

*continued*

### Illustration 1.2

3. Geographic location (e.g., percentage living in Midwest or South)
4. Parent education level (e.g., percentage with less than eighth-grade education)
5. Age (e.g., 8 years, 6 months)

A 9½-year-old Caucasian girl living in the north central United States whose father is a high school graduate would be an example of a quota to be filled. More than 2,200 children were selected, each filling a specific quota.

would rise. At the other end of the spectrum, individuals with IQs of 130–134 might find their scores dropping into the 125–129 range when tested with the newer version. Such a drop might exclude participation in a program for gifted or accelerated learners.

## SCRUTINIZING PSYCHOLOGICAL TESTS

Quantifiable, objective psychological tests have other advantages over informal assessment. Published psychological tests can have their worth evaluated in empirical, scientific ways by measuring their reliability and validity.

### Reliability

Generally speaking, psychological tests can be thought of as attempting to measure traits (e.g., intelligence, math aptitude, altruism). One goal of assessment is to measure these traits as accurately as possible. Long ago, mental measurement theoreticians worked out logic about how traits could be measured confidently. (For an excellent discussion, see Kaplan & Saccuzzo, 1982.) It is argued that psychological tests never measure traits with complete accuracy, that some "error" is always involved. This error prevents the test score from being an exact reflection of the "true score" for the trait under consideration. A hypothetical true score exists but is never attained through testing. *Reliability* is concerned with how much error is involved in measurement or how far observed scores depart from the true score.

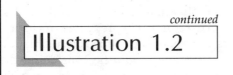

One way to handle the error problem is to take several or repeated measurements of the same trait rather than just one measurement. If factors like fatigue, motivation, and rapport with the examiner are operating to produce errors, then repeated measurements should allow these factors to negate each other. In a situation like this, the average of two measurements could be considered the best "true score" estimate. Repeated measurements would not only allow a more accurate score estimate, but also would provide an index of testing procedure reliability.

***Standard Error of Measurement*** By testing once and then retesting with the same instrument (called *test–retest reliability*), two important statistics can be generated. The first is the standard error of measurement. The second is the reliability coefficient. *Standard error of measurement* is produced by testing, retesting, and then calculating how closely the two scores agree. (In theoretical terms, the standard error of measurement is the standard deviation of the scores generated by this procedure for a single person, if that person were tested several times.) The standard error will be small if scores are similar on repeated administrations. This would imply that each measurement must be fairly close to the true score, hence without much error, and hence reliable. A large standard error implies that scores varied widely on repeated administrations. In this case neither measurement is close to the true score; hence much error is being measured, and there is poor reliability. Standard error of measurement has practical application. Using logic worked out mathematically by measurement theoreticians, the standard error statistic allows psychologists to find out how close the observed score is to the true score, within certain limits of confidence. For instance, the Wechsler Intelligence Scale for Children–III is a highly reliable instrument. The standard error of measurement for the Full Scale IQ is approximately 3. This means that, using previously developed logic, the chances are that two out of three times the true score is within $\pm 3$ points of the observed score. Using a less reliable test that contains more error, the standard error would be larger. For instance, the Peabody Picture Vocabulary Test–Revised (Dunn & Dunn, 1981) has a standard error of measurement of 7. This means that the chances are two out of three that the true score is within $\pm 7$ of the observed score using this test. Standard error, thus, is an extremely useful statistic for making practical decisions about how much confidence to place in a score.

***Reliability Coefficient*** A more general index of reliability is the *reliability coefficient.* The reliability coefficient can be calculated by using the same test–retest data used to calculate the standard error of measurement mentioned above. Determining reliability involves correlating each individual's score on the first administration of a test with the score on the second administration. If the two administrations agree, then it is assumed that the measurement instrument is detecting the true score and little error. If, however, the two administrations do not agree, then it is assumed that much error is being measured; therefore, the measurement instrument has reliability problems. Because the reliability coefficient is expressed as a correlation coefficient, the index can range from 1.0, indicating a perfect agreement between the two administrations, to 0, indicating no relationship. Most reliability coefficients fall somewhere between these two values, with scores ranging from 0.80 to 0.90 generally considered acceptable for practical use. In addition, there are other methods for calculating reliability coefficients. One method involves correlating two separate forms of the same test with each other; another method involves correlating one half of the items on a test with the other one half from the same test. These methods index numerically how accurately traits are being measured by producing a reliability coefficient (ranging from 1.0 to 0) just as with the test–retest method.

One more point must be made in regard to reliability: When all other factors are equal, longer tests are more reliable than shorter tests (Lyman, 1971). Long tests have enough items so that a single confusing item or a momentary attention lapse will not distort a child's total score. Longer tests have more items, which is equivalent to taking repeated measurements and averaging the scores. This practice of repeated measurements, as discussed previously, provides a better estimate of the true score and thus better reliability. As is seen in subsequent chapters, major differences exist in the reliability of published tests. Some long tests have excellent reliability, whereas some short tests are so deficient that they have been dubbed "quick and dirty" by those in the trade.

## Validity

Although reliability is important, examined alone it is not adequate evidence of a test's worth. For example, a test claiming to measure intelligence can be quite reliable (measuring some trait consistently and without error) but have absolutely nothing to do with intelligence, the trait that is supposed to be measured. Psychologists want their tests to be both reliable and valid. Validity answers the question "Does the test measure what it claims to measure?" There are several types of validity.

***Content Validity*** This method of assessing validity consists of examining test items and rendering a judgment about whether the items are measuring what they claim. For instance, assume authors devised a test of general intelligence that consisted entirely of mathematics reasoning items. Although math reasoning is one aspect of intelligence, the test does not contain enough different items to be considered a test of general intelligence. This test would have low content validity as a measure of intelligence. It might have adequate content validity as a measure of basic mathematical reasoning, or it might become an adequate measure of verbal intelligence if some items dealing with verbal analogies and some vocabulary items were added.

Content validity is especially important for achievement tests. As contrasted with ability tests, for which it is assumed the background of an individual who is tested provides some preparedness for the test items, achievement tests make sense only when the individuals who are tested have been exposed to instruction on the test's subject. Seventh-graders who are taught in their natural science curriculum about weather, elementary chemical compounds, and insects would be at a disadvantage if achievement test items dealt with human anatomy and geology. For these pupils, a test composed of anatomy and geology items would have poor content validity because the test would not measure the information that the students learned. The same test, however, may have adequate content validity for a school with a different science curriculum that focuses on anatomy and geology.

Published achievement tests, because they are designed for national use, can never perfectly match local schools' curricula. Nonetheless, school psychologists (or other diagnosticians who assess academic skills) can take steps to ensure that published achievement tests and each child's instructional history agree by reviewing instructional goals and the content of achievement tests. If an adequate match of instructional history to test content is not possible, then the validity of achievement test scores is diminished for a particular child. The scores, however, are not useless (a sufficiently discernible core curriculum exists in the United States to allow national tests to be developed with some validity). Even if adequate standardized achievement tests are used, informal, curriculum-based testing is often performed by educators to guarantee adequate sampling of local schools' instruction. Such assessment may occur at the onset of the diagnostic process and may continue as long as the child is being taught. This informal testing is complementary to more formal psychometric testing and performs a somewhat different function—to guide and monitor instruction. A detailed discussion of the topic of curriculum-based and informal educational testing is beyond the scope of this book. (For more detailed information, see Shinn, 1989.)

***Construct Validity*** Like content validity, *construct validity* renders a judgment; but unlike content validity, it relies on more sophisticated logic and observations rather than on simple item inspection.

Construct validity begins with an explanatory variable, or construct, designed to explain behavior. Examples of such constructs are *intelligence, depression,* and *anxiety.* Each of these constructs, according to the theorist who promulgates it, is believed to possess certain characteristics: Intelligence predicts achievement in a variety of situations, is not entirely the result of experience, and is stable; anxiety is related to degree of stress and is relatively unstable across time. An instrument's construct validity can be checked by creating experiments to see how scores change under different conditions. For instance, scores on an anxiety test are expected to rise if subjects are put in stressful situations (e.g., told they are about to take a difficult, impromptu quiz). Similarly, scores on an anxiety test are expected to decrease if a drug with known anxiety-reducing qualities is administered. If researchers found that these responses did occur under specific conditions, then the construct validity of a test of anxiety would be enhanced because it would then be evident that the test does in fact measure anxiety. Therefore, with construct validity a judgment is involved, but the judgments are not as straightforward as those used to assess content validity.

***Predictive and Concurrent Validity*** Two methods that demonstrate validity by correlating tests with independent criteria are *predictive* and *concurrent validity.* It is assumed that psychological tests predict independent, external criteria that might include specific behaviors (e.g., suicide attempts), general traits (e.g., scores on other psychological tests), or certain future outcomes (e.g., graduation from college). IQ tests are a classic example of instruments that are expected to predict the future. IQ tests were originally constructed to determine which beginning pupils were likely to succeed (those who should be left in the general academic curriculum) and those who were expected to fail (those to be channeled into an alternative curriculum). The worth of these IQ tests could be demonstrated empirically by showing that they predict school achievement. The evidence can be collected easily by computing a coefficient that correlates IQ scores for pupils as they begin school, with their subsequent achievement measured by achievement test scores, classroom marks, or teacher ratings. The higher the correlation, the greater is the test's predictive power, and the more valid the test is in placement. The essence of predictive validity is that current test scores foretell some independent criterion in the future.

Concurrent validity is nearly identical to predictive validity, except that an outside criterion is assessed at the same time the test is administered. Often a preexisting or well-established test is used as the criterion with which a new test is correlated. For example, an author may develop his or her own intelligence scale. To demonstrate the test's worth, the author administers it to a group of elementary pupils along with a standard test, recognized as a valid measure of intelligence, such as the Wechsler scale. If the new intelligence scale correlated highly with the standard, recognized test, the author would have established the test's worth by concurrent validity. Obviously, concurrent validation depends on identifying a suitable external criterion, such as the Wechsler scales.

Historically, research on the utility of psychological tests has been of this type—correlations between psychological tests and some other criterion that could also be quantified along a continuum, such as grade point average or scores on another psychological test. In the 1980s and 1990s, psychological tests have been drawn into other areas of scientific inquiry where conditions are classified as either present or absent, rather than along a continuum (in measurement terms the former is referred to as a *continuous variable,* the latter a *dichotomous variable*). Attention-deficit/hyperactivity disorder (ADHD), a condition that is receiving a great deal of consideration among educators and the general public, is such a condition. After an evaluation by an expert diagnostician, children can be deemed to have the disorder or to not have the disorder in a yes/no, or dichotomous, manner. As of 1997, the determination of ADHD is made by expert opinion in accordance with an explicit list of symptoms; psychological tests are not the basis for making the diagnosis of ADHD. Not surprisingly, investigators have sought to determine if psychological tests of attention or impulse control have a role in helping clinicians establish a diagnosis of ADHD. A study conducted in 1994 by Barkley and Grodzinsky shows how tests might be used in this regard and, more pertinent to this chapter's purpose, how this type of measurement information can be presented to help diagnosticians in their daily decision-making capacity.

Barkley and Grodzinsky studied 47 children—24 with ADHD and 23 without ADHD—who had been evaluated by several tests potentially capable of identifying ADHD. Test findings were summarized as two types of probabilities to facilitate comparisons between tests. The first type of probability is whether an atypical score on a psychological test is consistently associated with the presence of ADHD. This is called *positive predictive power* and is calculated by establishing a ratio based on the number of children who acquired an atypical score on the psychological test as the value for the denominator and the number of these children who were diagnosed with ADHD as the numerator. This is the probability of a child actually having ADHD if the test results indicate that ADHD is present. A second probability is *negative predictive power,* which is whether a normal test score is consistently associated with the absence of a condition, in this case the absence of ADHD. Negative predictive power is calculated by a ratio with the number of children who acquire a normal score on psychological testing as the denominator and the number of these children who were diagnosed as not having ADHD as the numerator. The result is the probability of actually not having ADHD when the test scores indicate that ADHD is absent. Scores organized in this manner (i.e., as positive predictive power and negative predictive power) reveal patterns that cannot be detected from other statistics often used in conjunction with psychological tests, such as the correlation between test scores and ADHD diagnoses or average values of various psychological tests for children with and without ADHD. In Barkley and Grodzinsky's study, almost all of the tests had neither adequate positive predictive power nor negative predictive power to be of clinical use. Of the tests that did work, however, findings must be used cautiously because an atypical score and a typical score do not help the diagnostician equally.

Barkley and Grodzinsky found that a test of sustained attention and impulse control, the Gordon Diagnostic System Vigilance task (see Chapter 9), had excellent positive predictive power. Children with abnormal scores on one dimension (total correct) of the Gordon Diagnostic System had a 92% probability of having ADHD. Even stronger findings were associated with another dimension (commission errors) of the Gordon Diagnostic System. In Barkley and Grodzinsky's sample of children, there was a 100% probability of having ADHD if an abnormal score occurred on the commission errors dimension. One might quickly assume that the Gordon Diagnostic System Vigilance task is an extremely valuable test for detecting ADHD. However, the negative predictive power value of the Gordon Diagnostic System Vigilance task proved to be less helpful. Barkley and Grodzinsky found, for instance, that if a child received a normal score on total correct he or she had a 63% chance of not having ADHD (but a 37% chance of having ADHD). For the other dimension of this test, commission errors, only a 59% negative predictive value was determined (41% with normal test scores had ADHD). In clinical practice a test like the Gordon Diagnostic System certainly has utility, but the test is valuable only if the diagnostician understands the advantages and limitations of the test. An atypical score tells the diagnostician that ADHD is extremely likely; a typical score imparts far less information. The point, however, is to demonstrate that psychological tests can be extremely useful in making everyday decisions but that research of a test's validity, specific to the intended use, is generally a prerequisite for clinical application.

Even findings like these that were derived under carefully formulated research conditions may not be directly applicable under other, slightly different, real-life circumstances (Elwood, 1993). In this study roughly one half of the subjects had ADHD, roughly one half did not. Thus, the probability of any one child who has ADHD drawn randomly in the study would be 50%. This prior probability, or *base rate* of the disorder among those under investigation, is also critical in determining how much confidence to put in test results (and, indeed, in all types of diagnostic information). Although there may be 100% positive predictive power among children when their composition is evenly divided between children with ADHD and children without ADHD (50% base rate for ADHD), what would happen if a group of unselected 8-year-olds, such as all 8-year-olds from a typical public school, were examined using the Gordon Diagnostic technique? Under these conditions, the prior probability of ADHD would be approximately 3% (the base rate for ADHD in the general population), rather than 50%. Under these circumstances it is easy to see that, in all likelihood, a positive finding on the Gordon Diagnostic technique would be much less of an assurance that the child has ADHD than is true in the research study. After all, most children do not have ADHD and a positive finding may be erroneous. The prior probability, or base rate, issue has been long discussed (e.g., Meehl & Rosen, 1955) but only imperfectly practiced as psychologists frequently lack information about the prior probability of a particular outcome. Still, the wise psychologist considers these types of information when attempting to establish diagnoses. As is seen in the issue of predicting suicide discussed in Chapter 2, not all outcomes are equally acceptable, and, thus, clinical judgment and human values have to be added to the statistical considerations discussed above.

## Test Titles and Their Implications

Psychological tests claim to measure an astounding array of traits, skills, and capabilities. Tests have titles ranging from "auditory discrimination" to "written language." Unfortunately, a test title is often a poor guide as to what that test or portion of that test measures. Two misconceptions often occur when it is believed that a test's content is described by its title. The first of these is the *jingle fallacy*—the mistaken notion that tests with the same title measure the same thing—and the second is the *jangle fallacy*—that tests with different names measure different things (Messick, 1983). For example, both the Kaufman Test of Educational Achievement (K–TEA) (Kaufman & Kaufman, 1985) and the Peabody Individual Achievement Test–Revised (PIAT–R) contain subtests of spelling. These subtests with the same title illustrate the "jingle" fallacy. On the K–TEA, a child is required to spell dictated words using a pencil and paper. In contrast, on the PIAT–R, a child chooses the correct spelling of a word from four possibilities spoken by an examiner. One may argue whether both of these tests measure spelling; few would agree that both measure the same skill, despite the spelling title affixed to both. The "jangle" fallacy may be understood by considering three tests that have titles implying that they measure different things. Intelligence, achievement, and aphasia purportedly can be measured by very similar, if not virtually identical, items depending on the type of test and depending on the author's intention. For example, the Kaufman Brief Intelligence Test "Expressive Vocabulary" subtest (Kaufman & Kaufman, 1990), the Wechsler Individual Achievement Test "Oral Expression" (Psychological Corporation, 1992), and the Multilingual Aphasia Examination "Visual Naming" (Benton, Hamsher, & Sivan, 1994) each contain items that require a child to, in part, name what is seen in a picture. According to their titles alone, one might think, incorrectly, that three different attributes were being measured.

Because psychologists use tests to make decisions about children, it goes without saying that psychologists must be aware of important test characteristics, such as reliability and validity. It is equally important, however, for psychologists to be aware of precisely what each test measures. Consumers of psychological test information must understand that test interpretation is not always as easy as it appears on the surface. Merely taking test names at face value often results in falling victim to the jingle and jangle fallacies. As seen in Chapter 9, in order to fulfill professional responsibilities, psychologists must do more than simply administer tests and report scores. Interpretation is required if test findings are to be used to help children. Sometimes those who receive written psychological reports are puzzled that test names and their associated numerical values do not agree with intuitive assumptions. Perhaps in those instances the psychologist is providing interpretation that goes beyond simple test names and is avoiding the jingle and jangle fallacies.

## PSYCHOLOGICAL TESTING AS SCIENCE

Although the foregoing discussion outlines only the most basic psychological testing principles, the implications should still be clear. Much of psychological testing is science. Tests focus on observable, objective, quantifiable behavior. They strive to produce results that can be subjected to scrutiny by peers. Research on psychological testing is reported in highly technical journals in a format conducive to criticism, investigation, and replication. The principles and procedures associated with testing are embedded in a carefully thought-out system called *psychometric theory* (Nunnally, 1978). Research often combines observation, logic, and powerful statistical methods—the signs of a mature science.

As seen in subsequent chapters, some test instruments use all of the best procedures outlined thus far. For instance, many standardized ability, achievement, and personality measures have excellent psychometric properties, such as large and well-selected norm groups, objective administration and scoring, refined standard score reporting systems, and outstanding reliability and validity data. The advantages associated with these refinements are both logically evident and empirically substantiated, as is shown in the remainder of the book. However, some personality measures, particularly the so-called projective techniques, lack many of these refinements. Yet, because projective techniques are part of the broad area of psychological testing, these techniques are similarly scrutinized for empirical evidence of worth. As a result, proponents of even relatively unrefined projective techniques have been forced to sharpen their research focus and further develop their instruments to accommodate peer criticism, leading to additional knowledge of the suitability of these techniques.

Finally, psychology as a science interfaces with psychology as a profession when psychological tests are used. Responding to its scientific roots, professional psychology has established standards for test instruments and for practitioners. For instance, *Standards for Educational and Psychological Testing* published by the American Psychological Association (1985) sets guidelines for standardization, norms, reliability, validity, interpretation of scores, and even use of computer scoring systems. Professional psychology training standards have been set forth to ensure knowledge of basic psychology principles, measurement theory, and specific training with individual measurement techniques.

All this implies that, as a science, test development requires more than simply putting some test items together and calling them a test. Likewise, appropriate test use involves substantially more than picking up a test manual and reading administration instructions. With a proliferation of test instruments and the appearance of test data in ever-broadening realms of everyday life, the consumer of psychological testing needs to be armed with knowledge. Understanding the principles in this and subsequent chapters will help the consumer of psychological tests acquire this knowledge.

## SUMMARY

Psychological tests, or mental measurements, share a set of procedures and principles that afford advantages over less structured assessment. Psychological tests emphasize uniform administration and objective scoring. With inconsistency and subjectivity removed from assessment, diagnosticians can more confidently assume that observed differences among children's scores reflect real differences in the trait being measured (e.g., level of development).

Most psychological tests are scored numerically. These numbers can be manipulated statistically to show exactly where any individual child stands compared to a representative norm group of children who have taken the test. Standard scores (e.g., T-scores, IQ scores), percentile ranks, and age and grade equivalents are the most common methods of score reporting. These scores are collectively referred to as derived scores.

Because they are objectified and quantified, psychological tests are easily researched. Investigators have developed empirical ways to measure test reliability to ensure that traits are being measured with a minimum of error. Test validity can also be measured empirically, by item inspection (content validity), by studying test score changes in differing situations and noting agreement with theory (construct validity), or by correlating tests with outside criteria (concurrent and predictive validity).

### Study Questions

1. Psychological tests that are administered in uniform fashion and are objectively scored offer what advantages over less formal assessment procedures?
2. Why do psychologists generally prefer to quantify test results?
3. What advantages result when a norm group exists with which an individual's score can be compared?
4. What general term can be used to describe age equivalent, percentile rank, and standard scores?
5. What problem might result if a very small norm group were used?
6. Reliability refers to what? How is this different from validity?
7. Is standard error of measurement associated with reliability or validity? What problem results if standard error is too large?
8. In your opinion, would a "spelling test" that requires a child to copy words from an adjacent page have high or low content validity? Why?

## Chapter Two

# Making a Referral

Making a referral for psychological testing may seem easy, but if the process is to culminate in useful results, then the referral process may require some effort and skill on the part of the person making the referral. A successful referral begins when a referring agent poses a well thought-out question for a psychologist to answer. Clarity of thinking and precision in asking a referral question can ensure that the examining psychologist does an adequate job. Poorly thought-out referral questions result in useless psychological reports. Psychological evaluations are too expensive and too time consuming to have them miss the mark. This chapter provides ideas for formulating better referrals in order to receive more useful evaluation findings.

### PUTTING THE PROBLEM IN BEHAVIORAL TERMS

The first step in making a good referral is putting the problem in behavioral terms. This means finding out exactly what the child does (or does not do) that is a problem and stating this in specific terms. Many referrals are weak because the referral agent has not identified, in his or her own mind, exactly what the problem is. If the psychologist asks why Johnny is to be tested, then he or she might be told, "Johnny has a 'poor attitude' and 'emotional problems.'" These statements are weak because they describe generalities rather than specific behaviors. A "poor attitude" means different things to different people. This lack of uniformity of meaning leaves the examining psychologist unclear about exactly what to look for. Naming specific behaviors is more useful for the psychologist. For example, the statements can be strengthened to read, "Johnny refuses to complete household chores, such as cleaning his room and emptying the trash.

When reprimanded by parents, he either flies into a rage or cries uncontrollably." The second statements are superior to the first because they identify and report Johnny's problem behaviors. A vague referral might begin, "Mary has classroom problems." But, stated in behavioral terms, it might read, "Mary is unable to complete any written assignments. She becomes restless and refuses to continue after 5 minutes of written work. Her handwriting is illegible." The stronger statement reports precisely which problem behaviors Mary performs and which desirable behaviors she fails to perform.

Evaluating psychologists are thankful for any behavioral statements of the problem that they may receive. Generally, the more they receive, the happier they are. If you wish to make a friend for life, then tell the psychologist the following information:

1. When the problem behaviors occur
2. In whose presence or under what circumstances they occur
3. How frequently they occur
4. Exactly what form the behaviors take

For example, a thorough behavioral description might look like this:

> Parents have become increasingly worried about their 7-year-old son, Will. Two or three times a day he seems to forget what has just been said to him. He seems worse at night and particularly when company visits. His mother thinks his expression looks blank when people are talking to him. His mother has commented, "It seems like Will spaces out and just can't seem to remember."

## FORMULATING HYPOTHESES

After putting a problem in behavioral terms, the next logical step is formulating hypotheses about what might be producing the problem. At times, of course, the individual requesting the psychological testing does not have any idea what is causing the problem. Lack of plausible explanations for the problem behavior may be the reason the referral was made originally. Most often, however, the person requesting or making the referral, whether it be a pediatrician, teacher, or parent, has at least a hunch about why the child is behaving in a certain way or what might be wrong. The referring person might hypothesize that Johnny has a behavior problem because Johnny feels like a failure and is depressed. Maybe Mary has problems with written work because of visual perception problems, or perhaps she simply has eyesight problems.

To help the examining psychologist, the referring person might check out as many explanations as possible with data already available. Examples of available data might include work samples, behavioral observations, health records, information from parent conferences, or informal parent contact. The referral agent's own thinking will help determine exactly what questions he or she wants answered by the psychological evaluation. In Mary's case, her pediatrician may speculate that her difficulty stems from either low visual acuity (poor eyesight) or poor visual perception. Assume that a quick, in-office screening shows no gross acuity problems. Also assume that the physician interviews Mary's mother and learns that Mary never enjoyed art work and has a long history of sloppy school papers with letter reversals. In this case, the hypothesis of low visual acuity is weakened, while the hypothesis of visual perception problems is strengthened. Often referral agents develop, check out, discard, and then reformulate hypotheses as they look at a case. Sharing hunches, intuitions, and hypotheses with the examining psychologist will help him or her know how to proceed. Having thought through and informally considered as many hypotheses as possible will help the referral agent with the most important task, asking an explicit referral question.

## ASKING AN EXPLICIT REFERRAL QUESTION

The best guarantee that a referral agent will receive useful findings from psychological testing is to pose questions about a specific concern regarding the client. Yet most psychologists feel lucky if they get a referral question at all. Often a psychologist begins with a vague and noninformative request to "please do a psychological evaluation." As is seen in subsequent chapters, there is no such thing as "a psychological evaluation." Instead, there are many different psychological test batteries, each tailored to answer questions posed in a referral. When a psychologist begins with a vague request, he or she is forced to track down the individual who has requested the psychological testing and find out exactly what is wanted. This is especially cumbersome in certain settings, such as schools, where a referring teacher usually has detailed, current information that a psychologist inevitably needs to address the referral question. It is obviously more efficient to include such information as part of the referral question. In less favorable situations, the psychologist is forced to proceed immediately without clear information and risk addressing the wrong concern.

Some requests are more specific than the general "do a psychological evaluation" but are no more helpful. These requests tell the examining psychologist what to do rather than what questions to answer: "Please give the Wechsler IQ test to this child." "This boy needs an MMPI and a Rorschach." Requests of this sort are usually inappropriate because they presume that the person making the referral knows better than the psychologist which tests are best suited for which situations. Of course, few individuals asking the psychologist for assistance know enough about the intricacies of testing to successfully make directives like these. The teacher, pediatrician, or other referral agent does not need to impress the psychologist by providing names of particular tests when requesting a psychological opinion. Furthermore, requests for specific tests are weak because they fail to inform the psychologist about the real concern. That is, the person initiating the referral does not really want an MMPI (Minnesota Multiphasic Personality Inventory), but wants to know if his client is depressed, or psychotic, or showing early signs of juvenile delinquency. Unfortunately for this referral agent, a general request for an MMPI or a Rorschach might not say as much as is needed about depression, psychosis, or juvenile delinquency.

If the referral agent has identified the problem in behavioral terms and has thought through hypothetical reasons for the problem, he or she is in an excellent position to formulate questions, such as, "Johnny refuses to complete household chores such as cleaning his room and emptying the trash. When reprimanded by parents, he either flies into a rage or cries uncontrollably. Do you think he is depressed? Would he be a candidate for treatment? What type?" Mary's referral may take this form: "Mary is unable to complete any written assignments. She becomes restless and refuses to work after 5 minutes of drill. Her handwriting is illegible. I suspect visual perception problems. What do you think is causing her low written-work productivity and poor handwriting?" Anyone who formulates such detailed referral questions will make the psychologist's day! Many nonpsychologists, in fairness, lack detailed information about a child's behavior at the time they make a referral. They know only that general learning or adjustment problems exist. Other referral agents are inundated with work and are too busy to track down information that may help the psychologist. Nonetheless, a clear, answerable question will go a long way toward ensuring that the referral agent gets some usable test findings. The following questions are examples of acceptable one-liners:

1. "Does this student have mental retardation?"
2. "Is this girl emotionally stable enough to stick with a posthospital diet?"

3. "Is this boy bright enough to make it in vocational welding school?"

In general, if the referral agent cannot think of at least a one-line referral question, then the case is inappropriate for psychological testing. Although this fact seems ridiculously self-evident, it nonetheless is often overlooked: Psychological evaluations only answer questions; without a question there is no need for an evaluation.

## REFERRAL QUESTIONS FOR WHICH PSYCHOLOGICAL TESTING IS NOT THE ANSWER

Despite having explicit, behaviorally defined descriptions, there are some referral questions for which psychological testing simply is not the answer. Testing could be an inappropriate response because of the nature of a referral question, a lack of compatibility between the type of information sought and the type of information yielded by tests, or the unwarranted amount of evaluation time that would be consumed by trying to answer a question. Typically, referrals for which testing is not the best answer tend to take one of three forms: 1) attempts to determine the cause of a present problem (etiology), 2) attempts to predict the future status of a problem (prognosis), or 3) attempts to simply unload a difficult or uncertain case.

### What Caused This Problem? (Etiology)

Psychological tests are most useful in describing current status. They generally are not designed to determine what caused a problem. If a person asks questions about causation, the lack of answers may often be disappointing.

Much of the inability to determine specific causes has to do with the nature of behavior itself. That is, behavior has multiple confounded causes as well as imperfectly related causes and effects. When two variables are related, and this relationship holds over time, it might be assumed that *A* causes *B* or that *B* causes *A*. Such a situation is most often found in the natural sciences and is usually a precise, predictable relationship that is statistically measurable and powerful. For example, *A* is the volume of gas in a container and *B* is the pressure. As the volume of gas (*A*) decreases, the pressure of the gas (*B*) proportionately increases. Therefore, changes in *A* predictably cause specific changes in *B*. In measurement, however, an alternative explanation or cause (C) always exists and must be excluded before it is assumed that *A* causes *B* or that *B* causes *A*.

This C variable is especially prevalent in behavioral science investigations. For instance, earned income (*A*) is related to years of education (*B*), but it could be argued that *B* does not cause *A*; they are both strongly influenced by socioeconomic status (C). That is, those born to low socioeconomic status lack both opportunities for good education and, ultimately, good jobs. Lack of education, perhaps, does not affect earned income as much as being born to a different social class does.

Behavioral science investigations also show that many identifiable causes, rather than a single cause, often come together to produce behavior. In the natural sciences, a change in *A* (volume of gas) is all that is necessary to produce a change in *B* (pressure of the gas). In the behavioral sciences, things are not often so simple. Traits such as measured intelligence, for instance, are caused by multiple factors, including genes inherited from parents, prenatal nutrition, perinatal course, quality of home environment, and quality of school, to name just some of the factors. A change in any one of these variables may be sufficient or insufficient to effect a change in intelligence, depending on the contribution of each of the other factors.

Still further, many behaviors occur without any known cause or with only weak suspected causes; that is, often current information is inadequate to identify potential causes, or only relatively weak causes have been located. For instance, attention-deficit / hyperactivity disorder (ADHD) occurs in approximately 3% of school-age children (*Diagnostic and Statistical Manual of Mental Disorders* [DSM-IV]; American Psychiatric Association, 1994). There is an association between ADHD and birth trauma, but the association is weak (Nichols & Chen, 1981). There is also an association between family history of ADHD and its occurrence in children (Cantwell, 1972). In reality, most children with ADHD have neither a history of birth trauma nor a family member who has been formally diagnosed with ADHD. Most cases of ADHD occur with unknown etiology.

What does this discussion about causation have to do with referral questions? Often questions about causation are asked without appreciating the aforementioned limitations of determining causation. Consider these examples:

1. Billy is a 4-year-old child of low socioeconomic status who was born with "respiratory difficulties." His parents want to know if perinatal respiratory difficulties caused his current mental retardation (Stanford-Binet IQ = 67). Respiratory difficulties are related to mental retardation such that having perinatal respiratory difficulties increases considerably the likelihood of mental retardation. However, membership in lower socioeconomic levels also

greatly increases risk of mental retardation. More important, research implies that respiratory difficulties combined with low socioeconomic status result in even greater likelihood of low IQ scores than either condition acting alone (Broman, 1979). Finally, a certain number of children have IQs as low as 67 without any known cause. Although the chance is remote, it is arguable that Billy was destined to be one of these children. Considering these facts, it makes little sense to ask if Billy's perinatal respiratory difficulties "caused" his mental retardation and to expect an unequivocal answer.

2. Consider the example of an 8-year-old aggressive boy with shoplifting problems. Knowing that the boy experienced a concussion in a pedestrian/motor vehicle accident 2 years ago, his attorney now wants to prove brain injury and blame the boy's antisocial behavior on this injury. Testing shows the boy to have mild mental retardation, to act on impulse, and to have poor judgment. History shows that his parents are divorced, his father was abusive, and his mother left him unsupervised while she worked. Maybe head trauma (*A*) caused the antisocial behavior (*B*), but there are so many alternative explanations (*C*) that the attorney's contention is hard to unequivocally prove. Although testing yielded important information on the boy's current status, it did not conclusively answer the question of causation. In practice, there are times when *A* exerts such a predictable influence on *B* that a cause-and-effect relation can be confidently drawn. This is especially true when a pattern found on psychological tests is rare or distinctive and has few, if any, alternative possible causes.
3. Consider the case of a child with a history of typical intellectual and academic development who sustained a closed head injury in a pedestrian/motor vehicle accident. The child subsequently had a 2-week coma and limited use of the right side of his body, despite no fractured bones or trauma to the muscles. On evaluation the child was found to have IQ scores in the 70s, severely impaired memory, and extremely impaired strength and dexterity with his dominant hand. This pattern rarely occurs without a specific insult to the nervous system. There is an abrupt onset of the symptoms (listed above) following a closed head injury, and research shows that children who experience sustained coma are quite likely to have poor psychometric test performance. A cause-and-effect relationship between poor performance on psychological tests and injury to the brain as a result of insult can be assumed confidently in cases such as this.

Psychological tests offer objective, quantifiable information of great value in understanding children's characteristics and current status, but they have limitations, as do most other sources of information, if cause-and-effect influences are to be concluded.

## What Exactly Will Happen in the Future? (Prognosis)

As effective as tests are in objectively measuring current characteristics, they are not crystal balls with unblurred visions of the future. Test findings can help determine the probabilities of future outcomes (*prognosis*), but for any individual child, tests cannot provide unerring predictions of what will result, except in cases of the most atypical children.

This does not mean that tests are worthless for predicting future behavior. Tests, particularly those that are objective and quantifiable, almost always outperform intuition and clinical judgment in predicting what future behavior is likely to occur (Lanyon & Goodstein, 1982). Still, even under the best circumstances, prediction of future events is less than perfect. There are no perfect associations between test findings and future outcomes. In all instances in which tests are used to assign individuals to categories, some errors will occur.

Consider the example depicted in Table 2.1. If tests are used to predict which of a group of children will have mental retardation as adults and which will not, invariably some individuals will be properly classified (listed as "success"), and some will be misclassified (listed as "failure"). Looking at any child individually, there is no way of knowing for certain whether that child is properly classified. That is, it can be predicted that the child will have mental retardation or not, but there is no way to know for certain what the child's actual status will be until he or she reaches the age of 18.

By relying on research, however, psychologists sometimes know what the chances of success and failure are in classification. Although unequivocal statements about what will occur with any individual are seldom possible, the well-informed psychologist can sometimes give

Table 2.1. Classification successes and failures when predicting future mental retardation

| | Has mental retardation at age 18 | Does not have mental retardation at age 18 |
|---|---|---|
| Predicted to have mental retardation | Success | Failure |
| Predicted to not have mental retardation | Failure | Success |

probability statements about future outcomes. For example, hypothetically assume that children with IQs less than 40 at age 8 have an 80% mental retardation rate at age 18. If this were true, each child in this example would have an 80% chance of being diagnosed as having mental retardation at age 18. Any predicted outcome that has an 80% probability of occurring would be an example of an extremely powerful prediction and would probably come as close to an ensured outcome as is ever likely to occur with psychological data.

Many outcomes are much harder to predict. Prognosticating suicide, which has a very low occurrence rate, is a classic example of a difficult prediction. Take an example suggested by Lanyon and Goodstein (1982) (which illustrates a point by using hypothetical data and simplified descriptions of probability). If we know from past research that only 1 person with mental illness in 300 will commit suicide, then we could assume that each has a 0.3% chance of killing him- or herself. For any given patient viewed individually, this likelihood of suicide is reasonably low. But suicide is an extremely undesirable outcome, so most people in psychiatric care are watched closely. Assume that hypothetical research studies show that by using psychological tests, a subgroup of 30 people, who are at much higher risk for suicide, can be identified from these 300 people with mental illness. Also, assume it is reasonably certain that 1 of these 30 is the "real" suicide candidate out of the original group of 300. Although tests have helped enormously in locating this at-risk group, a dilemma is then created in planning for each individual. The 270 people who are not at risk can be treated in standard fashion with regard to suicide precautions. But what about the 30 who are at risk? They now each have a 1 in 30, or about 3%, chance of suicide. A decision needs to be made about what to do with each of these people. With a 3% risk of suicide, is it best to hospitalize or otherwise closely supervise each person for his or her own protection, or are such restrictions under these circumstances an unfair suspension of personal liberty? Ninety-seven percent of the at-risk group are not really going to commit suicide. Obviously, at this point the problem is a value judgment and is best answered by considering several factors that encompass more than just results from psychological testing.

## What Else Can Be Done with This Case?

When lodging a forthright referral for psychological evaluation, you and the examining psychologist share a common mission to seek information. Occasionally, teachers, pediatricians, and case managers make referrals for other less considered and appropriate reasons. Out of exasperation that a student is disinterested, disrespectful, and/or unreachable, a teacher sometimes requests psychological testing. Sometimes, too, a therapist will find a client with whom no therapeutic alliance can be established. A pediatrician may reach a frustration point after constant complaints about a patient's behavior, and then he or she will suggest psychological testing be tried. The frustration seems likely when it is believed that no suitable way to treat a problem exists.

Unfortunately, little of value will result from psychological testing when exasperation rather than a logical search for answers to pointed questions leads to the evaluation. Unintentionally or intentionally, referrals made out of desperation can actually harm children and their families because they tend to leave people more frustrated at the conclusion of the process than they were at the beginning. This is so because, of course, psychological testing is merely an evaluation tool; it is not a treatment, and it does not produce solutions when those charged with caring for a child are at their wit's end. In these situations, it is important for the referring professional to analyze in his or her own mind what questions need to be answered by testing. If no questions arise, then talking about the case with the examining psychologist before proceeding with a referral is wise. These steps can prevent an unneeded evaluation. Psychological testing should not be used when you can think of nothing else.

## SUMMARY

The best guarantee a referral agent has for obtaining useful psychological information is to ask a clear, specific referral question. Information in a referral should be written in behavioral terms that explicitly explain to the psychologist what has occurred and what the question is. The detailed nature of a referral is what directs a psychologist's testing. Vague referrals, such as "complete a psychological evaluation," lead to vague information of little value to the referral agent.

Psychological testing can provide a wealth of information, but it is not always appropriate in every situation. Issues such as causation and prognostication cannot be addressed conclusively; testing, however, is still superior to only intuition and clinical judgment. Psychological testing is not the answer for problem cases "dumped" on the psychologist either, or when there is no other solution or intervention available to the referral agent.

### Study Questions

1. Write an acceptable referral question using behavioral terms.
2. What are the limitations of psychological testing where the issue of causation is concerned?

3. What advantages can psychological testing offer with prognostication?
4. What is the "C variable," and what is its role in psychological testing?
5. What are some reasons that referrals that are inappropriate for testing seem to crop up in schools?

CHAPTER THREE

# Infant Scales

## Diagnosing Early Developmental Delays

Signs that child development is not progressing as expected can occur as early as infancy, sometimes even earlier, as when a baby is born with known risk factors. Parents naturally want to know as early as possible if their baby is "okay." Physicians and nurses who care for neonates also may share this concern.

Baby Smith checks out all right physically and neurologically, but did the difficult labor and delivery have some subtle effects that are as yet undetected?

How ready is 2-month-old Lynn to go home to her parents after spending her entire life in an incubator? How closely does she need to be followed?

Beyond the neonatal period, other questions arise. We suspect that 14-month-old Billy's low weight gain and poor appetite mean he has failure-to-thrive syndrome. Are there any cognitive and/or developmental signs of this syndrome?

What is 18-month-old Mark's cognitive ability after experiencing a near-drowning episode?

## DIAGNOSING INFANT DELAYS

### PL 99-457

Questions about neonatal and infant development are among the most difficult for psychologists and child specialists to answer. Much of this difficulty has to do with the nature of infant problems. Distinctions between, and diagnoses of, mental retardation and learning disabilities can be made with older children and are discussed in subsequent chapters of this book. With infants, however, delays and problems are more global than specific, or more delimited in nature. What can be assessed is an infant's current developmental status. Although a diagnosis of a specific learning disability is beyond the reach of infant assessment, a more general diagnosis of "at risk" for a learning disability is not.

Identifying infants who are at risk and providing immediate intervention, and thus better long-term prognoses, are primary objectives of federal legislation. As of 1986, PL 99-457, the Education of the Handicapped Act Amendments, sought to identify children from birth to 5 years of age who had developmental delays or who were at risk for a disabling condition for early intervention services (Gallagher, 1989). PL 99-457 was reauthorized in 1991 as PL 102-119, the Individuals with Disabilities Education Act (IDEA) Amendments. In 1991, the broader special education law, IDEA, stated that developmental delays may occur in cognitive, physical, self-help, language, or psychosocial development. The law also includes diagnosed physical or mental conditions that have a high probability of resulting in delay. Each state, however, is free to define developmental delays as it chooses. Some states may choose to use the range of categories listed in the federal definition, but others restrict developmental delays to fewer and more narrow categories. In infants, however, many of the conditions included in IDEA cannot be diagnosed with any degree of precision. Because of this, IDEA has a provision for a diagnosis of at risk, which is to be used with regard to infants in the birth-to-3 age group. For many conditions, "at risk" is the most that can be ascertained for children younger than age 3; specific delays in cognitive, language, or self-help areas, for instance, cannot be determined precisely until the child matures.

## Prediction

Determination of the status of at risk for delays is most fitting in infant assessment because it is based on *current* developmental status and also because psychological testing is not sophisticated enough to tell us more about this young age group. For many worried parents, however, the concern is not about current status but rather future status: "Is this permanent, or will he outgrow it?" "Will she be able to learn when she goes to school?" There are inherent limitations in predicting future functioning from infant developmental status; such limitations extend to even state-of-the-art assessment tools and the course of development itself.

To accurately predict future IQ scores from infant IQs is difficult. This was understood in 1933 by Nancy Bayley, developer of the Bayley Scales of Infant Development (BSID). Bayley conducted long-term follow-up of infants into adolescence, with repeated assessments. She concluded that mental measurement during the first few months was a poor predictor of later mental development (Bayley, 1933). Bayley's same general finding still holds true. Authorities working in the 1990s and reviewing more than 50 years of research continue to echo Bayley: "The results unequivocally show that scores on instruments of infant mental performance assessed during the first 18 months of life do not predict later IQ to any practical extent" (McCall, 1979, p. 707).

But why do instruments fail to predict later IQ? If intelligence, or mental ability, is a meaningful trait, should it not be measurable at an early age, and should it not be roughly the same when measured later? As early as 1933, Bayley answered "no." She recognized that mental ability is a different attribute, resting on unrelated functions in infancy as compared with childhood. She believed that there was insufficient overlap of functions and skills between infant scales and IQ tests measured until 2 years of age. Thus, according to Bayley, infant scales administered before 24 months cannot predict later IQ with much accuracy because the child is shifting from one type of function to another between these ages (Bayley, 1933).

## Developmental Course

Many researchers have argued that development proceeds through specific, somewhat independent stages. In addition, infants naturally experience developmental spurts and lags, such that the rate of progression through stages is not identical for all children. Gains in one stage may have little or no bearing on gains in the next. Development during the first 18 months of age is characterized by the acquisition of motor and sensory skills, and by relatively simple nonlanguage, nonsymbolic problem solving. Piaget has referred to this stage as the sensorimotor period (Hunt, 1961).

But what about diagnosis of mental retardation? Even if rapid or average development in infancy means little, doesn't retarded development in infancy mean something? Slow infant development can, and often does, signal something significant. With children who have developmental disabilities, the relationship between infant and childhood IQs is much stronger than for infants without developmental disabilities (Sattler, 1988). Infants who score below average on mental scales during the first 18 months of life are more likely to have mental retardation than those who score average or higher. For infants, a below-average score usually indicates a disturbance in basic neurological/physiological functioning. Given that, a low score is likely to result when there is an obvious case of mental retardation, such as when a known predisposing factor has been identified. Some very low scores, particularly when coupled with known pre- or perinatal risk factors, place the the child in a category of severely at risk.

With less severe infant delays, however, prediction is not so ensured that a child will have mental retardation because his or her infant scores are low. If mild mental retardation were forecast in childhood solely from infant scales, many children would be misclassified as having mental retardation, whereas some who turn out to have mental retardation would be missed. This is particularly true because poor environment may have little effect on early development of sensorimotor skills, whereas later symbolic and language skills may be greatly affected. Thus, some infants who will have mild retardation based primarily on environmental factors will not be assessed as having significant delays in infancy.

There are, however, cases of severe mental retardation that are quite detectable in infancy. The following is a case example of the diagnostic process involved when mental retardation is suspected.

> Annie, age 16 months at the time of assessment, was the fourth child born to a 38-year-old woman. Annie was referred for a developmental assessment by her pediatrician, who suspected Annie might have Down syndrome. The syndrome is caused by a chromosomal abnormality and often occurs in children born to older mothers. It carries certain physical characteristics and almost always results in mental retardation. Following confirmation of the suspected diagnosis, Annie was monitored closely during her first year. Although the mother perceived Annie's development as progressing typically, the pediatrician saw significant delays, such as missed milestones. At this point, Annie was referred for a psychological consultation to better assess her current status.
>
> In order to help both Annie and Annie's mother, the psychologist encouraged the mother to be present during Annie's testing; this not only allowed the mother to comment on Annie's performance but also allowed her to see just what tasks her daughter could or could not do at various age levels. The Bayley Scales of Infant Development were administered, and Annie received scores for both mental and motor development that were 3 standard deviations below the mean. In addition to sharing these findings with the mother, specific items were pointed out. For instance, "Annie tended not to look for an object when we hid it from her. Most 10-month-olds will wonder what happened to it and want to

look for it." The findings helped to establish just what Annie's developmental status was and also gave foundation to the pediatrician's concerns. The results were used to develop interventions, including activities for stimulation, enrichment experiences in the community, and early education programs.

Follow-up evaluation was arranged for the next year, when the Bayley Scales would be readministered to assess Annie's growth and developmental status relative to same-age children.

This example about Annie makes two important points regarding infant assessment. First, it shows the utility of using several pieces of information from several different sources. Studies have shown that various combinations of clinical information, infant assessment results, and perinatal factors are more effective at predicting delays in early childhood than they are when used separately (Honzig, 1976; Siegel et al., 1982). Second, it shows that development itself limits predictability of test findings. Practically all infants, including Annie, will show some degree of progress, although that rate of progress will vary from one individual to another. This ever-changing status means decreased stability of assessment findings, which in turn limits predictive power. Furthermore, the individualized nature of development mandates ongoing assessment and follow-up when making diagnoses such as mental retardation. It is with these cautions in mind that the ensuing discussion of infant assessment can be best understood.

## Evaluator Viewpoint in Infant Assessment

Assessment of infants is unique in that, unlike assessment of older children, evaluators cannot ask infants to answer test questions, manipulate concrete objects, or talk about their feelings and behaviors. Because infant assessment typically covers birth to 2 years of age, concerns are often focused on determining whether the baby can roll over, visually track, or display emotion toward the caregiver. Much of infant assessment is dependent on observational data, and much of the data comes from clinicians or informants such as parents, nurses, child caregivers, and other primary caregivers. Each of these informants brings a slightly different point of view to his or her observations and sees a narrow slice of the child's behavior rather than the whole. Consequently, measures and ratings based on behavioral observations can vary, depending on the source of the data. Such differences give rise to some general cautions regarding the test setting and the relationship of the informant, which should be kept in mind when using assessment information.

One item to consider is whether various informants produce wildly divergent ratings or overall agreement about the same child. If differences do exist, then to what are they attributable? Some informant factors to examine include differences in individuals' formal knowledge or training in child development, the presence of pathology or distress that might positively or negatively skew individuals' perceptions, and the level of awareness of (or attention to) the child's growth and development. Setting factors include day-to-day familiarity with the child, opportunities to know about several different aspects of the child (e.g., sleeping, eating, and feeding routines; play skills; interactions with several children; attention span), and availability of other children against whom to make judgments about behavior. For example, the babysitter might watch a child only two afternoons per week, thus missing napping or feeding routines. Some babysitters may be less tolerant of fussy baby behavior or may have no experience with children and view a child as exceptionally problematic. Thus, psychologists who evaluate infants often attempt to incorporate several viewpoints of behavior to form the most comprehensive picture of an infant.

## ASSESSMENT OF TEMPERAMENT

Traditionally, infant assessment has focused on areas of motor, speech and language, adaptive behavior, and personal-social development. An alternative viewpoint, temperament, has been added to this list. Although mothers have always known that differences in temperament existed, these differences have come to be viewed as a potential predictor of later development.

*Temperament* has been described as an individual's personality, constitution, or nature. Definitions have ranged from "biologically based differences among individuals in reactions to stimuli, in the expression of emotions, in arousal, and in self-regulation" (Hetherington & Parke, 1986, p. 85), to the way in which a child does something, as opposed to simply what the child does (Hertzig & Snow, 1988). Temperament is commonly viewed as a style that is present from an early age that seems to be constitutionally based. Beyond this, however, there are several different views. Some view temperament as consisting of the dimensions of emotionality, sociability, and activity (Buss & Plomin, 1984), whereas others view it in a very basic fashion of individual differences in self-regulation and reactivity that are then affected by the environment (Rothbart & Derryberry, 1981). Kagan (1989) views temperament as physiologically based and has begun to link to two different temperament styles (inhibited and uninhibited) to brain functioning. Like many researchers, Kagan finds temperament qualities to be variable across infants but relatively stable within a given individual.

The following mother's description of her two children illustrates temperament differences:

> From day one, this child was a handful! He would not sleep, threw up a lot—feeding was an awful time, and he never took regular naps. He was so fussy, too. Nothing seemed to soothe him. I would pick him up, and he would cry. I would put him down, and he would cry. I would rock him or sing to him—nothing worked. Even now, he is still like that. His preschool teacher says that he often seems irritable and does not seem to enjoy playing with the other kids. He gets frustrated and angry with them for no reason at all.
>
> Now my second child is not like his brother at all. He is such a funny little boy, really sweet and affectionate, but he seems so scared and timid. Around me, he likes to be cuddled and play games. We read stories and sing, but the minute someone comes into the room, he draws back, gets clingy with me, and will not talk! His Sunday School classes were really tough at first. He would not want to go in without me; he hung back by the door. Only now does he go independently and willingly answer questions if the teacher calls on him. He has never been a real problem, though, like his older brother.

This mother's descriptions illustrate how two children can have two very different styles.

Psychologists, as behavioral scientists, require a more precise study of the concept of temperament, however. For psychologists, there are two basic issues in temperament: 1) how these styles can be measured reliably, and 2) what value exists in assessing temperament. Some of the earliest work done to assess temperament was the New York Longitudinal Study, conducted by Stella Chess and Alexander Thomas beginning in the 1950s. Chess and Thomas (1977) identified nine categories of temperament, shown in Table 3.1. These nine categories were distilled into three behavior patterns: Easy-Child Pattern, Slow-to-Warm-Up-Child Pattern, and Difficult-Child Pattern.

Children in the Easy-Child Pattern tend to be relatively stable in terms of mood, are generally positive, are adaptive to new situations and changes, and have rhythmicity in the biological functions. Slow-to-Warm-Up children tend to display negativity and low adaptability

Table 3.1. Categories of temperament

| | |
|---|---|
| 1. Activity Level | Sits quietly or is restless; favorite types of activities |
| 2. Rhythmicity | Biological regularity of functions such as sleep, bowel movements |
| 3. Approach/Withdrawal | Response style to novel situations, new people |
| 4. Adaptability | Responses to changes in routine |
| 5. Intensity of Reaction | Degree of emotion shown or expressed |
| 6. Threshold of Responsiveness | Responds to minute bits of stimuli or requires a great degree of stimuli |
| 7. Quality of Mood | General state may be happy or sad, contented or dissatisfied |
| 8. Distractibility | Able to concentrate or everything catches child's attention |
| 9. Persistence | Effort or perseverance on hard, challenging tasks |

Adapted from Chess and Thomas (1977); Hertzig and Snow (1988).

when in new situations; however, this behavior appears to change and become more positive with repeated exposures to novel situations. Children in the Difficult Pattern can be best described as highly negative, moody, slow to adapt, withdrawn, and lacking rhythmicity in biological functions. As we will see when discussing stability of temperament, the Difficult Pattern has been the main focus of attention in temperament research.

In addition to parent interview, two other techniques used in temperament assessment include the parent questionnaire and direct observation. Some parent questionnaires utilize the Chess and Thomas (1977) concept of temperament with its nine variables. Questionnaires are generally the preferred method of assessment because of their ease and cost effectiveness (Bates, 1987). However, direct observation is useful in clinical settings and can easily be incorporated into play activities or direct questioning of the child. For instance, the observer can note the ease with which the child separates from parents (approach/withdrawal) or the child's favorite thing to do (activity level).

Parent interview, parent questionnaire, and direct observation all have limitations that warrant caution for anyone using or evaluating information derived from these techniques. Generally, concerns focus on validity and comprehensiveness of information. There is always the risk of receiving inaccurate information from a parent or inadequate information from a brief interview or observation. The best assessment of temperament is likely to come from a combination of all three methods: parent interview, parent questionnaire, and direct observation.

No matter how temperament is measured, additional concerns pertinent to temperament assessment in general include selection of behaviors to be measured and quantification of those behaviors. Behaviors that will be selected are often dependent on age, context, and basic developmental guidelines. For instance, a 10-month-old may cry when separated from a parent, and a 10-year-old may seem unnecessarily clingy when separated from his mother. Although both behaviors seem similar, both are not necessarily indicative of approach/withdrawal. Separation anxiety and fear of strangers is developmentally expected in a 10-month-old. Similarly, if the 10-year-old child just had an upsetting experience, such as being scolded or being in a near-miss car accident, the resulting clinging behavior would be context specific, rather than generally true. This is an example in which direct observation needs supplemental information from the parent.

Concerns with quantification of temperament assessment center on the system used, the person who is scoring, and the standard used for comparison. For instance, scores may not be comparable across the dozens of commercially available instruments. If a child is assessed at 4 months and later at 10 months, then changes in results may be due to the instrument *or* the child. In addition, there may be differences between a mother's and a father's ratings. Research indicates that there are low levels of agreement across instruments attempting to measure the same characteristics of temperament and that there is moderate agreement between parents' ratings, particularly with concepts such as the child's activity level and difficulty (Hertzig & Snow, 1988). Deciding on the standard for comparison is of particular importance for scoring: Is the child to be compared to siblings, peers, self, just one sex, both sexes, children of the same socioeconomic level, or of all levels? Although some of these standards may be addressed in the measure's instructions, those not addressed may still indirectly affect scoring. Ideally, the same standard(s) should be considered and applied consistently to all items or behaviors to be scored.

Another basic question involves whether it is of value to assess temperament. Attempts to answer this question have come from research on the stability of temperament across time. Again, it is the New York Longitudinal Study that provided some of the first answers to this question. Thomas and Chess (1986) examined the stability of temperament ratings both within their first age group (3 months–2 years) and between the first and second (1–5 years) age groups. Within the first group, mood, adaptability, intensity of reaction, and approach/withdrawal had the highest stability, whereas activity level and distractibility had the lowest. Comparisons between the first group and second group showed that adaptability, rhythmicity, and activity level had the highest stability, whereas approach/withdrawal, distractibility, and persistence had the lowest. Overall, however, there was little predictive validity from the first year to the fifth year, and relationships that did emerge were not of any practical significance.

Using parent questionnaires, McDevitt (1976) found similar findings: low to moderate stability for activity level, adaptability, intensity of reaction, and threshold of responsiveness from infancy to childhood, and statistical relationships that were of little practical significance. However, McDevitt did find interesting sex differences, with males showing stability for approach/withdrawal and mood and females showing stability for rhythmicity across infancy to 3–5 years of age.

In contrast to these analyses that examined singular temperament variables, examination of temperament patterns has provided more meaningful information. As mentioned previously, it is the Difficult-Child Pattern that has been the focus of much attention. In Thomas and Chess's (1986) study, only 10% of the children were found to fit the Difficult-Child Pattern; however, 70% of those children later developed behavior problems in early and middle childhood. Other researchers also have found a correlation between difficult infant temperament and later behavior problems (Rutter, 1977; Terestman, 1980; Wolkind & DeSalis, 1982). Two possible reasons advanced for this phenomenon are 1) because difficult children do not adjust well to environmental changes, they are predisposed to emotional/behavioral problems later in their lives; and 2) because difficult children are so tiresome to their caregivers, they are likely to become the object of their caregivers' frustrations (Hetherington & Parke, 1986).

Thomas and Chess (1986) have advanced a goodness-of-fit/poorness-of-fit concept for viewing interaction between a child and his or her environment. This concept takes into account the caregiver's temperament in addition to an infant's temperament. The parents' needs, expectations, and reactions to the baby should be examined. A good fit between the style of the infant and the style of his or her environment, or *consonance,* allows for maximum child development, whereas a poor fit, or *dissonance,* may result in maladaptive responses from both parent and child, and problematic child development (Hertzig & Snow, 1988). For example, parents may modify their responses to a difficult child either adaptively, through flexibility and understanding, or maladaptively, through anger and punishment. The parental response pattern may lessen or exacerbate the likelihood of later problems. Assessing goodness- or poorness-of-fit requires assessing both parts of the concept: the child and his or her environment.

All three temperament assessment methods—parent interview, questionnaire, and direct observation—are needed to assess both parts. Identifying the child's temperament is an important starting point for helping parents understand their child's behavior. Observing parents' styles, however, is equally important for teaching adaptive responses and modifying parent behavior toward the child. By focusing on both child and parent, their "fit" may be modified in a manner that allows for more positive development.

General conclusions on the stability of temperament are somewhat mixed and are subject to "widespread hedging" (Bates, 1987, p. 1113). Some of the more global and accepted dimensions, like activity and emotionality, show stability through infancy. Also, temperament patterns such as the Easy-Child seem more stable compared to the Slow-to-Warm-Up Pattern. As for long-term prediction, temperament is a moderately powerful predictor of future behavior, although it is certainly apt to be influenced by parental and environmental variables.

## BRAZELTON NEONATAL BEHAVIORAL ASSESSMENT SCALE

The Brazelton Neonatal Behavioral Assessment Scale (NBAS) is an extremely specialized instrument, and unless one works in a neonatal or pediatric setting he or she is unlikely to encounter it clinically. The instrument has, however, been used in several research projects. It was originally developed as a measure of neonatal status for use with infants having known risk factors or expected atypical development. Since its inception in 1973, the Brazelton has undergone revision as a result of extensive research and clinical use. A second edition Brazelton NBAS (Brazelton, 1984) has been developed, as well as two modified scales: Assessment of Preterm Infants Behavior (Als, Lester, Tronick, & Brazelton, 1982) and Neonatal Behavior Assessment Scale with Kansas Supplements (NBAS–K) (Horowitz & Linn, 1984). Of these, the NBAS–K is a frequently used modification.

Like its predecessor, the revised Brazelton continues to emphasize two primary areas of infant functioning: reflexive behaviors and social-emotional/attention behaviors. Its goal is to identify children who are at risk and determine which of the children require early intervention. The goal is not simply assessment of an infant, but assessment within the context of that infant's relationship with a primary caregiver (Brazelton, Nugent, & Lester, 1987). The assumption underlying the instrument is that an infant has "interacting developmental systems rather than static ones" (Brazelton et al., 1987, p. 811).

By focusing on the interactive nature of the infant, the Brazelton scale breaks with traditional infant measures, on which the focus has been solely neurological functioning. The instrument can be used with typically developing infants at 36–44 weeks' gestational age who require no medical supports.

The first area, reflexive behaviors, measures 20 items that are rated on a 4-point scale according to degree of intensity: 0 for no response, 1 for low, 2 for medium, or 3 for high intensity (see Table 3.2). Any absent or asymmetrical reflexes are noted as well. Deviant scores here are indicative of gross neurological problems, and infants obtaining three or more such scores are referred for detailed neurological evaluation.

The Brazelton scale's second area, social-emotional/attention behaviors, consists of 28 items (with 9 supplementary items that are "currently under investigation") (Worobey & Brazelton, 1990, p. 34) that are rated 1–9, with the midpoint representing typical behavior of a 3-day-old neonate (see Table 3.3). The items can be loosely organized

Table 3.2. Reflex behaviors on the revised Neonatal Behavioral Assessment Scale

| Reflex items | X | O | L | M | H | A |
|---|---|---|---|---|---|---|
| Plantar grasp | | 0 | 1 | 2 | 3 | |
| Hand grasp | | 0 | 1 | 2 | 3 | |
| Ankle clonus | | 0 | 1 | 2 | 3 | |
| Babinski | | 0 | 1 | 2 | 3 | |
| Standing | | 0 | 1 | 2 | 3 | |
| Automatic walking | | 0 | 1 | 2 | 3 | |
| Placing | | 0 | 1 | 2 | 3 | |
| Incurvation | | 0 | 1 | 2 | 3 | |
| Crawling | | 0 | 1 | 2 | 3 | |
| Glabella | | 0 | 1 | 2 | 3 | |
| Tonic deviation of head and eyes | | 0 | 1 | 2 | 3 | |
| Nystagmus | | 0 | 1 | 2 | 3 | |
| Tonic neck reflex | | 0 | 1 | 2 | 3 | |
| Moro | | 0 | 1 | 2 | 3 | |
| Rooting (intensity) | | 0 | 1 | 2 | 3 | |
| Sucking (intensity) | | 0 | 1 | 2 | 3 | |
| Passive movement | | 0 | 1 | 2 | 3 | |
| arms R | | 0 | 1 | 2 | 3 | |
| L | | 0 | 1 | 2 | 3 | |
| legs R | | 0 | 1 | 2 | 3 | |
| L | | 0 | 1 | 2 | 3 | |

From Osofsky, J.D. (Ed.). (1987). *Handbook of Infant Development.* New York: John Wiley & Sons, Inc., Copyright © 1987, reprinted by permission of John Wiley & Sons, Inc.

X = response omitted; O = response not elicited; L = low; M = medium; H = high; A = asymmetry of response.

Table 3.3. Behavioral items on the revised Neonatal Behavioral Assessment Scale[a]

| | |
|---|---|
| 1. Response decrement to light (1, 2, 3) | 14. Pull-to-sit (4, 5) |
| 2. Response decrement to rattle (1, 2, 3) | 15. Cuddliness (4, 5) |
| 3. Response decrement to bell (1, 2, 3) | 16. Defensive movements (3, 4, 5) |
| 4. Response decrement to tactile stimulation of the foot (1, 2, 3) | 17. Consolability (6 to 4, 3, 2) |
| | 18. Peak of excitement (all states) |
| 5. Orientation inanimate visual (4, 5) | 19. Rapidity of buildup (all states) |
| 6. Orientation inanimate auditory (4, 5) | 20. Irritability (all awake states) |
| 7. Orientation inanimate visual and auditory (4, 5) | 21. Activity (alert states) |
| | 22. Tremulousness (all states) |
| 8. Orientation animate visual (4, 5) | 23. Startle (3, 4, 5, 6) |
| 9. Orientation animate auditory (4, 5) | 24. Lability of skin color (from 1 to 6) |
| 10. Orientation animate visual and auditory (4, 5) | 25. Lability of states (all states) |
| | 26. Self-quieting activity (6 to 4, 3, 2, 1) |
| 11. Alertness (4, 5) | 27. Hand-mouth facility (all states) |
| 12. General tonus (4, 5) | 28. Smiles (all states) |
| 13. Motor maturity (4, 5) | |

From Osofsky, J.D. (Ed.) (1987). *Handbook of Infant Development.* New York: John Wiley & Sons, Inc.; Copyright © 1987, reprinted by permission of John Wiley & Sons, Inc.

[a]Numbers in parentheses refer to optimal state for assessment.

around orientation and responsivity to various stimuli, motor capabilities, and emotionality (i.e., excitement, cuddliness, consolability, irritability). These behaviors pertain to the newborn's ability to adapt to a new environment. This assessment assumes change is occurring, and as such it is recommended that a minimum of two assessments occur. Ideally, the first assessment should occur when the baby is 2–3 days old, the second at age 7–10 days, and possibly a third at age 14 days or at 1 month (Brazelton et al., 1987). While each assessment is occurring, the examiner should note conditions in the environment, such as light and noise, as well as any medical conditions, such as jaundice or medication, that would influence performance. The infant's initial state and his or her prevailing state throughout the assessment are noted as well.

In an effort to make the Brazelton NBAS appropriate for use with premature infants at high risk, a set of nine supplementary behavioral items (Worobey & Brazelton, 1990) has been added to the second edition, as mentioned above. Brazelton et al. (1987) stresses that these supplementary items are most appropriately used when an infant is 36 weeks' gestational age or older and/or is off medical supports and when the examiner specializes in infants at high risk.

The revised Brazelton scale is scored for the 20 reflexive behaviors and 28 behavioral items, plus the new supplementary items. Some scoring difficulty may result from the ordering of the scales. On the 9-point scoring scale, a midpoint score is favorable for most items;

however, on some items a higher score is favorable. The current edition of the NBAS has resulted in several approaches for score summarization, although it is pointed out that the "process" is of particular interest and no one summary score is derived from the instrument. One popular approach involves grouping the neonate's performance into four dimensions: interactive processes, motor processes, state control, and responses to stress. Performance on each dimension can be described as optimal, normal, or inadequate (Worobey & Brazelton, 1990).

## Reliability, Validity, and Utility

Because the Brazelton is unlike most other psychological instruments, it has a unique set of technical concerns, the first of which is related to problems of rater viewpoint. The Brazelton relies on the clinician to elicit an infant's optimum performance via interaction and observation. Consequently, random problems, such as an inopportune time for assessment, an unusually bad day for the infant, an incompetent examiner, or an incomplete observation would result in an artificially low score. A second concern is low test–retest reliability, which results from the ever-changing status of the neonate. Although Brazelton et al. (1987) acknowledge that this is not the most appropriate statistic to apply because of day-to-day changes, it nonetheless hampers efforts at long-term prediction because prediction depends on stable scores. A third concern is the lack of adequate norming. For the first edition of the Brazelton scale, only 54 healthy, problem-free infants from a single hospital were used as the norm sample. The sample size and single hospital reduce the representativeness of this sample; however, an effort is underway to establish a representative normative base comprising healthy, problem-free infants. A final concern is the specialized training that clinicians must undergo to administer the measure. This training is only offered at selected sites, typically large medical centers and universities. Thus, the limited availability of training means that the instrument does not have widespread use, despite its diagnostic value.

Aside from the preceding concerns, there is positive research evidence that validates the measure's use. Performance on the Brazelton NBAS has been investigated for the following clinical populations with findings generally reflecting the instrument's sensitivity: prematurity, smallness for age, jaundice, alcohol and other drug usage by mother, maternal diabetes, and maternal exposure to environmental toxins (Worobey & Brazelton, 1990). Behavioral differences have been observed repeatedly on the clusters of orientation, state regulation, reflexive behaviors, motor performance, and autonomic regulation. Infants at high risk tend to score more poorly than infants at little to no risk (Francis, Self, & Horowitz, 1987).

A similar picture emerges from studies using the Brazelton scale to measure the effects of maternal medication on the newborn. All clusters have shown the effects of medication, although factors such as type and dose of medication seem to mediate these effects. In a comparison study of lidocaine and chloroprocaine, two epidural anesthesias, healthy newborns were examined with the Brazelton at less than 5 hours of age and again at 3 days of age (Kuhnert, Harrison, Linn, & Kuhnert, 1984). At less than 5 hours of age, infants whose mothers received chloroprocaine received significantly better scores on the autonomic cluster. With age, however, all cluster scores except for state regulation improved.

Prediction research is one of the most frequent applications of the Brazelton scale. One prediction study used repeated assessments with the Brazelton scale to correlate those scores with Bayley Mental Developmental Index scores for 18-month-olds (Lester, 1984). Premature and full-term infants were given a series of evaluations with the Brazelton that yielded recovery curves or profiles. *Recovery curves* allow a clinician to see patterns of change in an infant's functioning across time. The Brazelton scores were combined with variables of socioeconomic status, neurological status, and a rating of medical risk. Together, this 3-variable formula was a strong and accurate predictor of the preterm infants' Bayley scores at 18 months of age. Other studies support these findings and show significant relationships between recovery curves and later assessment of infants' cognitive functioning (Seposki, Hoffman, & Brazelton, 1986). Based on such results, researchers stress that a single assessment is only useful for determining gross levels of dysfunctions; repeated assessments significantly improve predictive power.

## BAYLEY SCALES OF INFANT DEVELOPMENT–II

Those who work with young children are much more likely to encounter findings from the Bayley scales than the Brazelton scale. The Bayley Scales of Infant Development–II (BSID–II) (Bayley, 1993) is a measure of infant development designed for the age range of 1 month to 3½ years. The Bayley scales focus on ability as it relates to learning, problem solving, and conceptualization. The measure was initially developed in 1933 as the California First-Year Mental Test and was subsequently revised, incorporating the California Infant Scale of Motor Development, over a period of years. The scale formally designated the Bayley Scales of Infant Development appeared in 1969 and constituted the first in-depth and psychometrically sophisticated standardization of an infant scale. In its current form, the BSID–II yields scores for mental development, psychomotor development, and infant behavior. The original intent was to measure intellect at its very earliest stages; however, years of research have shown that infant measures are generally not predictive of later intellectual functioning. This is a generalized limitation in infant assessment, rather than a criticism of the Bayley scales, which are an effective tool for assessing developmental status.

The first area of the BSID–II, mental development, has 178 items that measure development by tapping the ability to vocalize and use language, habituate to stimuli, solve problems, classify, generalize, and use social skills (see Figure 3.1). Specific skills assessed vary greatly depending on the age and developmental level of the infant or child. For the youngest infants, rudimentary skills like visual inspection, habituation, and discrimination are assessed. Some of these neonate items tap intactness of neurological/physiological functions (i.e., coordinated vertical eye movements). The scale covers an age range in which marked growth is occurring, and accordingly, the items are graded for difficulty. The items progress toward increased conceptualization with later items evaluating concepts such as understanding prepositions. At older ages increasingly sophisticated vocalization, naming, perceptual, conceptual, and problem-solving tasks are included. Not surprising given the upper age range of 42 months, the BSID–II includes some items quite similar to preschool IQ tests such as the Wechsler Preschool and Primary Scale of Intelligence–Revised (WPPSI–R). BSID–II scoring of the mental development area yields a Mental Development Index, which is a standard score with a mean of 100 and standard deviation of 15. This score is numerically equivalent to IQ scores.

| | | | | | | | | |
|---|---|---|---|---|---|---|---|---|
| 6 months | 49. Smiles at Mirror Image | Seated | Mirror | 50 | | 41 | | |
| | 50. Responds Playfully to Mirror Image | Seated | Mirror | | | 49 | | |
| | 51. Regards Pellet | Seated | Sugar Pellet | (M) 41, (M) 32 | | | | |
| 4 months | 52. Bangs in Play | Seated | Spoon or Other Hard Object | | | | | |
| | 53. Reaches for Second Cube | Seated | 3 Cubes | 57, 58, 65 | | 45 | | |

Figure 3.1. Sample Mental Scale items from Bayley Scales of Infant Development–Second Edition. These are beginning items (relatively easy) for 6-month-olds and concluding items (relatively difficult) for 4-month-olds. 

| | | | | | | | |
|---|---|---|---|---|---|---|---|
| 10 months / 7 months **51.** Moves from Sitting to Creeping Position | Seated | Bell | | | 50 | | |
| **52.** Raises Self to Standing Position | Supine | Bell or Rattle | | | 47 | | |
| **53.** Attempts to Walk | Standing | | 60, 61 | | 46 | | |

Figure 3.2. Sample Motor Scale items from Bayley Scales of Infant Development–Second Edition. These are beginning items (relatively easy) for 10-month-olds and concluding items (relatively difficult) for 7-month-olds. (Copyright © 1993 by The Psychological Corporation. Reproduced by permission. All rights reserved.)

The second area, motor development, is composed of 97 items that require both fine and gross motor ability (see Figure 3.2). Essentially, the motor scale examines degree of control of the body and overall coordination. Overall coordination includes skills such as standing, sitting, walking, grasping, jumping, and various balancing actions. These are meant to be distinct from activities required in the mental development scale because the Bayley scales include preplanning and reasoning as components of mental activities but not of motor activities. From the motor scale, a Motor Index is obtained. Like the Mental Developmental Index, the Motor Index is based on a mean of 100 and standard deviation of 15.

The third area, infant behavior, comprises 30 items that measure the qualitative aspect of child's test behavior in a Behavior Rating Scale. Each item (see Figure 3.3 for an example of a single item) is rated on a 1–5 scale. The following summary dimensions scores are produced: Attention/Arousal, Orientation/Engagement, Emotional/Regulation, and Motor Quality. Each of these dimensions can be summarized by percentile ranks, which in turn can be converted to the following categories: "normal limits," "questionable," and "nonoptimal." Items assess considerations such as soothability when upset, interest in test material, orientation to examiner, fearfulness, persistence when attempting to complete tasks, adaptation of change in test

**10. Adaptation to Change in Test Materials**
1–42 months

Consistently resists relinquishing materials and/or refuses to accept new materials .......... 1
Typically resists relinquishing materials and/or refuses to accept new materials; makes one or two transitions easily .......... 2
Makes poor transitions half the time; makes good transitions half the time .......... 3
Typically relinquishes materials and accepts new materials; one or two poor transitions .......... 4
Consistently relinquishes materials and accepts new materials .......... 5

Figure 3.3. Sample Behavior Rating Scale item from Bayley Scales of Infant Development–Second Edition. (Copyright © 1993 by The Psychological Corporation. Reproduced by permission. All rights reserved.)

material, and control of movement. In this respect, the Bayley scale is like the Brazelton scale because they both assess the behavioral repertoire.

## Reliability, Validity, and Utility

The development of the BSID–II occurred in large part because the excellent norms of the first edition of the Bayley scales (1969) had become dated. The BSID–II's carefully selected standardization sample of 1,700 infants and young children confirmed that restandardization was warranted—the BSID–II produces Mental Scale scores about 12 less and Motor Scale scores about 10 less than those earned if the original scale were used. The psychometric properties of the Bayley attest to it being a sound, well-developed instrument. In the BSID–II, the sample was matched with census figures on race/ethnicity, geographic region, and parent education. This is accepted practice for any psychological test, but as infant measures go, it places the Bayley scale among those tests at the very top. Few, if any, infant ability measures have such a solid foundation. The use of standard scores for both the Mental and Motor Scales is convenient for making comparisons across scales. In addition, this format allows for direct comparison of an infant's developmental status to other infants the same age. (See Illustration 3.1 for a case study.) This, too, is an indicator of the Bayley scale's technical sophistication over other infant measures.

Studies have shown that the original Bayley scale has adequate reliability and validity. The original Bayley scale was assessed favorably for reliability with test–retest short intervals (Horner, 1980; Werner & Bayley, 1966). Information in the BSID–II manual implies that it also has adequate stability over short intervals. In contrast to these findings, however, a study showed instability across repeated testing (Horner, 1988) on the original Bayley scale. A group of 9-month-olds and 15-month-olds was tested with the Bayley scale twice at 1-week intervals and showed significant variation in scores. The authors found that there was a 50% chance of having a developmental quotient from a single administration differ from an optimal score by more than 1 standard deviation. This led to suggestions to use repeated assessments with the original Bayley scale rather than a single test administration. Using the resulting score from a single administration may lead to erroneous assumptions and decisions about a child. As long-term studies of BSID–II become available, the same suggestion may also arise.

The test manual contains information that will help make the BSID–II clinically useful. Information was derived from testing 370

## Illustration 3.1

Allen was born prematurely at 26 weeks' gestational age, with a birth weight of 1 pound, 3 ounces. He is the third child of a healthy 30-year-old mother and a 31-year-old father; there were no complications with their previous two children. There were no known reasons related to either the mother or child for the premature birth. Allen was immediately placed in a neonatal intensive care unit, where he remained for 6 months. Allen's first few months were characterized by instability, rather than a steady course of growth and improvement. The most significant problem was the immaturity of Allen's lungs, which required him to be placed on a respirator for 2 months. Attempts to wean him from the respirator were not successful, and he went into respiratory failure on three occasions. He was completely taken off the respirator during his third month but continued to require oxygen supplementation until 15 months of age. In addition to breathing difficulties, he experienced numerous colds and infections due to a poorly developed immune system. Feeding was also difficult, and Allen's weight fluctuated daily. This necessitated the use of steroids to aid his growth, which in turn caused other health problems. Much of his early care was a delicate balancing act of attempting to treat one problem without complicating another.

Throughout this early period, Allen's parents visited him daily, and on occasion his two siblings were able to visit as well. As much as possible (given health limitations), Allen's parents were nurturant and interactive; Allen was held, rocked, fed, sung to, talked to, and played with by his family. His parents also were able to take over many of the nursing care duties, which gave them even greater involvement. Generally, Allen was not a fussy infant, except when painful treatments were being administered. He seemed alert and responsive to his parents and nurses. During his fifth month, Allen's health began to stabilize, and he began to gain weight steadily. He was off the respirator, and oxygen was being used only as needed. After demonstrating stability for approximately 3 weeks, Allen was referred for psy-

*(continued)*

*continued*

# Illustration 3.1

chological testing to evaluate current developmental status and aid discharge planning. He was administered the Bayley Scales of Infant Development with the following results:

| | |
|---|---|
| Chronological Age: | 5.5 months |
| Corrected Age: | 1.5 months |
| Mental Scale: | 1-month difficulty level |
| Motor Scale: | less than 1-month difficulty level |

Allen passed the mental scale items at approximately the 1-month level and the motor scale items at slightly under the 1-month level. Despite marginally better mental than motor skills, it was clear that Allen's overall developmental progress was lagging behind that of other 5½-month-old infants. Whereas Allen's behaviors included being able to respond to his caregivers, make coordinated eye movements, and move his arms and legs in anticipation of being picked up, behaviors characteristic of typically developing 5½-month-old infants include being able to grasp objects in their hands, inspect play items, and work themselves into a sitting position. A more accurate age comparison, however, is to use Allen's corrected gestational age rather than his chronological age. Had Allen completed the usual prenatal course and been born as expected, his true age would be 1 month, not 5 months. A corrected gestational age takes into account the months of prenatal development not completed. Thus, correcting for his 4-month early birth gives a better indication of Allen's development. In such a light, he does not appear to have delays. Instead, his range of skills is in keeping with a 1½-month-old baby. Because of Allen's young age and brief period of stability prior to testing, follow-up assessment was recommended in 1 year. It was also recommended that Allen's parents continue to stimulate Allen at home, in much the same way as they had in the hospital. His siblings were viewed as a source of stimulation as well, and their interaction with Allen was strongly encouraged.

Allen continued to have periods of stability and instability throughout the next 12 months. He was hospitalized twice, once for respiratory failure and once for pneumonia. During each stay, however, he stabilized quickly. Other ongoing medical

*(continued)*

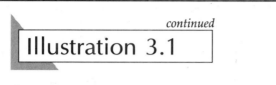

continued

## Illustration 3.1

problems included continued oxygen use and weight fluctuation. Temperamentally, his parents reported that Allen was still an easy child, provided he stayed healthy. When he was fussy and not feeling well, he could be comforted without too much difficulty. He was very responsive to family members and had developed play routines with his brother and sister. Parents also reported that Allen was starting to talk. His vocabulary included the family's names and those of their pet dog and cat.

Allen's follow-up assessment was conducted at 18 months of age. The Bayley scales were used again to determine Allen's progress as well as to make appropriate age comparisons.

| | |
|---|---|
| Chronological Age: | 18 months |
| Corrected Age: | 14 months |
| Mental Scale: | 11- to 12-month difficulty range |
| Motor Scale: | 8- to 9-month difficulty range |

As was true in his first assessment, Allen's mental skills were better developed than his motor skills. Although he demonstrated growth in all areas, he continued to be behind the average for his chronological age. Once again, however, he appeared within usual limits for his corrected gestational age. Although Allen's parents had indeed noticed progress, it was not commensurate with his chronological age. Nonetheless, this was clearly an encouraging sign, and his parents were urged to continue stimulating Allen. A 1-year follow-up evaluation was recommended for two reasons: 1) developmentally, Allen would begin acquiring a new set of skills different from the sensorimotor skills typical of earlier stages; and 2) test results obtained after 18–24 months of age have greater predictive value for later functioning.

From 18–30 months of age, Allen stabilized medically. Oxygen supplementation was no longer necessary, his weight steadily increased, and he successfully fought off colds during the winter. His parents reported that he was much like their other two children: "into everything, eats constantly, talks constantly, and fights with his brother and sister." Allen's 30-month evalu-

*(continued)*

*continued*

## Illustration 3.1

ation showed that, although his pattern remained the same, he had hit a growth spurt in terms of acquiring developmental skills.

| | |
|---|---|
| Chronological Age: | 30 months |
| Corrected Age: | 26 months |
| Mental Scale: | 25- to 28-month difficulty range |
| Motor Scale: | 15- to 18-month difficulty range |

For the first time, Allen passed mental scale items that were within usual limits for his chronological age. Language was the most notable area of improvement; his vocabulary had increased sizably. Motor skills were still behind, but again were in keeping with his corrected age. Overall, Allen had demonstrated significant growth in his first 2½ years, despite severe medical complications. At this point, preschool programs were discussed with the parents to facilitate Allen's learning, socialization outside of the family and future school readiness.

infants with diagnosed conditions: autism, HIV+, prematurity, prenatal exposure to drugs, asphyxiation at birth, Down syndrome, developmental delay, and chronic otitis media (middle ear infection).

In accordance with federal guidelines for infants and preschoolers who require special services, five areas of development (cognitive, physical, language and speech, psychosocial, and self-help) are enumerated. The BSID–II has attempted to include items in these areas. A seemingly good idea would be creation of a method of recording each child's performance in each of these areas. The BSID–II has done this by creating cognitive, language, social, and motor "facets," and the child's performance can be plotted in each to produce a pattern.

It is important to note that there are no true derived scores (e.g., standard scores) for these facets. Thus, diagnosticians lack a precise method of deciding if a child actually has delays in any one of these facets. The use of facets without exact scores for them has been criticized as confusing and potentially giving rise to misuse (Schock & Buck, 1995). This could be an important point if facet scores are to be used as a basis to determine whether children qualify for services

(Schock & Buck, 1995). It would appear wiser to rely on the BSID–II's derived scores of Mental, Motor, and Behavior and to forgo the potentially confusing facets for program qualification.

The BSID–II can be cumbersome and requires considerable practice for individuals to become facile with it. Because of this and the comprehensive scope of the instrument, the BSID–II is used primarily when problematic development is present or when an infant who is at risk is being followed; it is not typically used for routine screening purposes (Whatley, 1987). Overall, the original Bayley scale is widely accepted as the standard for assessment of infant development status (Francis et al., 1987; Goldman, L'Engle Stein, & Guerry, 1983; Sattler, 1988). The BSID–II appears to capitalize on the strengths of the original instrument with the advantage of adding new items and material and, most important, new norms.

## SCREENING INSTRUMENTS

Both the Brazelton and Bayley scales are examples of tools geared toward comprehensive assessment of atypical or problematic development. Not every child, however, requires such a thorough assessment. It is not feasible for a psychologist to routinely evaluate his or her very youngest patients with a Bayley scale to make sure they are "coming along okay." Nonetheless, there are children with problematic development who are frequently missed because of the subtle nature of their problems. The children often appear to be functioning typically, and difficulties are not detected during a visit to the pediatrician, or the children are not yet in school where a teacher or school nurse may spot delays. It is in these situations that *screening* (a brief assessment used to determine if a more detailed evaluation is required) is the preferred method of assessment. Because future outcome has much to do with early identification, there is ample justification to conduct screening.

Two measures presented here, the Battelle Developmental Inventory Screening Test and the Revised BRIGANCE® Diagnostic Inventory of Early Development[1], serve screening purposes by evaluating key areas of development in an efficient manner. The Battelle Developmental Inventory can be completed within 10–30 minutes, and the BRIGANCE Inventory in 15–20 minutes, depending on the child's ability. In addition, both measures have the advantage of being used repeatedly with a child as he or she ages, making it convenient to track progress. Another convenient feature of screening is that it often

[1]BRIGANCE® is a registered trademark of Curriculum Associates, Inc.

can be conducted by a variety of professionals, from psychologists to trained classroom teachers and child specialists.

Screening is efficient and useful in situations in which large numbers of children are involved, such as when screening incoming preschool and kindergarten children for possible delays or developmental disabilities. Similarly, screening is effective to help determine if a suspected weakness or delay warrants further, more in-depth evaluation. Often, simply screening a child yields enough information to adequately address a teacher's or parent's concern.

## BATTELLE DEVELOPMENTAL INVENTORY

The Battelle Developmental Inventory Screening Test, developed in 1984, was designed to avoid weaknesses present in other measures, such as the lack of utility of items for education and intervention purposes, unsuitability of the measure for use with children with developmental disabilities, and the inadequacy of standardization. It is a standardized, individually administered measure that can be used for screening purposes with children ages 6 months to 8 years. Although it is presented here as a screening measure, it should be noted that it can also be used as a more comprehensive full-length measure of a child's development from birth to 8 years of age. The screening test helps to identify children whose development seems to warrant more in-depth assessment. The Battelle inventory relies in part on a structured interview format for gathering information; consequently, it is subject to all of the concerns previously discussed regarding rater viewpoint. Information also comes from interaction with and observation of the child.

The Battelle inventory is organized into five major domains:

1. Personal-Social: Focuses on skills necessary for meaningful social interactions; includes adult interaction, expression of feeling/affective state, self-concept, peer interaction, coping, and social role
2. Adaptive: Focuses on task-related behaviors and self-help skills; includes attention, eating, dressing, toileting, and personal responsibility
3. Motor: Examines both large and small muscle use and control; includes muscle control, body coordination, locomotion, fine muscle, and perceptual-motor areas
4. Communication: Includes expressive and receptive forms of communication, both verbally and nonverbally
5. Cognitive: Includes skills that are primarily conceptual in nature, such as conceptual development, reasoning, memory, perceptual discrimination, and academic skills

From these five domains, a total of 96 items are administered for screening. Each item can be scored as follows: 2 for a response that meets specified criteria, 1 for an attempt that does not fully meet the criteria, or 0 for no attempt or a response that is quite poor. When the test is used for screening, age-equivalent scores are used. The Battelle inventory provides a complete range of standard scores, percentile ranks, deviation scores, and normal curve equivalents; however, these may be applied only to the full battery and not to the screening test. The authors state that the test is best used for screening after 5 months of age (Newborg, Stock, Wnek, Guidubaldi, & Svinicki, 1984).

A unique feature of the Battelle inventory is the special adaptation of the instrument for use with children who have sensory or motor impairments. Both general and specific guidelines are provided to adapt items in each domain. A study examined teachers' ratings of these adaptations to determine if they were appropriate to allow a child to give his or her best effort or maximum performance (Bailey, Vandiviere, Dellinger, & Munn, 1987). The highest rated adaptations were those for speech and lower body motor impairments; hearing and arm/hand impairments were given poorer ratings. The poorer ratings for selected disabilities indicate that the Battelle inventory may not be entirely suitable for use with every type of disability and that available adaptations simply do not meet a particular individual's need (Bailey et al., 1987). In general, teachers in the study viewed the adapted Battelle inventory as moderately useful, particularly for mild or moderate disabilities and for purposes of tracking progress and making same-age comparisons.

## Reliability, Validity, and Utility

The test developers for the Battelle inventory seem to have met their goals. With an eye toward relevant items that could be easily related to education, they employed the following criteria for item selection: 1) the importance of a behavior in typical functioning, 2) whether the behavior was regarded by professionals as a developmental milestone, 3) the agreement among practitioners that a skill be critical for a child to have, and 4) the degree to which a limited skill could be remediated by educational intervention (Newborg et al., 1984).

Standardization was accomplished by using 800 children, 100 at each age level. A normative base and availability of standard scores are necessary in order to make judgments about a child's relative standing. The only drawback is that these scores cannot be applied to screening results. Age-equivalent scores are used for screening, and these can be subject to misinterpretation by those not trained in assessment. Psychometrically, the Battelle inventory reports adequate reliability, and initial validity studies show significant correlations between the Battelle inventory and a variety of measures, including the Stanford-Binet Form L–M, the WISC–R, the Peabody Picture Vocabulary Test–Revised, and the Vineland Social Maturity Scale. A weak correlation was observed, however, between the Battelle Cognitive domain and the WISC–R Full Scale IQ. As noted by Sattler (1988), this weak correlation is difficult to understand and may in part be because of a lack of factor-analytic studies on the norm group of the Battelle inventory. There also has been recent criticism about use of the Battelle inventory as a norm-referenced measure for special services eligibility decisions because of difficulty calculating extreme standard scores in a reliable fashion (McLinden, 1989). The Battelle inventory received higher marks for use as a criterion-referenced measure (see Chapter 6).

In summary, the Battelle inventory appears to be a versatile instrument, with both screening and in-depth assessment uses, that provides information that satisfies norm- and criterion-referenced needs (Harrington, 1985). However, caution is urged when this inventory is used in norm-referenced fashion for making qualification decisions about early intervention services for children with disabilities.

One advantage of the Battelle inventory is the broad age range, which allows for repeated assessment of a child. The Battelle inventory contrasts with tests that are not continuous across such an age span, which leaves psychologists facing the problem of comparing apples and oranges because different tests are used to assess different ages. The Battelle inventory is likely to be most useful when interpreted in terms of overall status, rather than selective individual subdomains.

## BRIGANCE® DIAGNOSTIC INVENTORY OF EARLY DEVELOPMENT

The BRIGANCE Inventory is a departure from the previously discussed instruments in that it is criterion referenced rather than norm referenced, although norms have become available in supplemental study (Glascoe, 1995). Although the BRIGANCE Inventory is useful for assessment purposes, its value, as with most criterion-referenced tools, is identifying instructional objectives, serving as a guide for measuring those objectives, and providing an ongoing tracking system. The BRIGANCE Inventory is intended for informal assessment of several aspects of child development and is for children functioning at developmental levels from birth to 7 years of age. Major areas assessed, as revised in 1991, include preambulatory, motor skills and behaviors, gross motor skills and behaviors, fine motor skills and behaviors, self-help skills, speech and language skills, general knowledge and comprehension, social and emotional development, readiness, basic reading skills, manuscript writing, and basic math (Brigance, 1991). Within these major areas, there are subtests of sequenced developmental skills (see Figure 3.4). The BRIGANCE® Inventory permits various methods of administration to be used, such as observation, direct testing of the child, or reports from caregivers, child care workers, or teachers. In order to elicit a child's maximum performance, clinicians are encouraged to allow children to respond in any possible fashion, such as pointing, eye localizations, or verbalizing. Also, clinicians are encouraged to adapt materials to best meet the needs of the child in order to get a response.

## Reliability, Validity, and Utility

The 1991 update of the BRIGANCE Inventory was followed by a detailed study of its reliability and validity (Glascoe, 1995), which appears to produce generally favorable psychometric properties for the instrument. For example, this study presents information suggesting that the test has adequate sensitivity and specificity for identification of preschoolers and primary-grade children who have speech-language impairments, specific learning disabilities, and mental retardation (Glascoe, 1995). Moreover, there are now some normative data. As the BRIGANCE Inventory had generally been reviewed favorably as having adequate content and as being useful (but was criticized only on psychometric grounds), the minor revision of item content and organization that occurred in 1991 (Carpenter, 1995; Penfield, 1995), together with the advent of norms and reliability/validity data, will make the test even more popular.

As before, the strength of the BRIGANCE Inventory appears to lie in its ability to identify a child's pattern of strengths and weaknesses in several areas. The test items are representative of a curriculum appropriate for an early childhood program, and thus are easily linked to instructional planning and intervention (Bagnato, 1985). Another benefit of relating items to teaching and planning is that repeated assessments with the BRIGANCE Inventory can pinpoint areas of gains and losses. The obvious caution here is to avoid teaching to the test because the items are very specific. Some weaknesses that have been observed, including a lack of specific guidelines for how to make adaptations for individual children, have also apparently been addressed in the updated version.

# A. Preambulatory Motor Skills and Behaviors

| Assessment | Page | |
|---|---|---|
| | | Notes: ______ |
| A–3 | 11 | ***Sitting Position Skills and Behaviors:*** |
| | | 0–1 1. Head set forward with some control but also with some bobbing.* |
| | | 2. Steadies head but does not hold it erect.* |
| | | 3. Attempts to right self when tilted. |
| | | 0–4 4. Sits when supported. |
| | | 5. Sits briefly unsupported, may lean forward on hands. |
| | | 6. Sits steadily with little risk of overbalancing. |
| | | 0–7 7. Sits erect and unsupported for five minutes. |
| | | 8. Pivots. |
| | | 9. Goes from sitting to creeping position without losing control. |
| | | 0–10 10. Sits with enough balance and support to free hands for an activity such as pat-a-cake. 0–11 |
| | | Notes: ______ |
| A–4 | 15 | ***Standing Position Skills and Behaviors:*** |
| | | 0–3 1. Supports a small fraction of weight briefly. |
| | | 2. Lifts one foot (stepping movement) when held in a supported standing position. |
| | | 3. Supports approximately half of weight briefly. |
| | | 4. Supports most but not all weight. |
| | | 0–7 5. Supports full weight when balanced. |
| | | 6. Stands holding on to an object for support. |
| | | 7. Walks with both hands held. |
| | | 0–10 8. Pulls to standing position. |
| | | 9. Walks with one hand held (when led). |
| | | 10. Walks alone. |
| | | 1–0 11. Gets to standing position without support. |
| | | 12. Walks well and rarely falls. 1–3 |
| | | Notes: ______ |

*This is a "disappearing" behavior.

Figure 3.4. Sequenced developmental skills from the Revised BRIGANCE® Diagnostic Inventory of Early Development. (From Brigance, A.H. [1991]. *Revised BRIGANCE Diagnostic Inventory* [Birth to Seven Years]. North Billerica, MA: Curriculum Associates, Inc.)

## SUMMARY

Many of the questions in infant assessment have to do with future functioning; however, the state of assessment and assessment tools is much more limited at this age than at later ages. Most relevant for infant assessment is a noncategorical diagnosis of *at-risk status*, which is based on current developmental status. The identification of infants at risk for developmental delays is the goal of federal legislation, PL 99-457 and PL 102-119. In addition to provision of services to preschoolers, the laws mandate services for the first time for the birth-to-3 age group. Although future functioning cannot be reliably predicted from infant IQ measures, except in cases of very significant mental retardation, assessment of current functioning can occur as young as 2–3 days of age by using the Brazelton Neonatal Behavioral Assessment Scale.

Typically, the Brazelton scale is used when known risk factors are present or atypical infant development is expected. A large part of the Brazelton scale's value is in predicting future functioning from *recovery curves*, or profiles from repeated assessments over time. At older ages, cognitive assessment can be done with the Bayley Scales of Infant Development–II. The Bayley scale, a norm-referenced measure, is the recognized standard of assessment for young children because of its technical sophistication and comprehensiveness. Scores result for mental development, psychomotor development, and infant behavior. This scale was updated in 1993, which means that it will remain technically and clinically ahead of other infant tests for the foreseeable future.

Not every infant or toddler requires assessment with the Brazelton or Bayley scales. When infants are in need of screening rather than full-scale evaluation, the Battelle or BRIGANCE® Inventories may be used. The Battelle Developmental and BRIGANCE Inventories are both norm- and criterion-referenced. Although discussed in this chapter as a screening tool, the Battelle inventory can also be used for in-depth assessment. Although there are standard scores for the Battelle inventory, they are not applicable to screening results: Age-equivalent scores must be used instead. The measure appears psychometrically sound but does have some limitations that further research and practice will ultimately address. Because the BRIGANCE Inventory is criterion referenced, its greatest use is as a guide for planning and monitoring a young child's instructional program. Major areas addressed include language, knowledge, motor skills, and self-help. Social-emotional, or behavioral functioning, is not included, meaning that a supplemental measure is necessary to track progress in this area.

Developmental diagnosis in infancy is more limited than at older ages and is best when focused on a clear referral question about current status. In general, diagnostic ability is limited to mental retardation; diagnoses of milder delays in specific areas, or of learning disabilities, is not yet possible in infant assessment.

## Study Questions

1. What is the status of psychologists' abilities to predict future IQ from infant IQ?
2. In what situations would a BRIGANCE® Inventory be preferred over Bayley scales?
3. What are the strengths and weaknesses of the three main methods of temperament assessment?
4. What are the areas covered by the Brazelton scale, and how can results be used?
5. What role does rater viewpoint play in infant assessment?
6. How does early infant development correlate with later cognitive development?

## Chapter Four

# Preschool Tests

## Diagnosing Mental Retardation and Learning Disabilities

Parents frequently ask questions about child development. Teachers, social workers, physicians, and speech pathologists may encounter questions from parents, such as the following:

Is this little girl immature, or might she have mental retardation?
Is my 5-year-old Jimmy ready for kindergarten? He doesn't know his shapes and colors yet.
My son has two uncles with dyslexia. Will he have dyslexia?
Does it mean that something is wrong with my son because he is not yet talking at 3 years of age?
My 2-year-old is already counting to 20 and reciting the alphabet. Is he going to be gifted?

Besides questions from parents, professionals who work with children constantly see things that raise questions in their minds. A caseworker wonders if severe maternal deprivation has left 4-year-old Bobby delayed. A physician may wonder just how severe will be the impairments of a 5-year-old child with Down syndrome and what services the boy might require. A pediatric nurse may question if a 3-year-old child is too anxious to follow directions or if she simply lacks adequate language skills. A physical therapist may wonder how much cognitive ability a 5-year-old child has retained after neurosurgery. A teacher may wonder whether one of her pupils is showing the early signs of learning disabilities.

Nonpsychologists who have experience working with children can answer some of these questions independently. However, nonpsychologists will need assistance from psychologists to obtain acceptable answers to the other questions. Although not all of these concerns can be answered fully, they often should cause the child to be referred for psychological evaluation. Psychologists have developed a variety of tests to help answer these types of questions. This chapter covers the four broad groups of preschool tests of development: 1) global intelligence, 2) intelligence with subtests, 3) adaptive behavior, and 4) special ability. The chapter shows that most preschool developmental concerns can be thought of as questions about either mental retardation or learning disabilities.

## MEASURING INTELLIGENCE

Because IQ is such an emotionally laden concept, it is wise to review some facts about measuring intelligence before proceeding. In the past it was widely believed that intelligence was a fixed, unvarying attribute that, once accurately measured, would never change. Information from Chapter 3 shows that infant scales correlate poorly with childhood IQ scores. Although variations in individual development and predictions of later IQ increase after the second birthday, long-range IQ predictions are still far from perfect; for instance, longitudinal studies tracing children's intellectual growth show that most children's IQs change to some extent between childhood and adolescence, whereas other children's IQs change enormously. As a case in point, McCall, Appelbaum, and Hogarthy (1973) found surprisingly large IQ changes among children without disabilities, with an average change of 28.5 IQ points between 2½ and 17 years of age. In addition, changes were not a result of random fluctuation but tended to follow discernable, gradually changing courses that could be explained by algebraic formulas when examined retrospectively for 55% of children who changed significantly. Although many changes occur in children's IQs over time, IQ nonetheless remains one of the most predictable psychological traits. A variety of other studies shows the correlation between IQ at age 2 and adulthood to be approximately .40. Not until the child moves into the school year does the predictive power of IQ reach the point where forecasting of adult scores becomes reasonably ensured.

After examining a number of studies, psychologist Benjamin Bloom concluded that a 17-year-old's IQ can be predicted as he or she grows in the following way: with 20% accuracy at 1 year of age, 50% accuracy by 4 years, 80% accuracy by 8 years, and 92% accuracy by 13 years of age (Bloom, 1964). Does this mean that available preschool intelligence tests have somehow failed to measure "true" intelligence? The answer is no, not really. But research data have forced psychologists to rethink what is meant by intelligence and to state more explicitly what IQ tests measure.

Psychologists now recognize that what is called intelligence changes. Not only does an individual's position in relation to his or her peers change over time, but the processes described as intelligence are actually different at different ages. Chapter 3 discusses the enormous differences in functioning between the infant and toddler. Similarly, a bright 3-year-old shows ability in vastly different ways than does a bright 16-year-old. At age 3, a child is viewed as precocious if vocabulary size is larger than that of peers, if hand–eye coordination is superior to peers', and if the child has a few more simple concepts about size, color, and numbers than peers. Although attempts have been made, few IQ items that measure abstract reasoning or problem solving suitable for 3-year-olds have been devised yet. In contrast, a 16-year-old is viewed as bright because he or she understands abstract concepts and can reason through complex problems in a logical way. Although the early harbinger of these skills may be noted in the test performance of 3-year-olds, much content change and many developmental reorganizations occur before a bright 16-year-old emerges. It is a mistake to assume that those who do well on the concrete items at age 3 will always do well on the abstract reasoning items at age 16.

The concept of intelligence as measured by IQ tests has undergone other changes as well. A tacit assumption underlying much earlier intelligence testing was that tests somehow measure an inherent, fixed, biological trait—intelligence. A corollary to this assumption was that this trait was measured largely or completely independent of experience. In the term of geneticists, these tests were believed to be measuring *genotype* intelligence, or a pure biological trait that would predictably unfold as an organism matured. Most psychologists now view themselves as measuring *phenotype* intelligence. That is, psychologists measure intelligence as expressed in behavior, in the tradition of one of the earliest developers of intelligence tests, Alfred Binet (Weinberg, 1989). This expressed behavior reflects both genotypic underpinnings and predispositions, as well as the effects of experience. More than 80 years after intelligence tests were developed, it seems strange that so little emphasis was placed on experience and so much was placed on inheritance in the early interpretation of IQ scores. Psychologists now know that the influences of environment are neither so uniform across children nor so trivial that they can be ignored. It is presently recognized that intelligence tests measure a person's genetic potential *and* experiences, and that in many situations, experiences are as important or more important than genetics. Children encounter variations in the quality and nature of experiences provided by their families, neighborhoods, and schools as they grow, and these may substantially influence mental development (Neisser et al., 1996). In addition, the effects of nonshared family variables related to a child's birth rank and age of siblings has also come to be appreciated as important (McCall, 1987). The variations within and between families result in different rates of exposure to concepts, thinking styles, and problem-solving strategies that children incorporate into their own thinking. Experiences affect children's rates of mental growth. This is another reason that long-term prediction of IQ is difficult to accomplish accurately.

Finally, it must be pointed out that, in the 1990s, intelligence tests are not viewed as measuring potential in the strict sense of the word (Kaufman, 1994). This position partially reflects the recognition that long-term prediction is not what was once hoped for. More important, it reflects the recognition that there is no way to measure genetic potential independent of experience. All that present assessment devices are capable of measuring is behavior, which invariably and unavoidably reflects both genetic potential and experience. Psychologists no longer typically describe intelligence tests as measuring potential but rather speak of *current ability.* There remains an assumption that one's ability now predicts one's ability in the future, although not in the same unvarying way that the word "potential" connotes.

## GLOBAL INTELLIGENCE MEASURES FOR PRESCHOOLERS

### The Stanford-Binet Intelligence Scale: Form L–M

Global intelligence tests are designed to assess general thinking or problem-solving ability. They present results in the form of a single IQ score, rather than component scores such as those obtained in measuring language or perceptual skills. The classic Stanford-Binet L–M scale is the only suitable global intelligence test available for preschoolers, although in the 1990s it is used only rarely for clinical purposes. Nonetheless, a discussion of the Stanford-Binet L–M is in this volume because of the test's historical importance and because it remains frequently referenced in research reports. The Stanford-Binet L–M scale's principal value has been, and sometimes still is, in answering questions about across-the-board delays and mental retardation. In fact, this was the reason for developing the scale.

In 1905, the Paris public schools were interested in identifying children with low ability so that they could be channeled into special schools with simplified curricula. No suitable ability or intelligence tests were then available. Alfred Binet, a French psychologist, was hired to develop such a test. Binet's concept of intelligence and how it might be measured had enormous impact on the early mental measurement movement. Contrary to the thinking of his day, Binet recognized that measures of reaction time, sensory acuity, and attention span were not highly associated with overall ability and, thus, were not good items to include in his scale (Watson, 1968). Binet concluded that the best items measured judgment, comprehension, and reasoning. Consequently, his scale came to reflect these factors. Although some motor and memory tasks were used for younger children, abstract, judgmental, and reasoning tasks dominated the scale in general. This conception of intelligence as abstract reasoning, or problem-solving ability, continues to influence thinking about IQ and continues to be used as a working definition by most psychologists practicing in the field in the 1990s.

The original Binet scale was arranged in a series of graded tasks similar to those of the present Stanford-Binet L–M scale (Terman & Merrill, 1973) (see Figure 4.1 and Table 4.1). Then, as in the 1990s, the tasks differed in content at each age, with relatively more motor items at the 2- and 3-year levels, and relatively more language items at older

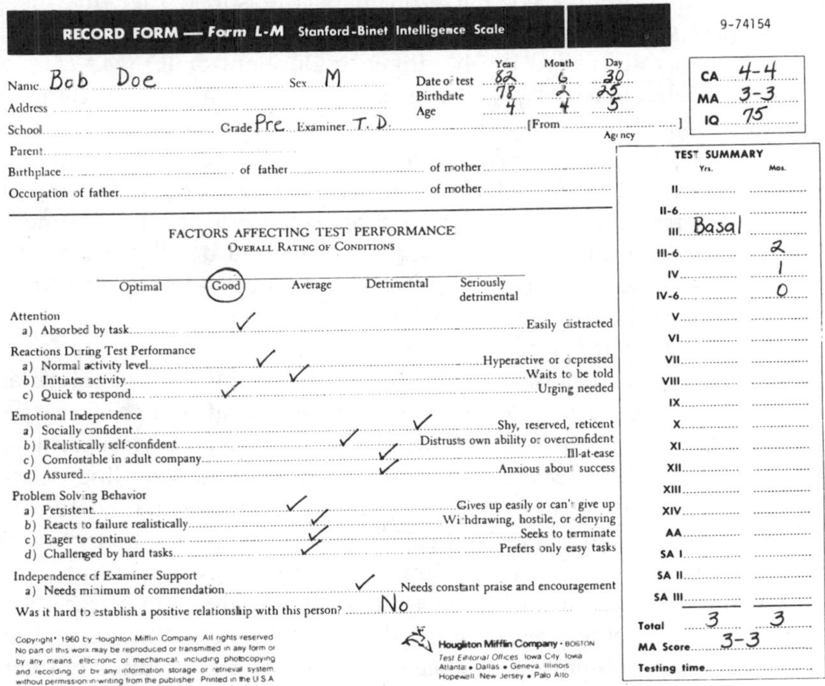

**RECORD FORM — Form L-M** Stanford-Binet Intelligence Scale

9-74154

Name Bob Doe Sex M

Address

School Grade Pre Examiner T. D. [From Agency]

| | Year | Month | Day |
|---|---|---|---|
| Date of test | 82 | 6 | 30 |
| Birthdate | 78 | 2 | 25 |
| Age | 4 | 4 | 5 |

CA 4-4
MA 3-3
IQ 75

Parent

Birthplace of father of mother

Occupation of father of mother

FACTORS AFFECTING TEST PERFORMANCE
OVERALL RATING OF CONDITIONS

Optimal (Good) Average Detrimental Seriously detrimental

Attention
a) Absorbed by task ✓ Easily distracted

Reactions During Test Performance
a) Normal activity level ✓ Hyperactive or depressed
b) Initiates activity ✓ Waits to be told
c) Quick to respond ✓ Urging needed

Emotional Independence
a) Socially confident ✓ Shy, reserved, reticent
b) Realistically self-confident ✓ Distrusts own ability or overconfident
c) Comfortable in adult company ✓ Ill-at-ease
d) Assured ✓ Anxious about success

Problem Solving Behavior
a) Persistent ✓ Gives up easily or can't give up
b) Reacts to failure realistically ✓ Withdrawing, hostile, or denying
c) Eager to continue ✓ Seeks to terminate
d) Challenged by hard tasks ✓ Prefers only easy tasks

Independence of Examiner Support
a) Needs minimum of commendation ✓ Needs constant praise and encouragement

Was it hard to establish a positive relationship with this person? No

TEST SUMMARY

| | Yrs. | Mos. |
|---|---|---|
| II | | |
| II-6 | | |
| III | Basal | |
| III-6 | | 2 |
| IV | | 1 |
| IV-6 | | 0 |
| V | | |
| VI | | |
| VII | | |
| VIII | | |
| IX | | |
| X | | |
| XI | | |
| XII | | |
| XIII | | |
| XIV | | |
| AA | | |
| SA I | | |
| SA II | | |
| SA III | | |
| Total | 3 | 3 |

MA Score 3-3

Testing time



Houghton Mifflin Company • BOSTON
Test Editorial Offices: Iowa City, Iowa
Atlanta • Dallas • Geneva, Illinois
Hopewell, New Jersey • Palo Alto

Figure 4.1. Stanford Binet Intelligence Scale, Form L-M. (Copyright © 1972. By the Riverside Publishing Company. Reproduced from *Stanford Binet Intelligence Scale, Form L-M,* by Lewis M. Terman and Maud A. Merrill with permission of the publisher.)

Table 4.1. Sample Stanford-Binet items

**Age Level II Years**

1. *Three-hole form board*—replace three figures in a form-board
2. *Delayed response*—remember location of hidden object
3. *Identifying body parts*—identify body parts on a paper doll
4. *Block building: tower*—replicate four-block tower
5. *Picture vocabulary*—identify by name pictured objects
6. *Word combination*—spontaneously emit one phrase of two or more words

**Age Level IV Years**

1. *Picture vocabulary*—same as Level II, Number 5, with higher standards
2. *Naming objects from memory*—recall and name removed object
3. *Opposite analogies I*—complete simple verbal analogies
4. *Pictorial identification*—select from a picture array objects that have been described verbally
5. *Discrimination of forms*—match geometric shapes with models
6. *Comprehension II*—explain the uses of common objects

*Source:* Terman and Merrill (1973).

age levels. Items were administered until there were no further successes at any age level, and then testing was terminated. A mental age was calculated by determining how far up the increasingly difficult scale the child progressed. Early on, it was reasoned that this mental age (MA) could be divided by the child's chronological age (CA) to produce a ratio called the Intelligence Quotient or IQ ($MA/CA \times 100 = IQ$). This was the beginning of the concept of IQ that remains into the 1990s. The average score was assumed to be 100, as it represented an exact equivalent between mental and chronological age. Scores below 100 indicated less than average rates of development, whereas scores above 100 indicated accelerated rates of development. The current Stanford-Binet L–M scale uses standard rather than ratio scores. This standard score system has a mean of 100 and a standard deviation of 16 (see Figure 1.4, on p. 9).

Binet's original test was a success in France. It was brought to the United States and restandardized, most notably by Lewis L. Terman at Stanford University in 1916 (Sattler, 1988), at which time the Stanford-Binet name was adopted. The test has been revised and renormed several times since with a thorough national sampling occurring in 1972. Because of its venerability, the test has extensive reliability and validity studies that show it to have excellent psychometric properties. The test is technically and statistically sound.

Although the Stanford-Binet L–M scale remains one of the most accurate and reliable preschool intelligence measures, the instrument is not without problems. It has been criticized on the grounds of overemphasizing, surprisingly, rote memory as well as verbal skills. The test has also been criticized for penalizing children who are creative. The language criticism is especially forceful concerning the evaluation of bilingual or bicultural children. The Stanford-Binet L–M scale's single IQ (see Figure 4.1) and its failure to break performance down into areas of strength and weakness is a substantial disadvantage. Furthermore, because the Stanford-Binet L–M tasks tend to be very structured and closed-ended (i.e., calling for a specific, limited response) the child's response style and personality are not as apparent as with other preschool instruments. Although a revised Stanford-Binet (Fourth Edition) scale is now available, the Stanford-Binet L–M scale still is used occasionally by psychologists if questions exist about middle-class, English-speaking children with general developmental delays or mental retardation.

## PRESCHOOL INTELLIGENCE SCALES WITH SUBTESTS

Delayed overall development is not the only concern that exists when assessing preschoolers. Just as is true with older children, preschoolers sometimes develop differently in various psychological spheres. Thus, one child might progress more rapidly linguistically than motorically, whereas the opposite might be true for another child. The Stanford-Binet L–M form, despite its other favorable characteristics, was unable to detect uneven development and to pinpoint narrow, limited-in-scope developmental problems. Three tests suitable for assessing preschoolers' overall development, and additionally appraising patterns of strengths and weaknesses, are presented here. They are the Stanford-Binet Intelligence Scale: Fourth Edition (Thorndike, Hagen, & Sattler, 1986), a virtually separate test from the Stanford-Binet L–M that retains the Stanford-Binet name; the McCarthy Scales of Children's Abilities; and the Wechsler Preschool and Primary Scale of Intelligence–Revised (WPPSI–R) (Wechsler, 1989). The Kaufman Assessment Battery for Children (K–ABC) (Kaufman, 1983) may also be used with this age group, but its primary use is with school-age children; this test is discussed in Chapter 5.

The advent of subtest scores offered considerable hope for better diagnosis, but also necessarily brought accompanying problems. Long tests, such as the Stanford-Binet L–M, that produce single scores are known to be quite reliable. As stated previously, the longer the test, the more reliable it is. When tests are divided into subareas, length is reduced. Reduced test length results in reduced reliability. This has the effect of undermining confidence in the differences between subtests because each may be so unreliable. Because reliability is a prerequisite for validity, each individual subtest is less likely to be a valid index of what it purports to measure. Logically then, predicting the future is even less sure for traits measured by individual subtests than for traits measured by full, long tests. The Stanford-Binet L–M administered at age 3 better predicts what that child's general thinking ability will be at 6 years of age than does a brief test of a specific skill (e.g., McCarthy Motor Index) administered at age 3 predict what his or her motor status will be at age 6.

## Stanford-Binet Intelligence Scale: Fourth Edition

The Stanford-Binet Intelligence Scale: Fourth Edition (Stanford-Binet IV) uses the Stanford-Binet name but different authors (the prior versions' authors are both deceased), a different format and scoring system, mostly different items, and a different, and more recent, standardization. About the only thing the two tests have in common is the name.

The Stanford-Binet IV is for individuals ages 2 years to adult. It provides scores in four areas: Verbal Reasoning, Abstract/Visual Reasoning, Quantitative Reasoning, and Short-Term Memory, plus a Composite score that is equivalent to a Full Scale IQ. Standard scores with means of 100 and standard deviations of 16 are available for each of the four areas. Each of the areas comprises one or more subtests; the exact subtests administered depend on the individual's age and his or her performance. The subtests have a mean of 50 and standard deviation of 8. (See Figure 4.2.)

The Stanford-Binet IV is well standardized, has excellent reliability, and has at least adequate evidence of validity. Unfortunately, because different subtests compose various areas (and the Composite score as well), the test is in fact many different tests, the exact composition of each depending on the child's age and ability level. Moreover, the Stanford-Binet IV has been criticized because psychological development at various ages may not agree with the authors' preconceived notions of how subtests ought to have been grouped to form area scores. This consideration has led one of the test authors, Jerome Sattler, to advocate an organization and interpretation different from the one spelled out in the test manual. Rather than following the manual's suggested groupings, which are based on what each subtest appears to measure, Sattler (1988) has suggested grouping subtests according to their intercorrelations. As an example of Sattler's recommendation, Memory for Sentences (a subtest in which the child repeats sentences held in short-term memory) would contribute to a factor called *verbal comprehension* (language thinking) for children ages 7 years and younger. Although this subtest appears to contain merely rote memory items, statistical findings imply that young children use language thinking to pass the items on this subtest, as they do on

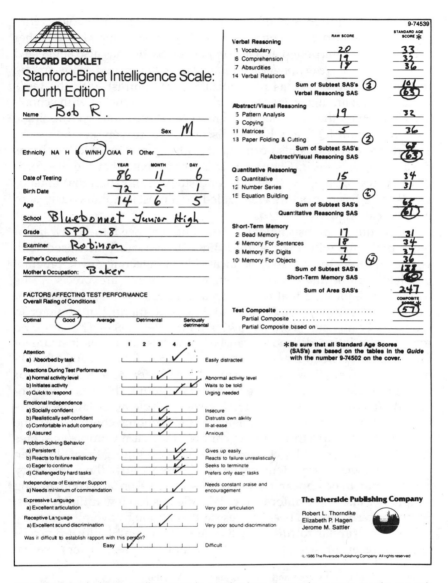

9-74539

STANFORD-BINET INTELLIGENCE SCALE

**RECORD BOOKLET**

Stanford-Binet Intelligence Scale: Fourth Edition

Name Bob R.

Sex M

Ethnicity NA H B W/NH O/AA PI Other

| | YEAR | MONTH | DAY |
|---|---|---|---|
| Date of Testing | 86 | 11 | 6 |
| Birth Date | 72 | 5 | 1 |
| Age | 14 | 6 | 5 |

School Bluebonnet Junior High

Grade SPD - 8

Examiner Robinson

Father's Occupation: —

Mother's Occupation: Baker

FACTORS AFFECTING TEST PERFORMANCE
Overall Rating of Conditions

Optimal | Good | Average | Detrimental | Seriously detrimental

| | RAW SCORE | STANDARD AGE SCORE * |
|---|---|---|
| **Verbal Reasoning** | | |
| 1 Vocabulary | 20 | 33 |
| 6 Comprehension | 19 | 32 |
| 7 Absurdities | 18 | 36 |
| 14 Verbal Relations | | |
| Sum of Subtest SAS's (3) | | 101 |
| Verbal Reasoning SAS | | 65 |
| **Abstract/Visual Reasoning** | | |
| 5 Pattern Analysis | 19 | 32 |
| 9 Copying | | |
| 11 Matrices | 5 | 36 |
| 13 Paper Folding & Cutting | | |
| Sum of Subtest SAS's (2) | | 68 |
| Abstract/Visual Reasoning SAS | | 63 |
| **Quantitative Reasoning** | | |
| 3 Quantitative | 15 | 34 |
| 12 Number Series | 1 | 31 |
| 15 Equation Building | | |
| Sum of Subtest SAS's (2) | | 65 |
| Quantitative Reasoning SAS | | 61 |
| **Short-Term Memory** | | |
| 2 Bead Memory | 17 | 31 |
| 4 Memory For Sentences | 18 | 34 |
| 8 Memory For Digits | 7 | 37 |
| 10 Memory For Objects | 4 | 36 |
| Sum of Subtest SAS's (4) | | 138 |
| Short-Term Memory SAS | | 60 |
| Sum of Area SAS's | | 247 |
| | | COMPOSITE SCORE * |
| Test Composite | | 57 |
| Partial Composite | | |
| Partial Composite based on | | |

*Be sure that all Standard Age Scores (SAS's) are based on the tables in the *Guide* with the number 9-74502 on the cover.

| | 1 | 2 | 3 | 4 | 5 | |
|---|---|---|---|---|---|---|
| **Attention** | | | | | | |
| a) Absorbed by task | | | | ✓ | | Easily distracted |
| **Reactions During Test Performance** | | | | | | |
| a) Normal activity level | | | ✓ | | | Abnormal activity level |
| b) Initiates activity | | | | | ✓ | Waits to be told |
| c) Quick to respond | | | | ✓ | | Urging needed |
| **Emotional Independence** | | | | | | |
| a) Socially confident | | | ✓ | | | Insecure |
| b) Realistically self-confident | | | ✓ | | | Distrusts own ability |
| c) Comfortable in adult company | | | ✓ | | | Ill-at-ease |
| d) Assured | | | ✓ | | | Anxious |
| **Problem-Solving Behavior** | | | | | | |
| a) Persistent | | | | ✓ | | Gives up easily |
| b) Reacts to failure realistically | | | | ✓ | | Reacts to failure unrealistically |
| c) Eager to continue | | | | ✓ | | Seeks to terminate |
| d) Challenged by hard tasks | | | | ✓ | | Prefers only easy tasks |
| **Independence of Examiner Support** | | | | | | |
| a) Needs minimum of commendation | | | | ✓ | | Needs constant praise and encouragement |
| **Expressive Language** | | | | | | |
| a) Excellent articulation | | | ✓ | | | Very poor articulation |
| **Receptive Language** | | | | | | |
| a) Excellent sound discrimination | | | ✓ | | | Very poor sound discrimination |
| Was it difficult to establish rapport with this person? Easy | ✓ | | | | | Difficult |

**The Riverside Publishing Company**

Robert L. Thorndike
Elizabeth P. Hagen
Jerome M. Sattler



Figure 4.2. Stanford Binet Intelligence Scale, Fourth Edition. (Copyright © 1986. By The Riverside Publishing Company. Reproduced from *Stanford Binet Intelligence Scale, Fourth Edition,* by Robert L. Thorndike, Elizabeth P. Hagen, and Jerome M. Sattler with permission of the publisher.)

subtests such as Vocabulary. For older children, however, the Memory for Sentences subtest does not correlate well enough with the verbal comprehension factor to allow it to be included there. Under these circumstances, tests such as the Vocabulary subtest would still be included in the proposed verbal comprehension factor for older children, but Memory for Sentences would now be grouped with other subtests to be interpreted as a *memory* factor. Sattler has also suggested that a *nonverbal reasoning/visualization* factor be created from among the various subtests. This reorganization, in contrast with the test's initial organization, is consistent with research conducted with school-age children on the Wechsler Intelligence Scale for Children (the single most important IQ test, which is discussed extensively in Chapter 5). This rearrangement is also congruent with research on such topics as dyslexia, as is seen in Chapter 5. It is unfortunate that the Stanford-Binet IV was created with such a confusing organization that amendments to its basic structure were called for almost simultaneously with its publication.

Consumers of psychological test findings need to be aware of other problems with the Stanford-Binet IV as well. When used with young children, the test may be incapable of detecting developmental problems; unfortunately, developmental problems are precisely the reason for requesting that testing occur for many young children. For example, it is impossible for a child 3 years, 0 months or younger to receive a Composite score as low as 68 (Sattler, 1988). Therefore, no mental retardation diagnoses can be made based on this instrument for children between 2 and 3 years of age. (See Table 4.2 for a breakdown of scores.) "Low" area scores, the basis for detecting subtle or mild problems, are similarly constrained for young children. This constraint effectively prohibits detecting such problems as language delays or visual-perceptual problems among young children. At the other end of the spectrum, young children may earn Composite scores as high as 164, but older children may score no higher than 149, even if they answer every item correctly. Consequently, the same very bright child may appear relatively less capable on a second testing simply because the Stanford-Binet IV scale has too few difficult items. Some concern has also been expressed that although overall summary values (i.e., similar to full scale IQ) agree between Stanford-Binet IV and Wechsler preschool full scale IQ among preschoolers, verbal

Table 4.2. Ability test scores and levels of mental retardation

| | Ability scores | |
|---|---|---|
| Retardation level | Stanford-Binet IQ McCarthy GCI | Wechsler IQ |
| Mild | 70–52 | 70–55 |
| Moderate | 51–36 | 54–40 |
| Severe | 35–20 | 39–25 |
| Profound | 19 and less | 24 and less |

*Note:* Wechsler scores below approximately 40 and McCarthy scores below approximately 50 are extrapolated.

scores earned by preschoolers "at risk" may differ (McCrowell & Nagle, 1994). This has led to speculation that the Wechsler preschool test (WPPSI–R) and Stanford-Binet IV are sampling slightly different verbal skills (McCrowell & Nagle, 1994).

In addition, among urban lower socioeconomic status school-age children, Wechsler and Stanford-Binet IV scores may not agree (Wechsler Intelligence Scale for Children–III averaged 9.4 points lower than composite Stanford-Binet IV), and the two tests may lead to different diagnostic conclusions (Prewett & Matavich, 1994).

For many good reasons the Stanford-Binet IV is among the most popular intelligence measures (Stinnett, Harvey, & Oehler-Stinnett, 1994; Wodrich & Barry, 1991). Still, nonpsychologists may be helped to remember the following: 1) The test's initial organization may be used in some instances, but Sattler's reorganization of scores into Verbal Comprehension, Visual/Spatial, and Memory factors may be used in others; 2) The test may be insensitive to young children's problems; 3) Children may score differently on this test than other ability tests; and 4) Both high- and low-score children may have score changes on later testing, based solely on peculiarities of the test.

## McCarthy Scales of Children's Abilities

A test that gained some popularity for assessing preschoolers after its 1972 publication was the McCarthy Scales of Children's Abilities (McCarthy, 1972). Like the Stanford-Binet IV scale, the McCarthy Scales provide an overall IQ equivalent (called the General Cognitive Index) with a mean of 100 and a standard deviation of 16. Also like the Stanford-Binet IV scale, the McCarthy Scales are composed of broad area scores (Index Scores with means of 50 and standard deviations of 10), each of which comprises narrow subtests (see Figure 4.3). McCarthy Scales are analogous to the Stanford-Binet IV in that both are well standardized, generally have good reliability, and have adequate evidence of concurrent and predictive validity. Also on the positive side, the McCarthy test items are attractive and the format is especially well suited for young children, so difficult-to-test children may be assessed. For instance, nonverbal, low-stress items are administered first, which allows rapport to be established before more demanding verbal items are introduced. The McCarthy Scales also include a separately interpretable Motor Index, which involves both fine and gross motor tasks. This feature, which allows psychologists to screen for delays that may warrant referral for more specialized assessment, is lacking from other preschool tests.

Unfortunately, some of the same limitations associated with the Stanford-Binet IV exist with the McCarthy Scales. The most severe of these limitations is that the General Cognitive Index (GCI) values of-

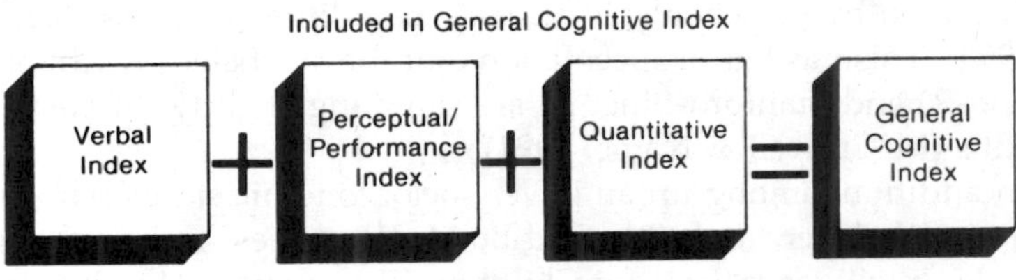

Figure 4.3. McCarthy Index Scores and their relationship to the General Cognitive Index.

ten disagree with the IQ values children earn on other tests. For example, children who have mental retardation score 20 points lower on the average on the McCarthy Scales than they do on the Stanford-Binet L–M scale (Levenson & Zino, 1979), and children with learning disabilities have McCarthy GCI values that range from an average of 8–15 points lower than standard IQ scores (DeBoer, Kaufman, & McCarthy, 1974; Goh & Youngquist, 1979). In a 1992 study, children with speech-language disorders were found to score 20 points lower on the McCarthy GCI than control group children, despite both groups having normal IQs on WPPSI performance scales (Morgan, Dawson, & Kerby, 1992). Concern that McCarthy GCI scores do not agree with other IQ test scores may preclude use of the McCarthy Scales for identifying learners with disabilities. This will become increasingly true unless the McCarthy Scales (copyrighted in 1972) are updated. In addition, the test does not have enough easy items to identify mental retardation among children 2½ years of age. No scores are reportable for GCIs below 50, regardless of the child's age; therefore, assessment of children with severe disabilities is further compromised.

Although the McCarthy Scales are designed for children from 2½ to 8 years old, most clinicians do not use the test with children 6 years old or older. At age 6 years, the Wechsler Intelligence Scale for Children–III (WISC–III), an excellent instrument with up-to-date norms, becomes appropriate. The WISC–III contains several judgmental tasks and social comprehension tasks that are absent from the McCarthy Scales (Kaufman & Kaufman, 1977). Finally, the McCarthy Scales have been criticized as having overlapping content among the various index scores and having insufficient reliabilities for the index scores to be interpreted as measuring distinct psychological abilities (Sattler, 1988). For example, an apparent numerical ability problem reflected in a child's test score may actually be due to the index's poor reliability or to that index's overlap with verbal skills, if a child has verbal impairments. Remedial plans targeting numerical skills may consequently be unnecessary. Thus, the McCarthy Scales may not only be inadequate to identify children with disabilities, but they may also fail to provide a profile useful for planning intervention. In summary, despite its appealing organization and format, and regardless of its early popularity, clinicians may increasingly supplant the McCarthy with other instruments; consumers may, thus, have less contact with this instrument.

## Wechsler Preschool and Primary Scale of Intelligence–Revised

The Wechsler Preschool and Primary Scale of Intelligence–Revised (WPPSI–R pronounced "whip-see") is a frequently used intelligence test for children from 3 years to 7 years, 3 months, although from age 6 years the Wechsler Intelligence Scale for Children–III (see Chapter 6) is used much more frequently. The WPPSI–R replaced the original WPPSI (Wechsler, 1967) with few item and format changes but with some changes in IQ values earned by examinees. The test has the same organization as the extremely popular WISC–III, which is discussed in detail in Chapter 5. Most of the subtests in the WPPSI–R are similar enough to those in the WISC–III that appreciation of one test's content is adequate to understand both tests. Likewise, the WPPSI–R's organization, array of scores, and usage is sufficiently similar to allow it to be understood and interpreted like the WISC–III.

There are some differences, however, in subtests between the WPPSI–R and WISC–III. Among the WPPSI–R Verbal subtests, there is no Digit Span subtest. Instead, an optional measure of short-term memory and auditory attention span, named Sentences, is available. A child's task here is to repeat verbatim increasingly lengthy and complex sentences. Raw score points are earned for accurate (i.e., without omissions, transpositions, additions and substitutions) repetition. Among the Performance subtests, a pencil-and-paper test that requires copying of increasingly complex geometric shapes is the fifth subtest used to calculate Performance IQ; there is no Picture Arrangement subtest on the WPPSI–R as there is on the WISC–III.

Although the original WPPSI and the WPPSI–R are highly correlated and are no doubt measuring mostly the same abilities (Wechsler, 1989), the scores between the two instruments are not directly comparable. Scores on the WPPSI–R tend to be about 8 points lower than those on the WPPSI (Wechsler, 1989). This finding is consistent with most other restandardizations of mental tests after a substantial time interval (22 years in this case); on average, children in the 1990s score better than their counterparts from 20 or so years prior.

As with all Wechsler scales, the test is well normed and has adequate, objective scoring criteria. There are adequate reliability and validity data. The WPPSI–R's scores tend to be more interchangeable with other IQ tests than do the scores on either the McCarthy Scales or Stanford-Binet IV. Although children may enjoy and attend better to McCarthy items, and although the WPPSI–R lacks separate motor and memory indexes, the WPPSI–R is often preferred by psychologists when important decisions about overall ability, such as the presence of mental retardation, must be made. Moreover, psychologists find that use of the WPPSI–R during preschool years dovetails smoothly with use of the WISC–III as children enter school and require reassessment. The interested reader is referred to the detailed section on the WISC–III in Chapter 5.

## MEASURES OF ADAPTIVE BEHAVIOR

Intelligence tests such as the Stanford-Binet IV, WPPSI–R, and the McCarthy Scales measure reasoning ability by putting a child through a series of tasks. The examiner observes the child's performance firsthand by requiring the child to either problem-solve or demonstrate previously learned skills. Adaptive behavior measures differ from intelligence tests in two ways. First, they assess the degree to which the child has actually mastered the living or adaptation demands expected of someone his or her age. That is, mastery of life tasks, rather than capability, is measured. Second, in contrast to measuring performance as the child is challenged by test items, adaptive measures rely on interviews of informants who have observed the child demonstrating skills in daily life. Like other psychological instruments, adaptive behavior measures strive for uniformity and objectivity, in this case by posing questions to the child's caregiver consistently, and by carefully codifying scoring criteria. The best adaptive behavior scales also produce standard scores that allow each child to be compared to a national sample. Unlike most psychological tests, adaptive behavior scales may be used without the examining psychologist ever seeing the child directly.

Practically speaking, adaptive behavior measures are frequently used as part of a battery that includes intelligence tests. They are used most typically if overall developmental status is questioned and mental retardation is suspected. Adaptive behavior tests are seldom used alone. Adaptive behavior scales prevent psychologists from relying on informal interviewing that may provide inconsistent results and may lead to overlooking some important aspects of development. By using these objective scales, psychologists can rely on explicit norms rather than base estimates of developmental status on their own implicit standards. Standardized adaptive behavior scales offer substantial advantages over the informal, less objective alternative. Many standardized adaptive behavior scales are available, and most attempt to measure similar aspects of behavior. As a group, the scales have been found to correlate reasonably well with one another, moderately with IQ, and poorly with academic achievement measures (Harrison, 1987). Two of the most frequently used adaptive behavior measures, the Vineland Adaptive Behavior Scales (Sparrow, Balla, & Cicchetti, 1984) and the AAMR Adaptive Behavior Scales (Lambert, Nihara, & Leland, 1993), are discussed in this chapter.

## Vineland Adaptive Behavior Scales

Among the best of the adaptive behavior scales are the (1984) revisions of the venerable Vineland Adaptive Behavior Scales. The scales come in three forms, varying in degree of detail and proposed setting. They are the Survey Form, the Expanded Form, and the Classroom Edition. The scales are administered by interviewing the parents, teachers, or caregivers of individuals ranging in age from birth to 19 years. Raw scores from various domains (Communication, Daily Living Skills, Socialization, Motor Skills, and Maladaptive Behavior) are converted to standard scores with a mean of 100 and a standard deviation of 15. There is also an Adaptive Behavior Composite score that uses similar scores. Figure 4.4 contains sample items.

The revisions of the Vineland scales have generally adequate evidence of reliability and some evidence of validity, at least partially based on the test items having appropriate content. When considering measures of preschoolers, there is acceptable agreement between measures of mental ability and adaptive behaviors (Roberts, McCoy, Reidy, & Crucitti, 1993). Questions have been raised, however, about the scales' standardization and the accuracy of standard scores across the broad age range (Salvia & Ysseldyke, 1985; Silverstein, 1986). Whereas the standardization sample may have departed slightly from targets for geographic location and parental education, the real problem is the lack of uniformity of scores across various ages. Depending on the child's age, means and standard deviations differ. Thus, comparing the same child's performance on reassessment is compromised, as is the accuracy of any composite score. Moreover, differences among do-

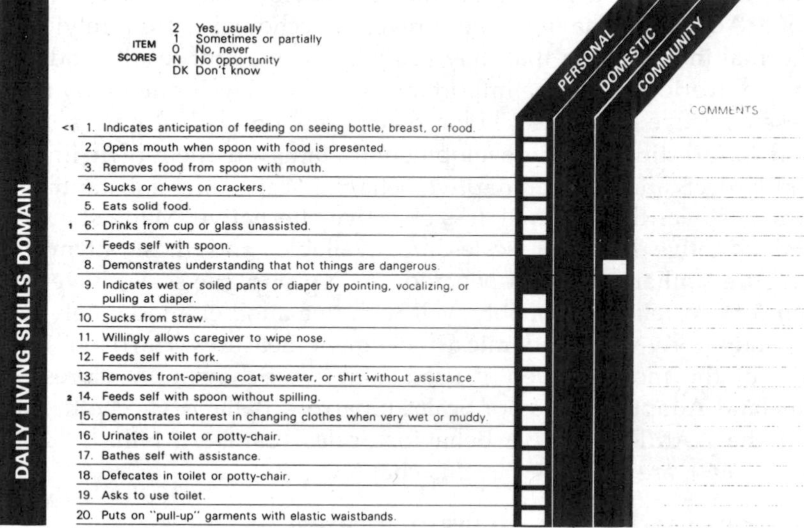

DAILY LIVING SKILLS DOMAIN

ITEM SCORES
2 Yes, usually
1 Sometimes or partially
0 No, never
N No opportunity
DK Don't know

PERSONAL DOMESTIC COMMUNITY

COMMENTS

<1 1. Indicates anticipation of feeding on seeing bottle, breast, or food.
2. Opens mouth when spoon with food is presented.
3. Removes food from spoon with mouth.
4. Sucks or chews on crackers.
5. Eats solid food.
1 6. Drinks from cup or glass unassisted.
7. Feeds self with spoon.
8. Demonstrates understanding that hot things are dangerous.
9. Indicates wet or soiled pants or diaper by pointing, vocalizing, or pulling at diaper.
10. Sucks from straw.
11. Willingly allows caregiver to wipe nose.
12. Feeds self with fork.
13. Removes front-opening coat, sweater, or shirt without assistance.
2 14. Feeds self with spoon without spilling.
15. Demonstrates interest in changing clothes when very wet or muddy.
16. Urinates in toilet or potty-chair.
17. Bathes self with assistance.
18. Defecates in toilet or potty-chair.
19. Asks to use toilet.
20. Puts on "pull-up" garments with elastic waistbands.

Figure 4.4. Sample Vineland Adaptive Behavior Scales: Interview Edition, Survey Form. (Vineland Adaptive Behavior Scales by Sara S. Sparrow, David A. Balla, & Domenic V. Cicchetti. © 1985 American Guidance Service, Inc., 4201 Woodland Road, Circle Pines, MN 55014-1796. Reproduced with permission of the Publisher. All rights reserved.)

main scores may be more apparent than real because of variable scores. For instance, does a 3-year-old with language domain scores of 82 have linguistic impairments if his or her other scores are all near 100? It might be contended that the 82 is merely an error resulting from poor equivalency among standard scores. In addition, there is considerable overlap among the various domains, with both Communication and Daily Living domains containing questions about the child's language skills, for example.

Despite these shortcomings, the Vineland Adaptive Behavior Scales allow psychologists to estimate adaptive behavior more accurately than would be possible if informal means were used. It is important to temper expectations about adaptive scales and to avoid expectations for them to measure development with precision or to pinpoint precisely children's relative strengths or weaknesses. Sometimes the Vineland is used in lieu of an infant mental test or a preschool IQ test. Although there certainly are positive correlations between the Vineland and these types of tests, tests such as the Bayley scales that actually evaluate the child's performance are likely to be better predictors of developmental outcome than Vineland scores (Raggio, Massingale, & Bass, 1994). As an adjunct to other assessment tools, adaptive behavior scales are nonetheless valuable.

## AAMR Adaptive Behavior Scales

A second set of frequently used adaptive behavior measures is the AAMR (American Association on Mental Retardation) Adaptive Behavior Scales (ABS). The ABS comes in two versions: 1) for children ages 3–21 years, the Adaptive Behavior Scale–School Edition (ABS–SE), and 2) for people with disabilities, a version simply entitled ABS. Both versions of the ABS consist of two parts. Part I assesses adaptive behavior in the sense of personal independence and development. Its content is therefore similar to the items that compose the Vineland Adaptive Behavior Composite. Part II is concerned with behavior related to emotional adjustment and, therefore, is not discussed here.

In its most recent form, Part I of the ABS–SE assesses nine domains of behavior, via informant ratings on items measuring skills and behavior related to independent functioning and competency: Independent functioning, Physical development, Economic activity, Language development, Numbers & time, Prevocational/vocational activity, Self-direction, Responsibility, and Socialization. To facilitate interpretation, scores can be collapsed into three broad factors: Personal Self-Sufficiency, Community Self-Sufficiency, and Personal-Social Responsibility, each reported in a standard score format. Finally, an overall composite score derived from these three factors can be calculated. Adding considerably to the instrument's utility is the fact that each child's score can be compared to norms for children in general school classes, for children with mild mental retardation, or for children with more severe mental retardation. Diagnostic decisions can be facilitated by noting which group of children has adaptive skills most like the child under consideration (e.g., the child's scores were at the third percentile for children in general classes but at the 45th percentile for children with mild mental retardation).

The version of the ABS that is suitable for residentially placed individuals is quite similar to the school version, but contains items that describe behavior unlikely to be seen at school (e.g., Domestic Activity) or that involve more severe symptoms (e.g., Self-Abusive Behavior).

Earlier versions of the ABS have been criticized for having weak psychometric properties (e.g., poor evidence of reliability, inadequate and unclearly defined norm groups) so that extreme caution must be exercised when using these instruments to make decisions about children (Sattler, 1988). There was concern about differences among raters; for instance, a special education teacher's ratings may contribute to lower adaptive scores than if others rate the child (Mayfield, Forman,

& Nagle, 1984). Updates of the ABS may have solved some of these concerns. Teachers may find that systematically examining those skills that the child has acquired and those that need yet to be taught is facilitated by these instruments, but if used to make placement decisions, the ABS is valuable mostly because it is superior to an informal interview.

## SPECIAL ABILITIES TESTS FOR PRESCHOOLERS

Tests such as the WPPSI–R and the Stanford-Binet IV scales are psychologists' principal tools for both assessing overall cognitive level and detecting intraindividual patterns of strengths and weaknesses. Consequently, if questions of this type exist, and certainly if important decisions are to be made about the presence of mental retardation or learning disabilities, then a thorough intellectual assessment is required. Special abilities tests may be used, however, to corroborate findings from more comprehensive tests or to help the psychologist more fully understand the child. Only two of many commercially marketed tests for preschoolers are discussed here, the Goodenough-Harris Drawing Test (Draw-a-Man) and the Boehm Test of Basic Concepts (Boehm, 1986a, 1986b). Several of the special ability tests discussed in Chapter 5 may also be used with preschool-age children.

### Goodenough-Harris Drawing Test (Draw-a-Man)

Consider the situation in which a child's WPPSI–R Full Scale IQ falls in the range for mental retardation, but the examining psychologist remains uncertain that the child has an intellectual impairment, as the test scores imply. Besides the obvious steps of collecting a developmental history and assessing adaptive skills, a psychologist would like to afford the child additional opportunities to demonstrate any cognitive strengths that have not yet been made apparent. Simply allowing the child to draw his or her best representation of a human being (i.e., drawing of a man or woman) is one additional assessment that may be accomplished. For some children, this task proves less confusing than responding to examiner requests to perform verbally and nonverbally. The advantage of reduced confusion may be especially important if the child is quite reticent or comes from a different lingual or cultural background.

It has been theorized for some time that children's drawings of familiar objects—the human form being perhaps the most universally familiar—reflect not only their motor and drawing ability but also reveal their conceptual sophistication (Goodenough, 1926). When this general supposition was coupled with an objective system to quantify drawings and was subsequently subjected to research, it was found that tests such as the Draw-a-Man test indeed could be used to help assess children.

Using a system devised by Harris (1963), children's drawings of men can be evaluated according to 73 pass-or-fail items (71 items for drawings of women) (see Figure 4.5). The raw scores from this procedure can be converted into standard scores, with a mean of 100 and standard deviation of 15, for children from 3 to 15 years of age. A representative norm group has been collected nationwide, and the test generally has adequate reliability, although it has rather weak concurrent validity with other intelligence tests and poor predictive validity if children in general are studied (Scott, 1981). The test may have real value, nonetheless, in instances such as those mentioned above (i.e., overcoming language barriers). A score that is close to average on the Draw-a-Man test may help convince the examiner that a child's WPPSI score may be unduly low. Careful scrutiny of other developmental information or further testing to supplement the WPPSI may then be necessary. Because the drawing tests can be scored fairly quickly (a briefer method than the 71- and 73-item options are also

Figure 4.5. Goodenough-Harris Draw-a-Man Test. Drawing by a 7-year, 7-month-old girl; standard score of 105.

available) and because it can be group administered, it has also been advocated as a screening instrument.

More recently Naglieri (1988) has developed a sophisticated scoring system for the standardized technique of drawing a man, a woman, and oneself. With considerable evidence of reliability and with contemporary norms, this test may have utility with its target age group (5–17 years), although Naglieri's work, like others' work in this area, has been criticized as being less suitable than other screening and brief tests (Kamphaus & Pleiss, 1991).

The reader is encouraged to contrast this developmental use of figure drawings to the projective use (typically called the Draw-a-Person test) reviewed in Chapter 7.

## Boehm Test of Basic Concepts

The Boehm Test of Basic Concepts, which comes in a Preschool Version for children ages 3–5 years (Boehm, 1986a) and in a standard version for children in kindergarten through second grade (Boehm, 1986b), can be used by psychologists much as the Goodenough-Harris is, although the Boehm tests measure extremely different aspects of development. The Boehm tests give the child a brief verbal direction, and the child responds by pointing to (or marking with a pencil, for older children) the correct part of a picture (see Figure 4.6). Unlike the Goodenough-Harris test's nonverbal content, the Boehm tests assess

Point to the cat <u>on</u> the box.

Figure 4.6. Sample item from the Boehm Test of Basic Concepts–Preschool Version. (Copyright © 1986 by The Psychological Corporation. Reproduced by permission. All rights reserved.)

primarily language and conceptual development. The concepts are related to size, direction, position in space, quantity, time, amount, and similar ideas that are typically acquired by preschoolers and kindergartners.

Originally, it was thought that the test would prove to be both a good predictor of early school success, which it was (Estes, Harris, Moers, & Wodrich, 1976), and that it would allow teachers to teach pupils new concepts. Psychologists recognized the potential for the test to supplement intelligence tests. Although almost all preschool intelligence tests produce verbal ability scores, they do so by using items that require the child to speak. The Boehm tests allow the child to demonstrate language and conceptual development without speaking. Consequently, the Boehm tests provide the child with an additional opportunity to score sufficiently high to rule out mental retardation. They also offer additional evaluation of language skills and, in some instances, may help to offer hypotheses; for example, a child who scores low on all WPPSI–R verbal subtests may be suspected to have pervasive language problems. However, if that child were to score in the average range on the Boehm tests, then the examiner may hypothesize that the child's problems may be more narrowly confined to those aspects of language that require expression. The Boehm tests, like individual subtests that compose IQ tests, are relatively brief and are somewhat unreliable; thus, interpretations like those made above need to be made cautiously.

The Preschool Version appears to have a generally adequate norm group and provides T-scores and percentile ranks according to the child's age. It also has some evidence of acceptable reliability and validity. Because the Preschool Version is clearly intended for individual administration, it is likely to be used frequently by psychologists. The version for older children is intended for group administration and does not provide standard scores by age; therefore, this version is less likely to find wide usage as part of an ability battery administered by psychologists. If used cautiously, either test may have value, as do tests such as the Peabody Picture Vocabulary Test–Revised that similarly assess language without requiring the child to speak. The Peabody Picture Vocabulary Test–Revised is also suitable for older children and is discussed in Chapter 6.

## DIAGNOSING MENTAL RETARDATION

Psychological tests are of clinical value only when used to answer referral questions. Although there are myriad questions about development, one of the most frequently asked during the preschool years is, "Does this child have mental retardation?" Often, however, those asking that a child be tested are aware that development is slow but lack such specifically focused questions.

Mental retardation can be diagnosed accurately during the preschool years, especially if the child is functioning in the range of most severe disability. By the time they reach the preschool years, children clearly manifest intellectual development in the form of planning, reasoning, and problem-solving ability so that they can be evaluated by intelligence tests. Preschool children also are expected to possess basic self-care and adaptive skills that are related to, but independent of, intellectual ability. Adaptive behavior assessment devices can measure this development. These two considerations allow for the accurate diagnosis of mental retardation during the preschool years.

## Definition of Mental Retardation

In 1983, the American Association on Mental Retardation (AAMR), an influential multidisciplinary group, promulgated a definition of mental retardation that was widely accepted: "significantly subaverage general intellectual functioning resulting in or associated with concurrent impairments in adaptive behavior and manifested during the developmental period" (Grossman, 1983, p. 11). This definition, together with its accompanying elaborations in the AAMR manual, meant that a diagnosis of mental retardation generally could be established among children with IQs less than 70 who manifested accompanying adaptive impairments, such as low scores on adaptive behavior measures like the Vineland.

The 1983 AAMR definition was revised—some would say drastically altered—by a new AAMR definition in 1992. There is concern among experts that the new definition may affect clinical practice and research in the area of mental retardation. In fact, the 1992 AAMR definition's authors were apparently intent on a drastic change when they stated: "This book will change the way you think about people with mental retardation" (cited in Hodapp, 1995, p. 24). The 1992 definition is as follows:

> *Mental retardation* refers to substantial limitations in present functioning. It is characterized by significantly subaverage intellectual functioning, existing concurrently with related limitations in two or more of the following applicable adaptive skill areas: communication, self-care, home living, social skills, community use, self-direction, health and safety, functional academics, leisure, and work. Mental retardation manifests before age 18. (AAMR, 1992, p. 1)

At first appearance many readers would wonder where this new definition departs from the old (1983) one. References to subaverage intellectual functioning and adaptive delays are still present. However, specifics have been altered: An apparently slight IQ shift has occurred, as outlined in the manual, with the old value of 70 replaced with the new value of 75; the global notion of adaptive delays has been supplanted by 10 skill areas of which only 3 must show "limitations." More important, conceptualization of mental retardation has been altered so that the condition is seen as a poor fit between the capabilities of the individual and the demands of his or her environment. This point is reflected in the elimination of the traditional levels of mental retardation (mild, moderate, severe, profound) and their replacement with the concept of "intensities of support." The intensities of support continuum (intermittent, limited, extensive, pervasive) is meant to indicate the amount of environmental support the individual requires from sources such as technology, other people, behavioral support, financial planning, and more.

Concern about the new definition's effect rather than its intention has been voiced in the community of psychologists and measurement experts (e.g., Hodapp, 1995). Although the notion of de-emphasizing the disabilities inherent in the individual and corresponding heightened emphasis on his or her need for services is laudatory, the effect of implementing the new standards may be negative rather than positive. Such implementation may be especially problematic for individuals with mild, rather than severe, disabilities and for children, rather than adults.

Consider first the evaluation of individuals with suspected mild disabilities (those with IQ scores around the traditional cut-off value of 70). Although a shift from the old threshold value of 70 to the new one of 75 may appear slight, it is in fact enormous regarding the number of individuals subject to identification. This fact arises directly from the nature of the IQ distribution (bell-shaped curve in form). Most individuals in a population score near the mean and even a slight shift of a cut-off value toward the mean results in a substantial increase in those who score above the cut-off value. If IQ values alone were to be relied upon, the shift from 70 to 75 would more than double the number of individuals eligible for mental retardation diagnosis. Said another way, there are more individuals with IQs between 71 and 75 than there are with IQs between 55 and 70 (Gresham, MacMillan, & Siperstein, 1995).

Of course, IQ score was not the sole criterion for diagnosis under the old system, and it is not under the new AAMR guidelines either. Individuals must also have adaptive delays. Here, too, problems with the definition not apparent on the surface may become evident when diagnosticians delve deeper into the practicalities of actual clinical diagnosis. Previous (1983) conceptualization of adaptive behavior as a more or less unitary construct has been exchanged for the notion that adaptive behavior is composed of several discrete and separate areas that are meaningfully distinguished from one another. The 1992 AAMR guidelines designate 10 such skill areas. Using the 1983 AAMR guidelines, diagnosticians could rely upon one of several standardized measures of adaptive behavior (Vineland Adaptive Behavior Scales) known to produce reasonably reliable and valid *composite* adaptive scores. The 1992 standards are unfortunate, whereas a limited number of instruments capable of accurately assessing global adaptive behavior do exist, adaptive behavior instruments corresponding to the 10 newly enumerated skills areas do not exist. Perhaps because these instruments are lacking, the 1992 AAMR guidelines indicate that clinicians' judgment can be used to determine adaptive deficiencies. Diagnosticians may, thus, merely use their own judgment about whether a child's adaptive skills are deficient in a particular area—a procedure that discards all the advantages associated with psychological testing (see Chapter 1) and seems fraught with potential problems. Also troubling is that the 10 skill areas have no empirical basis in research as being distinct from one another and, thus, there is little or no evidence that these skill areas are potentially capable of being assessed independently. Furthermore, several of the areas listed seem unrelated to childhood demands for adaptation (e.g., work, health and safety) (Gresham et al., 1995).

That so many more children might be labeled as individuals with mild mental retardation under the 1992 guidelines is made all the more troublesome because the "mild" distinction would be eliminated if the new diagnostic system were used. That is, a child with an IQ score of 73 who possesses some areas of adaptive integrity but who struggles, and thus requires help in language, academic, and motor coordination, simply would be labeled with "mental retardation." This is the exact same label as a child with an IQ score of 20 who has impairments in every adaptive area and requires institutional care.

Using the 1992 AAMR system, severity is denoted by the supports that the individual requires. There is, however, no track record of application for these distinctions in actual practice. Affixing distinctions about severity of disability under the 1992 system seems far more arbitrary than the numerical guidelines of the 1983 system (see Table 4.2). Moreover, the 1983 system resulted in most individuals who were diagnosed with mental retardation being identified as having mild mental retardation. A great deal has been learned about how modest these "mild" disabilities may be regarding long-term vocational adjustment and the prospect for success outside of school. In fact, some professionals have suggested that these individuals should be designated as "educationally handicapped" instead of mildly mentally retarded (Reschly, 1988). There is concern that these distinctions and the important data regarding their implications will be lost if the 1992 standards gain wide acceptance.

At the time of this writing, the 1992 AAMR definition and guidelines have not come to dictate clinical diagnosis. Only the changes associated with adaptive behavior (i.e., 10 skill areas rather than a single adaptive domain) were reflected in the influential DSM-IV (published in 1994). Most state laws continue to express the 1983 guidelines (70 IQ with concomitant delay in adaptive behavior). Some experts have suggested that AAMR may lose its position of prominence in the field of mental retardation (thus the 1992 definition will be discounted) (Gresham et al., 1995), that the definition will be ignored by researchers because it is "antithetical to science" (Matson, 1995), and that the field of mental retardation will move away from the definition as more is learned about the etiology of mental retardation (Hodapp, 1995). An effort is afoot for the American Psychological Association's Division 33 (a group with special interest and involvement in mental retardation) to write its own guidelines. Practically speaking, the levels of mental retardation listed below are likely to continue to be seen in clinical and educational settings, as is the traditional 70 IQ value.

Despite AAMR's proposed changes, in practical terms, most psychologists are still comfortable diagnosing a child with mental retardation during the preschool years only if he or she meets the criteria of low IQ and delayed adaptive skills, plus an additional criterion. This key additional criterion is significantly delayed development across all measured psychometric areas. If a child shows one or two areas of average or near-average functioning, then most psychologists are reluctant to conclude that the child has mental retardation, even though his or her overall IQ and adaptive skills are low. The assumption is that if a child is doing satisfactorily in a single area, then demonstration of skill may suggest considerable cognitive strength that has merely failed to be detected by other aspects of testing. The several other low areas of functioning may be artificially depressed by a lack of rapport with the test examiner, by the child's poor motivation during testing, or because narrow processing problems rather than overall cognitive delay kept ability scores low. For example, a preschooler who does well only on a few spatial/mechanical tasks, but does poorly on everything else (including other spatial/mechanical tasks and all language tasks) and earns an IQ score in the range for mental retardation, may have done so poorly solely because of language-processing problems that prevented him or her from understanding what was said. Despite low IQ scores, this child does not really have mental retardation but has a specific learning disability–type problem. Generally, the younger the child, the more hesitant psychologists are to diagnose mental retardation if one sub-area of functioning remains undepressed. This is to say that a certain amount of judgment, as well as reliance on test scores, is called for when diagnosing mental retardation in the preschool years.

Consider the example from Table 4.3. Both boys technically meet the definition of mental retardation, in that both have IQs below 70, have impairments in adaptive behavior, and are younger than 18 years. Yet, on some tests that require conceptual ability, Bob shows ability above the range for mental retardation. He also has evidence of doing better on motor-related developmental tasks than on language-related tasks. Bob's mother rates him as having delays in self-care or adaptive skills but also noted severe attention deficits and hyperactivity that may interfere with dressing, feeding, and toileting. Bob's diagnosis would probably be "at risk," "borderline delayed," or "delayed in language and attention," but probably not mental retardation. John's scores, in contrast, are uniformly low on all thinking and reasoning tasks, adaptive skills, and mastery of developmental milestones. John's diagnosis would be mental retardation, with a recognition that this diagnosis may be revised in the future.

Table 4.3. Comparison of two children with delays

| | Bob | | John | |
|---|---|---|---|---|
| Measures | Score | Range | Score | Range |
| WPPSI–R IQ | | | | |
| Verbal | 59 | Retarded[a] | 69 | Retarded |
| Performance | 73 | Borderline | 69 | Retarded |
| Full Scale | 69 | Retarded | 65 | Retarded |
| Vineland Adaptive Behavior Composite | 68 | Retarded, but motor higher | 68 | Retarded, but all areas equal |
| Goodenough-Harris Draw-a-Man | 83 | | 66 | |
| Development Milestone | | | | |
| Sit | 7 months[b] | | 11 months | |
| Walk | 13 months | | 19 months | |
| Tricycle | 27 months | | 37 months | |
| First word | 26 months | | 26 months | |
| Toilet self | 31 months | | Cannot | |
| Dress self | 49 months | | Cannot | |

[a]Indicates general range into which score falls.
[b]Indicates approximate age of acquisition.

## Diagnostic Designations of Mental Retardation

The foregoing discussion should not be taken to imply that mental retardation is a single, uniform disability. This is a false assumption because both the causes and manifestations (e.g., nature, degree of severity) of mental retardation vary considerably from child to child. Clinicians sometimes denote the etiology of mental retardation, when it is known and, despite AAMR's recent advice to the contrary, continue to specify levels of mental retardation. Abolishing levels of mental retardation would eliminate language that has proved helpful as it has become used commonly over many years; also lost would be important distinctions that have matured as clinicians and researchers have learned the characteristics associated with each level. Even though most individuals who have mental retardation have no identifiable biomedical condition (in fact, many are not evaluated by a physician as part of the diagnostic process), the option to assign a biomedical diagnosis can be important for prognostic and planning purposes. (See Wodrich, 1986, for a discussion of the role of biomedical diagnoses in psychological and educational assessment.) Some considerations do follow directly from biomedical diagnosis. Knowledge of biomedical conditions leads to direct intervention in some cases; for example, genetic studies are required for families in which fragile X syndrome is detected, and children with inborn errors of metabolism, such as phenylketonuria (PKU), must adhere to modified diets. In addition, in those instances in which an accurate biomedical diagnosis can be established, such as Down syndrome, a child's prognosis can be more accurately anticipated. This knowledge aids families and human services agencies in planning the child's future. Unfortunately, educational interventions seldom follow directly from biomedical diagnoses. That is, studies have yet to demonstrate that one child does better with curriculum A, whereas a child with an impairment of similar severity does better with curriculum B, simply because their biomedical diagnoses differ. Biomedical diagnoses do not allow teachers to assume that one child might require more language instruction, whereas another may benefit more from sensory stimulation. Taking the longer view, however, experts have suggested that addressing etiology as well as current manifestation is an essential step toward more sophisticated research that will ultimately lead to better intervention (Landesman & Ramey, 1989). Several common biomedical causes of mental retardation are listed in Table 4.4.

DSM-IV and similar systems also permit diagnosis on a second axis that addresses the child's level of mental retardation (see Table 4.2). It is essential to remember that a child's degree of impairment is

Table 4.4. Common biomedical causes of mental retardation

| Term | Incidence[a] | Cause |
|---|---|---|
| Down syndrome | 1/1000 | Extra #21 chromosome |
| Fragile X | .6 to 1/1000 males | Anomaly on sex chromosome X |
| Klinefelter syndrome | 1/1000 males | Extra sex chromosome(s) in male |
| Fetal alcohol syndrome | 2/1000 | Alcohol consumption by mother during pregnancy |
| TORCH | Varies | Intrauterine infection with toxoplasmosis, syphilis, rubella, cytomegalovirus, or herpes virus |

*Sources:* Batshaw and Perret (1992); McCoy, Arceneaux, and Dean (1996).
[a]Estimated incidence figures per live births.

a description of his or her current level of functioning. A widely held misconception is that mental retardation means lack of potential for future growth, and consequently an unchanging degree of disability over time. This supposition is unfounded, based on AAMR's diagnostic criteria, which address only current functioning, and by the fact that there are numerous reports of individuals whose statuses have changed dramatically over time, sometimes resulting in unexpectedly high levels of independence as adults (Koegel & Edgerton, 1984; Ramey, Yeates, & Short, 1984). Moreover, a child's developmental course may differ depending on etiology. Children with Down syndrome, for example, may appear less disabled early in their development, only to reveal relatively lower levels of functioning as they approach adolescence and adulthood (Graham, 1983). Although it is true that many children who are diagnosed as having mental retardation move from one level of disability to another between the preschool years and adolescence, many children do not. Outlined below are some of the considerations for each classification level, together with anticipated functional levels, should the child's ability status not change much between preschool years and adolescence.

***Mild Mental Retardation*** Mild mental retardation is the largest classification group, containing an estimated 85% of all individuals diagnosed with mental retardation according to DSM-IV (American Psychiatric Association, 1994). Children with disabilities in this range generally have none of the physical characteristics that are evident in children with more severe mental retardation and have the least degree of impaired sensorimotor development of all children with mental retardation. They are the group most likely to have mental retardation because of cultural-experimental factors and/or because of limited ability passed on genetically from parents. This fact is supported by the high number of cases in which an individual and his or her first-degree relatives have similar mild mental retardation (suggesting that relatives inherited the same general ability patterns and were exposed to the same degree of environmental stimulation). In contrast, individuals with more severe mental retardation show no such increased incidence of mental retardation among relatives, suggesting that factors such as insults and infection of the central nervous system, nonrecurring genetic errors, and similar causes not resulting from the common environment nor to common genes among siblings are responsible (Plomin, 1989).

Children with mild mental retardation often are not identified until they begin school. Parents may not see the child as having a delay and, in fact, there may be no apparent delays in the acquisition of developmental milestones. If separate educational designations are used, then most children in this range would be classified "educable mentally retarded" or "educable mentally handicapped," revealing the assumption that most of them are capable of learning the basics of reading, spelling, and arithmetic. Children who remain in this category throughout the school years generally learn academics to approximately a sixth-grade level. As adults, many, if not most, of these individuals live independently, filling mainly unskilled jobs, although they may require assistance during times of crisis and may need guidance regarding money management, employment, and childrearing. Some of these individuals are indistinguishable from their peers without disabilities, except that they are unable to keep pace academically. Consequently, the logic of using the mental retardation designation for individuals in this ability range, unless overwhelming evidence of extra-academic adaptive delays exists, seems questionable. The caveat on the use of this label would appear to be particularly appropriate if a child comes from sociocultural circumstances that differ from the mainstream (see Chapter 8). Although it is true that the mental retardation label is so highly stigmatized and its effects so potentially harmful that its casual use should be avoided, categorical issues are nonetheless complicated. For instance, most children scoring less than 70 on IQ tests are destined to encounter academic failure without special services, regardless of their ability to adapt outside of school. Yet most states provide services only for children who are labeled as fitting specific categories, such as mentally retarded or learning disabled, especially once they reach school age. Without labels, there are no special education services. Labels are potentially pernicious but so are years of school failure. In the final analysis, difficult choices often have to be made by diagnosticians who recognize both the cost of labels and their necessity as a ticket to essential services.

***Moderate Mental Retardation*** The category of moderate mental retardation consists of approximately 10% of all individuals diagnosed with mental retardation according to DSM-IV (American Psychiatric

Association, 1994). These children are much more likely than those with mild mental retardation to have an identifiable biomedical cause of their condition, although many children in this range (and those with more severe delays) still have no specific etiology associated with their disabilities. Because these children, and those with more severe disabilities, have a high incidence of neurological involvement and distinctive physical characteristics, their impairments are much more obvious to medical professionals during preschool years. Most are identified before they begin school simply by appearance, parent report, or delayed mastery of developmental milestones. One of the most salient developmental failures during the preschool years is delayed speech onset, and it is often this concern alone that brings children to health providers, such as pediatricians. Under these circumstances, it is important that children be given a comprehensive cognitive evaluation. Such an evaluation may reveal that not only is speech delayed but so too are all other aspects of development.

Almost all children with moderate mental retardation enter special education programs early in their school careers, and if designations are used, they would be "trainable mentally retarded" or "trainable mentally handicapped." Their school programs stress primarily nonacademic skills, such as self-care and basic vocational skills. Even with special services, however, most of these children will have significant disabilities as adults. By the teen years, most will use language for simple communication. As adults, many remain with their parents or live in sheltered group homes, performing routine and repetitive tasks, such as dishwashing. As they develop, many children with moderate mental retardation master the basics of self-care, such as grooming and eating, and participate in activities offered by community-based programs.

***Severe Mental Retardation*** Individuals in the severe mental retardation range constitute approximately 3%–4% of people diagnosed with mental retardation according to DSM-IV (American Psychiatric Association, 1994). Children with this degree of disability are almost always identified before they reach school age and generally have significant motor delays and little or no speech. The school curriculum for children with severe mental retardation often consists of self-care training that addresses skills such as eating, grooming, and toileting, but has little focus on academics except to teach a survival vocabulary (i.e., words such as stop, men). Some of these individuals master simple household tasks; however, most require considerable supervision, including assistance for self-care skills, such as tying shoes and bathing.

***Profound Mental Retardation*** Approximately 1%–2% of all individuals diagnosed with mental retardation are in the profound range (American Psychiatric Association, 1994). This group has the most obvious physical and neurological impairments. The delays of these individuals are almost always evident to parents during the preschool years. Training generally is concerned with sensory and motor stimulation. Many individuals with profound mental retardation require custodial care and close medical supervision for a variety of problems, including epilepsy and respiratory difficulties. Some individuals with profound mental retardation can develop self-care skills by adulthood and perform simple tasks while closely supervised in a sheltered workshop.

***Autism and Mental Retardation*** The group of children who are said to have autism and have accompanying syndromes sometimes called "pervasive developmental disorders" (American Psychiatric Association, 1994) represent a puzzling diagnostic situation because of an overlap with mental retardation. These children are not only delayed but also have distortions in development of basic psychological processes, such as social skills, language, attention, and perception. Language is often delayed or unusual (e.g., echolalic), there is a pervasive lack of responsiveness to others, and there is a bizarre response to various aspects of the environment (e.g., resistance to any change of routine). Because behavior or language problems dominate, professionals are sometimes reluctant to refer children with autism for intellectual testing. However, it is known that most children with autism have both the autistic disorder and mental retardation concurrently. In fact, 75% of children with autism are found to have IQs in the range of mental retardation (American Psychiatric Association, 1994). Both of these conditions need to be diagnosed and addressed in intervention, especially because the degree of intellectual impairment (as indexed by IQ) appears to have a substantial bearing on prognosis. In practice, it is wise to refer children who are suspected of having autism for intellectual testing.

## DIAGNOSING PRESCHOOL LEARNING DISABILITIES

The second main question referral agents ask about development relates to the presence of narrow, or delimited, developmental problems. Many times the question is simply posed, "Does this child have learning disabilities?" The referral agent does not expect that the child has global delays, as is the case with a child with mental retardation, but rather suspects isolated or limited developmental problems. Although most psychologists recognize what is being asked by the referral question above, nonetheless, the question is potentially confusing because the term "learning disabilities" has two meanings. An example of one meaning is the following: "This child has a learning disability; he loses information from short-term memory too quickly." That is, learning disability is used generically to indicate a narrow cognitive or information processing problem that interferes with learning. The second is a legal definition: "This child qualifies for special education; learning disability is the category of exceptionality." (See Chapters 5 and 6 for a more detailed distinction.) In many states, special education services for learning disabilities are not specifically mandated for children younger than 5 years of age although some preschoolers with this designation are served (Esterly & Griffin, 1987). Preschool children with disabilities are mandated to be served by IDEA although states may decide which categories will be served and how categories will be defined (Trohanis, 1989). Some experts have noted that since the federal guidelines that define learning disability call for an ability/achievement discrepancy, it becomes logically impossible for preschoolers to manifest the academic deficits necessary to be identified as learning disabled (Prasse, 1983).

Consequently, in most instances, questions about learning disabilities are really questions such as, "Does this child have psychological deficits that will cause him or her problems learning in school if they are not now corrected?" That is, the first definition of learning disabilities above is being used. Sometimes referral agents ask better-focused questions such as, "Does this child have visual-perceptual problems?" or, "Does this child have a linguistic deficit?" The more focused questions are preferred, of course, by psychologists.

What types of narrow psychological ability limitations can be detected during the preschool years? In general, any of the main ability areas assessed by preschool ability tests may constitute a significant impairment requiring special instructional considerations. For example, virtually all comprehensive preschool ability tests (WPPSI–R, Stanford-Binet IV, McCarthy Scales) include a language score. For obvious reasons, language impairments affect a child in multiple situations and, if uncorrected, will hamper academic progress. Similarly, most of the same tests contain a measure of nonverbal ability that includes items comprising spatial/mechanical, visual attention, and nonlanguage reasoning tasks. Problems in these spheres are predictive of school difficulties as well. Fine motor development is essential for adequate progress from kindergarten through the primary grades because writing is being taught. Consequently, visual-perception and fine motor tests are typically included in preschool batteries. Short-term memory, because integrity in this system is a necessary requisite for processing information into longer-term storage, is increasingly being assessed during the preschool years. Tests such as the Stanford-Binet IV and McCarthy Scales have multiple subtests to assess this ability. The K–ABC (Kaufman Assessment Battery for Children), discussed in Chapter 5, tests short-term memory extensively.

Many of the same issues of remedying ability impairments, identifying limitations that predict academic problems, and matching ability profiles to method of instruction, which are discussed in Chapters 5 and 6, also apply if preschoolers are assessed. Special considerations are also associated with preschool evaluation. First, psychological abilities are less stable during the preschool years than later in life. Thus, predicting that a child who has an auditory processing problem at age 3 will still have the same problem at age 10 is risky—far more risky than predicting that a similar problem will persist in a child from age 10 to age 17. Second, because it is sometimes difficult to convey directions to young children and to keep them attentive and motivated, it is difficult to assume that relatively narrow skills are being measured. For instance, consider a simple memory test, such as Bead Memory from the Stanford-Binet IV. The test is designed to measure short-term memory of visual material. Yet an inattentive child, who cannot comprehend simple directions or catch on to new tasks, is likely to score low, even though he or she may possess quite adequate visual short-term memory. Finally, because children at this age lack an academic history, it must remain speculative about whether measured processing problems will ultimately interfere with school progress. That is, there is no way to know for certain if a 3-year-old's memory problems will actually hold him or her back academically because that 3-year-old has not yet been exposed to academics. In contrast, this limitation does not occur with school-age children because it is possible to correlate history of school failure and processing problems, or to alternatively note the absence of such correlation. If an older child is succeeding academically, then there is generally little reason to be concerned about processing problems that surface during testing.

In short, diagnosis of learning disabilities is far less simple and certain during the preschool years than it is later in a child's life. Because of the psychological stigma attendant to any label, including "learning disability," many psychologists hesitate to affix a learning disabilities diagnosis unless the child's problems are severe and such a label is essential for acquiring special services.

As states have implemented more preschool services under PL 99-457 (see Fox, Freedman, & Klepper, 1989), and this trend continues under IDEA, some frequently used labels may be supplanted or simply not used. For instance, broad categories such as *developmental delay* may be employed and may subsume children with both general cognitive delays or more specific problems, such as physical or language impairments. More specific labels like *learning disabilities* may be used in other states to describe preschoolers and to sanction special education services for them (Snyder, Bailey, & Auer, 1994). Regardless of the labels used to designate children with disabilities, thorough, cautious assessment using the best psychometric instruments remains an important objective.

## SUMMARY

Psychologists have developed a variety of tests to help answer questions about preschool development. Intelligence tests can measure the emerging language, motor, conceptual, and reasoning skills that characterize preschoolers' development. The Stanford-Binet Intelligence Scale L–M is of historical significance as it was an early measure of general intelligence and provided reliable and valid global IQ scores. Today, tests like the Stanford-Binet Intelligence Scale IV, the Wechsler Preschool and Primary Scale of Intelligence–Revised, and the McCarthy Scales of Children's Abilities not only report global IQ but also break performance into subareas such as verbal and nonverbal development. Adaptive behavior instruments, which measure such behaviors as dressing and feeding, are an important complement to intelligence tests for preschoolers. The Vineland Adaptive Behavior Scales and the AAMR Adaptive Behavior Scales are two of the most frequently used adaptive scales.

Most referral questions about preschoolers deal with overall ability or with concern about more limited aspects of development, such as language. Consequently, preschool mental retardation and learning disabilities are two important concepts that are discussed in this chapter. Preschool mental retardation is an across-the-board delay, diagnosed by low IQ and poor adaptive functioning. Any of the accepted preschool intelligence tests, coupled with adaptive behavior scales, are useful in making this diagnosis. In contrast to mental retardation, preschool learning disabilities are diagnosed by a breakdown in limited psychological functions, such as visual perception or expressive language, whereas overall IQ is unaffected. Intelligence tests such as the Wechsler Preschool and Primary Scale of Intelligence–Revised and the Stanford-Binet IV scale, because they tap many important skills and report subtest scores for each, are extremely helpful in locating preschool learning disabilities.

## Study Questions

1. Why were children's intelligence tests first devised?
2. IQ originally was an expression of what ratio? IQ has subsequently become what type of score? What mean and standard deviation(s) are associated with IQ at present?
3. What advantages do intelligence tests with subtests afford over global intelligence measures? What disadvantages?
4. Contrast intelligence tests with adaptive behavior scales.
5. Which intelligence tests might be most appropriate for bilingual preschoolers? Which would be least appropriate? Why?
6. Why doesn't preschool IQ correlate better with adult IQ?
7. Why are children with mild mental retardation often diagnosed later than children with more severe mental retardation?

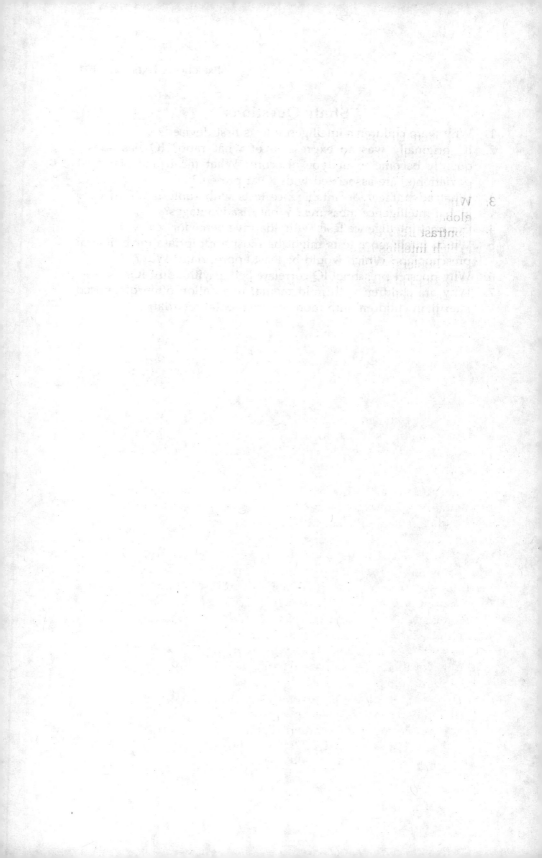

CHAPTER FIVE

# School-Age Intelligence and Ability Tests

Among children's principal tasks during the school years is to acquire academic skills. It is in instances when failure to learn occurs that school-age intelligence and ability tests have their greatest value.

Why does Mike always forget what he reads?
Is something wrong with Donnie? He is in the second grade and he still sometimes writes his letters and numbers backward.
Jim is struggling to keep up with his classmates in mathematics. Is he bright enough to do better?

As is discussed in Chapter 4, from its very inception, the history of mental measurement has been concerned with assessing children's intellectual ability. Consequently, some of psychology's best instruments are available to address concerns in this realm. Ability tests that are used to evaluate school-age children generally are concerned with the following: 1) verification that a child has sufficient intelligence to learn the school curriculum; 2) establishment of an ability level so that expectations for school achievement (including the detection of underachievement) can occur objectively; and 3) a search for a pattern of strengths and weakness so that educational plans, especially remedial instructional plans, can be developed. Also intimately related to the use of these tests are the diagnoses of learning disabilities and mental retardation.

This chapter discusses several frequently used intelligence and special ability tests, as well as how these tests may be used to address concerns similar to those mentioned above.

# INTELLIGENCE TESTS FOR SCHOOL-AGE CHILDREN

## Weschler Intelligence Scale for Children–III

The Wechsler Intelligence Scale for Children (Wechsler, 1991) has dominated assessment of school-age children for nearly 50 years and continues to do so in the 1990s, despite the advent of several new intelligence tests during the mid-1990s. Its recent updating (1991), which resulted in the Weschler Intelligence Scale for Children–III (WISC–III) that supplanted the Wechsler Intelligence Scale for Children–Revised (WISC–R) (Weschler, 1974), has helped to ensure its continuing popularity. Because of its acceptance as an important measure of IQ and because it is frequently the cornerstone of psychoeducational and neuropsychological evaluations, the WISC–III receives detailed inspection.

Unlike most children's tests, the WISC began as an adult scale. The test's author, David Wechsler, was a clinical psychologist who was involved in the mental testing movement in the U.S. Army before becoming chief psychologist at Bellevue Psychiatric Hospital. At Bellevue, Wechsler adopted a position that differed on several points from that of the authors of the then-dominant Stanford-Binet Intelligence Scale (Sattler, 1988). First, the notion of calculating IQ by dividing mental age by chronological age (a Stanford-Binet practice) was illogical for adults, according to Wechsler; Wechsler argued that the practice was inappropriate even for children. He contended that the best way to calculate brightness is to compare one's ability with the abilities of peers the same age, rather than to assess whether abilities were acquired sooner or later than peers. Both the Wechsler adult scales and the Wechsler children's scales (WISC) accomplished this. Second, Wechsler objected to the seemingly haphazard organization of Stanford-Binet items that resulted in little uniform item content across age levels. Instead, Wechsler advocated measuring various functions of intelligence so that the same types of items would constitute the test no matter what the child's age. Wechsler contended that it was important for children age 9, for instance, to receive the same types of items as children age 13. Only when this condition was met would individual findings be comparable regardless of a child's age. In addition, Wechsler grouped items together to form homogeneous subtests based on item make-up. Consequently, Wechsler's intelligence test became a series of subtests—an extremely important testing innovation. Subsequent to the development of the Wechsler scales, almost all newly developed intelligence scales for preschool-age (e.g.,

McCarthy Scales, discussed in Chapter 4) and school-age children (e.g., Kaufman Assessment Battery for Children, discussed in this chapter) comprised discrete subtests, each with homogeneous items.

Finally, because Wechsler was a clinician working in a psychiatric setting, he constructed his scale to elicit personality and observational data as well as intelligence scores. These features enhanced the popularity of the test because they often allowed psychologists to observe response styles, reactions to frustration, attention spans, facility with language, and a multitude of other considerations that contributed to understanding the person being examined.

In addition to constructing his line of intelligence scales (the Wechsler Adult Intelligence Scale, the Wechsler Preschool and Primary Scale of Intelligence), David Wechsler spoke widely on intelligence and its measurement. Wechsler defined intelligence as "the aggregate or global capacity of the individual to act purposely, to think rationally, and to deal effectively with his environment" (Wechsler, 1958, p. 7). Wechsler conceived of his instruments as measuring global ability with multiple facets, and he was opposed to equating general intelligence with general ability. The most recent test manual (Wechsler, 1991) makes explicit that the WISC–III does not measure all aspects of intelligence nor does it measure intelligence per se: "[T]he intellectual abilities represented in the scale may be essential as precursors of intelligence behavior" (p. 2), but other factors such as personality and outlook determine how ability is expressed. However, those who have come to use Wechsler's scale have both redefined his instrument as a measure of ability and, at times, have attempted to look at separate functions without focusing on general intelligence. In the 1990s, research on *human information processing,* the use of sophisticated statistical techniques to study the organization and interrelations of abilities, as well as concern about cultural bias, has resulted in questions about the adequacy of the Wechsler's theoretical basis. Some psychologists have suggested reorganizing the WISC–III's global scores into narrower clusters for more meaningful interpretation. Others have suggested finding alternative, and presumably superior, intelligence tests. Nonetheless, many practitioners continue to prefer the WISC–III because of all the information it can tell them about children.

***WISC–III Verbal Scales*** The WISC–III contains Verbal and Performance sections (see Table 5.1), each of which is discussed separately, followed by a discussion of how the subtests are grouped together for interpretation. For the most part, the WISC–III Verbal subtests are similar to one another in that each consists of questions asked orally by the examiner and answered orally by the child. One Verbal subtest, Digit Span, is an auditory task but does not consist of

Table 5.1. Organization of the WISC–III

| Verbal subtests | Performance subtests |
|---|---|
| Information | Picture Completion |
| Similarities | Coding |
| Arithmetic | Picture Arrangement |
| Vocabulary | Block Design |
| Comprehension | Object Assembly |
| (Digit Span) | (Symbol Search) |
| | (Mazes) |
| Verbal IQ = composite of five Verbal subtests (Digit Span excluded) | Performance IQ = composite of five Performance subtests |
| Subtest mean = 10 | IQ mean = 100 |
| Subtest standard deviation = 3 | IQ standard deviation = 15 |

typical questions per se. Vision is not required for any of the Verbal subtests; therefore, children who are blind can be assessed (older children are asked to read six brief Arithmetic items, but the examiner can read for them, if necessary). Verbal subtests are described below (see Kaufman, 1979, and Sattler, 1988, for more detailed descriptions).

*Information* The Information subtest consists of 30 questions requiring knowledge and recall of general factual information. Test confidentiality prohibits revealing exact items, but the following questions approximate WISC–III Information subtest items:

"How many ears does a dog have?"
"During what month is Christmas?"
"On what continent is Korea located?"

Most items can be answered with a single word. Whereas this subtest is relatively weak as a measure of reasoning, it does measure verbal knowledge and a child's sensitivity to and retention of information around him- or herself. It also has important implications for classroom learning. Children who lack simple factual information often cannot follow classroom discussion and fail to understand background ideas found in curriculum material; for instance, a 12-year-old who is unaware of the location of Korea or, perhaps, is uncertain of the exact meaning of the concept "continent" might be expected to struggle when geography lessons of any type are presented, especially those involving Asia.

*Similarities* The second Verbal subtest, Similarities, consists of 19 two-word combinations. A child is presented the word combinations and asked how they are "alike" or "the same." The following pairs approximate WISC–III Similarities items: "hamburger" and "pizza" (both are food or both can be eaten); "river" and "lake" (both are bodies of water); "gasoline" and "coal" (both are sources of energy or power). Some credit is awarded for identifying concrete, simple similarities between the concepts, but more points are credited for producing abstract responses showing higher conceptual ability. For example, children who liken gasoline to coal because they both "make fire" would receive less credit than children who state that gasoline and coal are both sources of energy, have power, or contain carbon bonds.

Conceptual ability and reasoning are required for a high score on this subtest, particularly for older children. In practice, a high score often identifies good verbal-conceptual ability even if some other verbal scores are low. That is, the child who scores high on the Similarities subtest may well be a good verbal thinker even if he or she has not been exposed to and retained some common general information or vocabulary words needed to score well on other Verbal subtests.

*Arithmetic* The Arithmetic subtest's name connotes measurement of achievement, such as acquired academic skills, and indeed there is some overlap with standardized achievement tests. Although mathematical in nature, Arithmetic items stress the use of concepts and problem solving rather than rote computation so as to emphasize the ability, or intelligence, aspect of arithmetic. Consisting of 24 items, the Arithmetic subtest deals with simple counting, number concepts, and solution of story problem. The following items are similar to those found on the Arithmetic subtest:

"Bob had two balloons and a friend gave him one more. How many does he have now?"

"Jenny had six cookies. If she gave one third of them away, how many would she have left?"

"If four doughnuts cost $1.20, how much would six doughnuts cost?"

The Arithmetic subtest does measure reasoning and problem solving to some extent but does not correlate especially well with other verbal subtests. The test is important because it can help identify children who have problems with concentration or distractibility, retention of material presented verbally, or glaring mathematics deficiencies.

*Vocabulary* In the Vocabulary subtest, the child's task is to provide verbal definitions of 30 words that are presented orally. The following are examples of the types of vocabulary words that children might be asked: "cow," "hurry," "lever," and "estuary." Credit is earned for definitions that not only show familiarity but define the vocabulary word in a precise, conceptually clear way; for instance, "lever" might be defined as "a stick for pushing things," which would show familiarity with and understanding of the term. But, a child who describes a lever as "a rigid instrument for prying that allows increased power because of its length" has a more abstract, higher conceptual understanding of the term. This second child would be credited more points and would ultimately earn a higher Vocabulary subtest score than would a peer who gives concrete, imprecise definitions. Quality of thought rather than sophistication in verbal expression is credited so that a child who uses poor grammar or confused syntax is not penalized.

The preceding example (defining "lever") suggests that the Vocabulary subtest, despite its simple appearance, is an excellent measure of conceptual and thinking ability. It is obvious that the child who knows vocabulary words and fully appreciates underlying concepts is in an enormously favorable position in school as compared to peers without this advantage. Research tends to confirm this subjective impression and shows the subtest to be an excellent measure of general cognitive ability and an important predictor of school success (Sattler, 1988). Consequently, a child's results on this subtest, as well as all measures of language skills, should be examined closely for deficiencies when school failure occurs.

The Vocabulary subtest is also an excellent source of data for the concrete response style that often characterizes children who have mental retardation. Although familiar with a vocabulary word, children with mental retardation often lack a clear conceptual grasp. The following is a hypothetical exchange between an examiner and a child with mental retardation:

Examiner: "What is a cow?"
Child: "A cow can be led."
Examiner: "Tell me more about a cow."
Child: "You can lead it to Grandma's."
Examiner: "What else can you tell me about a cow?"
Child: "Sometimes it doesn't want to go."

The child's responses reflect a poverty of content. Although all these statements are true of cows, the child's description hardly captures the essence of a cow, nor does it distinguish a cow from a horse, a dog, or even a little sister.

*Comprehension* The Comprehension subtest contains 18 items dealing with practical reasoning and judgment. Items consist of verbally presented questions similar to these:

"What should you do if you walk to school one morning and find your classroom door locked?"

"What are some reasons why we shouldn't steal?"

Responses are examined for quality of judgment, reasoning, and problem solving. Responses that are socially acceptable earn higher scores than less acceptable responses. As "social acceptability" is culturally (and subculturally) related, this subtest has been particularly criticized for being culturally biased. However, intuitive notions about cultural differences do not always find support in empirical research. (See Chapter 8 for a discussion of nonbiased assessment.)

Although the Comprehension subtest is a reasonable measure of language functioning, it does not appear to measure reasoning, problem solving, and conceptual ability as well as some other verbal subtests do. Empirical research bears out this subjective impression (Sattler, 1988). Nonetheless, valuable diagnostic information is often gathered by observing a child's responses to Comprehension items, some of which are emotionally laden. "Why shouldn't we steal?" might precipitate an angry verbal outburst against authority from one child or a recounting of severe physical punishment at the hands of an abusive parent from another child. A timid or anxious child might respond to the locked door situation with, "Sit down and cry for Mom." The Comprehension subtest represents most clearly Wechsler's knack for posing questions that both measure intellectual functioning and elicit important personality and emotional information.

At times, the Comprehension subtest is also valuable for detecting language processing problems. Children who have auditory processing impairments fail to sort out, retain, or understand these sometimes lengthy items. These children may look blankly and say, "huh," or ask to have items repeated over and over. Others respond as if they have heard or remember only a portion of the question. For example, the locked school door question may be responded to with, "Find out who broke the door," or, "See if I could fix it," revealing a misprocessed message. Repeated errors of this sort would cue the examining psychologist to check authority acuity and/or auditory processing more closely (Norman-Murch & Bashir, 1986).

*Digit Span* The Digit Span subtest consists simply of a series of random numbers (e.g., 1, 7, 8; 2, 3, 9, 5) presented orally by the examiner. The child's task is to hold the numbers in short-term memory and then repeat them in the correct order; both forward and backward series are used.

Wechsler believed that the Digit Span subtest had so little to do with higher conceptual and reasoning ability that he decided not to include results from this subtest in the calculation of IQ scores. Empirical research has substantiated Wechsler and shown poor correlation between this subtest and general ability. Nonetheless, psychologists frequently administer the subtest to determine how well a child concentrates and retains rote information. Such information may have diagnostic significance in some cases of learning or attention problems.

A child's Verbal IQ score is a composite of his or her performance on five Verbal subtests (excluding Digit Span). This score is a reasonably reliable and broad-based measure of the child's thinking, reasoning, problem-solving, and conceptual ability with language. Because language skills are called for in school and will be called for increasingly as the child progresses through the grades, the Verbal IQ score is an extremely important index, as is seen later in this chapter.

***WISC–III Performance Scales*** Verbal subtests make up half of the WISC–III, and Performance subtests make up the other half. Five Performance subtests are routinely administered, with optional sixth and seventh Performance subtests also available. The Performance tasks contrast with the Verbal subtests in that each requires little or no language. Performance tasks allow the child to show his or her intellectual ability by manipulating objects, pointing, or copying. Even a child who is deaf and nonverbal can complete most WISC–III Performance section items.

*Picture Completion* The Picture Completion subtest consists of 30 color pictures of common objects or everyday scenes. Each picture is missing an element, and the child's task is to point out or name the missing element. Figure 5.1 is an example of a Picture Completion item similar to those found on the WISC–III.

Although locating missing elements from drawings seems on the surface simply to require attention to detail, the task also requires higher cognition that becomes evident to examiners after observing many children confronted with these items. Before locating the missing element, the child must possess a concept of what the whole might be, and then must check to see if key elements are present. With simple scenes this may be done more or less automatically by simultaneously processing the entire picture, but with more complex scenes, a more sequential thinking, checking, and responding approach is needed. Research suggests that more than superficial attending skills are in fact measured, as the subtest has been found to be moderately associated with general cognitive functioning (Sattler, 1988).

*Coding* On the Coding subtest, symbols or codes associated with marks or numbers are copied by the child as he or she works as quickly as possible (see Figure 5.2). The goal is to complete as many symbols as possible in 2 minutes. Credit is earned solely for each symbol produced. Children who memorize the code and work quickly earn the most credit. Therefore, the subtest measures memory and psychomotor speed but is a poor measure of higher cognitive

Figure 5.1. Simulated WISC–III Picture Completion item. (Reproduced by permission from the Weschler Intelligence Scale for Children–Revised. Copyright © 1971, 1974 by The Psychological Corporation. All rights reserved.)

processes and intellectual ability; this supposition is born out statistically. Coding has low correlation with Full Scale IQ and with Performance IQ.

Although weak as a contributor to IQ, the Coding subtest nonetheless provides valuable information in many instances. Children with hand–eye coordination problems often make severe distortions of their symbols, lose their place, or become extremely frustrated. Children who are unable to memorize visual, nonverbal information also

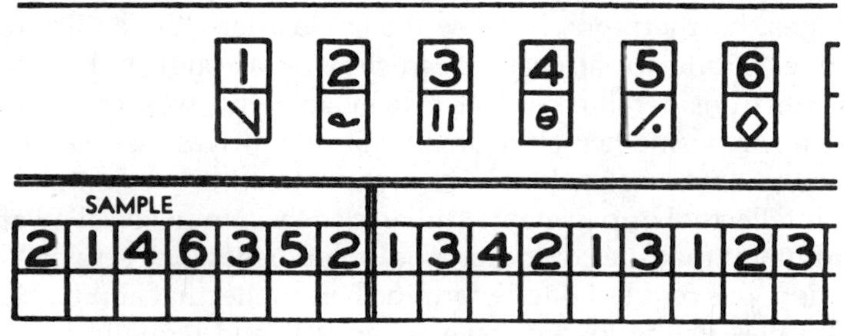


Figure 5.2. Simulated WISC–III Coding item. (Reproduced by permission from the Weschler Intelligence Scale for Children–Revised. Copyright © 1971, 1974, by The Psychological Corporation. All rights reserved.)

tend to do poorly on this subtest. In some instances, this proves to be important diagnostic information because these same skills are required in many primary school classrooms. Problems with the Coding subtest, when coupled with additional information, may also raise the possibility of attention problems.

*Picture Arrangement* The Picture Arrangement subtest consists of 14 cartoon-like sequences. Each sequence is presented to the child in a disarranged order, and the child's task is to study the pictures and place them in the correct order. Credit is assigned for accuracy of arrangement as it agrees with a predetermined logical order. Bonus points are given for rapid, correct arrangement.

Reasoning and problem solving seem to be clear requisites for correct arrangement of the pictures. Bright children earn more points because they appear to 1) examine the pictures and conceive of one or more possible logical story sequences, and 2) check the hypothesized arrangement for logic as they work (i.e., bright children self-monitor their hypothetical story sequences with a recognition that several possible arrangements might exist). The brighter child seems to recognize that among the several possible arrangements, he or she must settle on the one that others also would view as logical. Less bright children seem to conceive of few if any possible story sequences and/or fail to check their stories for logic that might be cogent to others. For these reasons, the Picture Arrangement subtest is credible as a measure of intellectual ability, capable of distinguishing bright children from less bright children. Picture Arrangement has been found by research to be an adequate, but not superior, measure of general ability.

The Picture Arrangement subtest also has unique diagnostic value. Children are required to position the pictures in sequence from left to right (spatially) and must arrange them from beginning to end (temporally)—abilities lacked by some children who have learning disabilities. Furthermore, because the subtest taps the ability to read sometimes subtle social cues, it can provide a rough index of social judgment. Consider the case of a teenager who was continually in trouble for exposing herself to small children. It was assumed that the girl, who had experienced brain injury in a boating accident, had such severe intellectual impairments and was so lacking in social awareness and judgment that she could not modify her behavior. A psychological evaluation was requested to determine her intellectual ability. Her Full Scale IQ was in the low-average range (84) and, equally important, her Picture Arrangement subtest was above average (12). This information implied that the girl probably could recognize what was occurring in social situations and had considerably more social intelligence than was previously assumed.

*Block Design* As the name implies, the Block Design subtest consists of several blocks that a child uses to reproduce 12 designs presented by an examiner. Credit is earned for correct reproduction, with additional credit available for speed.

Although perceptual skills are involved, the Block Design subtest also measures conceptual, planning, and reasoning abilities. Brighter children often respond to the design task in an organized, systematic way. They seem to recognize quickly that the four blocks presented to them must align in a 2 × 2 matrix and that each block must be solid white, solid red, or red and white diagonal. They use logic to work out each element of the matrix to match the model. Less bright children appear to have no plan, make 1 × 3 or 1 × 2 grids (trying to throw one block away) or simply try to make the blocks "look like" the model without any plan. These children work more slowly, haphazardly, and inaccurately, and therefore tend to earn less credit. Not surprisingly, Block Design has the highest degree of association with general cognitive ability of any of the Performance section subtests, which substantiates the notion that it is a valuable contributor to Full Scale IQ.

Block Design can also be an important source of more specific diagnostic information (Sattler, 1988). Children who have visual perception impairments often make incredible distortions of the designs, including the expected rotations and reversals of designs that many people associate with learning disabilities. Children who have attention-deficit / hyperactivity disorder (ADHD) tend to work impulsively and carelessly, often failing to check their work for accuracy. Children with poor frustration tolerance quit, gently push the blocks back across the table to the examiner or occasionally explode and throw the blocks on the floor.

Because Block Design involves no language and because the blocks are generally free of any cultural considerations and connotations, it is probably the least culturally affected of the WISC–III subtests. As a result, psychologists might consider using the Block Design subtest to obtain a global assessment of a child from a vastly different culture (e.g., Cambodian immigrant) if such information were required. One caveat exists, despite the culture-free appearance of Block Design. Cultural attitude and socialization experiences have been shown to affect even such basic skills as perception and the ability to break up large objects into component parts and then to reorganize the parts (see Royer & Feldman, 1984).

*Object Assembly* The Object Assembly subtest consists of five puzzle-like objects that are presented to a child in a disassembled fashion (see Figure 5.3). The child's task is to construct the puzzles as quickly as possible; credit is earned for accuracy and speed.

Figure 5.3. Simulated WISC–III Object Assembly item. (Reproduced with permission from the Weschler Intelligence Scale for Children–Revised. 

As with Block Design, Object Assembly requires a certain amount of visual-perceptual and spatial-mechanical ability, but also to some extent the Object Assembly subtest measures reasoning and problem-solving abilities. Brighter children possess more concepts and their concepts are more detailed; this allows greater likelihood that the disassembled object is recognized initially, giving the child an internal mental model against which to check his or her assembly. The bright child also tends to be flexible and often tries alternative arrangements if initial attempts are unsuccessful. Valuable diagnostic information about perceptual development, planning ability, flexibility, task persistence, and frustration tolerance can be gained from scores and observation of the Object Assembly subtest.

*Symbol Search* The Symbol Search subtest was introduced with the publication of WISC–III (it had not been in the earlier WISC versions), and it is an optional subtest. The task confronting a child is to look at a novel geometric shape(s) (one shape only for younger children, two for older) and determine whether the shape(s) also appear in a grouping of shapes placed to the right of the original design. If the child can locate the same shape in the grouping, he or she marks a "yes" box; if not, he or she marks a "no" box. The task is to complete as many items as quickly and as accurately as possible. Points are credited for correct items, and there are penalties for mistakes. The task obviously has relatively little to do with higher-level cognitive ability but seemingly measures speed, attention, and persistence. Its interpretation is discussed below.

*Mazes* The Mazes subtest, optional and seldom administered, consists of 10 paper-and-pencil mazes that a child must find his or her way out of without entering blind alleys or taking shortcuts through walls. Some perceptual-motor, planning, and judgment skills are necessary for success. Statistically, however, this subtest is a relatively poor measure of general cognitive ability and correlates poorly with the nonverbal ability measured by the other Performance section subtests.

***Performance Subtests Composite Scores*** A child's composite score on the five Performance subtests (excluding Symbol Search and Mazes) produces a Performance IQ score. Performance IQ represents the child's ability across a variety of nonverbal reasoning, problem-solving, spatial/mechanical, and perceptual tasks. In some ways, Performance IQ can be thought of as practical, everyday, nonacademic ability. A child's score here may be used to predict how he or she might do in a hands-on, nonverbal curriculum, such as woodworking or drafting—far better than would the Verbal IQ score.

## Interpreting the WISC–III

IQ tests in general, and the WISC in particular, have long been criticized for their use and the manner in which they are interpreted. A leading advocate of mental testing and author of several tests, Alan Kaufman, has outlined the contemporary position regarding WISC–III usage and interpretation. His basic tenets (Kaufman, 1994) reflect the view of many psychologists and help to dispel some widely held negative stereotypes about IQ testing. Kaufman's tenets are listed below:

1. "The WISC–III subtests measure what the individual has learned" (p. 6). That is to say that the WISC–III is in some manner an achievement test indicating those skills and capabilities that have been acquired both by virtue of certain life experiences and by virtue of inherent aptitude.
2. "The WISC–III subtests are samples of behavior and are not exhaustive" (p. 7). This statement indicates that IQ is not necessarily the same as "total intellectual functioning." This is so because there are many skills not measured by the WISC–III; even those skills that are measured must be interpreted in light of the child's life history and circumstances.

3. "The WISC–III assesses mental functioning under fixed experimental conditions" (p. 8). The uniformity and objectivity integral to the WISC–III permit invaluable comparisons of children with age peers. However, such objectivity may limit the test's usefulness if interpretation ends once scores are produced. The WISC–III is most useful if interpretation is concerned with the reason a particular pattern was earned as well as its implications for helping the child.
4. "The WISC–III is optimally useful when it is interpreted from an information-processing model" (p. 10). Information processing recognizes the need to receive, integrate, store, and output information. By reviewing the demands implicit in performing various WISC–III tasks, diagnosticians can learn much about an individual child's strengths and weaknesses. This is one of the principal purposes for using psychological tests with school-age children.
5. "Hypotheses generated from WISC–III profiles should be supported with data from multiple sources" (p. 13). Although WISC–III is often a beginning place for interpretation, alone the WISC–III is generally insufficient to reach final conclusions about a child's capabilities and limitations. Other tests, background information, and observations are almost always required.

The traditional way to summarize scores, and thus to begin interpretation of the WISC–III, is to produce Verbal, Performance, and Full Scale IQ scores. These scores may be interpreted separately because each is a reliable measure of functioning, owing in great part to the WISC–III's considerable length. IQ scores are so frequently used that the numbers often have meaning for the general public. For those unfamiliar with IQ ranges, Table 5.2 is a summary of David Wechsler's descriptive terms and the IQ ranges associated with each. Table 5.3 allows conversion from IQ scores and subtest standard scores to percentile ranks. Note that all Wechsler IQ scores have means of 100 and

Table 5.2. Wechsler's classification of intelligence

| IQ range | Descriptive term |
|---|---|
| 130 and above | Very superior |
| 120–129 | Superior |
| 110–119 | High average |
| 90–109 | Average |
| 80–89 | Low average |
| 70–79 | Borderline |
| 69 and below | Mentally deficient |

*Source:* Wechsler (1974). (From the Wechsler Intelligence Scale for Children–Revised. Copyright © 1971, 1974 by The Psychological Corporation. Reproduced by permission. All rights reserved.)

Table 5.3. Conversion from IQ and standard scores to percentile ranks

| WISC–R IQ | WISC–R Subtest standard score | Percentile rank |
|---|---|---|
| 145 | 19 | 99.9 |
| 140 | 18 | 99.6 |
| 135 | 17 | 99 |
| 130 | 16 | 98 |
| 125 | 15 | 95 |
| 120 | 14 | 91 |
| 115 | 13 | 84 |
| 110 | 12 | 75 |
| 105 | 11 | 63 |
| 100 | 10 | 50 |
| 95 | 9 | 37 |
| 90 | 8 | 25 |
| 85 | 7 | 16 |
| 80 | 6 | 9 |
| 75 | 5 | 5 |
| 70 | 4 | 2 |
| 65 | 3 | 1 |
| 60 | 2 | 0.4 |
| 55 | 1 | 0.1 |

standard deviations of 15; all subtests have means of 10 and standard deviations of 3. Although tables such as these help provide reference points for various IQ values, interpretation of scores is the responsibility of the examining psychologist. Written reports should convey the implication of findings, not simply values of the scores.

It is important to remember that the subtests measure different abilities. Verbal IQ measures many of the prerequiste vocabulary, word knowledge, language understanding, and verbal reasoning skills necessary for school success. Conversely, Performance IQ is a broad-based measure of nonverbal capability that taps a variety of visual attention, perception, and planning skills, plus reasoning and problem-solving skills. The Full Scale IQ, as a composite, represents a broad sampling of both verbal and nonverbal capability and is particularly useful for judging overall development.

For some time researchers have been applying sophisticated statistical techniques (e.g., factor analysis) to the WISC to determine how the various subtests group together. This work has demonstrated that groupings other than the simple Verbal/Performance dichotomy may exist. In the WISC–III manual, an alternative arrangement of scores (see Table 5.4) was presented that includes a statistical rationale for the groupings based on how closely the individual subtests interrelate. For many children, indexing verbal capability via the "Verbal Comprehension" factor and nonverbal reasoning ability via the "Per-

Table 5.4. WISC–III subtest composition of factor-based scale scores

| Factor I Verbal Comprehension | Factor II Perceptual Organization | Factor III Freedom from Distractibility | Factor IV Processing Speed |
|---|---|---|---|
| Information | Picture Completion | Arithmetic | Coding |
| Similarities | Picture Arrangement | Digit Span | Symbol Search |
| Vocabulary | Block Design | | |
| Comprehension | Object Assembly | | |



ceptual Organization" factor makes the most clinical sense. This arrangement often seems to give a truer appraisal of cognitive capability because it removes the subtests that can be influenced negatively by less intellectual considerations, such as concentration and speed. In turn, this arrangement allows two additional factors "Freedom from Distractibility" and "Processing Speed" to be spun off and interpreted independently from the cognitively loaded Verbal Comprehension and Perceptual Organization factors. The WISC–III manual permits scores with means of 100 and standard deviations of 15 to be produced separately for each of these factors.

Practically speaking, this method of grouping scores may be quite helpful for children with attention and various learning problems. The thinking capability of children with special problems often can be seen more clearly by reviewing Verbal Comprehension and Perceptual Organization factor scores; judgment about the ability–achievement discrepancy necessary for a learning disability designation (see Chapter 6) may make more sense in this light. The difficulty that some children have with tasks that require careful attention or sustained concentration also may be evident in low scores on "Freedom from Distractibility." However, the Freedom from Distractibility factor cannot be used to make a diagnosis of attention problems in that such a procedure lacks the positive and negative predictive power required for sound clinical practice (Barkley, 1990; Semrud-Clikeman, Hynd, Lorys, & Lahey, 1993). Children who work too slowly because of cautious and/or deliberate styles, who process visual material slowly, or who are simply clumsy with a pencil (Coding and Symbol Search subtests both involve use of a pencil) may also benefit from this alternative method of score organization. Hints at their difficulty may be evident by examining their Processing Speed factor; their cognitive capability can generally be better appreciated by examining their Verbal Comprehension and Perceptual Organization scores with the negative influence of poor scores on Coding and Symbol Search removed. The advent of separate factor scores is helpful for clinicians and the rationale for separate scores is presented in the test manual (see Illustration 5.1). However, whether the factor scores manifest in the manner that one might predict when data are collected from actual clinical populations or whether the factors even interrelate in the assumed manner remains somewhat controversial (Smith & Gfeller, 1995).

Beyond the interpretation of broad IQ and factor scores as discussed above, it generally should be remembered that individual WISC–III subtests are short and relatively unreliable—a fact that limits interpretation.

Sometimes diagnosticians are tempted to compare one subtest with another and to conclude that, "Johnny is better at picking missing elements (Picture Completion) than he is at memorizing associations and rapidly copying elements (Coding)," because he scored one or two scale score points higher on Picture Completion than Coding. Besides the fact that distinctions among skills such as these probably have limited practical importance, such distinctions cannot be made because the subtests lack sufficient reliability unless score differences are very large. The difference of a few scale score points generally is a result of chance or random fluctuation. The competent psychologist interprets subtest differences cautiously and refers to statistical tables that provide numerical cutoffs when in doubt.

Reasonable caution notwithstanding (see the sections on "Diagnosing Mental Retardation" in Chapter 4 and "Diagnosing Learning Disabilities" in Chapter 6), psychologists' observations during WISC–III administration can often afford important clues about the nature of children's learning and developmental problems. During the time (more than 1 hour) that is needed for administration, the child is required to understand spoken language, to reason with words and verbal concepts, and to express thoughts with language. Failures in any of these important domains can be noted. Similarly, the child must see, actively perceive, think about, and manipulate physical objects. Deficiencies here may also be noted. If a child experiences failure and frustration, his or her reaction can be noted. A child's ability to plan, organize, sustain concentration, and sit still also can be observed. His or her ability to meet and to work with a stranger and, importantly, his or her responses to emotionally laden questions (especially Comprehension) can provide key personality clues. All of these are bonuses to the objective test scores produced by the WISC–III. More is said later in this chapter and in Chapter 6 about how these scores are used to diagnose mental retardation and learning disabilities.

Realization that children were appearing brighter on the WISC–R as it became more dated was a principal impetus for the extremely

## Illustration 5.1

Those interpreting the WISC have long been concerned with differences between Verbal IQ and Performance IQ. When large differences exist between these scores, the information can be used to plan for the child. For instance, a child with a Verbal IQ score 20 points higher than his or her Performance IQ score would be expected to do better on language-related tasks than on hands-on tasks. Unfortunately, the Verbal and Performance Scale grouping of subtests was determined by judgments of test author David Wechsler about the types of items each subtest contained. More recent, sophisticated statistical techniques have allowed the various subtests to be grouped based on how they intercorrelate, rather than on what they appear to measure. Subtests that are highly correlated with one another, or clustered together, may be assumed to measure a common trait, especially if the subtests' content appears to be similar.

With publication of the WISC–III, the four-factor solution discussed on page 118 became available. Consider the following example and how the regrouping of scores into Verbal Comprehension, Perceptual Organization, Freedom from Distractibility, and Processing Speed factors makes for more understandable and usable interpretation.

Tim is a 7-year-old first grader, who was retained in kindergarten because of poor acquisition of readiness skills and an inability to complete assigned classwork independently. Poor progress in the first grade led to a psychological evaluation, which included the WISC–III. The examining psychologist noted that Tim required verbal items to be repeated, was inattentive on nonverbal tasks, was easily frustrated, and was extremely restless. Many of the same observations also were reported by his current classroom teacher.

*(continued)*

*continued*

## Illustration 5.1

Tim earned the following scores on the WISC–III:

| Verbal subtests | | Performance subtests | |
|---|---|---|---|
| Information | 7 | Picture Completion | 10 |
| Similarities | 7 | Coding | 7 |
| Arithmetic | 3 | Picture Arrangement | 11 |
| Vocabulary | 9 | Block Design | 10 |
| Comprehension | 4 | Object Assembly | 10 |
| Digit Span | 5 | Symbol Search | 6 |

Verbal IQ 78 Performance IQ 98 Full Scale IQ 86

Although examining the traditional Verbal and Performance IQs suggests that Tim has adequate nonverbal skills but has problems with language, such an interpretation disguises some important additional distinctions. If his scores were reorganized into Verbal Comprehension, Perceptual Organization, Freedom from Distractibility, and Processing Speed factors, then his scores would become 83, 102, 67, and 83, respectively. Interpretation based on these values continues to show the significant nature of Tim's language problems and that he has intact spatial/mechanical skills but has severe problems concentrating and working persistently on tasks. He also worked relatively slowly and inefficiently at perceptual tasks that required concentration and use of a pencil.

Supplemental evaluation of Tim consisted of the Personality Inventory for Children (PIC) (see Chapter 7), classroom observation, and rating forms designed to assess attention, impulse control and hyperactivity (ADHD) that were completed by parents and his classroom teacher. Tim's PIC had a single elevation, the Hyperactivity Scale, and, similarly, his teacher-completed ADHD rating forms were consistently elevated. Tim seldom attended to the teacher when directions were given in the classroom, he worked carelessly when seatwork assignments were provided, he left his seat frequently, and he was distracted by pupils seated near him. Even in small group settings, Tim's

*(continued)*

*continued*

## Illustration 5.1

teacher found it necessary to repeat directions to ensure that he understood.

Although just a small part of a comprehensive evaluation (hearing and vision screening must also take place as a minimum requirement), the foregoing information nonetheless contains some clear implications. Tim requires modified procedures if he is to progress adequately in school. Among the recommendations might be the following:

1. Reduce obvious distractions in the immediate work area and keep Tim seated away from high traffic areas.
2. Highlight the written matter Tim is to attend to by using colors or bolder type fonts.
3. Secure Tim's attention and insist on eye contact before verbal directions are stated.
4. Speak slowly, using simple vocabulary and augmenting directions with gestures or demonstrations where possible.
5. Stress language development as part of Tim's curriculum, and encourage parents to foster language growth at home.
6. Teach Tim to respond with a slow tempo and to scan options prior to responding.
7. Consider referral for trial of medication, especially if other interventions fail.

lengthy and expensive re-norming process accompanying publication of the WISC–III (see discussion on the importance of contemporary norms in Chapter 1). Most of the differences appear to be a result of changes in children's proficiency on WISC Performance items over time. Caution about assigning students to special services categories is required (Post & Mitchell, 1993) in light of these score changes, with special caution required when students who were once found eligible for learning disability placement based on WISC–R IQ are no longer eligible based on lower WISC–III scores. These considerations, again, highlight that even the best-developed tests, such as the WISC–III, are merely tools that help professionals make judgments about the capabilities and characteristics of children. The tests themselves do not make decisions.

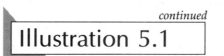

As was true of prior versions of the WISC, the WISC–III has technical data that are quite favorable. Psychometrically, the WISC–III Full Scale IQ has been shown to be both reliable and valid. Verbal and Performance IQ scores also have adequate psychometric properties, although the shortened length of each reduces reliability, meaning that these scores must be interpreted more cautiously than Full Scale IQ scores. For instance, the standard error of measure for Full Scale IQ scores averages ±3.20 IQ points, whereas the average is ±3.53 and ±4.54 for Verbal and Performance IQ scores, respectively. An extremely thorough and representative national norming sample completed for the WISC–III was recently collected, which is an important consideration for producing accurate scores (see Chapter 1). Differences on retesting may be evident among children in special services if the WISC–III is used for re-testing and the WISC–R for original testing. Average differences of eight points lower Full Scale IQ on the WISC–III versus the WISC–R are likely for some students in special services (Bolen, Aichinger, Hall, & Webster, 1995; Wechsler, 1991).

Other technical aspects of the WISC will help clinicians in that the WISC–III manual contains studies of the test applied to many important special populations; among these populations are children with mental retardation, learning disabilities, reading disorders, ADHD, conduct disorders, epilepsy, speech-language disorders, hearing impairments, as well as children with gifted capabilities. The manual also contains information that not only should help psychologists but also should help them better convey information about test performance to consumers: For example, the percentage of children who earn various Verbal/Performance IQ differences is discernible (e.g., "This particular child scored 25 points poorer on Verbal than Performance IQ—that event occurs among only 4.9% of children in the standardization sample"). Furthermore, formulas worked out in common between the WISC–III and Wechsler Individual Achievement Test (WIAT, see Chapter 6) help to make the WISC–III extremely valuable in the common task of identifying children eligible for learning disabilities services, even if subsequent research does not precisely replicate findings reported in the test manual (e.g., Slate, 1994).

## Woodcock-Johnson Psycho-Educational Battery and Woodcock-Johnson Psycho-Educational Battery–Revised (Tests of Cognitive Ability)

The Woodcock-Johnson Psycho-Educational Battery–Revised (Woodcock & Johnson, 1989) includes Tests of Cognitive Ability that may be administered alone to assess capability (much as an IQ test) or, more commonly, used in conjunction with the popular Woodcock-Johnson Tests of Achievement. The Tests of Cognitive Ability are suitable for children 2 years and older. When both ability and achievement components of the battery are administered, a detailed pattern of strengths and weaknesses emerges, and the information can be used to determine the presence of discrepancies necessary for learning disability designation. Only the cognitive abilities portion of the Woodcock-Johnson Psycho-Educational Battery is discussed here. The achievement portion of the battery is discussed in Chapter 6.

The Woodcock-Johnson was extensively revised in 1989–1990 to match a detailed model of ability (Horn-Cattell). To relate to the seven abilities outlined in this model—Fluid Reasoning, Comprehension Knowledge, Visual Processing, Auditory Processing, Processing Speed, Long-Term Retrieval, and Short-Term Memory—the basic cognitive battery encompasses seven subtests. The diagnostician, however, can include additional subtests by tapping the 14 supplemental tests available that match the model (Cummings, 1995). When this information is combined with the extensive information available from administration of the achievement battery, an amazingly large array of information becomes available. The Woodcock-Johnson can produce many types of scores including scores recognizable to most test consumers, such as standard scores with means of 100 and standard deviations of 15, as well as percentile ranks. Some of the instruments' more exotic scores generally require interpretation by a diagnostician with considerable measurement expertise.

The revised Woodcock-Johnson has been praised for excellent standardization, excellent reliability and validity information, inclusion of studies of clinical populations in the manual (e.g., children with learning disabilities, mental retardation), the luxury of ability and achievement tests being generated from the same standardized sample (which reduces potential measurement error in discrepancy determination), and adherence to a sophisticated model of ability (Cummings, 1995; Lee & Stefany, 1995). Some psychologists do not use the Woodcock-Johnson cognitive tests because the tests were not included in their training or because the tests' format, which consists of easels with individual pages without the familiar hands-on subtests of WISC–III, seems foreign. Although the Woodcock-Johnson contains some tasks of a promising nature, the battery may be underutilized. However, because of the tests' positive qualities, consumers may encounter the Woodcock-Johnson Tests of Cognitive Ability, especially in school settings.

## Kaufman Assessment Battery for Children (K–ABC)

The Kaufman Assessment Battery for Children (K–ABC) (Kaufman, 1983) was touted by its publisher (American Guidance Service) as a landmark in the history of mental testing. It was claimed that the instrument would result in the first true assessment of "ability" (which the authors contended is uncontaminated by experience) and "achievement" (which the authors defined to include ability and the products of past experience) in the same battery. Moreover, the K–ABC purported to provide a nonbiased assessment of ability that would minimize children's prior differences in experience and result in roughly equivalent performance among children from different racial/cultural backgrounds. Perhaps most important, the instrument claimed to be based on an empirically supported theory of mental processing that allowed assessment to be closely linked to subsequent intervention. This final feature offered special hope for children with learning disabilities—the principal group for whom the battery was developed.

The theory on which the battery rests has its roots in one of the world's most famous neuropsychologists, Russian A.R. Luria. The combined tradition of Russian developmental psychology and the first-hand study of innumerable cases of individuals with brain injuries led Luria to describe two distinct methods of how humans process information—simultaneously and successively. A Canadian research psychologist, J.P. Das, was influenced by Luria's work and proceeded to find or develop tests that called for either simultaneous or successive processing (Reynolds, 1981). Simultaneous tasks can be described as those that

1. Synthesize separate elements in a whole
2. Have all portions of stimulus material surveyable at once
3. Often deal with relationships or have spatial overtones

In contrast, successive tasks are those tasks that

1. Stress serial order
2. Have stimuli for which all portions are not surveyable at once
3. Often rely on a system of cues to consecutively activate components (Das, Kirby, & Jarman, 1975)

Research and conceptualization that continued along this line became known as the Das-Luria model. Alan Kaufman, who had helped develop the McCarthy Scales and helped revise the WISC–R, together with his wife, Nadeen Kaufman, were obviously influenced by the Das-Luria model when they developed the K–ABC.

The test battery itself consists of 16 subtests (see Table 5.5) designed to assess children from 2 years, 6 months, to 12 years, 5 months, of age. Mental processing subtests are designed to measure pure ability—apart from experience—and they form the battery's first portion, divided into a Sequential Processing Scale, a Simultaneous

Table 5.5. K–ABC subtests and description of item types

| Subtest | Item description |
|---|---|
| | Sequential Subtests |
| Hand Movements | Repetition of hand movement sequence made by examiner |
| Number Recall | Repetition of number sequences |
| Word Order | Touching of pictures of objects in order named by examiner |
| | Simultaneous Subtests |
| Magic Window | Identification of pictures exposed only a small portion at a time through slit in rotating window |
| Face Recognition | Short-term recall for faces |
| Gestalt Closure | Identification of objects depicted in partially completed inkblots |
| Triangles | Assembling pattern by using triangles |
| Matrix Analogies | Selection of choice that best completes pattern |
| Spatial Memory | Recall of location of pictured objects |
| Photo Series | Organizing photos of events in proper chronological order |
| | Achievement Subtests |
| Expressive Vocabulary | Naming pictured objects |
| Faces & Places | Naming pictured person, place, or fictional characters |
| Arithmetic | Arithmetic problem solving and conceptual understanding |
| Riddles | Inferring name of objects or concepts when given characteristics |
| Reading/Decoding | Letter and word recognition |
| Reading/Understanding | Following commands that are read |

Processing Scale, and a Composite Mental Processing Scale (a special Nonverbal Scale can also be produced by regrouping subtests). Each scale has a mean of 100 and standard deviation of 15. Subtests composing the mental processing portion of the battery tend to emphasize memory and concentration, with stimuli being presented either auditorily or visually. For instance, a Sequential Processing subtest, Number Recall, requires short-term memory for number sequences, whereas Face Recognition, a Simultaneous Processing subtest, taps the ability to remember and then locate, in a group, photos of faces that were just presented.

The second portion of the battery's subtests measures Achievement, defined by the Kaufmans as acquired skills and knowledge. Given this broad definition, Achievement subtests measure diverse skills, some clearly related to instruction in school, such as Reading/Decoding and Arithmetic. Others, however, appear to relate partially to experience but are also substantially tied to capability. In fact, several of these Achievement subtests (i.e., Expressive Vocabulary, Riddles) appear to call for skills typically tapped by intelligence tests such as the WISC–III.

Some things are clear about the K–ABC. The standardization is generally viewed as adequate. Reliability, both measured by internal consistency and test–retest, is satisfactory. Concurrent validity studies comparing the K–ABC to other ability tests resulted in correlation values in the range hoped for by the test's authors. Intercorrelations among mental processing subtests offer some support for the sequential/simultaneous distinction. Clinical utility of the battery is substantially more controversial, however, with several critical weaknesses apparent.

First, the K–ABC's Processing Scales' emphasis on rote memory and attending skills may make questionable the validity of the battery as an ability measure. The Mental Processing Composite contains few subtests that require reasoning and problem solving of any type and virtually none that require verbal reasoning—an element almost universally recognized as important to include in ability measures. Even though the Processing Scales arguably consist of items that reduce the effect of prior experience, they do so at the expense of measuring relatively unimportant rote learning—the type of learning that most other intelligence tests have intentionally rejected (Sternberg, 1984). In fact, the K–ABC's Mental Processing Composite has a smaller mean difference between African Americans and Caucasians and between Mexican Americans and Caucasians than the WISC–R, but such a finding is irrelevant if the test measures unimportant constructs (Sternberg, 1984). Others have suggested the K–ABC measures as much general ability in both Caucasians and African Americans as other ability tests do (Naglieri & Jensen, 1987), and it may be no more culture-fair than traditional tests (Krohn, Lamp, & Phelps, 1988). Practically speaking, many children with learning disabilities have such poor concentration and attending skills that they appear to score inordinately poorly on the K–ABC.

Second, the distinction between processing and achievement can be argued to be arbitrary. Some Processing subtests appear to require considerable prior experience (e.g., Gestalt Closure), whereas some Achievement subtests appear to involve considerable aptitude (e.g., Riddles). Because learning disability identification requires a significant discrepancy between ability and achievement, the flimsy distinction between the two used by the Kaufmans makes this battery a poor choice for learning disability identification.

Research reported in the test manual shows lower scores for children who are gifted and higher scores for children who have mental retardation on the K–ABC than other ability measures such as the WISC–R. Subsequent research has also failed to find equivalency between the K–ABC and the Stanford-Binet L–M scale and the WISC–R for children who are at risk and those identified as having mental retardation (Bloom, Allard, Frank, Brill, & Topinka, 1988; Obrzut, Nelson, & Obrzut, 1987). Sattler (1988) has also pointed out that the K–ABC is virtually useless in detecting mental retardation among preschoolers. For example, some very young children who fail every K–ABC Processing item still are credited with Mental Processing Composite Scores above the 70 cutoff score to make a diagnosis of mental retardation. Information of this type implies that the test has severe clinical limitations.

Finally, the notion of sequential and simultaneous processing as measured by the K–ABC has been criticized for being insufficiently defined, inaccurately measured, and unsuitable for planning remedial intervention (Sattler, 1988; Sternberg, 1984). Some studies of clinical populations (e.g., children with autism) have also failed to produce expected simultaneous/sequential distinction (Stavrou & French, 1992). Criticism of the simultaneous/sequential distinction raises questions about the very uniqueness that the K–ABC's authors hoped would make their instrument valuable. Although the battery should be praised for its bold effort to offer something new and valuable for diagnosticians, Sattler's (1988) suggestion that the instrument should not be used to make important decisions about special children probably indicates a decline in use of the K–ABC.

***Kaufman Adolescent and Adult Intelligence Test (KAIT)*** The Kaufman Adolescent and Adult Intelligence Test (KAIT) (Kaufman & Kaufman, 1993) is sometimes mistaken for an upward extension of the K–ABC. In reality, it is distinct from the K–ABC; the KAIT is composed of different subtests (and item types) resting on a different conceptualization of mental abilities. Because it is designed to assess only individuals 11 years and older, the KAIT can focus on measuring high-level thinking, planning, and problem-solving skills that remain undeveloped (and hence unassessable) among younger children.

The KAIT explicitly ties its measurement of intelligence to the theories of cognitive psychology and neuropsychology. These theories delineate fluid intelligence ("the ability to solve *new* problems . . . that may involve symbolic, semantic and figural content") from crystallized intelligence that is closely related to and may be dependent on fluid intelligence but "relates closely to advanced education and acculturation" (Kaufman & Kaufman, 1993, p. 11). Crystallized intelligence subsumes much of the content of traditional intelligence tests such as the WISC–III and Stanford-Binet IV. The KAIT includes several subtests compatible with these established tests (Definitions, Double Meaning, and Famous Faces subtests). The example of a Double Meaning item in Figure 5.4 may strike the observer as being equivalent to a WISC–III Similarities item. Generally, the KAIT crystallized intelligence subtests (which consists of Definitions, Auditory Compre-

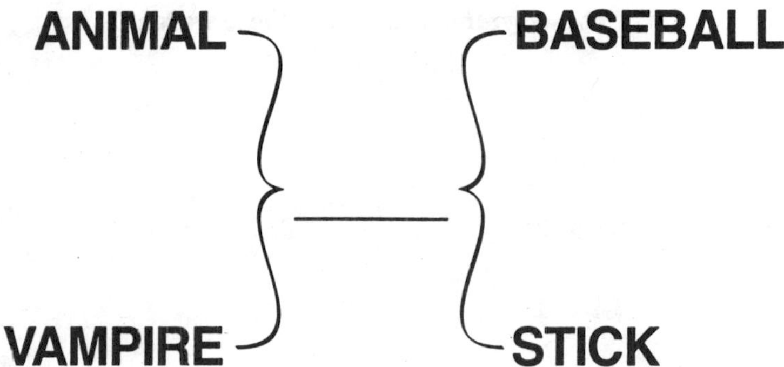


Figure 5.4. KAIT Double Meaning item. (Kaufman Adolescent and Adult Intelligence Test by Alan S. Kaufman & Nadeen L. Kaufman © 1992 American Guidance Service, Inc., 4201 Woodland Road, Circle Pines, MN 55014-1796. Reproduced with permission of the Publishers. All rights reserved.)

hension, and Double Meanings, plus an optional subtest, Famous Faces) seem to contain little that is new (in fairness, they were not intending to measure anything new). However, they do seem to require somewhat greater simultaneous mental manipulation of two sources of information for their solution than is true of some more familiar intelligence test items.

The more noteworthy aspect of the KAIT is its complex tasks, so-called fluid intelligence measures (which consist of Rebus Learning, Logical Steps, and Mystery Code, plus an optional subtest, Memory for Block Designs) (see Figure 5.5). Many of these tasks seem unlike those that children or teens would have encountered elsewhere in their day-to-day environment. The challenges for problem solving, inventiveness, and judgment certainly appear unique in the field of mental measurement. The fluid subtests (each of which has a mean of 10 and a standard deviation of 3) produce a Composite "Fluid IQ" that can be contrasted with "Crystallized IQ" and joined with it to produce an overall composite (IQs have means of 100 and standard deviations of 15). Besides emphasizing high-level cognitive skills, one of the fluid subtests (Rebus Learning) also requires learning across trials. That is, to solve the more complex items on Rebus Learning the individual must have acquired techniques on the easier items and must also retain specific knowledge (i.e., recall the words associated with various shapes). The requirement to acquire and use knowledge with repeated exposure also distinguishes the KAIT from other intelligence tests such as the WISC–III and Stanford-Binet IV.

Immediate and short-term recall as well as long-term storage and consolidation are also assessed on the KAIT. Such assessments are absent, or severely limited in scope and comprehensiveness, on most

**"These symbols stand for these words:"**

**Sleeping** Z

**Sees** >

**Girl** ‡

**Boy** †

**"Now read this:"**

‡ > Z †

Figure 5.5. Task similar to KAIT Rebus Learning.

other intelligence tests. For example, on the KAIT a separate Memory for Block Designs subtests exists. This allows examiners to determine a subject's capability to remember shapes that have just been seen. Scores on this subtest, like for each of the other subtests, are reported with a mean of 10 and standard deviation of 3. Far more unique are the delayed recall subtests: Rebus Delayed Recall and Auditory Delayed Recall. Memory assessment on these subtests occurs after 25–45 minutes by requiring the child or teenager to read phrases or sentences using previously learned rebuses or to answer questions about previously heard passages. Thus, the psychologist can compare the individual's performance on tasks that require immediate memory with tasks that require delayed memory. These comparisons may be extremely helpful clinically.

The KAIT appears to have a role in mental measurement of children and teenagers. The KAIT would seem especially valuable when previous assessment with instruments like the WISC–III or Stanford-Binet IV might be doubted. Examples would be children who score poorly but are judged by parents or teachers to be brighter. In these instances, the KAIT's unique ability to measure alternative aspects of intelligence (e.g., the fluid abilities) may prove instructive. Likewise, in instances in which parents or teachers believe that cognitive deficits exist but are apparent neither on traditional IQ nor achievement tests, the KAIT may help. Closely linked to this latter point is the assessment of children with traumatic brain injury (TBI) or other acquired neurological conditions. The KAIT is explicitly linked to neuropsychological theory and, as some preliminary research implies, sensitivity to neuropsychological dysfunction, although the number of children/adolescents studied to date is limited (Dumond & Hagberg, 1994). Still, the KAIT may have a special role in adding to the range of assessment tools used by psychologists who only rarely assess individuals with TBI. This would be especially true in public school settings, where most school psychologists lack access to cumbersome and costly neuropsychological test batteries and where they may not have had detailed training in using such instruments. Using the KAIT may be helpful. In addition, the KAIT is extremely well standardized and has detailed studies of reliability and validity included in the test's manual—considerations sometimes lacking from formally designated neuropsychological tests for children (see Chapter 8).

## MULTISUBTEST MEASURES OF INFORMATION PROCESSING

The WISC–III, the Stanford-Binet scales, the Woodcock-Johnson Ability test, and the K–ABC and KAIT ability tests report first and foremost a composite cognitive score or IQ. Thus, to a considerable extent, they are concerned with comparisons among children in terms of overall ability. Consequently, among the primary uses of these tests are the determination of mental retardation and the assessment of overall ability so that possible underachievement can be detected. In contrast, several tests have been developed to look almost exclusively at intraindividual differences. That is, they examine subtest patterns that might give clues to strengths and weaknesses so that planning can occur, with little or no regard to overall cognitive ability. Although on the surface such a purpose is quite laudable, how these tests as a group actually perform needs careful scrutiny.

### Illinois Test of Psycholinguistic Abilities

The Illinois Test of Psycholinguistic Abilities (ITPA) (Kirk, McCarthy, & Kirk, 1968) was based on a model of human information processing that posited receptive, associative (or thinking/conceptual), and expressive skills. The use of this test in the 1960s and 1970s helped to direct attention toward intraindividual differences and helped to create a mindset of examining scores from an information processing point of view. Although with each passing year the test seems to be used less frequently, it is still included here for historical reasons and because it continues to be used as a supplemental measure among young children (ages 2–10 years). At any rate, according to the ITPA approach, each type of processing could be assessed by providing the child tasks that required either primarily auditory input and language output (called the *auditory-vocal channel*) or visual input and motor output (called the *visual-motor channel*). The authors then constructed subtests designed to measure each of these skills in a discrete fashion; that is, independent of the effects of other skills. When a profile of skills was plotted, it was hoped that various combinations of information-processing problems would be evident for any given learner; for example, a child might perform relatively poorly on both auditory-vocal (i.e., answering verbally posed nonsense questions) and visual-motor input tasks (i.e., matching pictured objects to their appropriate category) and would be said to have receptive processing problems. Another child might score more poorly on all the visual-motor tasks (reception, association, and expression) than on the auditory-vocal tasks, with resulting speculation about a pervasive visual-motor processing problem. Six other subtests were also developed to examine more habitual or "automatic" processing, such as the child's method of forming plurals or irregular verbs.

This test gained considerable popularity during the early 1970s, no doubt based on the intuitive plausibility of its underlying information processing model. Empirical scrutiny of the test, however, has been unfavorable, and the ITPA has been declining in use among psychologists ever since the empirical data were presented. Studies have shown no evidence that the test actually measures the separate skills in the fashion for which the authors had hoped. In fact, some have even questioned if the test represents anything other than an ability (IQ) test that just is titled differently from most (Waugh, 1975). The representativeness of the normative sample has been questioned as well. Moreover, the test uses a peculiar standard score system (mean = 36, standard deviation = 6), and when a composite score (called a *psycholinguistic quotient*) is calculated, the antiquated and unacceptable method of dividing mental age by chronological age, then multiplying by 100 is employed.

## Detroit Tests of Learning Aptitude–Third Edition (DTLA–3)

With the original first published in 1935, the Detroit Tests of Learning Aptitude–2 (DTLA–2) (Hammill, 1985) received its first updated norms in 1985 and has had further reorganization and some updating of norms again in 1991 (Hammill, 1991). The updated version, the Detroit Tests of Learning Aptitude–Third Edition (DTLA–3), produces a "General Mental Ability Composite" that is much like a full scale IQ, and a novel "Optimum Composite" consisting of a child's four highest subtests, which is designed to indicate a child's performance under the best of circumstances (Schmidt, 1994). This score has been criticized on logical and psychometric grounds as potentially misleading (Mehrens, 1995).

However, it is likely that most examiners will be interested in domain scores, rather than composite scores, such as Linguistic, Attentional, or Motoric (mean = 100, standard deviation = 15), or scores on 1 of the 11 individual subtests (mean = 10, standard deviation = 3).

The DTLA–3 has improved norms, but the techniques used to establish them are not as refined as those that pay careful attention to all important demographic variables like tests such as the WISC–III do (Schmidt, 1994). Norms from two separate editions of the test (DTLA–2 and DTLA–3) are blended on some subtests. Some of the reliability and validity information for the DTLA–3 appears satisfactory, but questions about stability of scores and construct validity have been raised (Mehrens, 1995).

Some caution regarding tests like the ITPA and Detroit is in order. Despite their titles, tests like the Detroit and ITPA measure general ability in a fashion like IQ tests. That is, much of what is measured is IQ even if it is not called IQ. Sometimes these tests are used by nonpsychologists who are comfortable performing evaluations so long as "intelligence" tests are not employed, as intelligence testing is viewed as part of the practice of psychology. This is a deference to professional boundaries that is nominal rather than substantive. If important decisions are to be made about children, including whether they should be placed in special programs, then it is advisable to use the best instruments and not to be influenced by tests' titles. Tests of ability and tests of intelligence may be measuring pretty much the same thing. Many of the tests discussed in this chapter have important adjunctive and supportive roles, even if they are not used as the principal instruments to establish a child's general intellectual capability. The wise diagnostician understands what each test measures and selects a battery than can help to completely and confidently answer the referral question at hand.

## SPECIAL ABILITIES TESTS

### Tests of Memory and New Learning

As the astute reader has probably already noted, there are important capabilities required for school learning and satisfactory performance in life that are beyond the pale of intelligence testing. Even bright people sometimes lack important capabilities whereas even those with low IQs sometimes show a knack for certain academic or life tasks. A recent spate of instruments, several satisfactorily planned, carefully developed, and well-suited for practical use, have become available. Two of them, the Wide Range Assessment of Memory and Learning (WRAML) (Adams & Sheslow, 1990) and the California Verbal Learning Test–Children's Version (Delis, Kramer, Kaplan, & Ober, 1994), are discussed here. Three older instruments that receive wide usage are also discussed—the Bender Visual Motor Gestalt Test, the Rey-Osterrieth Complex Figures Test, and the Peabody Picture Vocabulary Test–Revised.

***Wide Range Assessment of Memory and Learning*** The WRAML, suitable for children from 5 to 17 years, has been well received by diagnosticians seeking to expand information beyond that provided by basic intelligence tests such as the WISC–III. As a complementary instrument to intelligence tests, the WRAML can be used as a quick screener for memory problems, or as a more detailed tool to help determine where a breakdown in learning may be occurring. It may be used rarely as an alternative rather than a supplement to intelligence tests (if the examiner already has information about the learner's general ability).

Four subtests—two nonverbal and two verbal—can be administered in about 20 minutes and provide a reasonable measure of immediate recall. The first nonverbal subtest (Picture Memory) consists of pictures of common scenes, which the child is allowed to study for 10 seconds. The child is then shown the original scene again but this time with alterations. His or her job is to identify the alterations and mark them with a pencil. Obviously, memory is required; little motor output and no verbalization are required for correct responding. The second nonverbal test (Spatial Memory) is similar to the first, but here the child studies geometric figures located in various portions of a configuration. Five seconds of exposure is followed by a 10-second delay after which the child attempts to draw the figures from memory in their proper locations. Points are credited for accuracy and a degree of detail contained in the drawings. Although no verbalization is called for, the child must be able to draw. The spatial aspects of this task also separate it from the Picture Memory subtest.

Two verbal subtests, Verbal Learning and Story Memory, are included in the basic four WRAML screening tests. Verbal Learning consists of fairly long lists of unrelated, single-syllable words (13 words for younger children, 16 for older) that are presented aloud at a rate of one word per second. The child's task is to recall as many words as possible. There are four repetitions of the entire list in this manner with the child's ultimate score depending on total words recalled across the four trials. Story Memory is more straightforward wherein the examiner reads a child two brief stories. The child's assignment is to recall as many of the elements as possible.

Each of these subtests produces standard scores with means of 10 and standard deviations of 3, so that children can be compared to same-age peers for immediate memory ability. A cumulative score for these four subtests (mean = 100, standard deviation = 15), termed the "Memory Screening Index," is also available. This cumulative score can be quite instructive because there are many clinical instances where a child scores well on intelligence tests but scores poorly when asked to register, store, and recall information from short-term memory. Comparisons with the WISC–III IQ and subtest scores are facilitated because both the WRAML and WISC–III use the same units of measure.

The WRAML contains other useful elements as well; there are several other visual memory and learning tests to supplement Picture and Spatial Memory. Cumulatively, they can establish children who may have deficient ability to register and retrieve data that are seen. Likewise, additional measures of language and auditory processing exist. Some of these (e.g., Sentence Memory) demand exact recall of what was heard, including the precise words in faithful order. Children with phonemic processing problems have been documented to have far greater rates of severe reading problems and dyslexia. This subtest may help in the identification and understanding of such underlying problems, although there appears to be little research on this aspect of the WRAML.

The same is true of tests such as Sound/Symbol, which mimics the process of matching sounds with symbols that takes place as one learns to read. In this test, various novel shapes are matched with individual sounds (e.g., the shape } might be associated with the sound "cha") (in experimental psychology this is called "paired-associate" learning). After practice, the child is asked to recall the sound when only the shape is presented. This format allows the examiner to see how readily the child can learn to match sounds and shapes. This type of task, which demands actual learning with practice, contrasts with many psychometric tasks that merely require recall of what is already known or use of previously acquired reasoning skills applied to mildly novel situations. The Sound/Symbol subtest asks that previously unknown shapes become associated with previously unknown sounds in what approximates truly novel learning. Information about learning of this type can help offer hypotheses about why a child is not learning better in school. It may also help in neuropsychological evaluations when it appears that a child retains previously learned skills but may have difficulty with new learning. It is hypothesized that novel learning ability is particularly vulnerable in children with acquired neurological disorders such as TBI.

The latter six subtests (beyond Picture Memory, Design Memory, Verbal Learning, and Story Memory that make up the memory screening portion of the battery) can be grouped to produce the following summary scores: Verbal Memory, Visual Memory, Learning, and General Memory, each with a mean of 100 and a standard deviation of 15. Research has questioned how accurate these groupings are (Gioia, 1991); some subtests seem especially prone to influence from attention problems (Haut, Haut, & Franzen, 1992). Most diagnosticians will make their own analyses based on the unique demands of each subtest. Like the other techniques discussed in this chapter, interpretation requires skill and knowledge and does not lend itself to the easy application of formulas. Summary scores should be taken with a grain of salt.

***California Verbal Learning Test–Children's Version*** Another of the well-developed and carefully standardized measures of ability of recent vintage is the California Verbal Learning Test–Children's Version (CVLT–C), suitable for children from 5 to 15 years old. Narrower in scope than the WRAML (assessing only verbal list learning) but more theoretically sophisticated, the CVLT–C is especially popular among pediatric neuropsychologists (see Chapter 8) but may also find school uses. The authors (who are mostly identified with neuropsychology) designed their instrument to address "strategies and processes involved in learning and recalling verbal material" (Delis et al., 1994, p. 1). To measure these strategies and processes, complex methods of recording children's responses and extremely detailed score production techniques were required. Research has suggested important aspects of memory that the authors sought to capture: the consistency with which learned information is recalled, the amount of interference that occurs when conflicting material is learned both before and after memorization, the degree to which the learner organizes material into meaningful categories to aid retention, and the ability to monitor one's own responses so that introducing wrong elements or repeating oneself is recognized and controlled.

To approximate the practical kinds of memorization that might occur in the real world, each child is told to pretend that he or she is going shopping. The child is then given a "Monday list" of items to purchase (e.g., ice cream, flowers, newspaper, cookies). Recall, consisting of stating as many items as possible (without regard to list order), follows. The same Monday list is re-presented four more times, with a recitation of remembered items following each presentation. After the fifth presentation and recall trial of the Monday list, a single presentation/recall trial of a separate Tuesday list occurs. Immediately thereafter, the child again is given the opportunity to recall as many items as possible from the Monday list—the list he or she had previously heard for five trials. After a one-half hour delay (to be filled with nonverbal measures) the child is, without prior warning, asked to recall the Monday list a final time. At the conclusion of the CVLT–C administration, the examiner reads a long list of items that might appear in a store, and the child indicates whether each was or was not on the Monday list.

A vast array of scores can be derived from the child's performance, with the scoring process greatly aided by the use of a computerized summary program. Even then, making sense of the scores and appreciating their implications is difficult. Unless one uses the test fairly frequently, the scores can be confusing. The summary score for the number of words from the Monday list recalled across trials 1–5 is fairly straightforward—a T-score is used (mean = 50, standard deviation = 10). All other scores are Z-scores (mean = 0, standard deviation = 1). Scores such as Tuesday versus Monday Trial 1 (reported as Z-score) convey little inherent meaning. In reality, however, the score here shows how readily the child memorized a list at the outset of testing versus learning a second list; the second learning task is more difficult because the list learned previously can interfere. This phenomenon of prior learning hindering later learning, referred to as *proactive interference,* has been studied extensively in experimental psychology. Furthermore, factors such as these are understood from a neuropsychological viewpoint—certain patterns of strength and weakness may help the diagnostician understand the nature and severity of impairment when neuropsychological evaluations are conducted. Other comparisons illuminate the presence of *retroactive interference.* This is the type of interference that makes it hard to learn something, subsequently learn something new, and then still be able to recall the first task well.

Other scores reflect the degree to which material is forgotten over time and whether the child uses effective strategies for organizing material that later must be recalled. Recall versus recognition distinctions are also deemed important because they help the psychologist determine whether failure is occurring due to defective encoding or due to defective retrieval of previously encoded material. In this regard, the CVLT–C ties together much of what has been learned about the complex and multifaceted nature of memory (Moscovitch, 1992;

Squire, 1987) and its measurement for clinical purposes. Thus, on the one hand, distinctions of this type can be particularly helpful to neuropsychologists who may be concerned about damage to structures necessary to encoding (i.e., hippocampus), which are often vulnerable to disruption in children with partial seizures. On the other hand, structures essential for creating an active strategy for searching and retrieving are also localized, to some extent, and may be vulnerable in other situations (e.g., TBI). Educational and rehabilitation strategies may depend on information that the CVLT–C can provide.

The CVLT–C manual contains information about the tests' reliability and correlation with other verbal tests as evidence of concurrent validity. More important is the information about how various clinical populations perform on specific aspects of the CVLT–C, such as rate of learning and overall level of recall, among children with Down syndrome, Williams syndrome, and ADHD. Moreover, for a test of this type the CVLT–C has a sufficiently large and representative norm group.

***Bender Visual Motor Gestalt Test*** The Bender Visual Motor Gestalt Test (Bender, 1946) was devised by Loretta Bender before World War II to assess the visual-motor functioning of adults. It was discovered that adults with brain injury had difficulty drawing the particular set of designs Bender was using. Later, it was found that the test could index the development of visual-motor maturity of typically developing children and suggest which children may have delays in this area. The Bender Gestalt test often is used as a supplement to the WISC–III, in order to assess visual-perceptual skills and hand–eye coordination. Because the test is nonverbal, nonthreatening, and quick to administer (about 5–10 minutes), it is often used as a warm-up before the more demanding WISC–III. The Bender Gestalt test consists of nine geometric figures, each on its own 3″ × 5″ card. The child is given a pencil, a blank 8½″ × 11″ piece of paper, and the cards one at a time, with a request to copy each onto the paper (see Figure 5.6).

Most psychologists score the Bender drawings for 27 possible errors using a system devised by Elizabeth Koppitz (1963). This system affords better reliability than impressionistic scoring and allows standard scores to be derived from norm tables. Some of the types of errors for which figures may be scored using the Koppitz system include the following:

1. Distortion of shape (any of a variety of severe distortions)
2. Rotation (generally, any figure rotated 45 degrees or more)
3. Integration (generally, figures overlap or figures fail to meet)

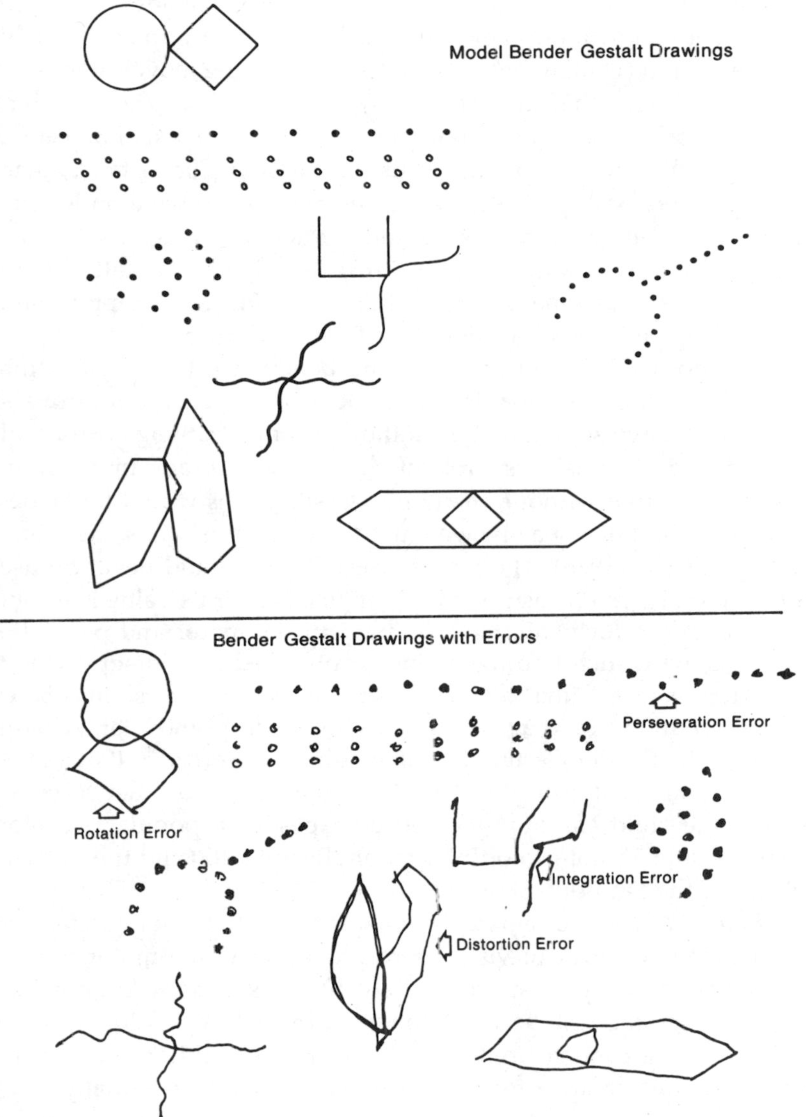


Figure 5.6. Model Bender Gestalt drawings and illustrations of Koppitz errors. (Reprinted, with permission, from *A Visual Motor Gestalt Test and Its Clinical Use* by Loretta Bender, Copyright and distributed by the American Orthopsychiatric Association, Inc.)

4. Perseveration (generally, overproducing elements of the design)

Koppitz norm tables show that children make progressively fewer errors as they grow older. This orderly and systemic decrease in errors provides some intrinsic evidence of validity for the Bender Gestalt test as a measure of visual-motor perceptual maturity (Koppitz, 1963), but it is the obvious content of the Bender—challenging, novel shapes that must be drawn—that appeals to psychologists. The test does have adequate concurrent validity with other measures of visual perception but marginal ability to predict academic success. For instance, many kindergartners with poor Bender scores turn out to have no learning problems and may even be substantially above average by the time they reach eighth grade (Koppitz, 1973). The Bender Gestalt test, and similar tests of this type, are poor at detecting visual perception problems among children older than 8 or 9 years (Sattler, 1988).

Diagnosing brain injury from the Bender Gestalt test has long been an area of interest for clinicians but is also an area of controversy. Researchers have shown that even though some drawing errors could be used to distinguish a sample of children with brain injury from a group of children without, many misclassifications would be made if the Bender Gestalt test alone were used to distinguish those with brain injury (Koppitz, 1975). The Bender Gestalt test should never be used independently as a measure of brain injury. The test's value is its ability to suggest which children may have visual-motor and perception problems, with such findings to be corroborated and integrated with other data before a final diagnosis is made. The reader should be especially cautious of diagnosticians who make grand claims based solely on the Bender Gestalt drawings (Bigler & Ehrfurth, 1981). There are similarities between the Bender Gestalt and two other tests that require the child to copy geometric shapes—the popular Developmental Test of Visual-Motor Integration (Beery, 1982) and the Copying subtest of the Stanford-Binet IV.

***Rey-Osterrieth Complex Figures Test*** The Bender Gestalt test can provide an index of visual-perceptual and visual-motor integration for children up to approximately 10 years of age. At about this age, however, the task becomes too easy; most 10-year-olds draw the designs without much trouble, and even those children with visual-perceptual or visual-motor problems may produce essentially error-free design renderings.

The Rey-Osterrieth Complex Figures Test (Osterrieth, 1944) represents a more difficult pattern, one capable of challenging the visual-motor and visual-perceptual skills of older children and adolescents (and even adults) (see Figure 5.7). Although the design is standard, the procedures surrounding use of the test are not. Some proponents of the Rey-Osterrieth have advocated an initial design-copying phase,

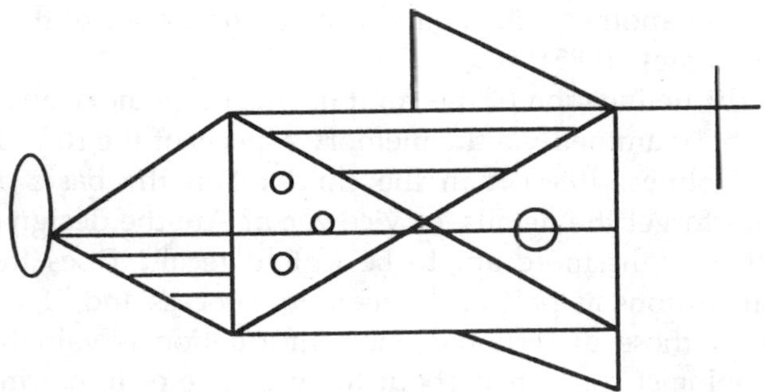

Figure 5.7. Configuration similar to Rey-Osterrieth Complex Figure.

followed without prior warning by an immediate recall phase (during which the design is redrawn from memory only) and a 30-minute delayed recall phase (Bernstein, Helmus, Kammer, Prather, & Rey-Casserly, 1994). Others have suggested only an initial drawing phase and a 30-minute recall. Almost all have recognized that the design's complex nature permits gleaning valuable observations. Thus, examiners may note the sequence of drawing from start to finish (by starting the child with a red marker, followed after 45 seconds by the use of a blue marker, and so on). Such information may help the examiner understand the child's organization and planning skills, in addition to visual-related skills per se.

In addition, the Rey-Osterrieth is popular as part of a neuropsychological battery. Observations made during administration about factors such as the child's attention to various aspects of a figure (e.g., more attention to elements on the right than left) or whether the execution is more wholistic and planful versus detailed and piecemeal may give clues about the nature, severity, and location of neurological impairment. For example, an individual with a cerebral lesion of one side of the brain often begins to draw on the same side of the drawing as the lesion and ignores elements opposite the lesion. Individuals with right-hemisphere impairment often produce designs that are not only poor in overall quality but are fragmented and appear that the individual was overly concerned with an isolated element. Some neuropsychologists contend that the Rey-Osterrieth taps planning, organization, problem solving, and nonverbal memory when the test is used to its fullest capability. Even when preteens reach the level at which most can reproduce all parts of the design, important information can be obtained by noting the differences that continue to distinguish one child from another—the ablity to plan and organize the drawing (Waber & Holmes, 1985).

Similarly, delineation of the components of memory and their integrity can be examined via the memory aspects of the Rey-Osterrieth (Waber & Holmes, 1986). Can the child retain the basic design in memory but forget the details, or vice versa? Are the design elements on the left or right more apt to be lost to recall? Does the design undergo distortions as part of the memory process and, if so, what is the nature of these distortions? Such information is valuable to the neuropsychologist concerned about the presence of impairments and whether they may be primarily anterior or posterior, in the left or right hemisphere, or involve structure at the cortical or subcortical level (see Chapter 8). Even without speculating about neurological dysfunction, psychologists seeking explanations for school failure often find these details worthy. Thus, the Rey-Osterrieth Complex Figures Test can provide excellent information at several levels when used by an experienced psychologist or neuropsychologist.

Unfortunately, the complexity of the Rey-Osterrieth design and the corresponding multitude of patterns of copying it make objective scoring difficult. Research (Akshoomoff & Stiles, 1995a, 1995b) has suggested that previously developed scoring techniques are inadequate for their intended purposes and that norms necessary to permit interpretation are either inadequate or nonexistent. The Rey-Osterrieth seems to be finding wide usage in the 1990s, but diagnostic conclusions should be tempered until refinements in normative basis and scoring occur.

***Peabody Picture Vocabulary Test–Revised*** In contrast to the Bender Visual Motor Gestalt Test, the Peabody Picture Vocabulary Test–Revised (PPVT–R) (Dunn & Dunn, 1981) is concerned with linguistic capabilities. The test was devised and standardized by Lloyd M. Dunn, who was then (1959) at George Peabody College. Among the original purposes of the PPVT–R was assessment of the ability of children who are nonverbal, those who have mental retardation, and those who have cerebral palsy. Dunn realized that even though these children might not be able to express themselves verbally, they might be able to select from among choices by pointing, or indicate agreement or disagreement by nodding yes or no. Dunn then developed a series of plates, each containing four pictures (see Figure 5.8). A list of vocabulary words was developed that was spoken to the child. The child was asked to simply point to the picture corresponding to the spoken vocabulary word. Children with insufficient motor control to point could nod agreement or disagreement as the examiner pointed

Figure 5.8. Sample Peabody Picture Vocabulary Test–Revised item. (Peabody Picture Vocabulary Test–Revised © 1981 by Lloyd M. Dunn & Leota M. Dunn. American Guidance Service, Inc., 4201 Woodland Road, Circle Pines, MN 55014-1796. Reproduced with permission of the Authors. All rights reserved.)

to each of the four choices. Revised in 1981, the PPVT–R has two forms, each with 175 items. A standard score (mean = 100, standard deviation = 15), age equivalent, and percentile rank scoring system are available for individuals from 2½ years of age to adulthood.

A thorough national sample has provided adequate norms. There is some evidence of satisfactory reliability and of concurrent validity with Verbal IQ scores, but less with Performance IQ scores (Appelbaum & Tuma, 1977). PPVT–R scores tend to depart from WISC–R scores for children with mental retardation (Beck & Black, 1986) and for other children in special services (Candler, Maddux, & Johnson, 1986), even though the test is fairly highly correlated with other ability tests for these groups. Validity may be poorer for children outside the cultural mainstream (Covin, 1977).

Another concern is the use of the test in clinical practice. In some instances, the PPVT–R has been used as an index of general ability. (In fact, before its revision, the test reported an "IQ" score.) As a measure of general ability, the PPVT–R has unacceptably poor content validity. Only familiarity with word meaning is assessed, and there is no demand for reasoning, problem solving, or use of conceptual skills. To base a diagnosis of mental retardation on the PPVT–R, or to make any important decisions based solely on scores from this instrument, would be a grievous error. In fact, its scope is deemed by some (e.g., Groshong, 1987) to be too narrow for most of the requirements of oral language comprehension assessment, and it should be supplemented routinely with measures of sentence comprehension.

Nonetheless, the PPVT–R has value. Often, children are suspected of having delays, but there is neither time nor need for an in-depth assessment. For example, an 8-year-old child is seen on a pediatric ward before scheduled surgery. The child is frightened and reticent, yet his impending surgical procedure needs explanation. The medical staff need to know if the boy can understand what is being said to him. In a case like this, the PPVT–R is a valuable screening instrument. Within 10 minutes, an assessment can estimate whether the boy has enough receptive language to comprehend what he is being told. At other times, the PPVT–R is valuable when used as part of a multitest battery.

Occasionally, a particularly shy child might earn an average WISC–III Performance IQ but might have a low Verbal IQ. Such results leave questions about whether the child's tentativeness and shyness or possible language delays caused the low Verbal IQ. Because the PPVT–R indexes vocabulary size without requiring the child to speak, it can help resolve such questions. In conclusion, the PPVT–R is suitable for screening and supplemental purposes, but is no substitute for an individual intelligence test such as the WISC–III.

## LEARNING DISABILITIES AS PROCESSING PROBLEMS

The concept of learning disabilities has a rather short history; in fact, the term apparently was coined by special educator Samuel Kirk in the early 1960s (Kirk, 1962). It is seen in Chapter 6 that the concept of learning disabilities has a specific legal definition. Nonetheless, in general conversation, "learning disability" has a less precise meaning that implies a problem in some aspect of information processing. In contrast to a lack of overall ability, a *learning disability* is thought of as a narrow deficit that affects the child in only limited ways or limited settings, most typically in school. Intraindividual differences are consequently important to those who think of learning disabilities in this sense.

In fact, diagnosticians once hoped to identify children with learning disabilities by the very presence of large or conspicuous intraindividual differences. For example, if a child had excessive scatter among subtest scores on a test like the WISC–III, it was thought that uneven development in thinking or information-processing skills was being demonstrated and that this denoted a learning disability. Research by Kaufman (1976) and others, however, has shown rather conclusively that scatter is common even among children without disabilities, and it could be considered rare only if extreme. Practically, large differences among subtests are often of little significance unless they fit a discernible pattern or such scatter can be shown to predict severe underachievement—the operational definition of learning disabilities discussed in Chapter 6.

## Subtest Patterns that Predict Learning Problems

A test capable of predicting which children are destined to have trouble learning in school would be extremely valuable. For the same reasons, an ability test with subtest patterns or characteristics distinctive to children with learning disabilities would also be valuable. Often parents ask that their preschooler be administered a learning disabilities test or that their school-age child be given a dyslexia test. Unfortunately, there are no psychological tests that predict with absolute certainty who will develop these problems. There are, however, some test patterns that are frequently associated with severe learning problems. That is, some generalizations can be made even though there is no assurance that a child with any particular pattern will have problems.

***Severe Reading Problems and Dyslexia*** If a test to detect *dyslexia* (a general term denoting severe failure to learn reading, not explainable by lack of experience or sensory impairments) were available, the general public would no doubt expect it to check for mirror writing or some sort of severe visual-perception problem. The notion that seeing letters and words backward causes reading failure is a widely held assumption (Vellutino, 1987). If a well-developed test to tap this skill were available, then this line of thinking goes: Dyslexia could be detected by its characteristic pattern or could be conclusively ruled out. In the 1990s, however, reading is recognized as a complex skill that develops over time, with different psychological abilities more important at some stages in the developmental process than at others. Moreover, different children appear to employ different strategies to accomplish the same reading task. These considerations imply that no single psychological ability or skill is always predictive of impending reading failure. The reading process is too multifaceted and changes too much over time to permit such a simple diagnosis.

Nonetheless, researchers have studied those psychological patterns most frequently associated with dyslexia, or severe underachievement in reading, and have reached some general conclusions.

The results are surprising to many because research actually shows that linguistic, language, and auditory processing problems are far more frequently associated with reading failure than are visual-perceptual problems.

Some facts are known about dyslexia: It is more common among boys, it tends to run in families (is heritable), and many children who ultimately develop it have less developed linguistic and auditory memory capabilities as preschoolers. During the school years, children with dyslexia are noted to have difficulty with simple word recognition (i.e., reading single words in isolation as is required by tests like the WIAT Word Recognition; see Chapter 6). The principal impairment that prevents word recognition skills from developing appears to be at the phonological (i.e., sound) level of language processing. That is, many of these children have severe and unusual difficulty hearing, remembering, and reproducing sounds. As they begin to learn to read they struggle to learn to associate sounds with letters (one crucial aspect of phonics reading) or to blend isolated sounds into complete words (another aspect of phonics). As a group, children with dyslexia have especially great problems reading so-called non-words (letter combinations that are pronounceable but do not form an actual English word, such as "cof" or "lak"). Interestingly, research shows that non–word-reading impairments are especially heritable (Rack & Olson, 1993). The particular difficulty associated with reading such non-words makes sense if the underlying impairment is indeed phonological. Reading meaningful words in isolation proves less difficult because the child can rely on both sight-word capability and recall from prior encounters with the real words. To pronounce non-words, though, the child must rely exclusively on the sounding out, or phonics approach. Research has also shown that as non-words become less similar to real words (i.e., do not fit into a word family such as "fap," which is easy because it fits into a family with real words: lap, map, sap), they become even harder for individuals with dyslexia. No such change occurs for readers without dyslexia (Olson, Forsberg, Wise, & Rack, 1994). Furthermore, tasks that require pure-sound blending and manipulation or rapid naming show, on average, substantially lower scores for children with dyslexia than would be expected. A variety of tests of auditory and phonic processing measures have been developed as tools to study dyslexia, but most of these are not yet standardized, are lacking norms, and/or are not yet commercially available.

Recent large-scale and sophisticated studies of dyslexia have highlighted the nature of the language-related impairments that affect most individuals with the condition. The same studies, referred to cumulatively as the Colorado Reading Project (Olson, Wise, Conners, Rack, & Fulker, 1989; Olson, Wise, Conners, & Rack, 1990; Rack, Snowling, & Olson, 1992) also provide surprising evidence regarding the genetic basis of the disorder: By studying patterns among fraternal and identical twins with dyslexia and comparing their patterns, it was determined that the ability to read non-words was highly heritable. Other types of reading problems, such as inability to read by sight-word method or orthographically, was much less genetically influenced.

The most common pattern seen with dyslexia is to have WISC–III Verbal IQs substantially lower than Performance IQs and to have poor auditory memory, sound blending, and auditory discrimination skills. Children with this pattern may have histories that include early language delays. The hallmark of these children's reading and spelling efforts is an inability to use phonics. When they spell, these children may include all necessary letters, but the letters make no sense phonetically (e.g., exit = etix, slow = swol). Oral reading is generally a severe problem. Here, extremely common words that are learned as wholes through practice (e.g., were, look, run) may be read without trouble, but even simple unmemorized words may result in severe trouble. Because these children lack phonics skills to help them decode, they may have no idea what to do with an unknown word and may guess wildly based on initial sound or simply give up without responding. These children may also omit word endings, use synonyms in oral reading, and make strange, unphonetic guesses when spelling. Because they have relatively better visual and spatial/mechanical skills, these children sometimes overrely on their ability to revisualize whole words, and shy away from their inability to make the individual sounds associated with letters. Tests like the Woodcock-Johnson Word Attack subtest may be particularly revealing because it forces the child to read non-words. The phonological impairments associated with this type of dyslexia are evident in research studies, and these studies imply that psychometric tests ultimately may be used as part of a test battery. For instance, tests of naming speed (how quickly many items in an array of objects or numbers can be named), alliteration, rhyming, and similar skills in children seem to be associated with dyslexia (Fawcett & Nicolson, 1994; Gallagher & Frederickson, 1995; Wilson & Cline, 1995). At the time of this writing, however, few such tests are in wide clinical use. The types of test most often seen are those included in Illustration 5.2, a case example of a child with auditory-linguistic reading problems. As might be suspected, things are rarely this simple. Once readers learn to break the code and recognize words, language comprehension skills become quite important.

## Illustration 5.2

Joe, a 9-year-old fourth-grader, has a severe reading problem. Joe was brought for a psychological evaluation by his parents after conferring with the principal of the parochial school Joe attended. Despite having been tutored in reading since first grade, the boy was falling further behind and was now going to be retained. The parents wanted to know how bright their son was and why he wasn't reading.

Joe's developmental history was unremarkable until he entered school. He was born following a full-term pregnancy, without perinatal problems, and acquired developmental milestones at average ages. Repeated hearing and vision checks were within normal limits. Joe's parents, both of whom had attended college, enjoyed reading. An older sister was a B+ student who had encountered no school problems whatsoever. A paternal uncle had many learning difficulties in school and dropped out before high school graduation but now was a successful small businessman. There were no other family learning problems.

Joe had difficulty in school beginning in the first grade. Early sound discrimination drills proved frustrating to Joe. He also had problems learning simple tasks. For instance, at the end of first grade he had not yet learned all the "key words" designed to serve as phonic cues associated with letters (e.g., alligator for A, bumblebee for B). Phonics in particular continued to be difficult as he moved through the primary grades. In addition, teachers noted Joe's difficulty in expressing himself verbally in class. Handwriting was average; spelling tests after repeated practice with word lists were generally good, sometimes 100%.

When seen for evaluation, Joe was a pleasant boy who seemed anxious (understandably so). He demonstrated good task persistence and attention span as he completed the evaluation tasks. Even subjectively, it was clear that Joe had language-processing problems. For example, when asked where his father worked, Joe replied, "Yes," suggesting that he mistook the question for, "Does your father work?" Other verbal information ei-

*(continued)*

*continued*

## Illustration 5.2

ther seemed lost from memory or was not fully grasped. Five times during the WISC–III Arithmetic and Comprehension subtests, Joe asked to have items repeated. Such errors frequently denote significant auditory-processing problems, especially when hearing acuity is intact.

Examination scores were consistent with subjective observations. Joe earned the following test scores:

**Wechsler Intelligence Scale for Children–III**

| Verbal scales | | Performance scales | |
|---|---|---|---|
| Information | 7 | Picture Completion | 10 |
| Similarities | 8 | Picture Arrangement | 11 |
| Arithmetic | 7 | Block Design | 10 |
| Vocabulary | 8 | Object Assembly | 11 |
| Comprehension | 9 | Coding | 9 |
| Digit Span | 6 | | |

Verbal IQ=86 Performance IQ=101 Full Scale IQ=92

**Peabody Individual Achievement Test–Revised**

| Test | Standard score |
|---|---|
| Mathematics | 98 |
| Reading Recognition | 71 |
| Reading Comprehension | 75 |
| Spelling | 83 |
| General Information | 89 |
| Total Test | 83 |

**Wide Range Achievement Test–III**

| Test | Standard score |
|---|---|
| Spelling | 73 |
| Arithmetic | 104 |

*(continued)*

*continued*

## Illustration 5.2

Below are Joe's responses to an informal reading and an informal spelling task. Note the extreme sound-symbol deficits seen throughout.

Reading test: *Bob's bicycle was new, but his brother's was old.*
Joe's reading: "Bob's (don't know) was new, but had both was old."
Reading test: *In springtime the birds return from the South.*
Joe's reading: "In (don't know) the ball takes far the some."

| Spelling test | Joe's responses |
| --- | --- |
| red | red |
| run | run |
| open | opne |
| jumping | kamping |
| large | narn |
| agree | une |
| start | sratt |
| forest | forest |
| direction | drnone |

Joe obviously has a learning disability. Although his intellectual ability is adequate, especially his Performance IQ, he has a breakdown in language processing—one of the basic psychological processes required to read. He seemingly has auditory discrimination, auditory comprehension, and auditory memory problems, in some combination. He also, apparently, does not reason as well when presented verbal problems as he does on spatial, nonverbal problems.

Academically, his skills have suffered the most in phonics. When he reads, he sometimes recalls whole words, but when this fails he has few phonic or word-attack skills to fall back on. He does not use context clues from the story to help him decode,

*(continued)*

*continued*

## Illustration 5.2

perhaps because he fails to follow the meaning of the story he is reading—a problem often seen in learners with language impairments. When spelling, Joe again shows tremendous phonic deficiencies. He either seems to recall a word in toto, or else produces a wild guess devoid of any semblance of phonics. To the extent that he has succeeded in school thus far, he has probably relied on revisualization of entire words. His ability to retrieve whole-word configurations probably explains his relative success on weekly spelling tests, which he simply overlearns through practice. Similarly, he does not do nearly so poorly on the PIAT Spelling test, on which he is only required to recognize the correctly spelled word from among four choices.

Without special assistance, Joe is destined to continue to accrue even greater frustration. As he moves beyond the fourth grade, not only will he experience failure in phonics, but his reading difficulties will have an effect on almost all other subjects because students are now expected to read directions and write answers on worksheets. Moreover, the boy's language impairments will likely prevent him from understanding the concepts and ideas found in upper elementary curricula. As more instruction centers around verbal discussion, he will be further disadvantaged. A remedial program calling for language development and intensive clinical reading drills was suggested. Joe transferred to the local public school, where he was placed in an extended resource program (4 hours per day) and provided with these services.

Accordingly, among more able readers (who may still be behind) language comprehension rather than phonological processing may be important (Vellutino, Scanlon, & Tanzman, 1994). Thus, even among children with predominantly linguistic-based dyslexia, the diagnostician must be prepared to assess many important component skills.

A second, less common pattern is seen among children with dyslexia that involves visual-spatial processing problems has also been described in the literature (Newby, Recht, & Caldwell, 1993). Large-scale studies of poor readers have shown much less evidence of this type of disorder and have failed to show the genetic/heritable pattern for this type of reading problem that seems to characterize the phonic type (Pennington, 1991). The literature is less clear about the psychometric characteristics of the children in this group, but it appears that they have lower WISC–III Performance IQs than Verbal IQs and often have associated problems, such as confusing letter sequences, reading slowly (word-by-word), reversing letters (e.g., "b"s and "d"s, words such as "was" and "saw"). These children tend to do poorly on visual-motor perceptual tasks such as the Bender Gestalt or Rey-Osterrieth test. Language tends to be adequate or better, and they show none of the auditory discrimination problems that characterize the first group.

Reading and spelling are difficult for the group with visual-spatial difficulties because they cannot revisualize entire word configurations. The sight vocabulary of instantly recognizable words that most readers acquire during the elementary grades seldom fully develops for this group. Because these children are unable to revisualize entire word configurations, they often read accurately but excruciatingly slowly, sounding out words letter by letter. Sometimes there is no instant, whole-word recognition, even with extremely common words (look, were, etc.). When spelling, they may not be able to see all of the letters in their mind's eye, and consequently, they may spell words incorrectly but produce all sounds in the correct order and make phonetic sense (e.g., right = rite, talk = tawk, champagne = shampain). It is hypothesized that this group of children, therefore, overrelies on the ability to hear sounds and sequence them properly and avoids the problem of revisualizing entire units almost completely. Most experts contend that this type of dyslexia is far less prevalent than the auditory-vocal type and may constitute only 5%–10% of all children with dyslexia (Boder, 1971).

The third, or residual dyslexic group, is less clear-cut in terms of psychological profile, and less well agreed upon by researchers. As a group, these children appear roughly equivalent on WISC–III Verbal and Performance IQ scores. They may, however, do poorly on Arithmetic, Coding, Information, and Digit Span subtests (Holcomb, Hardesty, Adams, & Ponder, 1987). These subtests measure a combination of memory, sequential ability, and academic-related skills that may be lacking, and thus contribute to impaired reading. Some researchers (e.g., Boder, 1971) contend that the residual group of children with dyslexia are definable because they lack both the auditory-linguistic and visual-spatial abilities to learn reading, and thus are the most difficult to teach and have the poorest prognosis.

Challenged with academics, these children exhibit the dual impairment of poor phonics and poor whole-word revisualization. When spelling, they may fail to recall letters, may write phonetically bizarre words, or both. Sometimes they may stumble on even the simplest words (was = waas). Their reading may also contain many errors, including poor word-attack skills and failure to recall high-frequency words. Because this group appears to have few information-processing strengths to which to turn, they often are the readers with the most disabilities. This mixed group may constitute approximately 10%–20% of children with dyslexia.

***Severe Arithmetic and Mathematics Problems*** Arithmetic disorders occur less frequently than reading disorders, and their occurrence interferes with fewer areas of academic functioning. For these reasons, far less research has been conducted to determine the cognitive and information-processing factors associated with arithmetic disorders than with reading disorders.

Much as is the case with reading, competence in arithmetic requires many diverse perceptual, memory, and thinking skills, all of which go through developmental changes as the child grows. As a result, no single profile can define those who fail to develop mathematical reasoning and computational competency. Unlike reading, however, critical abilities in mathematical reasoning appear to be related more to nonverbal or spatial/mechanical abilities than to language (Rourke & Findlayson, 1978). For instance, Hartje (1987) has suggested that spatial ability impairments, such as severe disorders of spatial exploration, spatial visualization, and spatial orientation, often lead to a severe inability to perform arithmetic calculations (in severe cases, sometimes called acalculia or dyscalculia). Such individuals often misalign vertical columns when working multiplace problems and have difficulty "carrying," as an example. A similar but far more detailed explanation of the sources of errors in mechanical arithmetic (e.g., computing various problems on the WRAT–3) has been advanced by Rourke (1989). Rourke's detailed research on nonverbal learning disabilities (see Chapter 8) includes findings showing that problems with computational arithmetic are frequently associated with this disorder. As a group, children with nonverbal learning disabilities make errors for spatial and visual reasons (e.g., confusing alignment of columns in a multicolumn problem or mistaking a plus sign for a multiplication sign). But the stumbling blocks to success in computational arithmetic are not exclusively visual or spatial. Other problems occur because of underlying impairments associated with nonverbal learning disability: procedural errors (taking the smaller of two numbers from the larger regardless of their position in a subtraction problem), failure to shift set (so that once the child begins subtracting, he or she continues to do so even if subsequent problems call for addition), graphomotor impairments (difficulty producing legible numerals), poor recall of facts (e.g., multiplication tables), and poor judgment and reasoning (the child records an answer to a computational problem by blindly following procedures; he or she fails to check the answer for plausibility). Rourke speculates that these impairments occur because the child with a nonverbal learning disability has impaired right cerebral hemisphere functioning, and the right hemisphere is especially important in performing the operations necessary to compute arithmetic problems correctly. Even more severe neurological impairment is implicated in some children with severe arithmetic difficulties. For these few children, brain dysfunction causes not only arithmetic problems but may also involve finger agnosia (inability to distinguish which finger is being touched), confusion of right–left orientation, and a severe inability to write. In some cases, dyslexia was also present in this cluster of symptoms, called Gerstmann syndrome (Benton, 1987).

Most children with severe arithmetic disability, however, do not have a neurological syndrome, nor do they necessarily always lack component cognitive or information-processing skills. Nonetheless, psychologists often encounter profiles with higher WISC–III Verbal IQ scores than Performance IQ scores and associated problems on the spatial tasks such as the Bender Gestalt test or the Rey-Osterrieth Complex Figures test and no evidence of reading problems. Some authorities believe this means a minimal level of visual/spatial skill is necessary (but alone not necessarily sufficient) for success in arithmetic (Barkley, 1981).

***Language Disorders*** Children whose psychological profiles show them to have severe verbal or language impairments are most likely to have difficulty learning in school because almost all academic skills are predicated on linguistic competency. Generally, the farther one progresses in elementary school, the more verbal skills become important for success (Satz, Taylor, Friel, & Fletcher, 1978). Tests like the WISC–III are excellent for identifying general impairments in language and also provide the diagnostician an opportunity to observe various aspects of language functioning. Some experts believe that, rather than indexing overall language competencies, standardized tests can identify quite specific patterns of strength and weakness, but this supposition remains controversial. Nonetheless, tests for such skills as language comprehension, language expression, and various aspects of auditory processing are available and are used by both speech-language pathologists and psychologists, although it has been cautioned that many of these instruments have inadequate psychometric properties (Norman-Murch & Bashir, 1986). Other important aspects of speech, such as voice quality, articulation problems, and stuttering, may also predict school problems, but diagnosing these problems seldom involves standardized psychological tests. Most often this type of assessment falls in the domain of speech-language pathologists.

***Written Expressive Disorders*** Perhaps more than any other skill taught in school, a child's capability to express him- or herself in writing requires a changing array of psychological abilities as he or she grows. In the early elementary years, written performance is mostly conceptualized by teachers as the ability to write legibly and spell accurately. Tests such as the Bender Gestalt test tap fine motor and visuospatial integrity, and consequently suggest who may have problems with handwriting. As is true with reading failure, either auditory-linguistic or spatial-mechanical impairments may contribute to early spelling problems. For instance, low WISC–III Verbal scores may be associated with lack of adequate phonic skills applied to spelling; low WISC–III Performance scores may be related to lack of whole-word revisualization when spelling. Of course, there are children with low scores in either of these areas who still manage to spell adequately. Linguistic problems such as errors in grammar and syntax or word finding may also underlie written expression problems (Vogel & Konrad, 1988).

After the basic mechanics of manuscript and cursive writing are mastered, and after a child has learned to spell, general language and cognitive competencies are most important to written expression. This is because teachers beyond the elementary years tend to evaluate students according to the organization and coherence of exposition and the sophistication of the language used. Thus, psychologists might expect to see general language and conceptual problems as the predominant contributors to later shortcomings in written expression. Even this is not necessarily what is actually found among older school children with written expression disorders. A study of 99 children (age 9–15 years) with writing disorders were found with four main clusters of impairments: children with fine motor and language problems, those with visual/spatial problems, those with attention and memory impairments, and those with sequencing problems (Sandler et al., 1992). As with many complex human behaviors, written expression may be hampered by impairments in an innumerable array of narrower perceptual information-processing and thinking abilities. However, no one particular impairment always predicts the inability to learn to convey thought through writing.

## GENERAL CONSIDERATIONS ABOUT ABILITY PATTERNS

Although it is true that the psychological patterns outlined above frequently predict academic problems, unfortunately prediction is far from perfect. For example, whereas many children with dyslexia have severe phonological processing impairments, many children who have phonological processing impairments do not have dyslexia. Consequently, diagnosticians cannot assume that all children with low Verbal IQ scores and problems with auditory discrimination or auditory memory will ultimately be diagnosed with dyslexia. Such an assumption would be faulty because it would result in over-identifying many children who will never have such reading problems. Equally troublesome, children free of any of the psychological profiles listed above still sometimes have dyslexia. It is therefore impossible to assume that certain academic problems will not develop based on an apparently trouble-free ability profile. That is, using ability profiles as predictors of learning disabilities inevitably results in missing some children with problems and incorrectly identifying some children without problems. Not every child with dyslexia fits into one of the typical cognitive profiles; some occur without a cognitive pattern that seems to explain their inability to learn. This finding should not be surprising, if one considers that each academic problem may have complex, multiply determined origins. Available psychological instruments cannot possibly assess every conceivable contributing ability. Even among those abilities that can be assessed, full understanding of their contributions to learning academics may be lacking. Moreover, noncognitive factors such as motivation and quality of instruction obviously are requisite to classroom success, but these are not part of a typical assessment of cognitive and information-processing skills, nor are they typically considered in conceptualizations of such problems as dyslexia.

What value accrues, then, to a profile of ability tests? First, although cognitive profiles cannot make unerring predictions, such profiles can nonetheless identify those who are severely at risk for learning problems. But more important, psychological profiles are often used for planning classroom instruction. Used in this fashion, individual children's profiles can help to decide how to teach academic skills and where to address efforts to remedy weak skills. It is these two latter areas that are discussed next.

### Differential Diagnosis and Prescriptive Teaching

Differential diagnosis and prescriptive teaching is a very broad notion that, in its general form or with minor variants, has been called such things as the diagnostic-remedial approach, prescriptive teaching, and ability and process training. A key assumption of this position is that profiles of psychological abilities are crucial to educational planning because they imply which skills are to be taught or in which fashion basic academic instruction should occur. Those who hold that ability profiles are crucial can be divided into two broad camps, with each emphasizing different content of instruction. One group of diagnosticians focuses on remedying weak processing skills by stressing the training of underlying abilities. In contrast, a second group primarily is concerned with teaching academics and holds that cognitive testing implies the best methods of teaching each child. Consider what each of these two approaches might suggest should be done with a child who is reading poorly, has substantially superior Performance IQ compared to Verbal IQ scores, excellent Bender Gestalt drawings, but clear problems with short-term auditory memory and remembering the sounds that are associated with shapes, such as might be detected on a test like WRAML. That is, this child has strong spatial/mechanical skills or a preferred visual-perceptual mode of learning.

## Remediation of Weak Abilities

Basic attention, perceptual, memory, and cognitive skills obviously underlie the ability to learn academics such as reading. Should any of these abilities be a deficit in a child who is failing to learn, then remediation should start with these component abilities rather than with academics per se. Such a position affords considerable logical appeal, especially at first glance. For instance, the child mentioned above first might be taught sound discrimination through practice sequences that involve distinguishing like sounds from different sounds, with each trial followed by feedback. Or the child might be drilled to memorize series of objects named aloud, with the requirement to repeat the correct sequence. Training like this strengthens deficit skills so that the child is ultimately more able to learn academics, according to the advocates of this approach. It is argued that without first remedying the necessary processing skills, academic instruction is destined to proceed slowly or to fail.

Despite the apparent plausibility of this position, it has been criticized soundly on several grounds (see Arter & Jenkins, 1979, for a detailed discussion). First, many of the "information processing" tests used to locate skills in need of remediation are too unreliable to be used. As a result, instructional time may be spent teaching abilities that are not actually in need of attention. This is especially likely to occur if large test batteries comprising relatively unreliable tests were administered. Under these conditions, several test scores would be likely to appear low simply because of chance. Second, there is little empirical evidence that, once weak processing skills are identified, remedial drills actually improve underlying abilities. Arter and Jenkins (1979), for instance, reported that only 24% of well-designed research studies showed improvement in the targeted ability after children receive training. Third, and most important, when children receive remedial training of abilities, they tend to do no better than children who receive only academic instruction, if academic outcomes such as reading proficiency are used as criterion measures. That is, the attempt to correct deficient processing skills appears to do little or nothing to enhance the child's bottom-line academic success. As a result, the emphasis on remedial training of deficit abilities in the hope of creating better academic outcomes has lost favor since the late 1970s.

In the early 1990s, however, there appeared to be some exceptions to this general rule. Specifically, children with severe phonological processing impairments may benefit from training in sound segmentation; this training may actually generalize to reading and spelling, thus diminishing the prospect of long-term reading failure (Ball & Blachman, 1991). Studies that have investigated training phonological process training, nonetheless, have generally found the most benefit to reading and spelling skills when training drills approximate real-world learning tasks and include practice in making actual sound (phoneme) and grapheme (letter associations) (Felton, 1993). Phonological processing skills may represent such a crucial link to reading success that they represent a unique case. Taking a far broader view and relying on a more sophisticated model of information processing, a prominent Canadian researcher, J.P. Das, has presented some evidence that training component skills may influence academic performance (Das, 1993; Das, Mishra, & Pool, 1995). Such comprehensive approaches to training cognitive abilities do not appear to be in wide usage at this time and their ultimate empirical support is unclear.

## Matching Academic Instruction to Learners' Profiles

Some researchers have contended that a carefully collected profile of psychological abilities is important for classroom planning because it allows strengths to be used and weaknesses to be avoided. This approach has been called *capitalization of strengths* (Cronbach & Snow, 1977) and *circumvention* (Hartlage & Telzrow, 1983). Rather than attempting to train basic cognitive processes, time should be spent in direct academic instruction; instructional experiences should be selected that either allow the child to use his or her best abilities or to be taught so as to minimize demands on weak underlying abilities.

Children with relatively better visual-perceptual ability might be provided tangible objects to be grouped and regrouped in order to help fix concepts while learning addition and subtraction, rather than relying on verbal memorization of facts. Children with linguistic and auditory impairments (such as the child mentioned above) might be taught reading in a fashion that deemphasizes the need to make sound discriminations, memorization, and production of subtle sounds. Some researchers (Jorm, 1979) have suggested that children with auditory impairments learn more readily if "whole-word" or "look-say" reading methods, rather than phonics methods, are used.

In their comprehensive 1979 review, Arter and Jenkins criticized this approach, as they did the remediation of deficit abilities approach, as having little empirical justification. Studies accomplished at that date tended to find no better academic acquisition, regardless of whether the method of instruction was matched to children's information-processing strengths. In the 1980s and 1990s, however, models of human intelligence and information processing have been developed that are far more sophisticated and research based than the intuitive models on which some tests and some intervention programs previously were based. Consequently, some researchers have contended that when contemporary, research-derived approaches to matching abilities and instructional techniques occur, this approach does improve academic learning (Hartlage & Telzrow, 1983).

Even in the absence of compelling research support, many educators continue to use psychological test findings to help plan instruction. When working with individual learners, a decision must be made about which skills are truly impairments, what impact these impairments might have on teaching academics, how amenable to remediation ability impairments prove to be in this individual child, and which approach might be best attempted initially for each child. Individualization with a close eye on the acquisition of skills, set against a backdrop of logic and empiricism, must guide educational decisions. It is disappointing that research findings have failed to provide the unequivocal support that one would hope to find for remediating deficit component abilities or for matching methods with learner aptitudes. Nonetheless, psychological tests are now used and will continue to be used to assist in planning instruction.

## SUMMARY

Psychologists are able to assess school-age children with test instruments that are more sophisticated, more reliable, and more valid than those used for infants and preschoolers. Of the increasing array of tests that are available today, the Wechsler Intelligence Scale for Children–III remains the dominant instrument, not only because of its utility in diagnosing mental retardation and learning disabilities, but also because it provides useful personality and observational data.

In some instances, tests such as the Kaufman Assessment Battery for Children, Kaufman Adolescent and Adult Intelligence Test, or the Woodcock-Johnson Psycho-Educational Battery–Revised (Tests of Cognitive Ability) are administered in lieu of, or to supplement, the WISC–III. More often, the WISC–III is supplemented by measures of special ability such as the Bender Visual Motor Gestalt Test, the Peabody Picture Vocabulary Test–Revised, Wide Range Assessment of Memory and Learning, or California Verbal Learning Test–Children's Version, or measures of information processing such as the Detroit Tests of Learning Aptitude–3. Some of these tests are also used for screening or to answer specific questions that do not warrant an in-depth intellectual assessment.

Each of these tests, used alone or especially in combination, may help detect information-processing problems that may underlie academic failure in reading, arithmetic, language, or written expression. How each learner's unique pattern of strengths and weaknesses is used to plan for academic instruction is controversial, however, with little empiricial proof that training of deficient information processing abilities or that matching instruction to learners' strengths differentially affects academic skill acquisition.

The intelligence tests discussed in this chapter are helpful if used as part of a battery to determine eligibility for special education services. A discrepancy between ability (IQ) and academic achievement is necessary for a learning disability designation; IQ scores below 70 with concomitant adaptive delays are necessary to qualify for services for children with mental retardation (see also Chapter 4). For both diagnoses—learning disability and mental retardation—measures of academic achievement, discussed in Chapter 6, are indispensable.

## Study Questions

1. What are the content differences between the WISC–III Verbal and Performance subtests?
2. If a child earned a 10 on the WISC–III Information subtest and an 11 on the Arithmetic subtest, why might it be wrong to say he or she has more general information knowledge than arithmetic capability?
3. Special ability tests are best used for what purpose? How might they be misused?
4. What configuration of psychological abilities (or deficits) is most often associated with severe reading problems or dyslexia?

5. What is meant by capitalization of strengths or circumvention? Provide an example of an academic task that might employ this strategy for a child with a severe language problem.
6. Identify a classroom task that would probably be difficult for a child with low scores on the WISC–III Performance subtests and the Bender Gestalt test.

CHAPTER SIX

# Tests of Academic Achievement

The intelligence tests discussed in Chapter 5 are concerned with assessing children's overall ability to think, solve problems, and reason, or with more narrowly defined aspects of this composite, such as receptive language or memory. These tests focus on ability. Achievement tests, in contrast, are designed to measure how well academic skills have been learned. The products of academic instruction, rather than the processes underlying learning, are the targets of academic achievement measures. Academic achievement tests are helpful in answering questions like the following:

How do Paul's academic skills compare to his classmates'?
Does Janet have sufficient reading comprehension skills to work with the eighth-grade textbooks she is asked to read?
Is Juan's underachievement so severe that he might qualify for learning disabilities special education services?

## INDIVIDUAL AND GROUP TESTS CONTRASTED

Anyone who doubts the importance of achievement tests should note the number of references to popular tests, such as the Iowa Test of Basic Skills, in the media. News stories about achievement tests, however, almost always reflect concern about the status of the United States on group measures of academic competence (often cited as in decline). Tests of this type are administered to large segments of the school-age population (e.g., all pupils attending public school in a given state) or to slightly more narrowly defined groups (e.g., all students planning to attend college). The inferences that are often drawn from these tests are how well *groups* of students have learned classroom instruction. Armed with such information, various school districts, states, or even countries might attempt to ascertain how effectively students are learning.

Individual achievement tests, in contrast, are most often applied to only those children for whom there is some concern about learning status. Used as part of a battery of tests, individual achievement tests can help determine if a child is in fact failing to learn and may describe the nature of the learning problem, can help establish eligibility for special services, or can even guide remedial efforts. This chapter describes some of the most frequently used individual achievement tests and demonstrates their use in practical situations.

## CRITERION-REFERENCED ASSESSMENT

Most of the tests discussed thus far in this text are designed to compare an individual's performance with a norm group (see Chapter 1). However, sometimes educators find that comparison among individuals is unimportant, whereas knowing precisely which skills specific pupils have mastered is crucial. In these instances, criterion-referenced assessment may be used; that is, evaluators compare how much a pupil has learned with regard to some standard or criterion, rather than with other pupils.

Criterion-referenced assessment has advantages in certain educational situations. First, educators can define exactly which skills are to be learned and, after instructing students, evaluate the success of the instruction. For instance, teachers can test recently taught material and find the percentage of learners who have mastered each skill. Findings can be used to re-emphasize material that the entire class has yet to master; or, for the individual child, can reveal those skills that need additional individual work. Because criterion-referenced tests are made to match the curriculum that is being taught, there is close agreement between instruction and assessment (Hannafin, 1986). Because testing can occur frequently and the tests are made by teachers themselves, fairly large numbers of items can be devoted to each educational objective.

The disadvantage of this approach is its lack of a normative basis—a fact that generally precludes comparing pupils with one another. Consequently, it is impossible to tell whether a pupil is performing better than, comparable to, or poorer than same-age peers. Moreover, because IQ tests are norm-referenced, criterion-referenced achievement tests cannot be used to objectively compare ability with achievement. Thus, criterion-referenced data have limited use in making placement decisions, although it is argued that criterion-referenced testing should be considered along with norm-referenced achievement scores when identifying learners with disabilities (Wodrich, 1988).

Concern about reliability may also be present if criterion-referenced assessment occurs. It is essential that assessment of academic performance be reliable if accurate teaching decisions are to be made using test results. For instance, assume testing one day shows a child to have mastered all consonant blends, but testing the next day finds that the child has only 50% mastery of blends. Inconsistent findings of this type suggest a lack of test reliability and thus prevent teachers from making important suppositions, such as that the child has sufficient mastery of blends so that instruction can move on to the next skill. Unfortunately, because of the informal nature of criterion-referenced tests, many educators assume reliability is unimportant. Teacher-made tests must be sufficiently long, possess unambiguous items, and be consistently administered if minimal standards of reliability are to be assumed. Most published criterion-referenced tests ignore the issue of reliability altogether (Salvia & Ysseldyke, 1985). This is a major disadvantage of criterion-referenced tests compared to adequately developed norm-referenced tests.

Often, those who use criterion-referenced tests generate a numerical value for each of their test items, known as the *difficulty level* (Stodola & Stordahl, 1967). This numerical index merely indicates the percentage of pupils passing that item. If multiple-choice items are used, percentages of students selecting incorrect alternatives (called *distractors*) can also be calculated and can provide additional information about an examinee's patterns of response. Procedures of this type are called *item analysis*. Figure 6.2 (see p. 167) is an example of item analysis. Despite the fact that psychologists seldom use criterion-referenced tests, understanding this type of testing will help the reader understand those educational tests that psychologists do use.

## NORM-REFERENCED ACHIEVEMENT TESTING

It is no surprise that teachers hope almost all their pupils will pass test items measuring classroom learning. Everyone can do well in the criterion-referenced scheme because everyone is competing against an achievement standard rather than against one another. Quite the opposite case exists with norm-referenced testing; assessment occurs so that individuals can be compared with one another. Despite our wishes that everyone be above average, such occurrences cannot take place in the real world. Similarly, tests items composing standardized, norm-referenced instruments cannot be constructed so that everyone, or even nearly everyone, picks the correct answer.

Rather specific item difficulty levels are selected for norm-referenced tests. Items with a difficulty level of approximately 50% (i.e., half of the test takers got that item correct, half got it wrong) have been shown statistically to contribute to a widely spread distribution of score, which in turn makes distinction among individuals easier to detect (see Figure 6.1). Other factors besides a 50% difficulty level characterize good items for norm-referenced testing, and one of these is a desired value on a statistic called the *item discrimination index*.

The item discrimination index begins by identifying those individuals who did well on the entire test, say the top one third of scorers, and those who did poorly, perhaps the bottom one third of scorers (see Figure 6.2). Once these two groups have been identified, their performance on each test item can be studied. Ideally, each test item should be passed more readily by the top than by the bottom group. By comparing the difficulty level for each group, an index of how well the item discriminated those who generally knew much (top group) from those who generally knew little (bottom group) can be constructed. The item discrimination index simply subtracts the difficulty level for the bottom group from that of the top (.75 − .35 = .40 discrimination index). Items with fairly large discrimination indices contribute to a spread-out distribution and detection of differences among individuals. A weak discrimination index may suggest to the test constructor that the item should be excluded or checked for confusing wording or inaccurate construction.

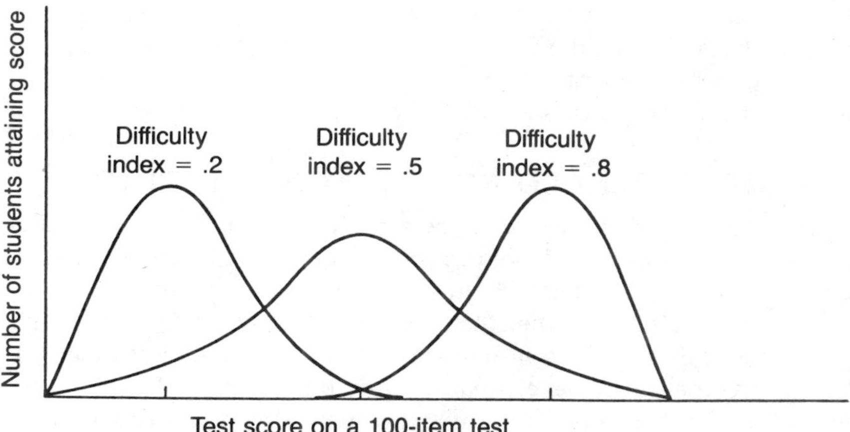


Figure 6.1. Test score distributions that would result if tests were constructed entirely of items having difficulty indices of .2, .5, or .8. (From Royer, J.M., & Feldman, R.S. [1984]. *Educational psychology: Applications and theory.* New York: Alfred A. Knopf; reprinted by permission.)

| (Top = upper 33%; Bottom = lowest 33%; 150 students total) | | | | | | |
|---|---|---|---|---|---|---|
| | | A | B* | C | D | E |
| | Top | 1 | 41 | 3 | 4 | 1 |
| **Item 1** | Middle | 4 | 26 | 10 | 7 | 3 |
| | Bottom | 9 | 16 | 10 | 10 | 5 |
| | | Difficulty Level = .55<br>Discrimination Index = .50 | | | | |
| | This item has adequate overall difficulty and is answered correctly by high scorers far more frequently than low scorers. It is probably a good item. | | | | | |
| | | A | B | C | D* | E |
| | Top | 4 | 2 | 20 | 19 | 5 |
| **Item 2** | Middle | 8 | 7 | 14 | 17 | 4 |
| | Bottom | 15 | 5 | 11 | 16 | 3 |
| | | Difficulty Level = .35<br>Discrimination Index = .06 | | | | |
| | This item proved almost as difficult for the high scorers as the low scorers. Option C may be confusing. This is probably a poor item. | | | | | |
| | | A* | B | C | D | E |
| | Top | 11 | 10 | 9 | 8 | 12 |
| **Item 3** | Middle | 10 | 10 | 12 | 7 | 11 |
| | Bottom | 10 | 9 | 11 | 9 | 11 |
| | | Difficulty Level = .21<br>Discrimination Index = .02 | | | | |
| | This items appears to be too difficult in that all groups of students were correct at only a chance level. | | | | | |

Figure 6.2. Example of item analysis. (*Correct response.)

Most of the tests discussed in the remainder of this chapter were carefully constructed of items with suitable item difficulty levels and discrimination indices. Equally important, these tests are standardized and norm referenced; their reliability and validity can be investigated, and the adequacy of their standardization sample can be evaluated.

These points notwithstanding, standardized achievement tests do have weaknesses. Foremost among these is the inability for test items to correspond precisely with the curriculum that local schools are teaching. Criterion-referenced tests, in contrast to norm-referenced tests, overcome this problem by having teachers create *tables of specification* defining what has been taught and the manner in which teaching has occurred before designing tests. This content validity problem that plagues norm-referenced tests can be mitigated to some extent.

For instance, it has been suggested that local schools, or entire districts, also create tables of specification to evaluate the match between the local curriculum and standardized, norm-referenced achievement tests used by school psychologists to identify learners with disabilities (Salvia & Ysseldyke, 1985; Wodrich, 1988). A high degree of correspondence between achievement tests and instruction ensures content validity of the test, a sine qua non for adequate achievement measurement (see Chapter 1 for a discussion of validity). Good and Salvia (1988) have demonstrated that a poor match between curriculum and such popular tests as the Wide Range Achievement Test (WRAT), Peabody Individual Achievement Test (PIAT), California Achievement Test, and Metropolitan Achievement Test has an effect on test scores. They argue that no one achievement test is suitable in all school districts.

Similarly, questions must be raised about the number of items devoted to each important skill that the school is teaching. Even if an achievement scale's content corresponds closely to classroom teaching, there still may be so few items that many important skills are left unassessed. This, of course, is an unfavorable situation. It is important for nonpsychologists (primarily teachers) to be aware of these considerations and to assist psychologists with adopting achievement tests suitable for local purposes.

## LEARNING DISABILITIES DEFINED

Achievement tests can be used to answer many of the questions similar to those posed at the beginning of this chapter. When psychologists are involved, however, achievement tests are often administered as parts of multitest batteries in order to detect the presence of learning disabilities. The definition of learning disabilities in school settings has a more specific meaning than the general designation used in Chapter 5. In almost all 50 states, the term *learning disabilities* has a legal definition. Demand for learning disabilities services is keen among the many children who are failing in school. As a result, an objective definition of learning disability is desirable so that diagnosticians can apply uniform standards for whom will be provided or denied these services. In addition, a learning disability diagnosis technically establishes that the child has a disability that requires special education, a designation for which carefully outlined due process procedures (such as informed parental consent and confidentiality of records) must be followed.

The federal definition for learning disabilities is as follows:

> A disorder in one or more of the basic psychological processes involved in understanding or in using language, spoken or written, which may manifest itself in the imperfect ability to listen, think, read, write, spell, or do mathematical calculations. The term (learning disabilities) includes such conditions as perceptual handicaps, brain injury, minimal brain dysfunction, dyslexia, and developmental aphasia. The term does not include children who have learning problems which are primarily the result of visual, hearing, or motor handicaps, of mental retardation, emotional disturbance, or environmental, cultural, or economic disadvantage. (PL 102-119, 20 USC 1401 [a][1])

Additional federal guidelines clarified this imprecise definition. These guidelines specified that a pupil must have a significant discrepancy between ability (typically established by IQ testing) and academic achievement in one of the following areas:

1. Oral expression
2. Listening comprehension
3. Written expression
4. Basic reading skill
5. Reading comprehension
6. Mathematics calculation
7. Mathematics reasoning

Following these guidelines, virtually every state has established its own definition of learning disabilities, and many have developed explicit standards that must be met if pupils are to qualify; in most states, a significant ability–achievement discrepancy is the principal criterion. A requirement for basic processing disorders such as perceptual, linguistic, or memory deficits, although lacking an agreed-upon method of identification, is nonetheless a criterion in 18 states (Chalfant, 1989). Underachievement due to sensory or motor disabilities, cultural/economic disadvantage, or emotional or mental impairments precludes the use of the learning disability term. From a practical point of view, the magnitude of ability–achievement discrepancies has generally been the critical consideration for a learning disabilities designation (Berk, 1984; Ysseldyke, Algozzine, Regan, & McGue, 1981). Only those children with "severe" ability–achievement discrepancies were to be eligible for learning disabilities services. But how were such discrepancies to be quantified? The answer to this question was key in determining who would be eligible to receive a learning disabilities designation and the valued services afforded by the label.

A simple approach to quantifying discrepancies would be to locate children who have average IQs but who score below grade level on individual achievement tests. This approach, however, would identify exceedingly large numbers of pupils because roughly one half of all pupils are below grade level on any achievement subtest, and of this one half, many would turn out to have IQs in the average range (90–110, or higher). Some states, or local education agencies, attempted to maintain the simplicity of this approach, but demanded more stringent standards for underachievement, such as that a child must be two grade levels below current placement (e.g., a pupil in the fourth month of fifth grade would be expected to have a 5.4 grade equivalent; if achievement were below 3.4, then underachievement would be considered to be present). Unfortunately, grade equivalent scores are flawed for this type of comparison. The flaw is that grade equivalents fail to allow specification of how far below average a pupil is performing compared to same-age peers. For instance, the pupil mentioned above is 2 years below grade level, but it is unclear if this 2-year deficit would result in the 25th percentile with a corresponding standard score of 90, or the 5th percentile with a standard score of 82. The use of grade equivalents fails to clarify exactly how far below average the pupil's score actually falls. It is precisely this information that is essential for determining severe ability–achievement discrepancies.

Grade equivalents are now less frequently used (in fact, some achievement tests no longer provide them); they have been supplanted largely by standard scores. Standard scores have the advantage of being transformable to the same units of measure as IQ scores (e.g., having a mean of 100 and a standard deviation of 15). Even more important, standard scores permit psychologists to tell where a pupil's performance stands relative to his or her age-peers, rather than calibrate performance to some other age group as grade equivalents do. With IQ and achievement tests both converted to standard scores, ability–achievement discrepancy can be specified in standard score points. Some educational agencies, for example, require a 30 standard score point discrepancy. A child with an IQ score of 105 would therefore be severely underachieving if any achievement standard score were below 75. There is one large problem (and some minor ones, too) with this otherwise appealing approach.

First, the approach, since it seeks achievement scores that are lower than ability scores, on average will detect more discrepancies among those with above-average IQs and fewer among those with below-average IQs. This occurs because of a phenomenon known as *regression to the mean.* This occurs when a score that departs from the mean appears on one test, such as an IQ test, so that the same child's score on another test, such as an achievement test, is likely to be closer to average—regress to the mean. For example, if a child earns a WISC–III Full Scale IQ of 110, then it is likely that his or her scores on an achievement test will not be 110, but rather closer to the mean (100), such as 105. Similarly, if a WISC–III score of 90 were earned, the chances are that an achievement test score would not also be 90, but would be closer to the mean, such as 95. These examples hint at the problems of using simple difference scores—low scores have to overcome the effects of regression to the mean if an ability–achievement discrepancy is to manifest; for high scores, the regression to the mean effect actually makes it easier for discrepancies to be found.

Differences in reliability of tests is another problem with simple approaches such as absolute differences between ability and achievement tests (see discussion of reliability in Chapter 1). Unreliable achievement tests, because they lack consistency, prevent examiners from assuredly knowing a pupil's "true" achievement level. Thus an unreliable achievement test, one with a standard error of measurement of ±7 standard score points (assuming the mean is 100 and the standard deviation is 15) would present considerable uncertainty to a psychologist searching for a 30-point IQ–achievement discrepancy. Now consider the same unreliable achievement test used in conjunction with a relatively reliable IQ test, such as an instrument with a standard error of measurement of ±3. When deciding whether the pupil did better on the IQ or the achievement test (and determining the magnitude of the difference), both tests' reliabilities must be considered. *Difference scores* (i.e., scores derived by subtracting achievement tests scores from IQ scores) are less reliable than scores from either the IQ test or achievement test alone. Formulas to assess the reliability of difference scores have been developed; when applied to each combination of intelligence and achievement tests used to diagnosis learning disabilities, acceptable values should result (Cone & Wilson, 1981). Although many combinations of IQ and achievement tests have been scrutinized (e.g., WISC–III and WRAT–3; WISC–III and Woodcock-Johnson Tests of Achievement), unfortunately, not all combinations have been examined yet in this empirical fashion.

As more is learned about ability–achievement discrepancies, increasingly sophisticated methods for making accurate comparisons have come into use. In the late 1990s, a refined procedure using regression formulas is popular. This procedure takes into account factors such as the correlation between specific ability and achievement tests (an additional point of deviation in detecting differences), regression to the mean effects and, in some cases, differences in specific tests' reliabilities. By entering IQ scores into a formula, it is possible to tell precisely whether a student's reading comprehension score, as an example, is or is not discrepant from the reading achievement score predicted by the formula. Some states use general formulas for IQ versus achievement test scores; even better, tests like the WISC–III and Wechsler Individual Achievement Test (discussed later in this chapter) produce such an analysis when their scores are entered into a computerized scoring program.

Several conclusions can be drawn from this discussion, and it is important for nonpsychologists to keep these in mind: 1) Differences between IQ and achievement tests may be unreliable; 2) like all tests, brief achievement tests that contain few items tend to be unreliable; and 3) even with combinations of IQ and achievement tests that have fairly reliable difference scores, increasing the number of tests involved (e.g., using many achievement subtests) increases the risk that discrepant scores are due to chance. Using sophisticated statistical techniques can help establish whether various score values are truly discrepant from one another. In summary, the process of detecting severe ability–achievement discrepancies, despite its apparently simplistic nature, is technically demanding. The more those involved in the process know about the tests themselves, the tests' reliability and validity, and about achievement assessment, the better.

## MULTIPART TESTS OF ACADEMIC ACHIEVEMENT

### Wide Range Achievement Test–3

The current edition of the Wide Range Achievement Test, the WRAT–3 (Wilkinson, 1991), is the most recent revision of one of the oldest individual achievement tests, originally published in 1936. It is suitable for children age 5 years and older. Items have changed little in recent revisions, but the norms, a source of criticism previously, have been updated somewhat but not to acceptable levels if the test is used to compare to other achievement tests or to IQ (Mabry, 1995; Ward, 1995). The test consists of three subtests—Reading, Spelling, and Arithmetic—each with standard scores (mean = 100, standard deviation = 15), percentile ranks, and grade equivalent scores.

Unfortunately, the test has such narrow content that it cannot be used by itself to assess academic status. For example, the Reading subtest consists solely of individual words read orally by the pupil (for younger children letter recognition is also included). No passages are read, nor is reading comprehension checked. Moreover, the word lists are too short to adequately assess even basic sight vocabulary for most pupils (Witt, 1988). Arithmetic items consist almost exclusively of computational problems, and there are too few problems of each type to match the goals of most schools' instruction (e.g., only one or two items of each type). Also, adequate reliability has not been conclusively demonstrated (Mabry, 1995; Ward, 1995).

On the positive side, the WRAT–3 now has two roughly equivalent forms that permit combining the two to produce a more reliable score (or for retesting, although reliability is probably insufficient for this purpose). In addition, the requirement to work math problems independently for a sustained time interval (up to 15 minutes) may be more typical of the demands expected in class than some achievement tests (e.g., PIAT) that provide extreme structure and thus disguise attentional and persistence problems (Wodrich & Barry, 1988). Still, there is little evidence that the WRAT–3 has sufficient normative base, reliability, and content or construct validity to permit it to be used in other than an adjunctive or screening capacity (Mabry, 1995; Ward, 1995).

In general, the WRAT–3 should be used as a screening device or as one of several instruments, including those that are more thorough, when assessing children suspected of failing in school or as having learning disabilities or mental retardation.

## Peabody Individual Achievement Test and Peabody Individual Achievement Test–Revised

The Peabody Individual Achievement Test–Revised (PIAT–R) consists of Mathematics, Reading Recognition (oral reading of single words), Reading Comprehension, Spelling, and General Information (child answers orally posed questions) subtests and Written Expression (Markwardt, 1989). In its original (1970) form the test was one of the first individual achievement instruments to use an easel and a multiple-choice format, a technique that is now popular. With this technique, a child is presented a question or performs a task (e.g., reads a sentence) and is then presented with four choices, from which he or she selects the one believed to be correct (see Figure 6.3). This procedure is used for Mathematics, Reading Comprehension, and Spelling subtests. Standard scores (mean = 100, standard deviation = 15) may be reported for each subtest. A Total Test score, a composite of the five achievement subtests, is also reported in standard score format. The one exception to this rule is Written Expression where a developmental score that can range from 1 to 15 is assigned.

Some questions have been raised about PIAT–R. There is no requirement for mathematics computation using pencil and paper nor must pupils read sentences or passages aloud. The test's easel and multiple-choice format may prove far easier than classroom demands for inattentive and poorly organized children, and this fact may con-

A
See the boy with the hat.

Figure 6.3. Sample Peabody Individual Achievement Test, Reading Comprehension item. (Peabody Individual Achievement Test by Lloyd M. Dunn and Frederick C. Markwardt, Jr. © 1970 American Guidance Service, Inc., 4201 Woodland Road, Circle Pines, MN 55014-1796. Reproduced with permission of the Publisher. All rights reserved.)

tribute to fewer pupils being identified as having learning disabilities with the PIAT–R than with other achievement tests (Wodrich & Barry, 1988). The revised version has been criticized, however, for lack of validity information at the time of its publication (Kamphaus, Slotkin, & DeVincentis, 1990). Nevertheless, updated item content, new norms, and excellent reliability data (Kamphaus et al., 1990) mean the test is likely to remain fairly popular.

## Wechsler Individual Achievement Test

The "Wechsler" name has been so long and so intimately associated with intelligence testing (see Chapters 4 and 5) that it seems peculiar to see a "Wechsler" listing under the achievement test heading, especially since the test was published long after the death of its namesake, Dr. David Wechsler. Still the Wechsler Individual Achievement Test (WIAT) (Psychological Corporation, 1992) has become a popular instrument, and there are excellent reasons for its warm reception by the psychological and educational communities. This is easy to understand in light of one of the most crucial purposes of individually administered achievement tests—to determine whether there is a sufficient ability–achievement discrepancy to warrant consideration for learning disabilities special education designation under IDEA.

To accomplish this task, psychologists typically administer an intelligence test (WISC–III being the most common) and an individually administered achievement test. Most achievement tests suffer in this situation because although they are carefully standardized on large national samples of children, these standardization samples are not actually composed of the same children used to standardize the IQ test. Significantly, the WISC–III (i.e., IQ) and WIAT (i.e., achievement) were both administered to some of the same children (1,118 of them). This co-norming helps the diagnostician considerably in the crucial task of identifying underachievement; if WISC–III and WIAT scores are different from each other, those differences are not due to anomalies in the norming process. A computer scoring program permits score production on both WISC–III and WIAT and quickly tells the diagnostician whether IQ / achievement scores are truly statistically different from each other and, if so, how significant those differences are, and how often they occur in the standardization population. These facts help clarify which children are truly underachieving. The representativeness and size of the standardization sample are excellent, and the WIAT has been praised for meeting high psychometric standards regarding reliability and validity (Saklofske, 1992).

The WIAT has other advantages—one of which is its scope. Consider the various achievement subtests (each of which produce a standard score with a mean of 100 and a standard deviation of 15):

Basic Reading (pronunciation of words in isolation)
Mathematics Reasoning (concepts, vocabulary, and word problems)
Spelling (written responses from dictation)
Reading Comprehension (oral responses to comprehension questions after passage reading)
Numerical Operations (pencil-and-paper math calculations)
Listening Comprehension (receptive vocabulary and comprehension of orally presented passages)
Oral Expression (naming and oral explanations)
Written Expression (writing a passage in response to examiner request) [subtest used for children in grades 3–12 only]

This list corresponds directly with the areas of potential underachievement for learning disabilities outlined in the federal guidelines. In other words, not only does the WIAT provide a good comparison with IQ scores, but it provides measures of achievement in every one of the areas of potential underachievement that might permit a student to be identified as having a learning disabilities under IDEA (see p. 169). The WIAT's comprehensiveness precludes the need to administer several achievement tests (which themselves may have different norms), which frequently use different scoring systems (e.g., some achievement tests use standard scores with means of 10, standard deviations of 3; others use means of 100, standard deviations of 15; still others use grade equivalents only).

The WIAT's authors have also taken steps to make the subtests' content meaningful. Ideally, achievement tests comprise items that tap skills learned in a particular school class or in a particular curriculum. A close correspondence between the curriculum and the test constitutes content validity (see Chapter 1). Locally developed tests can accomplish this task fairly easily by adding or discarding tests' items to enhance agreement with what has been taught. National achievement tests cannot possibly match all the various reading and math curricula that are used in the various elementary schools in the United States, for example. However, the test items that compose the WIAT each are designed to match a bona fide behavioral objective drawn from a standard curriculum package. For example, the goal in a standard basal reading series may be to teach students to sound out multisyllabic words with double consonants by splitting consonants and attacking each syllable individually. The WIAT would include test items that matched this goal. Many achievement tests fail to strive for this degree of curriculum affinity.

Shortcomings that consumers might want to be aware of include the absence of school skill readiness level and extremely easy items in most of the scales that would make it hard to detect delays (and therefore ability–achievement discrepancies) among young children (Riccio, 1992). In an attempt to include easy items, some subtests include tasks that are much like ability tests (e.g., Listening Comprehension and Oral Expression have receptive and naming tasks like some special ability or IQ tests). Creating sufficiently easy achievement items and having those items correspond to the content found in more difficult achievement items from the same subtest is a problem that occurs among most standardized achievement tests, however. An equivalent problem exists at the upper end of several tests where insufficient numbers of difficult items exist to permit older children (13 years of age and older) to produce meaningful scores in the superior range (Riccio, 1992). Also, caution is suggested in interpreting the Listening Comprehension score in that some children may struggle on this subtest because of expressive, rather than receptive or listening, problems (Riccio, 1992). These problems are relatively minor compared to those of most other individual achievement tests, which lack many of the outstanding qualities of the WIAT.

The WIAT also contains a brief screening battery comprising Basic Reading, Mathematics Reasoning, and Spelling subtests. There are obvious problems with the scope of skills measured and with content of the Screening test; the problems here are much like those found with other brief, or screening, tests such as the WRAT–3.

## Woodcock-Johnson Psycho-Educational Battery and Woodcock-Johnson Psycho-Educational Battery–Revised (Tests of Achievement)

In Chapter 5, the Cognitive portions of the Woodcock-Johnson battery were discussed, but it is the achievement sections of this instrument (Woodcock-Johnson Psycho-Educational Battery–Revised: Tests of Achievement; Woodcock & Johnson, 1989) that appear to be most frequently used. The Tests of Achievement are reviewed in this chapter. Despite the authors' hope that the entire Woodcock-Johnson battery (i.e., cognitive and achievement sections) would be used to assess each child, it appears that many diagnosticians use the achievement subtests alone.

The achievement battery consists of 17 subtests that the authors suggest be grouped into four broad "cluster scores" for purposes of score generation and interpretation. The achievement clusters and their constituent subtests appear in Table 6.1. For each cluster, standard scores with a mean of 100 and standard deviation of 15, as well as percentile rank and grade equivalent, are available. Other more sophisticated scores may also be produced. Concern that some learners may have fairly circumscribed impairments has prompted the authors to generate separate tables that allow individual subtests, rather than the larger clusters, to be interpreted. This is an advantage, especially for a learning disability diagnosis, although some of the reliability of the clusters is sacrificed if shorter subtests are interpreted alone.

Table 6.1. Achievement clusters and subtests of the Woodcock-Johnson–Revised: Tests of Achievement

| | |
|---|---|
| Reading Cluster | Written Language Cluster |
| Letter-Word Identification | Dictation |
| Passage Comprehension | Writing Samples |
| Word Attack | Proofing |
| Reading Vocabulary | Writing Fluency |
| Mathematics Cluster | Punctuation and Capitalization |
| Calculation | Spelling |
| Applied Problems | Usage |
| Quantitative Concepts | |
| Knowledge Cluster | |
| Science | |
| Social Studies | |
| Humanities | |

Many diagnosticians like the content of the Woodcock-Johnson achievement subtests. However, it is unlikely that all educators will be satisfied with a reading assessment that requires no oral reading of sentences or passages and that measures reading comprehension by a cloze procedure (readers supply the missing word from context) rather than by answering comprehension questions. Local school personnel should examine content, especially in the knowledge cluster, to ensure agreement with their schools' curriculum. For many, the match will be deemed adequate.

The Woodcock-Johnson battery held considerable promise by developing a Cognitive and Achievement battery that was standardized on the same population. With the revised and updated Cognitive battery, the Woodcock-Johnson will probably be used more often to identify the discrepancies needed to qualify students as having learning disabilities. Much of the overall popularity of the system derives from the extensive measurement of academic skills that the battery now encompasses. Consider the issue of written expression as an example. Whereas the WIAT includes a single test of written expression that involves writing a story (with the capability to produce a somewhat broader index by including the child's performance on spelling of dictated words), the Woodcock-Johnson is capable of producing a composite score on written language that is derived from seven subtests that tap skills as diverse as simple spelling to as complex as proofreading for spelling, grammar, and punctuation errors. Moreover, the Woodcock-Johnson's writing tasks are suitable for primary grade children, whereas the Written Expression subtest of the WIAT is not.

Many other aspects of the Woodcock-Johnson are also extremely favorable. As mentioned in Chapter 5, the Woodcock-Johnson contains a standardized subtest that requires students to read non-words, a task that is especially difficult for many children with dyslexia. For older students, subject knowledge in the content areas of science, social studies, and humanities is assessed by three separate subtests. Features such as these have helped the Woodcock-Johnson become popular at high school and even college levels for the assessment of potential learning disabilities with later manifestation.

## Kaufman Test of Educational Achievement

Alan and Nadeen Kaufman not only hoped to redefine intelligence when they developed the Kaufman Assessment Battery for Children (K–ABC), but they also sought to create a valid achievement measure contained within the same battery (see Chapter 5). The achievement subtests of the K–ABC, however, have generally been rejected as having unsuitable content or for being too brief. The Kaufmans subsequently mounted a more extensive effort that has resulted in the Kaufman Test of Educational Achievement (K–TEA), although there was some item overlap with the K–ABC Achievement subtests (Radenich, 1986). The K–TEA, however, has generally been well received (Sattler, 1988).

The K–TEA provides a Comprehensive Form, for more detailed diagnostic purposes, and a Brief Form, for screening. The Comprehensive Form includes the following subtests: Mathematics Application, Mathematics Computation, Reading Decoding, Reading Comprehension, and Spelling. The brief form consists of the following subtests, comprising items that do not overlap with the comprehensive form: Reading, Mathematics, and Spelling. Standard scores (mean = 100, standard deviation = 15) are available for each of the subtests, for composite scores in mathematics and reading (derived from the two appropriate tests in each area), and for the entire battery, if the comprehensive form is used. The brief form provides scores for each subtest and an overall composite. Derived scores are produced in the typical fashion by comparing pupils with age peers or grade peers, but the authors have also generated separate tables for fall and spring testing, as pupils' performances differ depending upon the time of year they are tested. Grade equivalent scores are not available.

Most of the content of the K–TEA appears to be suitably matched to many school districts. The test has been found to correlate highly with popular achievement tests and to produce similar mean scores (Kamphaus, Schmitt, & Mings, 1986). Unfortunately, the only oral reading that is required consists of words in isolation, and this must be considered a significant shortcoming. Reading comprehension is assessed well for older children (answering questions orally or selecting from among multiple-choice items that the pupil must read him- or herself), but young children demonstrate their understanding by following directions (usually motoric and nonverbal) contained in the material read (with items like, "If you are a boy, raise your hand; if you are a girl, lower your hand"). It is questionable that such tasks effectively measure reading comprehension as it is taught in the typical elementary classroom. Although clearly superior in length to many individual achievement tests, the number of items assessing each important skill may be too few for some diagnosticians' liking. For example, there are six items measuring subtraction without regrouping. The K–TEA is often administered concurrently with the WISC–III so that ability–achievement discrepancies necessary for learning disability diagnosis can be found. However, empirical evi-

4

**Reading**
**decoding**

| Grade | Item | Stimulus | Response | Score | Prefixes & Word Beginnings | Suffixes & Word Endings | Closed Syllable (Short) Vowels | Open Syllable (Long) & Final e Pattern Vowels | Vowel Digraphs & Diphthongs | r-Controlled Patterns | Consonant-le Patterns | Consonant Clusters & Digraphs | Single & Double Consonants | Whole Word Error Type |
|---|---|---|---|---|---|---|---|---|---|---|---|---|---|---|
| | | | | | WORD PARTS | | | | | | | | | |
| 1 | 1 | S | | | | | | | | | | | | |
| | 2 | A | | | | | | | | | | | | |
| | 3 | n | | | | | | | | | | | | |
| | 4 | e | | | | | | | | | | | | |
| | 5 | b | | | | | | | | | | | | |
| 2 | 6 | to | | | | | | o | | | | | t | |
| | 7 | in | | | | | i | | | | | | n | |
| | 8 | here | | | | | | e_e | | | | | h r | |
| | 9 | four | | | | | | | | our | | | f | |
| | 10 | apple | | | | | a | | | | (p)le | | p | |

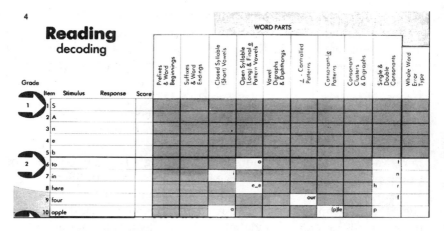

Figure 6.4. Kaufman Test of Educational Achievement, Comprehensive Form, portion of Reading Decoding Record Form. (Kaufman Test of Educational Achievement by Alan S. Kaufman & Nadeen L. Kaufman © 1985 American Guidance Service, Inc., 4201 Woodland Road, Circle Pines, MN 55014-1796. Reproduced with permission of the Publisher. All rights reserved.)

dence that the difference scores calculated by this procedure are reliable is not yet available.

On the positive side, the K–TEA has an excellent recent standardization. It has good reliability and adequate evidence of concurrent and construct validity. The authors' attempt to link diagnosis to teaching by including an analysis of the skills tapped by each item (see Figure 6.4) is also helpful, although most teachers will require additional informal assessment prior to beginning instruction.

In summary, the K–TEA appears to be an excellent member of the list of available individual achievement tests, and the test will probably continue to be used frequently by psychologists and educators.

## TESTS THAT MEASURE ONE ACHIEVEMENT AREA

The achievement tests discussed in this chapter are adequate for most psychologists' purposes. They help round out a comprehensive battery so that information about academic status can be integrated with intelligence, special ability, and social-emotional data. A comprehensive battery allows much to be concluded about a child's overall characteristics. These multipart tests of academic achievement are also valuable in objectifying ability–achievement discrepancies necessary for determining learning disability eligibility. The tests, however, are less helpful in delineating precisely those academic skills that have been learned and those yet to be mastered. If more specific information is required, then criterion-referenced tests administered by teachers, or more detailed standardized achievement measures administered either by psychologists or educators, may be used. The tests discussed below, KeyMath–Revised and the Gray Oral Reading Tests, Third Edition (GORT–3), are two of the many standardized achievement tests that measure single academic areas.

## KeyMath–Revised

An example of a test that assesses specific skills within a single academic area and that attempts to retain the rigor of standardization is the KeyMath–Revised test (Connolly, 1988). The KeyMath–R test comprises 13 subtests (e.g., Numeration, Addition, Time, Money) that are grouped into three broad content areas: Basic Concepts, Operations, and Applications. Standard scores (mean = 10, standard deviation = 3) are produced for each subtest and area, as well as a total test score (mean = 100, standard deviation = 15). The test's uniqueness is that it reports scores from circumscribed strands of academic skills, called *domains,* that constitute the various subtests. The mastery of small, clearly defined sets of academic skills can be tabulated, just as is the case with criterion-referenced testing, but each child's performance on these small domains has the advantage of being able to be compared with grade peers (see Figure 6.5). Such specific information can then, it is argued, be used to plan what to teach an individual pupil.

Unfortunately, the test's good qualities, including recent national standardization and good reliability for area and total tests scores, do

### SUMMARY OF DOMAIN PERFORMANCE

**BASIC CONCEPTS AREA**

| Subtest | Domain | Domain Score | Average Score (Table 16) | Domain Status | | |
|---|---|---|---|---|---|---|
| **Numeration:** (24 items) Ceiling Item 17 | Numbers 0–9 | 6 | 6 | W | (A) | S |
| | Numbers 0–99 | 4 | 5-6 | (W) | A | S |
| | Numbers 0–999 | 2 | 2-3 | W | (A) | S |
| | Multi-digit numbers and advanced numeration topics | 1 | NA | W | A | S |
| **Rational Numbers:** (18 items) Ceiling Item 6 | Fractions | 2 | 1-2 | W | (A) | S |
| | Decimals | 0 | NA | W | A | S |
| | Percents | 0 | NA | W | A | S |
| **Geometry:** (24 items) Ceiling Item 13 | Spatial and attribute relations | 4 | 6 | (W) | A | S |
| | Two-dimensional shapes and their relations | 4 | 4-5 | W | (A) | S |
| | Coordinate and transformational geometry | 0 | NA | W | A | S |
| | Three-dimensional shapes and their relations | 0 | NA | W | A | S |

Figure 6.5. KeyMath–Revised summary of pupil's domain performance. (KeyMath Revised by Austin J. Connolly © 1988 American Guidance Service, Inc., 4201 Woodland Road, Circle Pines, MN 55014-1796. Reproduced with permission of the Publisher. All rights reserved.)

not extend to the hoped-for use of domain scores. With very few items, each domain tends to be quite unreliable. Moreover, the test's hierarchical organization may also be questioned. For instance, why is the test divided into three areas instead of the traditional two areas of mathematics computation and mathematics concepts, which many other tests use and that the federal guidelines call for when assessing children with learning disabilities?

These criticisms notwithstanding, the KeyMath–R test can be used favorably by psychologists who require a reasonably thorough assessment of elementary arithmetic skills. The test's use will not be confined to psychologists, as special educators will find the alternate form capability and the availability of fall and spring norms helpful for testing after instruction has occurred. Even so, for many psychologists the test is too detailed, and for many special education teachers, informal, criterion-referenced tests of mathematics are preferable.

## Gray Oral Reading Tests, Third Edition

No educational capability is more important than reading, and no more frequent source of school failure exists than reading problems. As a result, many instruments that are devoted exclusively to assessing reading have been developed. Most of these are criterion-referenced tests that tap skills of oral reading and comprehension. These criterion-referenced tests are popular among educational diagnosticians because they have high correspondence to classroom instruction (e.g., Classroom Reading Inventory) (Silvaroli, 1986). Psychologists, as mentioned previously, prefer norm-referenced tests that produce derived scores (such as standard scores). An example of a test that combines the favorable content qualities of the frequently used criterion reading tests and the psychometric qualities of standardized tests is the Gray Oral Reading Tests, Third Edition (GORT–3) (Wiederholt & Bryant, 1992).

Like the criterion-referenced reading tests, the GORT–3 consists of a series of graded passages that are read aloud by the child while the examiner records errors, such as substitution, repetition, failure to pronounce, and reading rate, and asks comprehension questions related to the passage. The GORT–3 is a norm-referenced instrument, however. So unlike the criterion-referenced tests, errors and reading rate are numerically tabulated and compared to norm tables; comprehension is similarly quantified, and standard scores for reading rate, accuracy, and comprehension are generated, as is a composite *Oral Reading Quotient.* These scores have a mean of 10 and a standard deviation of 3; the oral quotient has a mean of 100 and a standard deviation of 15. Percentile ranks are also available.

The GORT–3 has been reviewed favorably regarding reliability and validity, and it has also been praised for improvements in the standardization sample (King, 1995; Kundert, 1995). Like its predecessor, the Gray Oral Reading Tests–Revised (GORT–R) (Wiederholt & Bryant, 1986), the GORT–3 has adequate content validity for most elementary school pupils, affords examiners the advantage of observing reading skills in considerable detail, and has helpful standard scores. Unlike many other reading measures, the GORT–3 is a much closer approximation of actual classroom reading. The test also appears suitable for identifying learning disabilities, as difference scores between the GORT–R and WISC–R are reliable, and the test seems more sensitive to reading problems than simple word lists like the WRAT (Wodrich & Barry, 1989). Given the importance of reading skills for school success and the high prevalence of reading disabilities, tests such as the GORT–3 would appear to be valuable tools to include in a comprehensive assessment of academic skills. Some researchers (Felton & Wood, 1989) have noted that reading learning disabilities are adequately detected only if multiple reading/spelling tasks are assessed, such as reading single words, decoding and encoding of real and nonsense words, plus reading of prose and answering comprehension questions. The GORT–3 may objectively index these latter two categories and be used with tests like the Woodcock-Johnson battery to render a comprehensive reading assessment. Use of the GORT–3 not only assists in detecting reading problems severe enough to qualify the pupil for special education services but also may be used to help plan what and how to teach the child.

## CASE ILLUSTRATIONS

Academic achievement tests have roles ranging from central to supplemental when used to help psychologists understand children. Three case studies involving standardized achievement tests follow.

### Alice

Alice is an 8-year-old in second grade who was evaluated after her classroom teacher referred her to the school psychologist. Her teacher had questions about whether a learning disability might be holding Alice back and whether she was eligible for special services. The teacher also sought input in planning for Alice in the classroom.

Background information was collected that indicated Alice was in good health and had no hearing or vision problems. Her mother told the school psychologist that Alice had been born following a full-term pregnancy and that she had slight neonatal jaundice for which she was treated with phototherapy before being released from the hospital at 5 days of age. Developmental milestones were generally attained at average ages, although Alice's mother stated that her daughter had relatively less interest in fine motor activities than her two older sisters did. For example, Alice reportedly never enjoyed cutting paper or coloring as a preschooler.

Educational history was reviewed, and it was found that problems had existed since early in kindergarten. Alice's report card contained notes stating that she had much difficulty learning letter names. She was clumsy in the classroom, often spilling things; she attempted to avoid art activities and had "sloppy" work. Her marks in arithmetic were average, but reading and writing marks were consistently in the "needs improvement" range. Many of the same comments were also evident in the first grade, although she was then doing so poorly that her teacher suggested her for grade retention. Alice's parents concurred, so she spent a second year in the first grade, this time with marks only slightly better than those from her initial first-grade year.

Alice is now a second grader, and unfortunately, she is still struggling to keep up in the classroom. Her handwriting is described as poor, and when she is fatigued her written efforts become almost illegible. She reportedly reads poorly and fails to retain skills from one day to the next. Although she performs adequately on some phonics worksheets, Alice is virtually incapable of reading any passage fluently. Her comprehension, even when her teacher helps her decode unknown words, is inadequate. Much of her work is not completed, and there are comments that she is showing increasing signs of "a defeatist attitude."

Alice was administered a battery of psychological and educational tests with the following results:

**Wechsler Intelligence Scale for Children–III**

| Verbal tests | | Performance tests | |
|---|---|---|---|
| Information | 12 | Picture Completion | 9 |
| Similarities | 12 | Coding | 7 |
| Arithmetic | 10 | Picture Arrangement | 7 |
| Vocabulary | 9 | Block Design | 7 |
| Comprehension | 13 | Object Assembly | 6 |
| Digit Span | 12 | | |

Verbal IQ = 107    Performance IQ = 82    Full Scale IQ = 95

**Bender Gestalt Test**

Koppitz Errors 9    Standard Score 71

(continued)

**Kaufman Test of Educational Achievement**

| Test | Standard score |
|---|---|
| Mathematics Application | 99 |
| Mathematics Computation | 81 |
| Reading Recognition | 80 |
| Reading Comprehension | 68 |
| Spelling | 72 |

**Gray Oral Reading Test–3**

| Test | Standard score |
|---|---|
| Oral Fluency | 4 |
| Comprehension | 3 |
| Oral Quotient | 61 |

The school psychologist who examined Alice noted that she began the assessment session enthusiastically but quickly became discouraged and complained that the problems were too hard and that she was stupid. Alice was especially perplexed and frustrated on the Block Design subtest of the WISC–III. Here she appeared confused by the spatial nature of the task and consistently misoriented the designs. She worked slowly on the Coding subtest and often lost her place. She reversed several of the designs on this subtest as well.

During academic testing, Alice made reversals on both the mathematics and spelling sections. She spelled only very simple words correctly but otherwise overrelied on phonics (e.g., spelled "said" as "sed"). Her severest weakness, however, occurred during oral passage reading. Alice read at an exceedingly halting pace, slowing to sound out virtually every syllable and often losing her place. Her voice was devoid of inflection, and she was unable to answer comprehension questions at a level better than chance.

At a meeting during which the school psychologist shared findings with Alice's teacher, her parents, and other members of the school's pupil personnel team (e.g., principal, school nurse, special education resource teacher), the following conclusions were drawn: Alice is eligible for special education services for children with learning disabilities. Her school history is replete with instances of failure in the classroom, and her lack of academic skills is substantiated by objective testing. Current testing found Alice to be a bright girl but to be severely underachieving. The 30-point standard score discrepancy between the Full Scale IQ score and the reading score is substantial and entirely consistent with classroom reports. Moreover, cognitive and special ability testing suggested visual-perceptual problems that are especially evident when she uses pencil and paper. In more general terms, Alice tends to do much better if words and oral language are involved than if tasks are hands-on or manipulative. As is true with many such children, phonics prove to be far easier than recalling words as whole units. Similarly, mastering an instantly recognizable list of sight vocabulary words proves very hard. Finally, it was concluded that Alice has visuospatial impairments that contribute to her being confused in situations that call for visual perception and visual organization.

Besides the technical and legal considerations of qualifying Alice for special services, the evaluation was designed to help describe her special needs. Among the suggestions for Alice were the following:

1. Provide instruction in sight vocabulary but confine instruction to an essential list that contains phonetically regular words or words that must be mastered to ensure smooth oral reading; instruction will probably require more practice (overlearning) and more review than is true of other learners.
2. Alice's excellent oral language competencies should be employed as a strength to help her read where possible; for example, she could be taught to ask herself questions about the meaning of passages as she reads and to use the context of a passage to decode unknown words.
3. Likewise, listening as opposed to reading should be used wherever possible; for example, listening to a classmate read worksheet instructions may be easier for her than reading directions for herself.
4. Reducing visual stimulation (e.g., by removing clutter from desktop, limiting the number of problems presented on a single page) while simultaneously enhancing stimulus value of material to be attended to (e.g., writing with magic markers, presenting academic material with various colors) may help prevent visual confusion.
5. Providing practice in discriminating confusing letters (e.g., "d" vs. "b"), and providing spatial orientation such as an arrowed line on a desk to be accompanied by verbal cue ("b always goes with the arrow") may prove helpful.

## Steven

Steven is a 7-year-old male referred by his classroom teacher because of poor academic progress. Steven is the youngest of five children; his father is an unemployed laborer. This is the third school Steven has attended. In kindergarten, he was viewed as slightly below average in all academic areas. He had some difficulty learning the phonics skills that were included in the kindergarten curriculum. No oral reading was taught during Steven's kindergarten. Steven's family moved to another state in the summer prior to his first-grade year. As a first grader, he was rated as slightly below average in most subjects, but as failing in reading. A basal reading series was used in this first-grade classroom, and oral reading was emphasized. There were few phonics drills.

Just before beginning second grade, Steven's family moved again, this time to a district in which most pupils performed above the national average. His second-grade teacher used both basal reading material and phonics drills, but the teacher was most concerned about Steven's lack of phonics skills. Because he was unable to decode unknown words, he had trouble reading second-grade level stories. He reportedly was experiencing some difficulty with a unit of story-type problems in arithmetic as well. Steven's handwriting was poor compared to peers but was much improved when he was prompted to work slowly and do his best. Much classwork was left uncompleted in class, and Steven's teacher found he was rarely motivated to do academics. Yet he was a popular child who did well in sports. Health and developmental data were unremarkable.

The local school psychologist administered a battery of tests that yielded the following results:

**Wechsler Intelligence Scale for Children–III**

| Verbal tests | | Performance tests | |
|---|---|---|---|
| Information | 10 | Picture Completion | 11 |
| Similarities | 11 | Coding | 12 |
| Arithmetic | 8 | Picture Arrangement | 10 |
| Vocabulary | 11 | Block Design | 9 |
| Comprehension | 9 | Object Assembly | 8 |
| Digit Span | 9 | Symbol Search | 9 |

Verbal IQ = 99 Performance IQ = 100 Full Scale IQ = 99

**Bender Gestalt Test**

Koppitz Errors 5 Standard Score 104

**Wide Range Assessment of Learning and Memory**

| | |
|---|---|
| Visual Memory | 10 |
| Design Memory | 9 |
| Verbal Learning | 10 |
| Story Memory | 8 |
| Memory Screening Index | 95 |

(continued)

**Personality Inventory for Children**

None of the clinical scales were elevated.

As part of the local school's comprehensive assessment, a master's level educational diagnostician administered the following test:

**Wechsler Individual Achievement Test**

| | |
|---|---|
| Basic Reading | 94 |
| Mathematics Reasoning | 94 |
| Spelling | 91 |
| Reading Comprehension | 96 |
| Numerical Operations | 87 |
| Listening Comprehension | 90 |
| Oral Expression | 99 |

Steven worked cooperatively but unenthusiastically during the assessment. He was attentive and well focused. He had no problems comprehending what was said, he organized his thoughts adequately, and his verbal expression was clear and effective. Steven worked adequately with pencil and paper.

Neither Steven's ability profile nor observations of his test behavior suggested problems with information processing. Whereas he scored 12 points below his Full Scale IQ on one of the seven achievement subtests, this ability–achievement difference is relatively small, especially considering that neither test is perfectly reliable. The regression formula that produces a predicted score for each WIAT subtest based on his WISC–III Full Scale IQ indicated that this difference is not statistically significant. There were no signs that short-term memory problems were holding him back. Perhaps more important, Steven's one low achievement score is in arithmetic, and arithmetic concerns have not been conspicuous in teachers' reports of Steven's academic failure. One may also question the match between the content of the WIAT subtest (computational problems) and the current instructional emphasis in Steven's classroom (arithmetic story problems). In addition, a review of Steven's educational history may lead the discerning reader to conclude that there are factors other than learning disabilities that may have contributed to his school failure. For instance, he has had three separate approaches to reading during his 3 years of school. He reportedly is unmotivated in class. Comparing him with his current classmates, who are described as unrepresentatively capable, may also accentuate minor academic problems.

Steven, unlike Alice, would probably be concluded by his school's staff to be ineligible for special education learning disabilities services. Nonetheless, several recommendations may be made:

1. A behavior modification system, to enhance classroom productivity by providing positive reinforcement for task completion, is recommended.
2. A review of both phonics skills and basic sight vocabulary is suggested. Because the WIAT is not sufficiently detailed to allow a careful analysis, a criterion-referenced test administered by Steven's teacher may be required. Remedial drills designed to teach missing skills will then be required.
3. Providing Steven success experiences as a means of building self-esteem would appear to be important. Perhaps highlighting his competency in sports would provide a means to accomplish this end.

## Mark

Mental retardation is, of course, sometimes diagnosed for the first time when a child is in elementary school. Many of the same considerations for preschoolers that were discussed in Chapter 4—the presence of a uniformly low ability profile and low scores on standardized adaptive behavior measures—are also important for school-age children. Academic achievement tests are also used when children of elementary school age are suspected of having mental retardation. When academic achievement tests are combined with the intelligence tests suitable for children of school age, which tend to be superior psychometrically to preschool tests, some of the most certain diagnoses of mental retardation occur.

Consider 7-year-old Mark. His parents had noticed few differences in the rates at which he and his older siblings acquired developmental skills such as walking, talking, independent toileting, and eating. In retrospect, they noted he may have been a bit slower to catch on to things than his siblings. Discernible differences did appear, however, when Mark started preschool. Here his teachers described him as a nice boy but severely "immature." He was held out of kindergarten until age 6 in the hope that 1 additional year of growth would solve the immaturity problem. He struggled academically in the first grade as well, but his teacher attributed many of his problems to poor effort. Finally, after a hearing and vision screening were passed, a psychological and educational evaluation was conducted at the end of his first-grade year. The following scores resulted:

**Wechsler Intelligence Scale for Children–III**

| Verbal tests | | Performance tests | |
|---|---|---|---|
| Information | 6 | Picture Completion | 7 |
| Similarities | 5 | Coding | 5 |
| Arithmetic | 3 | Picture Arrangement | 4 |
| Vocabulary | 5 | Block Design | 5 |
| Comprehension | 3 | Object Assembly | 4 |
| Digit Span | 7 | Symbol Search | 3 |

Verbal IQ = 69 Performance IQ = 70 Full Scale IQ = 67

**Vineland Adaptive Behavior Scale–Interview Edition**

Adaptive Behavior Composite 67

**Wechsler Individual Achievement Test**

| Subtest | Standard score |
|---|---|
| Basic Reading | 69 |
| Mathematics Reasoning | 74 |
| Spelling | 67 |
| Reading Comprehension | 66 |
| Numerical Operations | 70 |

Mark is a child with mild mental retardation and qualifies in most states for special education services. Students at his ability level usually master basic academic skills, and the skills are usually the focus of instruction during the elementary years. Even though the disability is a mild one, the diagnosis can be made with considerable assurance because of the quality of instruments available. Not only does the WISC–III have excellent qualities of reliability and validity, but it also offers multiple subtests, each of which affords Mark a chance to demonstrate his ability. In Mark's case, he scores uniformly poorly on all of these subtests. As would be true for preschool children, his low IQ score must be substantiated by impaired adaptive behavior. This substantiation is accomplished by interviewing Mark's parents and completing the Vineland Adaptive Behavior Scales based on their comments.

The Vineland scales assess important nonacademic aspects of development, but for school children the acquisition of academic skills is a conspicuous and critical developmental task. Consequently, if a youngster has mental retardation the disability should be reflected in failure to learn at a typical rate in school. Objective, norm-referenced tests of academic achievement represent the most effective method of documenting that these academic deficiencies exist. In Mark's case, his achievement standard scores are consistent with his ability scores. The achievement scores can be used by the examiner to substantiate the hypothesis that he lacks sufficient ability to succeed in school unless he is provided special education help.

Mark's case highlights an additional point. Children who are failing in school often do not receive prompt attention from psychologists or special educators. Like Mark, many of these children are assumed to be merely "immature" (an imprecise term that explains nothing), lacking motivation, or any of a number of "pet" explanations evoked by those involved with the child. Such explanations, however, represent only one of many possible explanations for school failure. An alternative possibility for each of these children is the presence of a learning handicap (e.g., a severe information processing disability, mental retardation) that logically should be ruled out. Unfortunately, there are many instances in which pupils with learning handicaps are referred for evaluation only after several years of school failure have occurred and the child's inherent enthusiasm to learn has been seriously eroded.

Consideration of learning problems as one explanation for school failure should always be entertained, and necessary referrals should be made in timely fashion. This is especially true if the child is doing so poorly that grade retention is being contemplated.

## SUMMARY

Psychologists generally use individual tests of academic achievement because using such tests allow a comprehensive picture of the child to emerge. Standardized achievement tests permit pupils' ability and academic levels to be compared objectively so that learning disabilities can be detected. Their use may also help substantiate the presence of mental retardation. Occasionally, psychologists use achievement tests alone to index academic levels of an individual learner. However, this latter concern is most often addressed by educators, some of whom may use the tests reviewed in this chapter.

Standardized achievement tests have the advantages associated with other psychological tests. They are capable of being examined for objective evidence of reliability and validity. They often allow standard scores to be generated, and these scores may facilitate comparisons among pupils and between test scores produced by the same pupil. Care must be taken, however, to ensure that the tests have adequate content validity; that is, they should agree with what is being taught in local classrooms.

Unfortunately, standardized individual achievement tests are generally not able to identify precise academic deficits or to guide precision teaching. Most of the achievement tests reviewed in this chapter have too few items assessing any particular skill for such purposes. Besides, many psychologists are neither trained to identify such specific skills nor do they see such an undertaking as part of their assessment responsibilities. In many cases, a more finely detailed educational assessment must follow psychological assessment and continue throughout the teaching process, if educational interventions are to be accurately focused.

## Study Questions

1. Contrast norm-referenced and criterion-referenced approaches to testing.
2. What are some common advantages that lead classroom teachers to select criterion-referenced testing?
3. State the advantages that norm-referenced tests have over criterion-referenced tests in identifying pupils with learning disabilities.
4. Why might a specific achievement test be suitable in one school district but unsuitable in another?
5. What advantages does the Wechsler Individual Achievement Test have over the Wide Range Achievement Test–3?
6. Why might a test such as the Gray Oral Reading Test–3 be preferred over the Peabody Individual Achievement Test–Revised?

## CHAPTER SEVEN

# Personality Measures

## Diagnosing Children's and Adolescents' Emotional Problems

The test instruments used for diagnosing children's and adolescents' emotional problems are amazingly diverse in their form, method of administration, and scoring, as well as in the information they produce. Some instruments require children to draw or tell stories; others depend on parents or teachers to rate the presence and severity of symptoms; and still others require the child or teenager to confirm or deny certain feelings, attitudes, or beliefs that are posed as objective questions. Moreover, there is no consensus about the label that should be used to describe these instruments: personality, behavior, adjustment, social-emotional, or affective. There is, however, some consensus on the uses of personality tests. Simply put, psychologists use personality tests to help identify, classify, or clarify.

For purposes of identification, tests are used to distinguish between children with emotional or behavior problems and children without. Conceptually, this is analogous to using IQ tests to identify children with mental retardation. Once scores reach certain threshold levels, then the diagnostician becomes increasingly convinced that the person may be classifiable. In the case of IQ and mental retardation, scores of about 70 typically are used as a cutoff. Of course, other sources of information, such as developmental and social history and adaptive behavior, would be expected to influence a final clinical judgment about a diagnosis (classification) as significant as mental retardation. The same holds true when identifying emotional problems.

Consider the real-life challenge of determining if a student has severe enough emotional problems to interfere with school performance and require special education services (i.e., in essence, the definition of "serious emotional disturbance" under IDEA; see p. 197).

Tests that produce composite or summary scores of adjustment, such as the Achenbach Teacher Report Form (TRF), or that describe in quantifiable terms how likely children with a particular pattern are to require special education services, such as the Personality Inventory for Children (PIC), offer huge advantages. To say that this individual child's composite adjustment score is at the 99th percentile or that the child's pattern is highly compatible with other students requiring special education placement, as the PIC does (see Table 7.1), helps the diagnostician to be confident that the student is properly identified. In the real world, objective information from quantifiable parent and teacher questionnaires proves invaluable, but these questionnaires too must be supplemented with the child's social history, classroom observations, or personal interview before clinical judgment about emotional disability can occur. Objective instruments prove most helpful in the problem of classification.

Classification expands upon simple identification in that an attempt is made to place individuals into known categories. The categories are assumed to possess common characteristics. The classic example of classification occurs when diagnosticians attempt to establish a diagnosis within a formal nosology system (e.g., DSM-IV, see p. 198). Assume that a classroom teacher has referred a student for evaluation and the initial data overwhelmingly point toward the presence of emotional and behavioral difficulties. The child seems to be aggressive with peers, noncompliant with teachers, and irritable. Although there may be consensus on the presence of a problem, its nature may be in dispute. Is the student more depressed or more oppositional and noncompliant? In this situation, diagnosticians may consult the criteria for various disorders in DSM-IV and, in this case,

Table 7.1. Similarity of child's PIC profile with various class placements

| Class placement | Correlation coefficients |
|---|---|
| General classroom | −.43 |
| Classroom for students with emotional disturbance | .08 |
| Resource/mainstream for students with LD | .06 |
| Self-contained special education for LD | .20 |
| Self-contained special education for students with mild mental retardation | .64 |

Adapted from Lachar & Gdowski (1985, 1989). A WPS report, Western Psychological Services, © 1985, 1989.

Individual student's PIC results can be compared with those children already enrolled in various programs to determine the degree of similarity. The values can be interpreted as correlation coefficients. This student's profile was dissimilar to children in general class placement without special services, only slightly similar to those with emotional disturbance or learning disability but much more similar to those children in self-contained classrooms for mild mental retardation. In some instances, this information can help with placement decisions. (LD = learning disability.)

might consider dysthymia (a mood disorder) and oppositional defiant disorder (characterized primarily by noncompliance).

The situation may also warrant use of psychological tests, especially multidimensional personality questionnaires. Tests such as the Minnesota Multiphasic Personality Inventory–Adolescent (MMPI–A), PIC, and Child Behavior Checklist (CBCL) contain several scales, each of which produces norm-referenced standard scores on a particular dimension of behavior, adjustment, or personality. Either singularly or in combination, these scales often generate recognizable score patterns that suggest specific diagnoses. Highly researched instruments such as the MMPI and PIC produce their own meaningful profiles that were developed and possess clinical significance independent of systems such as DSM-IV (see discussion of actuarial interpretation, p. 204). Much of the value of multidimensional personality questionnaires rests on their empirical, quantitative bases, which gives these techniques an edge over less precise diagnostic techniques such as interviewing. Even so, non-objective (so-called "projective") tests such as Thematic Apperception Test (TAT) and Rorschach inkblot technique sometimes play a valuable adjunctive role in classification.

Identification and classification of emotional and behavior problems can be accomplished without in-depth theorizing about personality development or even a cohesive theory about how psychopathology develops. Much of the logic for such practices is subsumed under the general principles and techniques of measurement discussed in Chapter 1. Similarly, the contemporary diagnostic systems, specifically DSM-IV, are atheoretical. They are valuable because they permit reliable diagnoses and afford a basis for collecting information about causes, natural history, and the effects of various treatment of specific disorders. DSM-IV does not explain why a disorder might occur or reveal how to correct it. It is in this final regard (theorizing about causes and establishing a treatment plan) that assessment that merely identifies and classifies is most lacking. To treat various conditions effectively, especially if treatment is nonpharmacological (does not involve medication), requires a theory of development, personality, and psychopathology.

It is in the final purpose for using personality tests—to clarify—that theories such as ego psychology, psychoanalysis, cognitive, and attribution theory have a role. Similarly, it is in the name of clarification that projective tests often have unique advantages. For example, assume that the above-mentioned student has an emotional problem (the identification issue) and that his condition falls into the category of oppositional defiant disorder (the classification issue). His treatment team is considering individual psychotherapy as one aspect of treatment, yet they are unsure about its value. The team would like to know if there are sources of frustration that fuel the child's anger, whether there are specific areas of his life in which he feels incompetent or threatened, whether there are perceived sources of nurturance (e.g., a parent, a friend) that can be capitalized on in therapy, and whether an inner drive to resolve his problems exists. Although objective personality techniques often have value in identifying and classifying, they may be severely limited in their ability to speak to issues such as these. In order to clarify, projective techniques, such as TAT, Rorschach, drawing, and sentence completion, may be required.

## CONSTITUENTS OF DISTURBED BEHAVIOR

Although there are several theoretical explanations for how disturbed behavior develops, the options are more limited when it comes to determining just what constitutes disturbed behavior. Of the two prevailing approaches used in the 1990s, one is a definition and one a classification system; IDEA provides a definition of disturbed behavior, and the *Diagnostic and Statistical Manual of Mental Disorders-IV* (DSM-IV) (American Psychiatric Association, 1994) provides a classification system. There are other systems in existence, but for all practical purposes, these two represent the mainstay. The reason has to do with the institutions each serves. IDEA is educational in its scope, and DSM-IV is psychiatric; therefore, between the two definitions, public schools and most mental health agencies and hospitals are covered. Very few service providers and provider agencies exist that do not operate within one of the two systems. Whereas these systems formally organize and categorize various disturbances, they are also the informal languages of their settings; that is, the terminology contained in each system has become the educational and mental health jargon of disturbances.

### Federal Definition

The Education for All Handicapped Children Act, PL 94-142, was passed as the 142nd law of the 94th Congress in 1975 and was reauthorized with the passage of IDEA (PL 101-476) in 1990. Its goal is to guarantee a free and appropriate public education in the least restrictive environment to all children with disabilities, ages 3–21. Additional rights included in the law are parental access to records, parental participation in the development of educational plans for their child, nondiscriminatory assessment practices and instruments, and the right to due process. The law outlines and defines disabling conditions for which special education services are to be provided such as learning disabilities, mental retardation, physical disabilities, sensory impairment (deaf, hard of hearing, visually impaired), and serious emotional disability. According to the law, *serious emotional disturbance* (SED) is defined as follows:

> The term means a condition exhibiting one or more of the following characteristics over a long period of time and to a marked extent, which adversely affects educational performance:
>
> 1. An inability to learn which cannot be explained by intellectual, sensory, or health factors;
> 2. An inability to build or maintain satisfactory relationships with peers and teachers;
> 3. Inappropriate types of behavior or feelings under normal circumstances;
> 4. A general pervasive mood of unhappiness or depression;
> 5. A tendency to develop physical symptoms or fears associated with personal or school problems.
>
> The term includes children who are schizophrenic. The term does not include children who are socially maladjusted unless it is determined that they are seriously emotionally disturbed. [IDEA, §121(a)(5)]

Two key points need to be highlighted about the SED definition. First, it mandates that the disturbing behavior(s) adversely affect educational performance. Second, it specifically excludes children who are "socially maladjusted" unless it can be shown that they also meet the criteria for SED. With both of these points, the federal definition is severely lacking by not providing criteria that help specify terms such as "adverse affect" and "socially maladjusted." Does adverse affect mean getting Cs when in fact the student is gifted and quite capable of getting As? Does it mean getting all Fs, or just poor performance on yearly achievement tests? Furthermore, the behaviors that produce this affect must exist over a "long period of time." Again, is this 4 weeks, 2 semesters, or 6 months?

Difficulties also arise when considering whether emotional-behavioral problems affect education. For instance, a child who is experiencing significant family problems may not be adversely affected in terms of school performance, in which case education services would probably not be provided. Education professionals have attempted to distinguish between mental health needs and school-based, educationally relevant needs, acknowledging that whereas many children may be in need of some kind of help, the services should not be educationally tied. These children might benefit from private counseling or family therapy but not specialized instruction in a separate setting outside the general classroom.

The second point—the meaning of social maladjustment—is the focus of a much larger debate. Many have taken it to mean behavior in which there is a chronic violation of societal rules and basic rights of others. In addition, there seems to be a control issue implied with this behavior pattern; namely, social maladjustment is believed to mean that a student has control of his or her behavior and willfully chooses to behave in such a manner. The presence of both of these factors (chronic rule violations by volition) is considered by some to rule out a serious emotional impairment. Such children may be called "behavior disordered," a categorization that probably would not warrant special education services according to this line of thinking. For consumers of special education services, including parents, children, and education professionals, this lack of uniformity leads to confusion and frustration. Not only do individual states differ on the SED issue, school districts within a given state vary, as do individual psychologists. Consequently, a child may receive service in Pennsylvania but not in Idaho, or within District A in Arizona but not within District B. All aspects of SED service, such as the amount of program time provided to the student and behaviors that meet eligibility requirements, are subject to this kind of variability by individual school districts so long as the definition remains imprecise.

## DSM-IV

DSM-IV, published in 1994, is a fourth-generation revision of the original DSM, that was developed in 1952 by the American Psychiatric Association. The manual is the primary classification system for psychiatric disturbances occurring in children and adults. Just as IDEA is the language of schools and special education, DSM is the language of hospitals and mental health. It is widely used by everyone connected with psychiatry, from trainers and prospective clinicians to insurance companies to hospital staff workers. DSM-IV is a comprehensive listing of more than 200 psychiatric disorders, each with its own code number and description. The manual does not espouse any particular theoretical view. Rather, descriptions of the disorders are primarily concerned with "essential features." The manual is organized around several major headings, including Disorders Usually Evident in Infancy, Childhood, or Adolescence; Schizophrenia and Other Psychotic Disorders; Mood Disorders; Anxiety Disorders; Sexual Disorders and Gender Identity Disorders; and Adjustment Disorders; among others. Within each heading, individual disorders and their subtypes are listed along with the following descriptors: associated features, age at onset, course, prevalence, familial pattern, and differential diagnosis. In order for a clinician to diagnose a condition, the behavior must meet the required diagnostic criteria for each disorder. For many disorders, the criteria are arranged menu style, in a way that some but not necessarily all criteria must be met. DSM-IV employs a multiaxial system of diagnosis that consists of five axes, each for assessment of a different area of the individual. Not every individual has a diagnosis on each axis, however. Axis I is where clinical syndromes such as Major Depression or Panic Disorder and learning disorders (e.g., Reading Disorder, Expressive Language Disorder) are recorded. Axis II is for personality disorders and mental retardation, and Axis III is for physical disorders and conditions. Axis IV is where psychosocial (e.g., death of a family member) and environmental problems (e.g., unsafe neighborhood) are listed. Axis V is a rating of global assessment of functioning, generally referenced to the individual's current level of functioning, ranging from 100 being superior functioning to 1 being grossly impaired functioning. Of the five, Axis I is usually the principal diagnosis, although Axes I, II, and III are considered to compose the official diagnostic assessment (see Illustration 7.1).

DSM-IV enjoys widespread use and is essentially the standard of the industry. However, it is not without criticism. Chief among these has been concern over reliability and validity (Knoff, 1986), which appears to have been improved with the 1994 publication of DSM-IV.

The DSM system has been criticized for the use of adult criteria to diagnose children with disorders like schizophrenia, mood disorders including depression and bipolar illness, sexual disorders, and personality disorders (Clarizio & McCoy, 1983). The manual states that the essential features of the disorders are manifested in roughly the same manner in children as they are in adults; hence, no separate categories are needed for lower ages. It is acknowledged, however, that there are some age-specific characteristics that apply when giving a child one of these diagnoses, and the manual does include them in descriptions of disorders. For example, a major depressive episode in a child might include irritable rather than depressed mood; rather than weight loss that may occur among adults, children may merely fail to make expected weight gains.

Although both DSM-IV and IDEA define disturbed behavior that applies to children and adolescents, the use of the definitions still remain separate in practice. Much of the difficulty in bridging the two approaches has to do with agencies and funding. For a school district to receive funding for a child with SED, the child must meet the criteria of IDEA; health care payments often require a DSM diagnosis. Also, SED as defined by educational law, and childhood disorders as defined by DSM, are not necessarily interchangeable. A child treated with a DSM-IV diagnosis of bipolar disorder may or may not be identified as having SED in the local school district, depending on that

## Illustration 7.1

### DSM-IV DIAGNOSTIC ASSESSMENT

Craig is an 11-year-old boy with a long-standing history of attention-deficit/hyperactivity disorder (ADHD) and a learning disability in math. In addition, he has asthma for which he regularly takes medication. Despite these difficulties, Craig has always done relatively well both at school and at home; there is no history of behavior problems. Craig's parents have recently separated, with no definite plans about either divorce or reconciliation. Craig and his siblings have remained with their mother; contact with the father is sporadic until he finalizes new living arrangements. Since the onset of the separation, Craig has been having significant problems at home and school, as well as increased asthma symptoms. Problems reported by his mother and his teacher include fighting with peers, verbal aggressiveness, defiance, irritability, and tiredness. The following diagnoses would be made of Craig:

Axis I: ADHD, developmental arithmetic disorder
Axis II: No diagnosis
Axis III: Asthma
Axis IV: Chronic health problems, parents' divorce
Axis V: 70

school's SED guidelines and subsequent determination of the special education multidisciplinary team. Similarly, an SED diagnosis alone is insufficient to imply the need for psychiatric or outpatient mental health services. The differences between systems, coupled with the public law's imprecise terms, make for trying circumstances for those attempting to secure services or determine placements for children. Ideally, such situations could be avoided by using supplemental data to bolster what is lacking in each approach, with the hope that relevant information will emerge and be of use to all agencies involved with a child.

Psychological testing has much to offer in such circumstances. Classification systems are based on accurate diagnosis, and psychological testing can help the diagnostician decide on a diagnosis. Treatment planning also follows from accurate diagnosis; therefore, a relevant, realistic treatment plan can result from testing as well. A good example of psychological testing's utility can be seen with an SED diagnosis. The diagnosis must reflect an unexplainable inability to learn as well as educational impairment. Intelligence and achievement levels generally must be assessed and learning disabilities ruled out as a cause of the educational impairment. Psychological tests can often establish and clarify these aspects beyond what observation or parent or teacher report can do alone. Within the DSM-IV classification, psychological testing also aids the diagnostic process. Questions of differential diagnosis often rest on data derived from testing. For instance, an associated characteristic of depressed adolescent males is antisocially acting out. These behaviors could easily be misinterpreted as indicating only a conduct disorder diagnosis. In the context of emotional/personality assessment, however, such symptoms can be more appropriately identified as part of a larger, different diagnostic picture. The in-depth nature of psychological testing and its analysis and interpretation often serve to bridge the two classification systems by providing data applicable in either situation.

## OBJECTIVE ASSESSMENT MEASURES

This section deals with two types of objective measures: self-report and informant (parent or teacher) report measures. These measures are objective in the sense that responses are quantifiable, and there is usually an existing body of research that supports the resulting personality profile types. Interpretation is not entirely qualitative or subjective on the part of the psychologist. However, because these measures rely on one person's viewpoint, they are open to potential bias or distortion on the part of the individual completing them. For instance, on the Minnesota Multiphasic Personality Inventory (a self-report measure), an individual may deny problems out of fear or embarrassment, thereby distorting the resulting profile. Similarly, on the Child Behavior Checklist (a parent-report measure), the parent may wish to have the child appear better or worse than he or she actually is. So, although objective measures yield scores and profiles that have empirical support, the perspective of each individual rater must always be taken into consideration when interpreting the results.

Strengths of objective measures include their time and cost efficiency for the subjects of the evaluation and the psychologists alike. Although some instruments may take a parent up to 2 hours to complete, they may take the psychologist only 20 minutes to score and interpret. That, compared to 2 hours of professional time that might be required to collect similar information, represents a considerable savings. Also, paper-and-pencil rating scales and inventories tend to be more reliable and valid than less structured clinical interviews.

## Minnesota Multiphasic Personality Inventory

The MMPI is a true/false self-report inventory, consisting of 566 items, which when scored results in a personality profile type. Probably no single instrument is more widely researched or written about than the MMPI. The MMPI was originally developed in 1937 by S.R. Hathaway and J.C. McKinley at the University of Minnesota. Three years later, the first norms came out and were based on a pool of 800 clinical subjects and 1,500 nonclinical (free of identifiable psychiatric problems) subjects who were drawn from hospital visitors, local clients from the University of Minnesota testing center, and medical patients. The scale was based on questions a psychiatrist or psychologist might ask in an interview, and as expected, people with various disorders responded differently from one another and from people without disorders. From these initial differences, researchers went on to empirically separate the groups such that each scale deals with either a type of mental disorder or a personality type such as Depression, Mania, or Social Introversion.

The traditional MMPI consists of 3 validity scales and 10 clinical scales. The validity scales are designed to guard against faking and defensiveness in a respondent's answers. The validity scales are the L or lie scale, for evaluating frankness; the F or infrequency scale, which includes items that are responded to in the same manner by at least 90% of nonclinical people; and the K, or defensiveness scale, which corrects for subtle or not-so-subtle test-taking defensiveness, and thus aids the test's discriminating power. Any extreme deviation is often reflected in the validity scales, making it hard for a person to beat the test by making him- or herself look drastically better or worse than he or she really is. The MMPI yields T-scores with a mean of 50 and standard deviation of 10. The 10 clinical scales are shown in Table 7.2. Rather than being referred to by their original name (e.g., Hypochondriasis), scales are typically referred to by their number, as in "she scored 100 on 2 and 65 on 9." The MMPI is scaled in an easily understandable way. The higher the elevation is on each scale, the more pathology is present. The only exception to this is the masculinity/femininity scale, where a high score means the patient has traits typically associated with the other sex. A high score by a male means that he has aesthetic interests, is likely to be sensitive, and tends to be dependent. A high score by a female means she tends to be independent and aggressive.

Table 7.2. MMPI clinical scales

| Scale | | Paraphrased sample item | High scores imply |
|---|---|---|---|
| 1 | Hypochondriasis | My head feels tender. (True) | Inappropriate concern with health |
| 2 | Depression | What happens to me doesn't matter. (True) | Sadness, depression, lack of energy |
| 3 | Hysteria | I get along with people even if they do bad things. (True) | Denial, expression of emotions, or depression somatically |
| 4 | Psychopathic Deviation | I never have been in legal trouble. (False) | Nonconformity, acting out, impulsivity |
| 5 | Masculinity/ Femininity | I like to collect flowers and to nurture house plants. (True for men) | For men: aesthetic interests, sensitivity<br>For women: assertiveness, independence |
| 6 | Paranoia | No enemies want to harm me. (False) | Interpersonal sensitivity, suspiciousness, guardedness |
| 7 | Psychasthenia | I am worried that my reading ability is not as good as it used to be. (True) | Overcontrol, overorganization, obsessive-compulsive |
| 8 | Schizophrenia | I often feel lonely even if other people are around. (True) | Emotional confusion, isolation, mental deterioration |
| 9 | Mania | I like to create excitement when I am bored. (True) | Hyperactivity, elation, overoptimism |
| 0 | Social Introversion | I am wounded when people criticize or scold me. (True) | Introversion, social apprehension, or isolation |

Adapted from Hathaway and McKinley (1943).

Interpretation of the MMPI uses an "actuarial" approach. When actuarial tables are used in life insurance, the intent is to place individuals into one set of categories and then determine what behaviors or outcomes are associated with each category; individuals may be categorized by age, current health status, and family history of diseases. Based on such data, probability of longevity is assessed and used to fix the size of the premiums. Similarly, individuals may be categorized by their MMPI profiles, age, and sex. The profile types can then be studied to find out what sort of behaviors such people engage in, such as a tendency for substance abuse or acting out. Profiles may be used for a variety of purposes, such as to determine how well someone may do in using a particular medication or whether juvenile delinquency or alcoholism is associated with a profile type. The actuarial approach begins by using a 2-point code. These 2 points are determined by selecting the two highest clinical scales (provided that the high scores are above 70 T-score). For example, 4–9 is Psychopathic Deviate (Scale 4) and Mania (Scale 9) or 2–0 is Depression (Scale 2) and Social Introversion (Scale 0). The code type is then looked up in one of several "cookbooks," which provide behavioral descriptors and interpretations that are based on actuarial data (see Illustration 7.2 for an example).

The traditional MMPI can be used with adolescents as well as with adults, but there are greater limitations for use with adolescents. The minimal reading level required for the instrument may be as high as ninth grade (Brown, 1986); this reading level limits using the test for many adolescents. The lowest norms extend downward to age 14, although research has begun looking at norms for 13-year-olds (Colligan & Offord, 1987). Frequently used adolescent norms (Marks, Seeman, & Haller, 1974) are becoming dated, as they were based in part on results from the original Minnesota sample plus supplemental data gathered in the mid-1960s (Archer, 1987). Although specific comparisons are difficult to make because of differences in selection procedures, the general finding is that adolescents today yield profiles different from adolescents of the Marks et al. (1974) norms. The cautious psychologist may want to use profiles that are plotted with both contemporary and older norms for comparative purposes (Colligan & Offord, 1987).

In 1989, 46 years after its publication, the original MMPI was updated (MMPI–2) (Butcher, Dahlstrom, Graham, Tellegen, & Kraemmer, 1989) with contemporary item wording, new norms, and several new supplemental scales. Importantly, whereas the original scale was suitable for adolescent use, the MMPI–2 was developed specifically for individuals 18 years and older, with no norms available for teen-

## Illustration 7.2

### EXAMPLE OF MMPI ACTUARIAL INTERPRETATION

The following information is based on actuarial interpretation of an elevated 6–8 profile on the MMPI.

For both adolescents and adults, a 6–8 profile suggests serious psychopathology. Associated behaviors for both populations include delusional thinking, feelings of persecution, paranoid ideation, and hallucinations. Individuals with this profile are socially isolated, and their behavior is often unpredictable. Thought processes are significantly impaired and accompanied by difficulties in concentration and schizophrenic ideation.

The following characteristics have been noted in an adolescent sample:

1. Physical punishment was the primary form of discipline; nearly half received beatings for misbehavior.
2. They frequently changed schools during their elementary years; 30% were in five or more schools.
3. They were not well liked by their peer group.
4. These adolescents showed little insight into their own problems.
5. More than half used drugs, usually in connection with a suicide attempt.

*Source:* Adapted from Archer (1987); Marks et al. (1974).

agers. Fortunately, at about this time an MMPI especially for teenagers, the Minnesota Multiphasic Personality Inventory–Adolescent (Butcher et al., 1992), was published. This test was the first version of the MMPI intended for adolescent usage. It contains norms specifically developed for adolescents and encompasses test items that have been revised to be sensitive to the adolescents' backgrounds and life experiences (e.g., questions about religious attitudes and sexual preferences have been omitted). But the MMPI–A has retained the basic 13 scales of the original MMPI. In addition, the MMPI–A contains psychometric advances not present in the traditional MMPI. For example, the characteristics measured by many of the MMPI scales, such as a tendency toward mania, are not distributed in the bell-shaped frequency distribution seen among IQ and some other ability scores. In addition, the distribution of the various MMPI scales tend to differ from each other (antisocial characteristic [Pd scale] may be differently distributed from tendencies toward mania [Ma scale]). In the traditional MMPI, T-scores (a form of standard score) were not equivalent across the scales; a T-score of 70 on one scale may be associated with a different percentile rank than a T-score of 70 on another scale (Archer, 1992). This problem was corrected in the MMPI–A by a technique called uniform T-score transformation procedures that should help clinicians better understand score values. The briefer form of the MMPI–A consists of 350 items, which is somewhat shorter than the original MMPI. A longer version allows scores to be produced not only on the standard clinical and validity scales but also on many so-called content-, supplemental-, and sub-scales. These scales are derived by reorganization of the tests' items in unique ways to permit investigation of areas of adjustment and personality not directly addressed by the standard scales (see Table 7.3).

Although clinicians will continue to use the critical features of actuarial interpretation and whereas it is assumed that much of what has been learned over the years with teenager and adult research on the MMPI will have some relevance to clinical use of the MMPI–A (Archer, 1992), MMPI interpretation for adolescents is not without potential problems. The new adolescent norms of the MMPI–A do not always produce the same values or even the same profile configuration as the adolescent norms for the traditional MMPI. This may leave diagnosticians in a quandary in that much actuarial information was derived using the traditional MMPI. Additional research (e.g., Archer, 1992; Archer, Stolberg, Gordon, & Goldman, 1986) has found that adolescents with significant emotional and behavioral difficulties may score below the commonly used 70 T-score clinical cutoff. Thus, a less stringent cutoff value may be necessary, and the diagnostician must rely on clinical judgment and other data sources to help produce accurate conclusions. Still, the advantages such as the capability to receive a detailed report for the clinician and an accompanying feedback document for the adolescent (which can be computer generated) will keep the MMPI and MMPI–A popular.

## Child Behavior Checklist

The CBCL is one of four measures developed by Thomas Achenbach and Craig Edelbrock (1983; Achenbach, 1991a) for assessing the prob-

Table 7.3. Abbreviated overview of the MMPI–A scales and subscales—Item regroupings

| | |
|---|---|
| *Basic Profile Scales (17 scales)* | |
| *Standard Scales* (13) | |
| (Traditional 3 validity scales and 10 clinical scales) | |
| Additional Validity Scales (4) | |
| *Subscales of F* Scale | $F_1/F_2$ |
| Variable Response Inconsistency | *VRIN* |
| True Response Inconsistency | *TRIN* |
| *Content and Supplementary Scales*[a] | |
| Content Scales[b] (Some of these also appear in MMPI–2) | |
| Anxiety | *A-anx* |
| Depression | *A-dep* |
| Health Concerns | *A-hea* |
| Anger | *A-ang* |
| Conduct Problems | *A-con* |
| Low Self-esteem | *A-lse* |
| Social Discomfort | *A-sod* |
| Family Problems | *A-fam* |
| Negative Treatment Indicators | *A-trt* |
| *Supplementary Scales*[c] (some of these also appear on MMPI–2) | |
| MacAndrew Alcoholism–Revised | *MAC-R* |
| Alcohol/Drug Problem Acknowledgment | *ACK* |
| Alcohol/Drug Problem Potential | *PRO* |
| Immaturity | *IMM* |
| Anxiety | *A* |
| Repression | *R* |
| *Harris-Lingoes and Si Subscales*[d] | |
| *Harris-Lingoes Subscales*[e] (some of these also appear on MMPI–2) | |
| Subjective depression | $D_1$ |
| Psychomotor retardation | $D_2$ |
| Denial of social anxiety | $Hy_1$ |
| Need for affection | $Hy_2$ |
| Familial discord | $Pd_1$ |
| Social imperturbability | $Pd_3$ |
| Self-alienation | $Pd_5$ |
| Persecutory ideas | $Pa_1$ |
| Poignancy | $Pa_2$ |
| Social alienation | $Sc_1$ |
| Lack of ego mastery, conative | $Sc_4$ |
| Bizarre sensory experiences | $Sc_6$ |
| Amorality | $Ma_1$ |
| Ego inflation | $Ma_4$ |
| *Si Subscales*[f] (some of these also appear on MMPI–2) | |
| Shyness/Self-Consciousness | $Si_1$ |
| Alienation-Self and others | $Si_3$ |

From MMPI-A: Assessing adolescent psychopathology (pp. 59–60), by R.P. Archer, 1992, Hillsdale, NJ: Lawrence Erlbaum Associates. © 1992; reprinted by permission.

[a]21 total Content and Supplementary scales.
[b]9 of the 15 Content Scales.
[c]6 total Supplementary Scales.
[d]31 total subscales.
[e]14 of the 28 Harris-Lingoes subscales.
[f]3 Si subscales.

lem behavior of children ages 4–16 years. The other measures are the Teacher's Report Form (Achenbach, 1991b, 1991d), the Youth Self-Report Form suitable for children older than 11 years (Achenbach, 1991c), and the Direct Observation Form (Achenbach, 1986). Both the CBCL and the Teacher Report Form allow an examiner to determine if significant deviation exists in the behavior ratings of the target child compared to behavior ratings of typical children. The CBCL is made up of 118 behavior items that parents rate either 0 for not true, 1 for somewhat or sometimes true, or 2 for very true or often true. The scale has a fifth-grade readability level and is not overly technical or overwhelming for parents. Three additional areas are assessed in an effort to balance the assessment of the child by finding positive attributes; the Activities Scale, the Social Scale, and the School Scale constitute the Social Competency Scale of the CBCL. The Activities Scale focuses on a child's sports, hobbies, jobs, and activities. The Social Scale focuses on a child's friendships, play, and membership in organizations, and the School Scale asks parents to rate their child academically and provide educational information about whether the child receives general or special education and how the student performs in school.

The behavior items and three supplemental scales are scored and plotted on a profile form that is age and sex specific—a nice feature when making comparisons about behavior. Derived scores for Social Competency are percentiles and T-scores, with the 10th percentile used as the cutoff; scores falling below this would be considered clinically significant. Behavior items are scored similarly, with percentiles and T-scores. Here, scores falling above a T-score of 70 or the 90th percentile are of clinical significance. The 118 behavior items are clustered into narrow groupings: schizophrenia or anxiety, depression, uncommunicative behavior, obsessive-compulsive behavior, somatic complaints, social withdrawal, hyperactivity, aggression, delinquency, cruelty, sex problems, and hostile withdrawal. These narrow groupings, in turn, are further clustered into two broad groupings: internalizing behaviors and externalizing behaviors. High points on any of the scales are not meant to yield a diagnosis but rather a thorough description of the child's behavior. A sample profile is shown in Figure 7.1 on pages 210–211.

The development of the CBCL used both clinical and nonclinical samples of children. Clinical samples were used to identify syndromes of problem behaviors and to construct the scales, whereas nonclinical samples were used to form a normative base. From a psychometric point of view, both samples are well constructed. In general, psychometric properties were given special attention in development of the

CBCL, more so than is usually the case with other childhood social-emotional measures (Freeman, 1985). Reliability data are more than adequate, having been assessed with several methods, including internal consistency, interrater, and test–retest methods. As for validity, correlations with other behavior checklists are also adequate. The CBCL has shown to discriminate between clinical and nonclinical children, with 18% misclassification with behavior and 16% with social competency (Knoff, 1986). More recently, using the CBCL and TRF together was shown to discriminate among children in the general population; specifically, those who require outpatient mental health services and those who have SED special education placements (Mattison, Lynch, Kales, & Gamble, 1993). The "total problems" values were most helpful in making discriminations. The CBCL has received positive endorsements for its empirical approach to childhood behavior problems (Freeman, 1985; Kazdin, 1989; Kelley, 1985; Knoff, 1986). Certainly its development, standardization procedures, and technical aspects are good. An added benefit is the supplemental forms that have been developed to complement the CBCL. Different perspectives of the child's behavior can be garnered by comparing ratings from one measure to another, such as parent ratings to teacher ratings on the TRF, or parent ratings to the clinician's own ratings from the Direct Observation Form, or when appropriate, parent ratings to self-ratings from the Youth Self-Report Form. These ratings, though, are frequently at variance with one another (Achenbach, McConaughy, & Howell, 1987). The CBCL can provide detailed information useful to many settings and professionals, but it requires a thorough understanding of the instrument on the part of the clinician. Overall, the CBCL represents a step forward in the assessment of childhood psychopathology.

***Teacher Report Form*** The TRF (Achenbach, 1991b; 1991d) is a companion form to the CBCL designed for teacher use in rating children's behavior problems. It is much like the CBCL in item content, development, and standardization. There are 118 problem behaviors that teachers rate, using the same 3-point CBCL scale of 0, 1, or 2. In addition to problem behavior items, teachers also provide information on demographics, academic history, ratings of academic performance, and overall functioning.

Scoring of the TRF yields a profile essentially like the CBCL. The narrow-band categories are similar to those of the CBCL and include withdrawn, somatic complaints, anxious/depressed, social problems, thought problems, attention problems, delinquent behavior, and aggressive behavior. An externalizing and internalizing factor score can also be obtained. Like its counterpart, the TRF has a well-standardized

# CBCL/4-18 Profile for Girls—Problem Scales

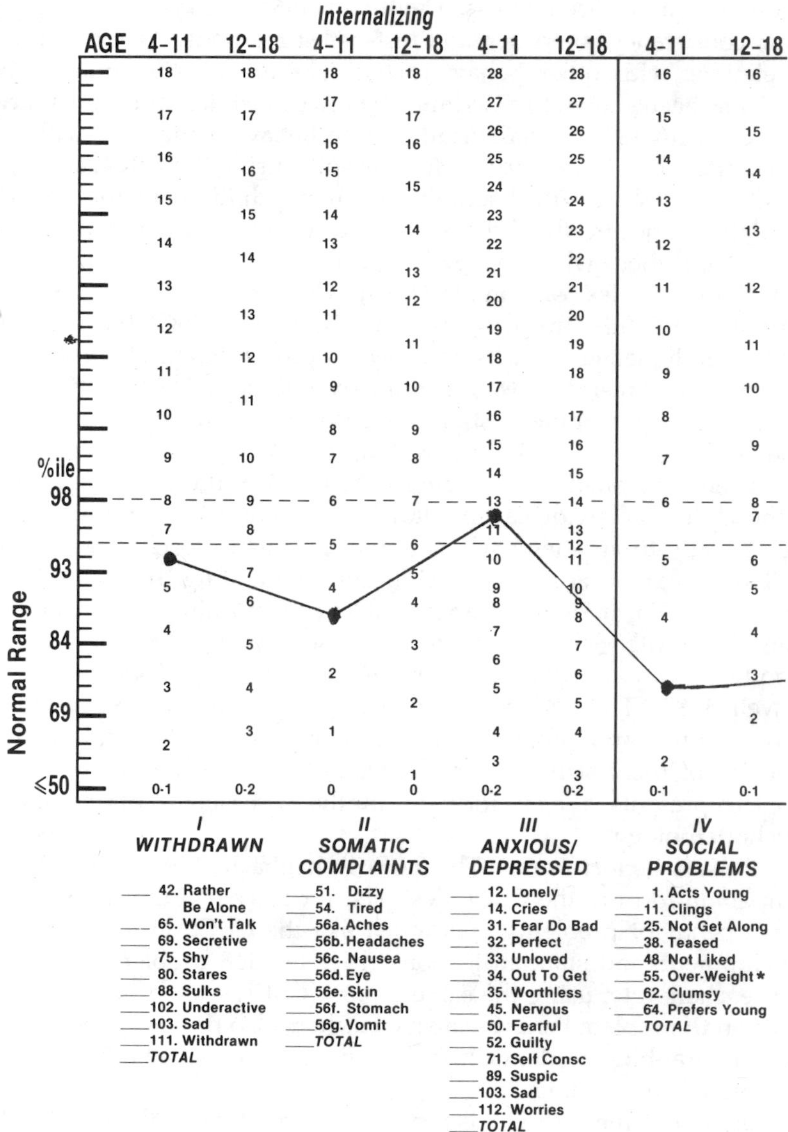


Figure 7.1. Profile for Problem Scales of Child Behavior Checklist. (From Achenbach, T.M. [1991]. *Child Behavior Checklist.* Burlington, VT: Author; reprinted by permission.)

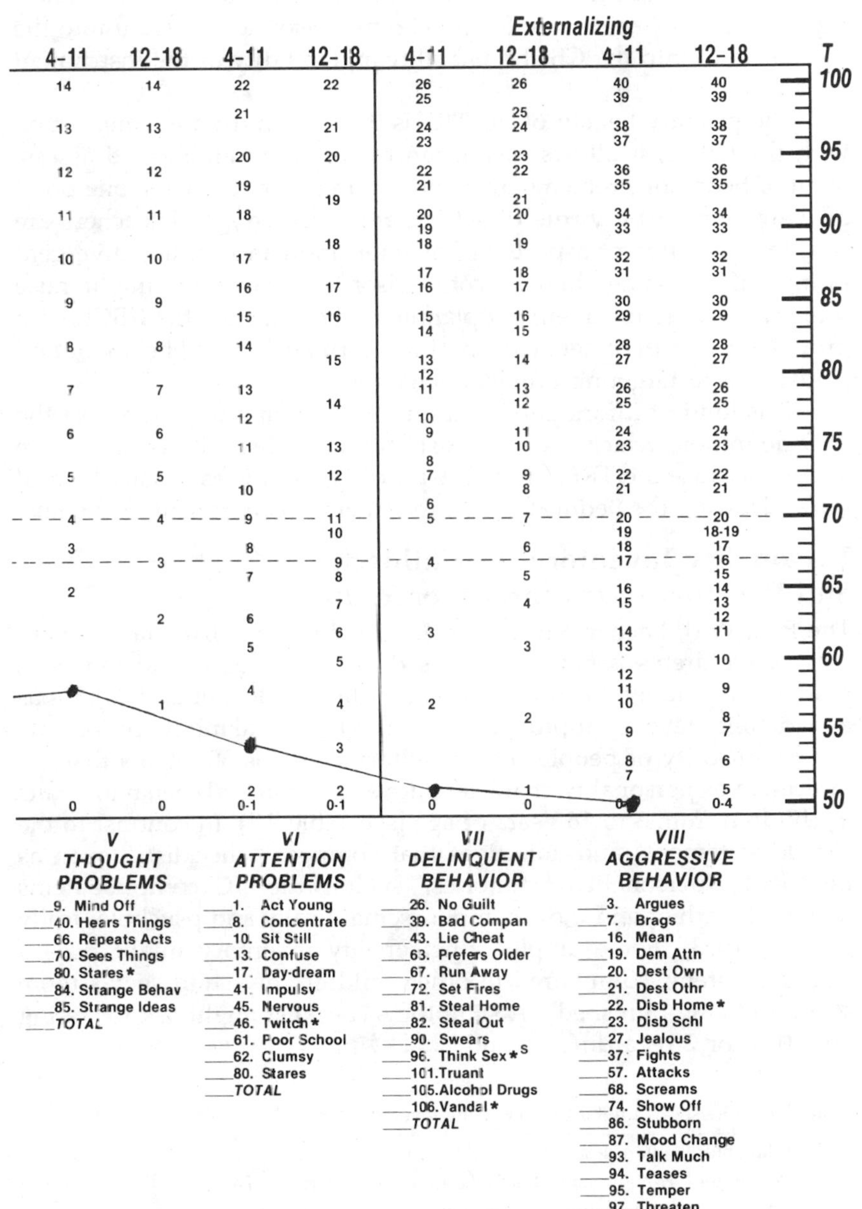
Externalizing
4-11 12-18 4-11 12-18 4-11 12-18 4-11 12-18
T
100
95
90
85
80
75
70
65
60
55
50
V
THOUGHT PROBLEMS
___9. Mind Off
___40. Hears Things
___66. Repeats Acts
___70. Sees Things
___80. Stares*
___84. Strange Behav
___85. Strange Ideas
___TOTAL
VI
ATTENTION PROBLEMS
___1. Act Young
___8. Concentrate
___10. Sit Still
___13. Confuse
___17. Day-dream
___41. Impulsv
___45. Nervous
___46. Twitch*
___61. Poor School
___62. Clumsy
___80. Stares
___TOTAL
VII
DELINQUENT BEHAVIOR
___26. No Guilt
___39. Bad Compan
___43. Lie Cheat
___63. Prefers Older
___67. Run Away
___72. Set Fires
___81. Steal Home
___82. Steal Out
___90. Swears
___96. Think Sex*S
___101. Truant
___105. Alcohol Drugs
___106. Vandal*
___TOTAL
VIII
AGGRESSIVE BEHAVIOR
___3. Argues
___7. Brags
___16. Mean
___19. Dem Attn
___20. Dest Own
___21. Dest Othr
___22. Disb Home*
___23. Disb Schl
___27. Jealous
___37. Fights
___57. Attacks
___68. Screams
___74. Show Off
___86. Stubborn
___87. Mood Change
___93. Talk Much
___94. Teases
___95. Temper
___97. Threaten
___104. Loud
___TOTAL

normative base. Percentiles and T-scores are derived for the TRF; behavior scores above the 98th percentile or a T-score of 70 are of clinical significance. The same care for psychometric soundness went into the TRF as went into the CBCL; reliability and validity of the instrument are satisfactory.

The primary benefit of the TRF is that, when used in conjunction with the CBCL, it allows a clinician to conduct multifaceted assessment of behavior problems by incorporating more than just one point of view. Simply by virtue of setting alone, parents and teachers are sensitive to different aspects of behavior and can produce divergent ratings of the same child. A comparison of viewpoints might raise important issues for treatment planning. The TRF, like the CBCL, also provides a wealth of detailed, specific information about behavior and lends itself to targeting problem behaviors.

This kind of information is useful in clarifying the strands of the SED definition, which, as they exist within the federal definition, are vague. Because the TRF relies on teacher input, it is especially helpful for addressing the "educational impairment" requirement of the law.

## Personality Inventory for Children and Personality Inventory for Youth

The PIC (Wirt, Lachar, Klinedinst, & Seat, 1977) is a true/false inventory of children's behaviors that is designed to be completed by a parent—preferably the mother (Lachar, Kline, & Boersma, 1986). It has a readability level of approximately fifth grade, making it appropriate for the majority of people. The inventory contains 600 items that are indicative of personality characteristics and emotional/behavior traits in children from 3 to 16 years of age (see Table 7.4). In contrast to the simple statements and adjectives that compose "checklists" such as the CBCL, "personality inventories," such as the PIC, comprise items that are lengthier and more complex semantically and psychologically (Lachar, 1993). For example, a personality inventory might pose a true/false item: "Compared to other children, my child seems more afraid of being punished." A symptoms checklist might ask for rating on a 0, 1, or 2 regarding "afraid."

Table 7.4. Questions similar to Personality Inventory for Children items

| |
|---|
| My son/daughter is often destructive with toys. (True or False) |
| My son/daughter has nightmares that wake him/her up. (True or False) |
| My son/daughter seems anxious about leaving me. (True or False) |
| As an infant, my son/daughter was seldom fussy or cranky. (True or False) |
| My son/daughter is cruel to animals. (True or False) |

*Note:* These are not actual test items.

In some ways, the PIC is very similar to the MMPI, in that it utilizes the concept of validity scales and clinical scales. On the PIC, there are three validity scales: the lie scale, which indicates denial of problems with the child; the frequency scale, which contains items that are rarely responded to in the normative sample and can indicate a random test-taking style; and the defensiveness scale, containing items designed to separate high-defensive parents from low-defensive parents. The 12 clinical scales are as follows:

Achievement
Intellectual screening
Development
Somatic concerns
Depression
Family relations
Delinquency
Withdrawal
Anxiety
Psychosis
Hyperactivity
Social skills

Not all 600 items need be administered to generate a profile. Various groupings are available, depending on the number of items used; shortened versions can be administered. The PIC is easily scored and uses T-scores with a mean of 50 and a standard deviation of 10. The higher the scores, the greater the likelihood of pathology, although the range of clinical significance varies scale by scale.

Like the MMPI, the PIC uses an actuarial approach. By conducting psychiatric interviews, family assessments, and school assessments on several types of children, researchers established behaviors and traits that are consistently associated with the various scales, such as depression or anxiety. For example, children with a delinquency scale score greater than a T-score of 99 are identified by those around them as showing a disregard for rules and societal expectations, both at home and at school. They have a high frequency of academic adjustment problems and are rated as hostile, defiant, impulsive, and as having poor judgment and lack of interest in school. They may manifest behavioral symptoms of stealing, lying, sexual acting-out, and participating in group delinquency activities (Lachar & Gdowski, 1979). Children with psychosis T-scores between 90 and 99 are described as socially isolated, emotionally labile, seeming in a fog, and demonstrating peculiar behaviors. Scores falling below 90, however, may show different attributes. By relying on an actuarial approach, the clinician can predict which behaviors and symptoms are associated with which profiles. By virtue of this research, diagnosticians can be assured that high scores not only represent rarity (in the sense that few children are rated in this manner) but also that these high scores reflect known types of problems among children who have been carefully studied in actual clinical situations (Lachar, 1993). The determination rests on empirical data and is not a subjective process on the part of the psychologist.

The PIC was developed over the course of several years and has generated numerous studies concerning its utility—both practically and technically. Strengths of the instrument include its empirical base and its use of an actuarial approach for interpretation. Reliability and validity appear adequate. It is easily administered and scored by the psychologist but is not especially efficient for the respondent. The PIC has been recognized for focusing on typical developmental problems in addition to more pervasive, disturbed behaviors of childhood psychopathology (Tuma, 1985). Also praised is the very large sample of subjects used for developing normative data.

Criticisms that have been leveled against the instrument, however, concern some of these very aspects. For instance, although a very large number of subjects (2,390) was used for standardization, an overwhelming majority of the subjects came from one single school district, and the remaining subjects came from one medical clinic, rather than the subjects coming from a sample that would have been nationally representative. Another criticism regards the time span involved in developing the instrument. The first test booklet was published in 1958, and from then until 1962, the University of Minnesota spearheaded the development of norms using a local sample (Reynolds, 1985). These norms may not be reflective of current children and adolescents. In addition, confusion has been noted regarding the manner in which T-scores are clinically significant at different levels for different scales, and there is confusion regarding differences in information between the PIC Manual and Monograph (Tuma, 1985).

The PIC now has a self-report companion instrument (for children in grades 4–12) called the Personality Inventory for Youth (PIY) (Lachar & Gruber, 1994). This instrument was developed by modifying PIC items so that they could be answered by the child him- or herself. After item development, try-out, revision, and norm-referencing, a 270-item inventory with a simple reading level (3.4 grade level) resulted (Lachar, 1993). Scales are used to be certain that the child is not being inordinately defensive or careless, or is not prone to exaggeration as the youngster describes him- or herself (Defensiveness, Inconsistency, Dissimulation, Validity). The main clinical scales are as follows:

Cognitive impairment
Impulsivity/distractibility
Delinquency
Family dysfunction
Reality distortion
Somatic concern
Psychological discomfort
Social withdrawal
Social skills

Several overlapping summary scales are also available. Initial information suggests that reliability (both test–retest and internal consistency) are adequate. More applied clinical research is forthcoming, although for now psychologists may find the PIY a helpful adjunct to the PIC. Not only can information from the PIY be used to compare with the PIC (and thus, perhaps, substantiate PIC findings) but the PIY may be able to gain access to internal feelings (e.g., anxiety/depression) that are known to the child but not to his or her parent.

## Behavior Assessment System for Children

The Behavior Assessment System for Children (BASC) (pronounced as "Basque") actually refers to several different techniques (Reynolds & Kamphaus, 1992). Much like Achenbach's CBCL and TRF, BASC contains multidimensional scales of adjustment completed by parents and teachers (referred to as simply Parent Rating Scales and Teacher Rating Scales and consisting of slightly fewer items than the Achenbach instrument). The BASC includes a Self-Report instrument and also an observation technique for recording various student in-class behaviors. Finally, a supplemental form can be completed by parents to indicate the child's developmental and medical history.

Among these, the Student Observation System (SOS) appears potentially quite helpful because it gives clinicians a fairly simple way to organize and, in some ways, quantify their observations of the student in the classroom. Such observations are frequently mandated as part of the evaluation process before students are enrolled in special programs. The SOS organizes classroom behavior into several categories of behavior—four categories of appropriate and nine of inappropriate. Categories include "Response to Teacher/Lesson" (basically appropriate academic behavior), "Inattention" (inappropriate behavior that reflects lack of attention but not disruption), and "Inappropriate Vocalization" (disruptive vocalization such as arguing or teasing), and there are fairly detailed definitions of each category to help the rater. These categories can be used to tabulate a student's behavior via a method wherein the observer makes a brief appraisal (i.e., notes what is occurring during a 3-second period) every 30 seconds. Such observations continue for 15 minutes. This method produces 30 brief snapshots of behavior tabulated by the various categories of appropriate and inappropriate behavior. Clinicians can rate subjectively the same 11 categories of behavior regarding the overall extent to which these behaviors occurred during the entire 15 minutes of observation. That is, at the conclusion of the observation period, judgments of never, sometimes, and frequently can be made for each category. This appraisal is more subjective than the tabulation mentioned above.

The SOS is not a norm-referenced psychometric technique, however. There are no tables with which to compare students' observations, and the SOS is not particularly connected to the other dimensions generated by BASC parent, teacher, or self-ratings. Still, clinicians can use SOS information for student-to-student comparison by randomly selecting classmate(s) who are performing the same tasks in the same class and then performing an equivalent observation on the classmate(s). Equally relevant, students' earlier performances can be compared with their later performances after various interventions are instituted. The authors are well aware of these points when they state some aspects of interpretation require "considerable clinical acumen" (Reynolds & Kamphaus, 1992, p. 40).

The BASC manual includes many sophisticated tables for comparing scores across various methods of rating; scales for comparing scores within a particular instrument are also available. There are even ways to plot a child's scores compared to norm groups from the general and clinical populations with severe problems. This latter method can help with differential diagnosis (i.e., to classify), whereas the former can help establish if a problem exists at all (i.e., to identify).

As appealing as it is to include all sorts of personality and behavior information into a single system, the enterprise can be more difficult than it might appear on the surface. In the case of BASC, three versions of Parent and Teacher reports are required to span the ages of 4–18 years (preschool, child, and adolescent versions). Composite scales evident at one age level may not be at another: Adaptability is absent for teens, Conduct Problems is absent for preschoolers, and Sensation Seeking is included on the self-report for teens but not on Parent or Teacher Report. Some of the scales fit nicely with DSM-IV terminology (Hyperactivity, Conduct Problems), but others do not (Atypicality). A clinical profile is presented in T-score form with high scores on dimensions such as Depression or Attention Problems indicating greater degrees of problems. In contrast, an adaptive profile is also presented on dimensions such as Adaptability and Social Skills with higher T-score values denoting more positive characteristics. Most of the scales have easily recognized and understood names that are reported in T-score format. There are also summary scores similar to the Achenbach scales (CBLC and TRF)—internalizing and externalizing problems. The clinician must rely on his or her skills to integrate these disparate sources of information into an organized picture; the BASC system appears capable of helping.

## PROJECTIVE ASSESSMENT MEASURES

The essence of projective techniques may be best revealed by a story. Showing his Rorschach inkblots to an upstanding member of the community, a psychologist encouraged, "Just tell me what you see in these cards." The seemingly stodgy solid citizen described the first card as, "Two naked women dancing seductively." The second card drew the response, "An enormous and beautifully shaped breast." The third card was described as, "A beautiful reclining nude." And so it went throughout the 10 cards. A bit exasperated, the psychologist finally commented, "I'm a bit surprised that you see such things in these cards." His patient responded, "So am I. Shame on you for showing me these dirty pictures!" This anecdote reveals a potential problem with projective techniques. "Normal" is a relative term. The respondent might argue that his or her responses are just as appropriate as anyone else's, including the examiner's. What are projectives? In formal terms, *projectives* are techniques relying on the *projective hypothesis,* which is that a person will project, or place onto an ambiguous or unstructured stimulus his or her feelings, thoughts, needs, conflicts, and attitudes. This is the primary assumption that underlies all projective techniques (Obrzut & Boliek, 1986). The other major assumption at work is that an individual's responses are true and are representative of his or her behavioral functioning in life. Thus when a psychologist makes inferences from test responses about personality and emotional status, they are assumed to be true of the person. Projective measures and the projective hypothesis are most closely linked to the psychoanalytic perspective wherein an individual's verbalizations, free associations, or dreams can all be taken as indicators of actual needs and conflicts. Within this model, the psychologist makes inferences about and interpretations of such information to the individual. Projective measures stand in sharp contrast to objective measures such as the MMPI and CBCL. Projective measures typically lack standard administration and scoring rules and certainly lack the quantifiable, norm-referenced results that their objective counterparts have.

Whereas there is little left to the examiner's subjectivity with objective measures, this is not so with projective measures, which instead rely largely on the experience and clinical insights of the examiner. Objective measures are backed by normative data or actuarial systems of interpretation. If five psychologists administered the MMPI to the same person, their interpretations would differ little. If, however, those psychologists administered a projective measure to the same person, their interpretations might differ appreciably. Because of such potential differences among practitioners, projectives can significantly affect the relevancy of diagnosis, treatment planning, and educational services, particularly in psychoeducational or biobehavioral models where these issues are of importance.

Projective measures can be quite controversial, and therefore, caution is in order. First, projectives are influenced by the developmental status of the child. Second, projectives should not be used with the expectation of generating fail-safe data nor should they be chosen with the hope of achieving psychometric soundness. These limitations beg the obvious, which is that projective measures should never be used alone as a basis for decisions about children. Four projective measures are presented in this chapter: 1) the Rorschach inkblot technique, 2) the TAT and associated thematic measures, 3) the incomplete-sentence methods, and 4) various projective drawing techniques.

## Rorschach Inkblot Technique

The Rorschach technique is one of the oldest projective measures in existence, having been developed by Swiss psychiatrist Hermann Rorschach in 1911. The test comprises a series of 10 standard inkblots that are shown, one at a time, to a person who then describes what he or she sees in the card (see Figure 7.2). That a test with such a loose, unstructured nature constitutes personality assessment has made the Rorschach inkblot one of the most controversial of all psychological tests. Many view the test as little more than palmistry, whereas others contend that only the Rorschach can truly assess deep and subtle aspects of personality and emotion.

Rorschach died before completing extensive studies on his instrument. Subsequent research over the years on issues such as administration, scoring, and interpretation has resulted in no fewer than five separate systems (Exner, 1974). The lack of uniformity among systems has precluded development of an integrated Rorschach and has also hampered research efforts. Depending on the system being used, a person is asked, "What might this be?" or, "Tell me what you see." As the person responds, the examiner records the entire response verbatim. This segment of the Rorschach is referred to as the *Free Asso-*

Figure 7.2. Example of a Rorschach-like inkblot.

*ciation* phase. After all 10 inkblots have been administered, the examiner then begins the *Inquiry* phase. In this phase, the examiner goes back through each of the individual's responses and asks which aspects of the inkblot were used to form the response, such as, "Where did you see it? What makes it look that way to you?" Once this process is completed, the Rorschach can be coded, scored, and interpreted. Although there is some difference among existing scoring systems, most generally use the following criteria:

1. Where is the location of the image? Did he or she use the entire inkblot or only a small detail?
2. What is the determinant? What caused the person to see what he or she saw?
3. What is the content of the image: animal, human, or nature?
4. How original or atypical is his or her description?
5. What is the form level of the response? Is there a basis for the response, or does the description seem to come from nowhere?

The information is then organized into broad categories that typically include Location, Determinant, Form Quality, Organizational Activity, Popularity, Content, and Special Scores (Exner, 1974). Within each category, there are smaller details that are also noted and recorded (see Table 7.5). By the end of this process, every verbal response has been translated into a series of codes that help explain just how the response was formulated. Besides coding the information in such a detailed manner, percentages and ratios can also be derived to describe the relationships among the categories.

Table 7.5. Sample Rorschach scoring categories and elements

| | |
|---|---|
| 1. Location: | W, whole blot<br>D, large usual detail<br>d, small usual detail<br>Dd, unusual detail |
| 2. Determinants: | F, form<br>M, figures in human movement<br>FM, animals in animal movement<br>C, color only<br>FC, color with definite form<br>CF, color with indefinite form<br>cF, form indefinite |
| 3. Content: | H, human figures<br>A, animal figures<br>At, human anatomy<br>Ad, animal anatomy<br>N, nature<br>Obj, objects |
| 4. Popularity: | P, popular response<br>O, original response |
| 5. Scores: | R, total number of responses<br>F%, percentage of F responses<br>Sum C, FC + CF + C |

The *Interpretation* phase follows, which is the most complex part of the Rorschach technique. Although scoring procedures and interpretation are not quite as developed as they are for the WISC–III, for example, there are still a few generalizations about Rorschach responses that can be made. One such generalization is that people who use the whole blot when forming their impressions tend to problem-solve and perceive the world globally, in terms of broad-based issues. Those who rely instead on small, unusual details within the blot to form their impressions tend to also focus on narrow issues and not see the "big picture" (Weiner, 1986). Another example concerns one particular inkblot that people almost universally identify as a bat. This identification seems to stem mainly from the gray/black shading of the card, because when the bat was shown in a bright color instead, people did not identify it as a bat (Exner, 1959). There is a striking difference, however, between those individuals who report the gray/black shading as their main determinant and those who are influenced by it, but do not state it as a determinant. Those people who actually identify the shading as a determinant are those likely to be depressed (Weiner, 1986). It is hypothesized that individuals who are depressed are especially responsive to the shading aspect because psychologically, the colors of gray and black are associated with feelings of sadness, dejection, and helplessness.

But what about interpretation of children's responses? What can be said about how children typically respond? Some psychologists are wary about using the Rorschach technique with children, but this caution is believed to be unwarranted by others (Weiner, 1986) because response styles may have the same meaning independent of age. This is not to say that developmental factors are meaningless, however. Indeed, Rorschach responses need to be interpreted along developmental lines. An example of this can be made with color-form (CF) and form-color (FC) responses in children. CF responses are based primarily on color, with form of the blot being secondary in importance; the opposite is true of FC responses. More CF than FC responses are taken to indicate lability and lack of reserve with one's emotions (Weiner, 1986). This type of emotional lability is not expected with adults but is more developmentally fitting for children. Seen in an adult, this response may be of concern, but in a child this response would likely be dismissed as developmentally typical. Therefore, whereas a ratio of CF over FC responses still indicates emotional lability versus emotional guardedness, the CF response pattern is developmentally more expected and accepted with children than adults.

Researchers have attempted to identify Rorschach responses associated with various childhood disorders (Exner & Weiner, 1982). Children or teenagers with schizophrenia typically have scores indicative of poor reasoning and thought processes, poor form level, and grotesque, unusual content. Depressed children respond to coloring and shading aspects of the inkblot, with a low number of responses overall, long reaction times to the stimuli, and poor organizational quality. Another category of childhood disturbance, anxiety-withdrawal, shows a pattern of responses with few human identifications and an emphasis on the color shading of the blots. Reviewing these indicators, it is arguable that a structured clinical interview and observation would reveal the same features more quickly, simply, and cheaply. With the onset of more behaviorally based assessments, the Rorschach technique is not as popular in the 1990s as it may have been in past times. The instrument is still used, however, in cases such as an extremely reticent child who can only provide simple descriptions of the blots. Such a situation may not be ideal, but it may be the only basis for making any statements about personality. In other cases, suspicious children who might purposefully distort their responses on other instruments might reveal themselves on the Rorschach. Most children avoid blatantly gory or crazy identifications but really have no idea how to go about distorting the Rorschach inkblot because of its ambiguous, unstructured nature. Whatever the use of the Rorschach, interpretations need to be viewed with caution.

The instrument should never stand alone as the basis for decision making with children.

## Thematic Apperception Test

Although both the Rorschach and the TAT are classified as projectives, they are actually very different instruments. The Rorschach technique is highly unstructured and ambiguous, using a series of inkblots, whereas the TAT is much more structured, using clear, identifiable pictures of children and adults. An advantage of the TAT is that children recognize and thus respond to the stimuli material more than they do to the nebulous inkblots.

The TAT was developed by Christina Morgan and Henry Murray in 1935 at Harvard University. It is a set of picture cards depicting people in activity or interacting with other people. Some cards depict very definite scenes or situations, whereas others show people and only imply activity or interaction. The test operates on the same assumption as the Rorschach test: namely, the projective hypothesis that a child will identify his or her needs, conflicts, thoughts, and feelings through the stimuli, which in this case are pictures. Murray viewed the instrument as being able to help identify a person's *needs* and *presses* (Murray, 1971). A need can be thought of as an internal mechanism—forces or desires within a person, such as a need to achieve. A press can be thought of as an external force that plays a role in a person's behavior in the environment, such as family factors or support systems. The concept of needs and presses is psychoanalytic in nature and hypothesized to be unconscious on the part of the individual.

Administration of the TAT is straightforward. The entire set of pictures consists of approximately 30 cards, with 10 usually selected. The cards are shown one at a time to the child, with the following instructions:

> This is a storytelling test. I have some pictures here that I am going to show you, and for each picture, I want you to make up a story. Tell what has happened before and what is happening now. Say what the people are feeling and thinking and how the story will end. You can make up any kind of story you want. Do you understand? Well, then, here's the first picture. (Murray, 1943, pp. 3–4)

As the child tells his or her story, the psychologist records it, asking questions as necessary throughout. There are several scoring systems that have been developed over the years, ranging from simple to complex. One system uses frequency tallies and weighted scores for identified needs and presses (Morgan & Murray, 1935), whereas another relies solely on content analysis (Bellak, 1947), and a third relies on quantifiable data derived by rating scales for each story (Eron, 1950).

In general, however, no formal scoring is done on TAT stories, but they are analyzed according to such basic criteria as 1) the thematic content of the story; 2) the identified hero and his or her needs, motives, feelings, and conflicts; 3) the hero's perceptions of the world around him or her; 4) the psychological defenses used by the hero; 5) the way the story is ended; and 6) if the story generally fits the picture in the card and has a basis in reality. The child's story-telling manner can also yield useful information on other aspects, such as the child's verbal expression abilities, general cognitive level of functioning, and organizational abilities.

Although the TAT appears simple to administer and analyze, this is not really the case. There are more subtle attributes of the test that a psychologist must be familiar with in order to gain an accurate picture of the child. Some of the picture cards have a *stimulus pull;* that is, they lead the subject in a certain direction. For instance, some of the scenes in the cards pull toward aggression, and an aggressive story theme would not be unexpected. Thus, knowing each card's stimulus pull is important in judging the psychological needs that are revealed in the story. Over time, the psychologist working with children develops an idea of which cards work best with which referral questions. Referrals having to do with suicide risks, for instance, might call for cards with some but not too much stimulus pull to depression. Stories would be evaluated for comments about depressed, incompetent, or helpless heroes, heroes who willingly accept punishments out of proportion to their actions, and negative story endings (Bellak, 1975). Illustration 7.3 contains examples of TAT responses.

Another caution with the TAT has to do with how well the themes children reveal correlate with their daily behavior. Although there may be strong tendencies revealed in the themes, these are mediated by social judgment and rules. The child who shows much aggression in his or her stories is not necessarily beating up everyone in school. A child may have learned a family value against violence and may avoid the violent stimulus pull of certain cards by creating peaceful, nonviolent stories. A second child may reveal few aggressive themes but not have any self-restraint against aggression or family values against it, and consequently show more frequent episodes of aggression. The second child would be judged as more likely to be overtly aggressive, whereas the first child would be less overt but probably more conflicted about aggression. Thus, TAT interpretations are not as simple as they appear and must take into account outside factors if they are to be accurately interpreted.

The TAT is a popular instrument for several reasons. It is an easy instrument to use, and it is well suited for children due to its social nature and nonthreatening task demands. In addition, the TAT can

## Illustration 7.3

### SAMPLE TAT RESPONSES

The following are three TAT stories in response to Card 3 for boys and men. The card shows a young person kneeling on the floor, head hung in despair, with a revolver on the floor nearby. These three stories show varying feelings of despair and the differing stresses that have led to it.

**Story 1** Doug is an 11-year-old male who was seen on the pediatrics unit because of abdominal pain. Extensive laboratory findings were negative. His responses show concern with body image and peer acceptance.

> Once there was a boy named Brian. Brian wasn't very happy because the kids at school made fun of him because he was fat. So Brian got tired of kids teasing him. He went on a diet. Two months later he was skinnier than they were. The kids said they were sorry for teasing him.

**Story 2** This story was composed by a bright 11-year-old male referred because of severe family problems. His stories show his anger toward his family, his feelings of rejection, and his isolation.

> A long time ago in South America, this little boy sassed back his mother. His mother spanked him and sent him to his room. He went to his room but climbed out the window by using an apple tree. When he finished climbing down it, he went over to his friend's house. His friend's mother would not let him spend the night, so he sat on the floor and cried himself to sleep. He felt that nobody liked him.

**Story 3** This story was composed by a 13-year-old female with incipient schizophrenia. Her stories show mental deterioration including confusion, extreme feelings of inadequacy, and general difficulty with mental organization.

> Is this contemporary? In this picture, she is hurt and depressed. She wants to pick up everything and go back and yell at them and make her point. She wants to let her emotions and feelings settle in. Go back and yell and settle everything. Also, she is thinking about the future. Thinking of going to sleep and how this will affect her life. Maybe how the changes will affect her husband. She hopes he won't get mad because of what she did. I think that's what most of us hope for out of life. [The examining psychologist then asks her what made the character mad or depressed.] He came home and yelled at her about money and about messing up with the kids. She just had one rotten day and not a bad week. Now she is upset.

help identify treatment issues in contrast to instruments like the Rorschach technique, which focus more on personality style. Of course, there are drawbacks to the TAT as well. First, a child can render the instrument worthless, simply by refusing to talk or by creating superficial stories that do little more than describe the picture. Second, it takes considerable experience and competence on the part of the psychologist to avoid inaccurate or misleading interpretations. Finally, as with the Rorschach, the TAT lacks an empirical foundation, which means that, as with all projectives, it should never stand alone when used to make decisions about children.

## Roberts Apperception Test for Children

The success of the TAT opened the door for development of other thematic measures. Some new measures were designed with children in mind, and their content reflects this. The Children's Apperception Test was modeled after the TAT in terms of administration and interpretation, but uses animal pictures rather than human pictures (Bellak & Bellak, 1949). The Blacky Pictures Test is a measure tied to stages of psychosexual development by using a series of picture cards, each representing a various stage (Blum, 1950). The picture content revolves around a family of dogs, of whom Blacky is the main character.

One of the newer thematic tests is the Roberts Apperception Test for Children (McArthur & Roberts, 1982). The Roberts test is an effort to combine both projective and objective aspects of assessment. Projectively, it is very similar to the TAT, in that it uses picture cards that require the subject to create a story. Instructions are also similar to the TAT, as is the sex coding of specific cards for boys and girls. However, the content of the picture cards of the Roberts test is different from the TAT. Here, the pictures have definite *child pull;* that is, they depict situations relevant to virtually all children, such as parental problems, aggression, observation of nudity, school situations, and peer interactions (see Figure 7.3).

Objectively, the Roberts test was created with a more standardized approach than most projective measures. There are 8 adaptive scales and 5 clinical scales. The 8 adaptive scales are termed as follows: reliance on others, support to others, support of the child, limit setting placed on the child, problem identification; and there are 3 resolution scales. The 5 clinical scales are termed as follows: anxiety (guilt, remorse, apprehension), aggression (verbal and physical), depression (sadness, dejection, physical symptoms), rejection (separation, isolation, jealousy), and unresolved. Additional data come in the way of noting atypical responses, card refusals, or maladaptive story endings. An Interpersonal Matrix can be generated from the scores, as well as

Figure 7.3. Illustrations representing themes depicted in Roberts Apperception Test story cards. (These are not actual test cards.)

an Ego Functioning Index, an Aggression Index, and a Level of Projection scale. The instrument uses T-scores and norms for the resulting scores, and profiles are specific to the child's age.

Normative data for the Roberts test was based on 200 "well-adjusted" children as compared to 200 children referred to clinics. Well-adjusted children scored higher on the adaptive scales but no differently from the referred group on the clinical scales of aggression, anxiety, and depression. This is certainly unexpected, given that aggression, anxiety, and depression are common reasons for referrals. In addition, there is not yet research to show that the Roberts test is a truly objective personality assessment tool. Although it attempts to combine objective and projective aspects, the Roberts test may in fact disenchant both camps: Those psychologists who adhere to a projective philosophy will not make use of the scoring system and normative data, whereas psychologists who adhere to an objective philosophy will find the objective system lacking in technical sophistication (Sines, 1985). Still, the Roberts test is noteworthy for its attempt to combine both aspects and is likely to be useful as a supplemental tool. It is not, however, the recognized standard of the storytelling tests, as the TAT seems to be.

## Incomplete-Sentence Method

The incomplete-sentence method is a technique rather than a single specific psychological instrument. Various forms of the technique are available, some suitable for children, some for adolescents, and others for adults.

Whatever the form, the incomplete-sentence method consists of a series of "stems" that are actually the beginning parts of sentences. Usually the stems focus on self-image, emotional status, and relationships with significant people. The respondent simply adds endings to the stems to form a complete sentence. Sample instructions are, "Complete this sentence to express your real feelings. Try to do every one. Be sure to make a complete sentence" (Rotter, 1950). Often the child is encouraged to work as quickly as possible so as to produce spontaneous, unguarded responses (see Illustration 7.4). Children 12 years of age or older usually prefer to write the responses themselves, but younger children do best if the examining psychologist reads the items and writes the child's spoken response.

Among the many variations of sentence completion techniques available, some have developed formal scoring systems. One such example is the Rotter Incomplete Sentence Blank (Rotter & Rafferty, 1950) in which every response is given a neutral, negative, or positive rating on the basis of how much conflict is present. The ratings are

## Illustration 7.4

### SAMPLE INCOMPLETE-SENTENCE BLANK RESPONSES

The following are three different children's responses to sample incomplete sentence blanks:

**Child No. 1** This preteen boy had a history of acting out impulses, conflict with authority figures, and failure to adhere to family rules.

I am ashamed . . . *of nothing.*
In school I . . . *think the teachers have favorites, which is unfair.*
People think that I need . . . *to control my temper.*
Sometimes I think about . . . *a new dirt bike and trailer.*
The worst thing that ever happened to me was . . . *I couldn't go to the lake.*

**Child No. 2** In contrast to Child No. 1, this child had a history of worrisomeness, tentativeness, and refusal to attend school, often complaining of stomachaches and nausea.

I am ashamed . . . *I failed spelling.*
In school I . . . *can't do the work.*
People think that I need . . . *to be more responsible and to not let myself down.*
Sometimes I think about . . . *being laughed at in front of the class.*
The worst thing that ever happened to me was . . . *when my dad almost got fired from his job.*

**Child No. 3** This child was evaluated because his parents were concerned about learning disabilities. No learning problems were detected and, in fact, the boy was found not to have significant emotional problems.

I am ashamed . . . *of cheating in Monopoly.*
In school I . . . *sometimes get bored.*
People think that I need . . . *to share with my brother.*
Sometimes I think about . . . *going on vacation with my family.*
The worst thing that ever happened to me was . . . *when my grandpa died.*

then given weighted scores that when totaled provide an overall adjustment score. Another measure, the Hart Sentence Completion Test for Children (Hart, 1972), can be scored by assigning a rating of neutral, negative, or positive to each content cluster tapped by the stems. A second system for the Hart test takes individual item ratings together to form a composite. All composite scores in turn are used to create a profile of the child. Although systems like this exist, incomplete sentences are usually regarded in an impressionistic fashion. Often the examining psychologist reads all of the sentences, making margin notes about repetitive themes or especially salient responses. This type of review is the most frequently used approach for interpretation. Another is to group items together that reflect similar content (Hart, 1986). Hypotheses are generated from the review and checked against important dimensions such as family functioning, self-concept, and areas of conflict.

Because incomplete sentences are used projectively and have an impressionistic quality, there are limitations regarding how they are used. Like so many projectives, psychometric standards are not present to any significant degree, making incomplete sentences a supplemental measure, never a primary one. The unstructured format and open interpretative process are also concerns because of variability from psychologist to psychologist in how they use incomplete sentences (Barnett & Zucker, 1985).

On the positive side, incomplete sentences are an efficient, inexpensive way to help get at personality dynamics. This is especially true when a child is particularly reticent. The task demand is not threatening, so that children and adolescents often reveal something of themselves when they might be reluctant to do so if a more straightforward instrument were used. Also, there is a common-sense appeal to the measure that attracts many users, regardless of theoretical orientation.

## Projective Drawings

The projectives discussed so far all involve language. But children often have immature language or are reluctant to talk. Nonlanguage techniques, such as drawings, have long been looked to as a window into the child's mind. Any of the drawings used by a clinician as part of a personality assessment battery may be referred to as *projective drawings*. Presumably, children's drawings are sufficiently unstructured so that the child projects him- or herself into the drawing. In addition to the nonlanguage aspect, projectives are frequently used to get a sense of a child's conflicts and perceptions both inter- and intrapersonally, and to help generate hypotheses and guide assessment

(Cummings, 1986). Although extremely variable, drawings often take one of four forms:

1. *Draw-a-Person* consists of a nonspecific request like, "draw a person, any kind of person you want. Be sure it's not a stick figure or cartoon person." The child is usually given a blank 8½" × 11" page on which to draw. Questions by the child are usually given loose answers to keep the situation ambiguous, thereby allowing for projection. After the first drawing, the child is asked to draw a second person, this one being the opposite sex of the first figure drawn.
2. *House-Tree-Person* consists of a house, a tree, and a person drawn separately by the child. After the three drawings are completed, a questioning phase begins in which the child can further describe or interpret his or her drawings (Buck, 1948). This allows the psychologist to gain additional insights. Buck also suggested a second administration, in which the child draws the figures with crayons. These figures are then compared to the pencil drawings.
3. *Kinetic Family Drawings* consist of a request for the child to draw a picture of "everyone in your family, including you, doing something." Administration is similar to the other measures, and a questioning session follows, much like that of the House-Tree-Person drawings.
4. *Kinetic School Drawings,* which are much like the Kinetic Family Drawings, instead consist of a request that the child draw a school picture and "show everyone doing something." Some instructions are more specific, such as "be sure and include the teacher, yourself, and a couple of friends." A second color administration is sometimes used, as in the House-Tree-Person drawings.

Clinicians often come to have a favorite drawing technique that they use to the exclusion of others. For instance, those who are interested in family relations may use the Kinetic Family Drawings. Those concerned with gender identification and differentiation may prefer to use the Draw-a-Person test, asking for drawings of both sexes. Those who believe in symbolism in drawings may favor the House-Tree-Person test. Some who are atheoretical or eclectic may request a single Draw-a-Person test, simply as a warm-up at the outset of an evaluation, and any personality data revealed would be considered strictly as a fringe benefit.

Interpretation of drawings is controversial. Philosophies range from considering even the smallest detail to be an indicator of clinical significance to evaluating the drawing as a whole and looking for gross-level distortions, to decrying the very existence and use of the drawings. Although there are elements common to the interpretation of just about all drawings, scoring systems have been developed that focus on the meaning of specific elements. According to Machover's (1949) system, a person's "body image," or how an individual views him- or herself, will be reflected in the drawings. The head of a drawing represents social communication and expression. Thus a psychologist working under these guidelines would pay particular attention to details such as open or closed eyes, the mouth, or an absence of details. The body parts are considered representative of interactions with the environment, and the positioning and appearance of hands, legs, and arms would be of interest. Machover's system of interpretation is projective in nature; thus, the drawings reflect the worries, conflicts, and feelings that an individual projected into the stimulus. Machover also focused on sexual identification, hypothesizing that the sex of the drawing is the sex identified with by the child.

Another interpretative system, which was developed by Koppitz (1968), categorizes 30 features into 3 groups: Quality Signs (i.e., shading of the face, size of the figure overall, integration of body parts), Special Features (i.e., arms clinging to body, legs pressed together, arm length, hand size), and Omissions (i.e., no neck, arms, mouth, ears). When one evaluates a drawing under Koppitz's framework, three questions should be kept in mind: 1) How did the child approach the drawing? 2) Who was drawn? and 3) What message seems to be contained in the drawing? (Koppitz, 1968). In addition, children's drawings are typically examined for any concerns relative to self-image, sexual identification, and emotional indicators of aggression, depression, and anxiety. In contrast to Machover's emphasis on sexual identification, the Koppitz system hypothesizes that children draw people who concern them the most. Koppitz (1968) cautioned, however, that interpretation should be based on the whole of the drawing, not merely isolated signs. Along with that, she urged consideration of the child's age, maturity, and cultural background as factors of importance.

More recently, a standardized technique has been developed to use drawings (man, woman, and self) to screen school-age children for emotional problems. Relying on prior research and a current norm group, Draw-a-Person: Screening Procedures for Emotional Disturbance (Naglieri, McNeish, & Bardos, 1991) provides T-scores and suggestions that further assessment is, 1) not indicated, 2) indicated, or 3) strongly indicated based on the child's drawing.

Children's drawings are a common tool in an assessment battery. Even though differences exist among professionals as to the most appropriate scoring or level of interpretation, most will nevertheless agree that disturbed children produce qualitatively different drawings from typical children. Although difficult to define precisely, the drawings of disturbed children seem aloof, bizarrely malformed, and nonhuman. Children with schizophrenia often produce the most bizarre drawings, whereas less disturbed children who may be socially withdrawn or have disordered thinking also produce figures that reflect this bizarre quality. Figure 7.4 shows sample drawings done by two disturbed children.

It should be obvious that any number of meanings can be extracted from a drawing, depending on whether a scoring system is used, which system is used, or the theoretical leanings of a psychologist. In addition, such nonpersonality factors as eye–hand coordination, maturation of the child, societal influences, motivation, and artistic ability influence drawings (Cummings, 1986). These factors influence the quality of a drawing but should not be subject to overinterpretation on the part of the practitioner. A drawing may help to develop hypotheses about a child, but alone does not render a child aggressive, depressed, schizophrenic, or oppositional. Human figure drawings are best used in conjunction with other pieces of assessment and historical information.

## A DISTURBED ADOLESCENT

Ron, a 15-year-old high school sophomore, was hospitalized in a psychiatric facility by his parents due to aggressive, acting-out episodes and, more recently, grandiose thinking. His psychiatrist referred Ron for a psychological evaluation to help answer the following questions: 1) Is Ron's behavior a response to a situational crisis, or is it a more

Figure 7.4. Human figure drawings by two disturbed children.

ingrained part of his personality? and 2) What is an appropriate diagnosis?

Background information on Ron reveals many educational and behavior problems. In school, he has had problems learning since first grade, and he continues to be extremely deficient in all academic areas. His school placements, however, have always been in programs for children with severe emotional disabilities because of his behavioral difficulties. His behaviors are long-standing according to his mother, dating back to approximately 2 years of age. She describes him as chronically aggressive (both verbally and physically), constantly in school and neighborhood fights, difficult to discipline, disobedient, and "disrespectful to his father and me." In addition, he is an uncoordinated, clumsy boy, which has caused much teasing from peers and frustration in sports and physical education classes. Consequently, Ron was not involved in organized sports while growing up, and in fact has very few activities. Recently, his mother has noticed that Ron is given to "exaggeration" when relating stories or events. Any questioning of his stories leads to outbursts, in which Ron yells and screams, slams doors, and sometimes throws things. After two such confrontations, he left the house and stayed out all night.

Because of his behaviors, Ron has always had difficulty developing friendships. It seems that the more peers neglect him, the harder he tries to gain their acceptance, and because he typically tries with immature, inappropriate behaviors, this results in further neglect or rejection. His mother acknowledges that Ron has a few friends, but "they're the kind we don't want him to have." His parents have tried to limit friendships, but this has largely been ineffective. He frequently changes friends; his mother cannot identify one consistent or best friend that Ron has had for any length of time. His poor selection of friends has led to sporadic police involvement since about age 13, resulting from stealing a car stereo on one occasion and shoplifting on another. Ron's parents hoped their son would finally be taught a lesson when the stereo theft resulted in a court appearance and mandatory community service. However, their frustration only intensified when Ron had another shoplifting charge a year later.

Ron's family constellation is revealing. He is the middle child of three boys; his older brother is 18 years old and his younger brother is 11 years old. The older brother, who just entered college after a very successful high school experience, is in many ways the "golden boy" of the family, in that he has been academically, athletically, behaviorally, and socially competent. The younger brother has the role of the "family clown" and receives much attention, laughter, and reinforcement for his behavior. Ron's brothers have become increasingly disinterested in him, and he has grown more resentful toward them. Ron has not enjoyed academic successes, or the smooth adolescence that his older brother had. Indeed, he has no readily observable strengths.

Over the past 3 months, Ron's behavior seemed to have taken a turn for the worse. Both school personnel and Ron's mother have noticed an increase in his aggressive outbursts and exaggerated, inaccurate stories. These problems intensify when Ron is being confronted about one of these behaviors. His stories are frequently aggrandizing and boastful, such as insisting that he stayed out all night, ditched classes to be with his girlfriend, punched his father in an argument, or meets a group of friends every morning before school. All such stories were proved to be untrue, yet when confronted with the factual information. Ron becomes even more entrenched. Ron's mother suspects a recurrence of stealing, in that she noticed money and some jewelry pieces were gone, although Ron has pleaded ignorance.

During an initial interview, Ron told grandiose stories and was restless and angry when challenged. Over the next two sessions, however, he was somewhat more subdued and pleasant. He spoke of his family and peer relationships in a superficial and guarded manner. Ron generally made socially appropriate statements and denied feeling any strong negative emotions toward his brothers. As for his criminal involvement, he tended to place the blame on peers, saying that it was not his idea, that he did not actually take anything, and that he had been sorry for these things.

Ron was given the MMPI–A, which resulted in a 4–9 profile; a clinically elevated T-score of 79 on 4 (Psychopathic Deviate) and a T-score of 73 on 9 (Mania). This profile type is frequently seen among adolescents and is associated with conduct problems of an antisocial nature. Characteristic behaviors of this code type usually include an unwillingness to accept responsibility for behavior, a tendency to act-out impulsively, a history of legal involvement and unstable personal relationships, and impatience and recklessness (Archer, 1987). This profile type is most often referred for behavioral health services as a result of defiance and disobedience toward parents, impulsivity, school truancy, and provocative behaviors. Many adolescents studied with this particular profile did not live at home with their parents; approximately 50% had legal involvement; and 83% had truancy or runaway problems (Marks, Seeman, & Haller, 1974).

This personality type tends to be very enduring and carries a poor prognosis for change. These individuals are not especially responsive to therapy. This finding, coupled with the chronic nature of Ron's behaviors, helped the psychologist conclude that it is unlikely Ron's behavior is merely a reaction to a situational crisis. Indeed, it is probably that his behavior pattern would have occurred without a disruption of the homelife and that it will continue with or without any therapeutic intervention. Ron's incomplete sentence responses show additional evidence of his personality style.

I am ashamed . . . *of nothing; well, I guess when I got busted for those thefts I was sorry.*
Girls . . . *love me, man! I have three different girlfriends.*
What bothers me . . . *is when kids tell lies about me, make up a bunch of crap. I beat up kids for doing that.*
When I grow up . . . *I'm gonna have a great job and make loads of money.*
The only trouble . . . *is the food here. It stinks!*
The happiest time . . . *is when me and my friends are out cruising.*
My nerves . . . *are cool. I'm keeping cool here, but there are a few kids though.*
At home . . . *I don't do much. I'd rather be out with my friends, having a good time.*
My greatest worry . . . *is I don't know. I don't worry about too much.*

Ron's incomplete sentences are significant because his responses fail to recognize the serious nature of his problems. Not only is he failing to express awareness, but he also gives no indication of wanting or needing to correct his behaviors. Diagnostically, Ron meets the DSM-IV criteria for a conduct disorder. Specifically, he has stolen, run away on two occasions, lied, been involved in a break-in of a car, and frequently been in physical fights. It is important that feedback to Ron's psychiatrist include this diagnosis, as well as some prognostic information. This will answer the question of a situational crisis and also provide important direction to Ron's course of treatment. Ron's DSM-IV profile would be as follows:

Axis I: Conduct Disorder
Axis II: No Diagnosis
Axis III: No Diagnosis
Axis IV: Conflict with parents, lack of close friends, involvement with court
Axis V: 60

## A PSYCHOSOMATIC CHILD

Joanna, a 6-year-old girl, had a history of numerous physical complaints, such as headaches, stomachaches, dizziness, and weakness. Although Joanna was seen frequently by her pediatrician, he could find nothing wrong. She had never had any serious illnesses as a child and was not especially prone to colds, earaches, or other childhood illnesses. After a lab work-up was negative, the pediatrician requested a psychological evaluation to see if Joanna was experiencing some type of adjustment problems that were prompting her physical complaints.

School history shows that Joanna is currently repeating first grade because of poor academic progress. So far this year, however, she is making good progress. Her absences, which average 1 day per week, were a concern to both her parents and her teacher given her history of grade retention. The teacher reported that Joanna frequently requests to see the nurse, but in these instances she can be directed back to work and usually involved again. There were no behavior problems to report, only that Joanna sometimes seemed sad when first arriving in the morning. Like her physical complaints, however, this disappeared once she was into her routine. She plays appropriately, although somewhat awkwardly, with a few little girls. She seems out of place among peers who formed ties before she had come to this class.

Joanna's family history was a bit more enlightening than her school history. Her parents had divorced about 2 months prior to evaluation; Joanna is their only child. Other than some confusion, Joanna did not display much reaction or reveal any immediate problems in response to their divorce. Her mother reports that Joanna is close to and has an equally good relationship with both parents. Her father currently sees her every other weekend, but Joanna wishes it were every weekend. One of her mother's complaints is that since the divorce her father has become a "Disneyland Dad" in an effort to "make up for" the divorce. She reports that he buys Joanna numerous treats and gifts and spends his weekends with her seeing movies, allowing her to play video games, and eating junk food. This has left her mother resentful because Joanna is hard to discipline.

The divorce also has forced Joanna's mother to change her work schedule from part- to full-time nursing and has caused a financial strain. This has meant longer days and increased time with a babysitter for Joanna. Her mother has also missed a lot of work because of frequent doctor's appointments and staying home with Joanna. She has demonstrated considerable concern over Joanna's complaints, something she attributes to her nursing background and not being one to "just let it go by."

Concerned about Joanna's behavior and social competence, the psychologist had the mother complete a Child Behavior Checklist. All scores on the Social Competence Scales fell below the normal range, more so regarding school where it is likely that her frequent absences are reflected in her low scores. Her mother rated her as not particularly active or social outside of school. Joanna does not belong to any clubs or organizations, such as Girl Scouts or after-school sports, nor does she play much in the neighborhood. Her main activity at home is watching TV; entertaining herself is difficult for Joanna. It seems that most of her socialization and entertainment comes from her parents, which sometimes becomes problematic. According to her mother, Joanna "nags and begs, saying, 'I'm bored, there's nothing to do.'" Her mother blames this on the time spent with her father. On the behavior profile part of the CBCL, the Somatic Complaints factor was in the clinically significant range at a T-score of 77, as was the Social Withdrawal factor at 70. Specific somatic complaints checked by the mother included dizziness, headaches, stomach problems, and feeling overly tired. The remaining factors were all within the normal range.

Based on the CBCL and Joanna's history of any medical factors having been ruled out, it is possible that Joanna's somatic complaints were either a disguised effort to secure her mother's attention and company or were stress related. It also seemed that Joanna had been rather successful in gaining her mother's attention; not only did her mother arrange to take her to the doctor's, but also stayed home several times with her. Likewise, Joanna's contact with her father seemed to increase the more she complained of illness. Presentation of this hypothesis to the mother, however, resulted in anger toward the psychologist for suggesting that Joanna was "faking" her symptoms. Citing her nursing background, Joanna's mother stated that she was certain that Joanna was ill and had her own ideas about the possible problem.

At this point the psychologist was able to convince the mother that projective testing might help them both better understand Joanna. The psychologist administered an Incomplete-Sentence Blank and Draw-a-Person tests, with the following results:

A mother . . . *takes real good care of me when I'm sick; she's a nurse, and she stays with me.*

At bedtime . . . *my mommy reads to me.*

What hurts me . . . *is my head and my tummy. Mommy says the doctor can make it better.*

A father . . . *is so much fun! I love my daddy; he got me a teddy bear and a new book when I was home sick. He gets worried when I don't feel good. He calls me.*

The happiest time . . . *is when we went to Disneyland for our vacation. I wasn't sick in the summer.*

At home . . . *my mom stays with me and we have fun.*

Other kids . . . *don't get sick like me.*

When I grow up . . . *I'm gonna be a nurse and help take care of sick kids.*

Joanna's sentences are telling, particularly about the family dynamics. Both of her parents rally around her illnesses with their time, attention, and gifts. When sick, Joanna is able to see or hear from her father more than just every other weekend, something she admittedly wants. Without being sick, it seems that Joanna has no other way to secure this. Practically speaking, sickness is the most effective tool to interrupt the normal pattern of her mom working and Joanna staying with a babysitter.

On a Draw-a-Person test, Joanna drew a small figure that she identified as a "grown-up lady." The central themes of her answers to the psychologist's questions were illness and attention. Joanna stated that her lady has a disease that no one can cure. Although this makes the character "sad," her happiness stems from her children, her husband, and, it is important to note, the concern they display about the illness. She identified the lady's fear as having no family to take care of her. The three wishes of her character were to be able to go away on a vacation with her family, to buy her family presents, and to have the family members play with her.

The psychologist again met with the mother to present Joanna's perceptions, and received both supporting information and continued skepticism. Upon reviewing the information, the mother agreed that there was significant energy devoted to Joanna but still believed it was for legitimate medical reasons. The mother did support the finding that Joanna's father was very available to her when she was sick but that the mother disapproved of him buying gifts every time. As for Joanna's awareness that sickness meant attention, the mother believed that any physical complaints needed investigation, not dismissal. When pressed about why the pediatrician could not find anything of a medical nature, Joanna's mother stated that he had not considered her own hypotheses about what could be wrong.

The mother's resistance to a psychosomatic interpretation of Joanna's behavior had significant treatment implications. A typical approach, such as working through a parent to help modify a child's behavior and substituting more appropriate methods of gaining attention, could not be readily implemented. How could the mother agree to overlook Joanna's symptoms and to provide attention systematically at other times if she still believed that Joanna had a yet-undiscovered medical problem? In order to facilitate treatment of Joanna, it was decided to gear initial interventions toward the mother. To this end, two steps were taken: 1) A meeting was held with the mother, the pediatrician, and the psychologist, in which the mother was able to receive direct information from the pediatrician about why her theories of Joanna's illnesses were improbable; and 2) a monitoring system was established, in which the mother tracked frequency and timing of Joanna's complaints, responsiveness of both parents, and shared activities or events with the parent.

Following 3 weeks of monitoring, Joanna's mother was much more amenable to viewing her daughter's behavior in a psychosomatic light, based on the conspicuous patterns that emerged. At that point, a set of behavioral interventions was developed for both parents to implement directly with Joanna. The emphasis of the interventions was three-fold: 1) to help her parents acknowledge their daughter's need for attention and to provide it when Joanna was not behaving "sickly," thus introducing more appropriate ways of seeking attention; 2) to teach her parents to both dismiss and redirect Joanna's complaints and behavior, thus reducing these behaviors; and 3) to begin refocusing her socialization away from her parents and into age-appropriate activities with peers, thus reducing her dependence on her parents as the sole source of socialization.

## A SCHOOL REFERRAL

Nicole is an 11-year-old, fifth-grade student who was referred to the school psychologist by her classroom teacher. According to the teacher's report, Nicole is having behavior problems in the classroom and on the playground, has strained peer relationships, and has deteriorating work performance. The classroom teacher wants to know if Nicole is eligible for a program for children with SED and what interventions she can use to help the student.

The mother identified problems that have been evident since Nicole's early childhood. She said that Nicole is "a bossy kid, real tough with other little ones in the neighborhood, but yet real sensitive, too . . . cries when she's upset or feeling hurt." For her, Nicole has always been a handful to manage, and she has sought help from various counselors here and there, as well as from their family doctor. Nothing has proven to be especially effective, and she believes that Nicole has only gotten worse over the years.

Nicole has one younger brother, Pete, who is 3 years old. The parents divorced shortly after Pete's birth, when Nicole was 9. The father has since remarried, and now has four sons in his new family. Nicole *is uninterested* in visitation, because even though her father is supposed to see her and Pete every other weekend he often cancels, making the time between visits about 4–6 weeks. Her mother reports that Nicole is extremely jealous of her stepbrothers and feels forgotten and abandoned by her father. Nicole's jealousy and resentment have apparently carried over into her relationship with Pete, which is now characterized by her mother as bossy and physically aggressive.

Nicole's school history was relatively problem free until this year. Although she was sometimes aggressive with other children, she seemed to respond to discipline. However, she has not responded this year. She recently caused several playground incidents, received detentions, and had meetings with her mother and school officials. When dealt with individually, Nicole frequently blames incidents on other children or becomes defensive and simply denies her actions. Afterward, however, she cries and apologizes for "being a bad girl." Nicole has no identified group of friends; she usually wanders about the playground in search of a playmate. She'll stay with a group for only a few minutes until she becomes bossy or aggressive and the group leaves her. This scene is repeated over and over again, each day. In class, she talks "incessantly, to anyone" according to the teacher, and asks repeated, off-task questions such as, "What's for lunch today; when we do math, will you help me; are we going on a field trip soon?" The teacher has speculated that Nicole is trying to keep her near for attention and security.

Academically, Nicole had typically been an A/B student, but this year her grades reflect a steady downward trend. For the first quarter, she received all Cs and one B; the second quarter, she received two Cs and four Ds; and she currently is failing two classes. Her work completion has dropped, her homework has been incomplete, and her "continuous" questioning and talking has interfered with productivity. The teacher has modified the amount of work required and lowered the level of Nicole's homework, but to no avail. In addition, group-task situations are difficult, as a result of Nichole's tenuous peer relationships.

Upon evaluation with a WISC–III, Nicole earned a Verbal IQ of 118 and a Performance IQ of 110, indicating a more-than-adequate ability level for success in a general classroom. On academic testing, however, she revealed a loss of skills of approximately 6 months to a year. Her Woodcock-Johnson battery scores all fell below average, clustered around the late–third- to mid–fourth-grade level. This is supported by her teacher, who reported that Nicole's behaviors, including talking and not completing work or homework, has impeded her learning and thus is not at a fifth-grade–skill level. A Teacher Report Form showed significant elevations on depressed, immature, and aggressive factors. Some of the behavior items noted were that Nicole was often moody, felt picked on, appeared sad, was argumentative, was impulsive, became easily frustrated, and had poor peer relationships. Nicole's incomplete sentences test reflected some of these factors, as well as other central concerns:

I want to know . . . *why my dad is the way he is.*
The happiest time . . . *is when my dad took me to Disneyland.*
I can't . . . *do anything right.*
I am sorry . . . *that no one likes me; I don't have friends.*
What bothers me . . . *is my dad. He makes me so mad.*
I feel . . . *mad when kids pick on me and won't play with me. I want to kill them when they do that.*
I wish . . . *I could be like everyone else, smart, cute, get good grades—not be goofy or trip over things.*
A father . . . *should be loving and caring and understanding.*
A mother . . . *can be mean but helps you get through things.*

When asked what three wishes she would most like to have granted, Nicole responded as follows: 1) to have friends, 2) to have a father who cares, and 3) to be like normal kids. It is evident from her responses that Nicole sees herself as abnormal and is clearly aware of her peer problems. Her sentences reflect a poor self-concept, feelings of anger toward people who shut her out, and no indication of how to address or alter her situation. Obviously, her father plays a big part in Nicole's life and affects her day-to-day functioning. On TAT cards, Nicole's stories corroborated findings from the Teacher Report Form and Incomplete Sentences:

Card 1: Well, this kid has to practice his violin and he hates it. So he's just sitting there, thinking what else he wants to do, like play outside, but the neighborhood kids are mean to him and that makes him mad. Then his mom yells at him to practice again, but he just keeps sitting there.

Card 2: This girl came to visit her dad. She hasn't seen him in a long time. She's all grown up now but hasn't seen him since she was little. That's his wife and they're having another baby. She used to be sad when she didn't see him, but now it don't matter cause she's grown up.

Card 5: It's a mother checking on her kids to make sure they're not doing anything wrong. They're playing a trick on her though, 'cause they don't like it when she checks on them so they're hiding from her.

Card 7: This girl's mother is reading a story to her, only the girl would rather go play with her doll. She's hoping the mother stops soon, or else she'll just tell her to stop.

Card 13: This man and his wife were sleeping except he couldn't sleep. They had a big fight and he yelled at her and hit her. He thinks he might divorce her now—he's not sure though because they got kids and if they divorced, they'd be real sad. His wife was crying, but now she's asleep.

Does the evaluation information indicate that Nicole is eligible for a program for children with serious emotional disabilities? From an educational standpoint, her learning certainly seems to be adversely affected. She is not achieving commensurate with her ability, as she once was. Evaluation results gave no indication of a learning problem; Nicole had no impairments in visual-motor coordination, attending skills, or reasoning ability, nor was there any difference in her ability with verbal and nonverbal material—all typical characteristics of learning difficulties. Instead, her recent backslide seems a result of behavioral factors. Emotionally, Nicole is experiencing depression, low self-concept, anger about her father, and a lack of friends. Given that she is such a bright girl, it is no surprise that she is highly cognizant of her father's behavior and is acutely aware of her peer problems. Unfortunately, she has no coping method available to her other than aggression. Her depression and poor self-concept are further compounded when her only method, aggression, fails to achieve her goals.

Based on a review of all the data, the school's special education team decided to recommend Nicole for the program under the SED definition. The federal government guidelines, which call for an inability to build satisfactory interpersonal relationships with peers or teachers and a general pervasive mood of depression, were most applicable to Nicole. Program goals included helping Nicole deal with her depressive feelings about her family situation and peer status. Individual counseling was suggested because of her strong verbal capabilities. It was believed that because these feelings were at the root of her aggressive behaviors, this should be the primary focus. A second step was then to help to establish the link between her feelings and behaviors and to develop more socially appropriate coping skills by having her participate in a social skill training group.

## SUMMARY

A psychologist's tools for assessing disturbed behavior include objective inventories and projective devices. Objective inventories may be in the form of self-report (e.g., MMPI–A, PIY) or may be completed by parents (e.g., CBCL, PIC) or classroom teachers (e.g., TRF). These inventories are standardized, norm-referenced measures that, when scored, yield quantitative data such as standard scores or percentile ranks. The personality profiles that result from objective measures are based on empirical research. Some profile types have been well researched and allow psychologists to make predictions about future outcome or response to treatment. Strengths of objective measures include their time and cost efficiency and also their advantage over projective devices in prognosticating behavior.

Projective techniques rely on the projective hypothesis rather than on empirical research, standardization, and norm-referencing. The projective hypothesis is that an individual will project onto a vague stimulus his or her conflicts, feelings, and needs. In contrast to the objective nature of interpretation of measures like the MMPI or CBCL, interpretation of projective measures is largely inferential. Common projective measures include 1) the Rorschach inkblot technique, in which a person describes what is seen in a series of inkblots; 2) the Thematic Apperception Test and the Roberts Apperception Test for Children, which are story-telling measures that use picture cards as the stimulus; 3) the incomplete-sentences method, in which a person completes partially written sentences; and 4) human figure drawings, where the child may be asked to draw a person, his or her family, home, or classmates. Projective measures are widely used, but typically in conjunction with objective assessment tools. Because they are controversial and lack psychometric soundness, projectives are not primary measures for making placement or classification decisions about children.

## Study Questions

1. Discuss the differences between objective and projective measures.
2. Which theoretical orientation is the primary influence on DSM-IV?
3. What is a serious emotional disturbance, and how is it defined?
4. When are human figure drawings preferred over story-telling tests?
5. What is actuarial interpretation? What are its strengths?
6. What are potential drawbacks to self-report and parent-completed measures?
7. Compare the classification system of DSM-IV with the federal law IDEA.

## CHAPTER EIGHT

# Neuropsychological Assessment of Children and Adolescents

Recent increases in the understanding of brain function and the behavioral concomitants of brain dysfunction have spurred neuropsychological assessment. Although the use of traditional psychological tests to assess children overlaps appreciably with the use of neuropsychological tests, there are nonetheless important differences and distinctions between the two approaches. This chapter briefly describes some of the basic assessment tools and purposes of neuropsychological assessment with children. It is likely that neuropsychological measurement will exert an increasingly powerful influence on the assessment of children in the future.

Is Robert showing signs of brain injury after he was involved in a car–pedestrian accident?

Has surgery to remove a malignant brain tumor affected Ellen's psychological functioning? Which abilities are most affected?

How much has Phillip's status improved in the 3 months since a near drowning? How can his progress be monitored in the future?

Answers to these questions obviously involve assessing brain functions—a pursuit typically assigned to neurology, a branch of medicine. Although neurology continues to be concerned with brain–behavior relationships, a rapidly growing branch of psychology, neuropsychology, is also addressing this relationship. The application of techniques from this field, called clinical neuropsychology, is important for consumers of psychological testing to understand.

Historically, physicians trained in neurology have been concerned about disease processes such as structural-anatomical, chemical, or electrical abnormalities of the brain (Rosenberger, 1986). Patients' behaviors, both as observed directly during examination and as reported from examinee history, often help the physician make accurate diagnoses. Neurological examinations, however, tend to look for obvious physical features of disease or damage. If neurologists assess behavioral manifestations, then they tend to examine simple reflexes of sensory and motor status, with higher intellectual processes being assessed only grossly and informally (Rosenberger, 1986). With the advent of sophisticated neuroimaging techniques that include computed tomography (CT), magnetic resonance imaging (MRI), and positron emission tomography (PET), which allow observation of the anatomy of the brain and, in some cases, its actual physiological functioning, most neurologists perform even fewer behavioral assessments in their offices than was once the case. Simultaneous with these developments, neuropsychological techniques that formalize behavioral observations of brain functioning and focus on higher brain functions (i.e., those associated with the cerebral cortex) have become available to perform roles complementary to and collaborative with neurology.

Neuropsychological assessment is concerned with measuring psychological performance that is associated with brain functioning. What are the unique attributes of neuropsychological tests, and how are these tests used to make decisions about children? After all, traditional intelligence tests (e.g., the WISC–III) measure functioning mediated by the central nervous system, but they are not in themselves identified as neuropsychological tests. Likewise, the WISC–III is sensitive to brain injury—an additional hallmark of neuropsychological tests.

Work with adults who have sustained an obvious brain injury, such as wounds to the head or cerebral vascular accident (stroke), is a starting place for understanding neuropsychological testing. Some adults with brain injuries experience intellectual decline as a result of their injury, as indicated by diminished postinjury Full Scale IQ scores—a fact that has long been known (see, e.g., Morrow & Mark, 1955). Clearly, IQ tests are sensitive to some forms of brain injury in adults. Nonetheless, many people with documented brain injury have no discernible IQ decline but instead have subtle changes in their ability to deal with the world. Some of these changes are evident on individual IQ subtests (if not on Full Scale IQ); others are detectable only by careful observation or by requiring performance of quite specialized tasks that involve sensory or motor performance comparisons of one side of the body with the other. Pioneers, such as A.R. Luria in the Soviet Union, and Ward Halstead and his student Ralph Reitan in the United States, investigated innumerable psychological functions to determine which were related to brain injury. Many of their assessment techniques, in their original form or as modified by subsequent investigators, have come to be used in clinical practice. By expanding testing to include some of these specialized tasks—many of which are not included in traditional IQ tests—professionals have gained sensitivity in detecting brain dysfunction. Not only have investigators found that special tests help to identify people with brain injury, but they also found that some tests may help locate the site of damage. Such findings are possible because, in the mature brains of adults, damage to certain brain centers may result in predictable patterns on neuropsychological tests.

After many clinical trials and some controlled research, clinicians began to use batteries of special tests to help determine both if brain injury had occurred in adult patients and to speculate on the location of that damage. Among the uses of these adult neuropsychological batteries were the following: 1) to locate the exact site of brain lesions, 2) to determine whether the brain injury was likely or unlikely in equivocal cases, 3) to profile strengths and weaknesses so that a post-injury rehabilitation program could be developed, and 4) to monitor return of functioning by repeated testing after an injury. A similar list of goals for children's neuropsychological testing was developed when batteries for children were created (Hartlage & Telzrow, 1986). Unfortunately, attainment of these goals is far more controversial if children rather than adults are the subject of evaluation.

Detecting neuropsychological impairments in adults is far easier than in children because it is assumed that unless adults' brains are injured, or unless they have been extremely deprived, adults can perform a wide range of tasks quite adequately. Should an adult lack some very basic capability, then his or her performance tends to clearly stand out as unusual. For instance, almost all adults can distinguish which of their fingers is being touched while they are blindfolded. The inability to do so is rare in adults and is highly suggestive of brain malfunction. Failure on this task typically allows the examiner to assume that the adult subject had once acquired this skill and can no longer do it because of a nervous system change or deterioration. In contrast, children are far more likely than adults to fail a finger localization task. This is because children must acquire this skill as they develop, and some typically developing children have not yet acquired the nervous system maturity necessary to perform the task. Nonetheless, among children, poor performance on a standardized version of this task (Tactile Finger Recognition Test, see p. 250) may be a sign of brain injury. Finger localization errors may provide compelling evidence of brain dysfunction in adults but only help offer hypotheses that a problem exists in children.

Two important differences between children and adults cannot be overemphasized when considering neuropsychological testing. First, children's nervous systems are still undergoing growth (and are subject to spurts and plateaus in developmental rate), and thus deficits may reflect delay but not damage. Second, children are far more difficult to test than adults. For instance, is 7-year-old Robert's poor performance on the Tactile Finger Recognition Test due to damage to his nervous system that may have been sustained in an automobile accident, or might this performance merely reflect slightly delayed development that is unrelated to the accident? Other possibilities are that Robert simply did not understand the examiner's directions or that he was distracted during the task, which adversely affected his performance. Distractibility and problems following directions are common among 7-year-olds and fail to indicate delays of any type; they certainly do not constitute neuropsychological impairment signifying brain malfunction. Isolating neuropsychological functions in children and measuring each without the contamination of other skills—especially in young children (i.e., those younger than 10 years)—is difficult, and consequently, inferences about brain injury with this group must be made cautiously. Examiners encounter many of the same problems when using nearly all neuropsychological tests with children. Although poor performance may suggest brain dysfunction, it also may result from normal variations in development. Abilities other than those intended to be assessed by any particular test may contribute to poor performance, thus making definitive measurement of narrow abilities difficult.

Despite the problems mentioned above, two neuropsychological batteries for children have gained popular usage in the United States. Both are time consuming to administer and can be accurately interpreted only by psychologists who have special knowledge of nervous system functioning and neuropsychological assessment.

## HALSTEAD-REITAN AND REITAN-INDIANA BATTERIES

The Reitan-Indiana Neuropsychological Test Battery for Children (Reitan, 1987) is suitable for children from 5 to 6 years of age, and the Halstead-Reitan Neuropsychological Test Battery for Older Children (Reitan & Wolfson, 1992) is for those from 9 to 14 years of age (see Table 8.1). Both of these batteries are downward extensions of adult batteries, although some unique tests had to be developed to assess younger children. These batteries and their clinical uses were refined over a period of years by Reitan and his associates as they worked with patients suffering from nervous system diseases and injuries.

Table 8.1. Summary of Reitan-Indiana[a] and Halstead-Reitan[b] batteries[c]

| Test name | Battery | Skills assessed |
|---|---|---|
| Seashore Rhythm Test | HR | Attending, auditory perception, sequencing |
| Speech-Sounds Perception Test | HR | Attending, auditory perception, visual integration |
| Trail Making Test | HR | Flexibility, scanning, symbolic appreciation |
| Sensory Perception | HR, RI | Attending, sensory perception |
| Strength of Grip | HR, RI | Upper extremity motor strength |
| Lateral Dominance | HR, RI | Right/left preference |
| Category Test | HR, RI | Concept formation, problem solving, flexibility |
| Tactual Performance Test | HR, RI | Sensorimotor ability, problem solving, organization |
| Finger Tapping Test | HR, RI | Fine-motor speed |
| Aphasia Screening Test | HR, RI | Expressive and receptive language, spatial, reading and writing ability |

[a]RI = Reitan-Indiana.
[b]HR = Halstead-Reitan.
[c]Optional Reitan-Indiana tests consist of Matching Pictures Test, Individual Performance Tests, Marching Test, Progressive Figures Test, Color Form Test, and Target Test.

## Halstead-Reitan Neuropsychological Test Battery for Older Children (9–14 Years)

The Halstead-Reitan Neuropsychological Test Battery for Older Children is frequently used in its complete form even though it is quite time consuming. Use of the complete battery permits several summary scores to be produced for children from 9 to 14 years of age. Some sense of the Reitan approach can be discerned by reviewing the battery's components as outlined below under several headings. Most components come from Reitan and Wolfson's own test material; a few come from the WISC, which is administered as part of the battery.

***Motor Functions*** Four tests are administered to assess motor functioning.

*Finger Tapping Test* Children work with mechanical counters that permit precise tabulation of the oscillation of a single (index) finger. Children are instructed to work as quickly as possible. Their score is the number of taps completed within 10 seconds (averaged across five trials). Taps for dominant and nondominant hands are calculated separately.

*Strength of Grip* Children hold a dynamometer in their dominant and nondominant hands for two trials each. Performance is measured in kilograms of pressure for each hand when the child is instructed to squeeze with maximum strength.

*Name Writing* Time required for a child to write his or her first and last name is measured for both dominant and nondominant hands.

*Tactual Performance Test* Children are blindfolded and presented with six geometric shapes and a formboard with indentations corresponding to each shape. Without ever seeing the shapes or the board, children must insert the shapes into the board as quickly as possible with first their dominant hand, then with their nondominant hand, and finally with both hands together. Times are recorded for each trial separately, but the total time required to complete all three trials is used for calculating motor performance using the Halstead-Reitan system.

***Sensory-Perceptual Functions*** The four tasks involving sensory-perceptual functions have much in common with standard neurological examinations.

*Bilateral Simultaneous Sensory Stimulation* Despite the task's name, the Bilateral Simultaneous Sensory Stimulation task actually begins with stimulation to either one side of the body or the other (unilateral). The examiner touches the child's right or left hand while the child is blindfolded, and the child must determine which hand is touched. Similarly, the examiner makes noise on the side of either the right or left ear or to the right or left of the visual field (including above, below, and at eye level) with the requirement for proper recognition of the stimulus' location. For children who pass these tasks (most do), trials of simultaneous stimulation to both sides of the body (bilateral) are interspersed with unilateral stimulation. The examiner notes any "extinctions," which occur if the child ignores or fails to attend to a stimulus to one side of the body if both sides are stimulated simultaneously (i.e., reports unilateral stimulation when bilateral stimulation actually occurred). That is, a child may indicate that only the right hand was touched when actually both right and left hands were touched at the same time (this would be an extinction with the right hand).

*Tactile Finger Recognition Test* The blindfolded child is touched on each finger four times in an irregular sequence (total of 20 trials with each hand). The score is the number of errors (i.e., report of wrong finger) with each hand. (Errors are sometimes referred to as indicative of "finger dysgnosia" or "finger agnosia.")

*Fingertip Number Writing Perception Test* While blindfolded, each child has single-digit numbers (e.g., 3, 5, 6) written on his or her fingertips by the examiner using a standard pencil. The task is to discern which number was written. There are 20 trials with each hand; the number of errors with each hand constitutes the child's score. (Errors are sometimes referred to as indicative of "agraphesthesia.")

*Tactile Form Recognition Test* Without looking, the child feels a geometric shape (e.g., square) and indicates his or her recognition of it by pointing to that shape in an array presented by the examiner.

The child's score is the number of errors made during eight trials with the right hand and during eight trials with the left hand. (Errors are sometimes referred to as indicative of "astereognosis.")

***Visual-Spatial Skills*** Scores from several previously administered WISC performance subtests are included in the assessment of visual-spatial skills:

*WISC Picture Arrangement* See page 112.
*WISC Block Design* See page 113.
*WISC Object Assembly* See page 113.

*Trail Making Test–Part A* The child is presented an 8½″ × 11″ page with numbers 1–15 dispersed throughout the page. The child's task is to begin at number 1 and use a pencil to connect each of the numbers together in sequential order as quickly as possible (the effort results in the making of a trail). Elapsed time to complete the task is the child's score.

***Attention and Concentration*** There are two tests used to measure attention and concentration.

*Seashore Rhythm Test* The child's task on the Seashore Rhythm Test is to listen to a tape recording of 30 sets of rhythmical patterns and to indicate whether each set is the same or different. The child must keep pace with the presentation and indicate on an answer sheet whether the sets are the "same" or "different." The child's score is the number of correct answers.

*Speech-Sounds Perception Test* The child listens to a voice on a tape recorder that pronounces non-words, each consisting of an initial consonant, a double vowel "ee" as the middle syllable, and a final consonant sound. On a corresponding sheet the child selects from among these choices by circling the correct answer. For example, the voice on the tape may say "feeg." From among the written choices, "beeg," "leet," and "feeg," the child must mark his or her selection. There are 60 items; the score is the number of errors made.

***Immediate Memory and Recapitulation*** Only two scores are included in the assessment of immediate memory and recapitulation, and both come from a task the child completed at the conclusion of the Tactual Performance Test (see above).

*Tactual Performance Test–Memory* The child is asked to draw the shapes (using standard pencil and paper) that he or she handled while blindfolded during completion of the Tactual Performance Test. Score is the number of shapes properly recalled (six points possible).

*Tactual Performance Test–Location* After the child's performance is scored for correct recall (see preceding paragraph), it is scored again for proper location of the recalled shapes. A total of six points is possible on this test if the child recalls the proper location of each shape.

***Abstraction, Reasoning, Logical Analysis***

*Category Test* See description later in this chapter.

*Trail Making Test–Part B* The Trail Making Test–Part B is similar to Trail Making Test–Part A except that the task here is to alternate between number and letter sequences as the trail is made. For children in this age range, numbers 1–8 are placed on the page as are letters A–G. The child begins at 1 and proceeds to A, from A to 2, from 2 to B, from B to 3, and so on sequentially until reaching the end. The child's performance is measured in elapsed time.

*WISC Coding* See page 110.

***Aphasia Screening Test*** The brief Aphasia Screening Test measures a mixture of items, many related to language functioning (aphasia is defined as "a deficit, due to cerebral impairment, in the ability to utilize language symbols [receptively and / or expressively] for communicative purposes" [Reitan & Wolfson, 1992, p. 821]). By noting the child's performance on naming, repeating, reading, spelling, arithmetic computing, direction following, and drawing tasks, errors leading to suspicions of brain dysfunction can be noted. When various types of problems are observed (e.g., central dysarthria, which is defined as "deficit, due to brain impairment, in the ability to enunciate words; characterized by an omission, addition, or transposition of syllables" [Reitan & Wolfson, 1992, p. 376]), points are assigned. These points are later used in calculating scores that index the child's dysfunction, as is discussed below.

## Reitan-Indiana Neuropsychological Test Battery for Children (5–8 Years)

The Reitan-Indiana Neuropsychological Test Battery for Children (5–8 years) generally consists of tasks like those of the battery for 9- to 14-year-olds in simplified form. However, some tasks have been added that parallel other children's tests. These include Star Drawing and Concentric Square Drawing, which are similar to other children's shape drawing tasks. There are some unique tasks too, such as Marching for dominant and nondominant hands, which requires the child to demonstrate motor speed and accuracy with the entire arm while using a writing tool (rather than using the hand alone), and Marching Circles, which requires bilateral hand and arm movement while following a tempo set by the examiner.

The following tests are administered to determine level of performance, which is combined with right–left differences and scores from the Aphasia Screening Test to produce a total Neuropsychological Deficit Scale, as discussed below.

***Motor Functions*** The following four tests measure motor functions:

*Finger Tapping Test* (dominant and nondominant hands)
*Marching Test* (dominant and nondominant hands)
*Marching Test Circles*
*Tactual Performance Test*

***Sensory-Perceptual Functions*** The following four tests measure sensory-perceptual functions:

*Bilateral Sensory Perception*
*Tactile Finger Recognition Test*
*Fingertip Symbol Writing Test*
*Tactile Form Recognition Test*

***Alertness, Concentration, and Recapitulation*** The following test measures alertness, concentration, and recapitulation:

*Tactual Performance Test—Memory and Localization*

***Visual-Spatial Abilities*** The following five tests measure visual-spatial abilities:

*Matching Figures Test*
*Matching V's Test*
*Star Drawing Test*
*Concentric Squares Drawing Test*
*Target Test*

***Abstraction, Reasoning, Logical Analysis, and Integration Skills*** The following four tests measure abstraction, reasoning, logical analysis, and integration skills;

*Matching Pictures Test*
*Category Test*
*Color Form Test*
*Progressive Figures Test*

In an attempt to produce a battery that is linked to brain function and dysfunction, Reitan (1987) and Reitan and Wolfson (1992) have included tests that measure abstract reasoning and conceptual ability and language, as do traditional intelligence tests, but they also emphasize motor, sensory, attention, laterality, and perceptual skills far more extensively than traditional IQ tests. The laboratory work of Reitan and his co-researchers demonstrated that adding these measures to traditional cognitive tasks resulted in a more comprehensive view of the psychological functions performed by the brain. Many of the scales that compose both the adults' and children's batteries are based on experimental laboratory techniques that are modified for clinical use.

Reitan's group also found that abilities more closely linked to intelligence tests such as language and spatial/mechanical abilities have value as part of neuropsychological batteries, but these tasks were often modified to detect severe problems. For example, the Aphasia Screening Test, part of the batteries administered to both older and younger children, contains items much like ones that might be seen on the Stanford-Binet Intelligence Scale: Form L–M or on the WPPSI–R.

People taking the Aphasia Screening Test perform very simple naming and drawing tasks. In contrast to traditional ability tests, which comprise items of moderate difficulty so that subjects can be dispersed along a normal continuum, the Aphasia Screening Test is composed of easy items that are failed only by children (and especially adults) with substantial impairments. Moreover, the Aphasia Screening Test items are designed to elicit distinct symptoms of brain dysfunction. Naming objects seen in pictures, for example, is designed to check for dysnomia (an impairment in the ability to name common objects); the drawing task is targeted at constructional dyspraxia (an impairment in the ability to construct or draw simple spatial configurations, characterized by distortions of spatial relationships) (Reitan & Wolfson, 1987). The former condition is most often associated with damage in the left cerebral hemisphere, and the latter with right hemisphere damage, especially to areas of the frontal lobes.

As is true of all Reitan batteries, interpretation of the battery for children ages 9–14 is complicated. Briefly, Reitan has suggested that four approaches be used to organize data and make inferences about the functioning of children's nervous systems: level of performance, pattern of performance, right–left differences, and pathognomonic signs (Selz, 1981). Inferences based on level of performance are possible because levels of performance that are below certain cutoff values have been shown by research to be consistently associated with brain injury. Consequently, summarizing the child's performance on the entire battery and comparing that performance with normative tables allows conclusions to be made about the presence and severity of damage. The Neuropsychological Deficit Scale is the overall composite score for the Halstead-Reitan Battery. It comprises scores from the Motor Functions; Sensory-Perceptual Functions; Attention and Concentration; Immediate Memory and Recapitulation; Visual-Spatial Skills; and Abstraction, Reasoning, and Logical Analysis areas mentioned above, which are added to values for performance on the Aphasia Screening Test and unusual findings suggestive of lateralized impairments (right–left differences as mentioned below). In this system, points are assigned for poor or pathological performance, thus the fewer points assigned the child, the less the presence of neuropsychological impairment. As shown in Table 8.2, there are large differences among children with brain damage, children with learning disabilities, and the control group in each of the areas, with the exception of Attention and Concentration in which children with learning disabilities performed even worse than children with known brain impairment. The Neuropsychological Deficit Scale, the overall cumulative value, shows large differences between a group of children with a variety of neurological impairments (e.g., traumatic brain injury, brain tumor) and control group children without neurological disease (mean value for children with brain damage is 67.34 as contrasted with 30.43 for the control group). Cutoff scores for assigning children to one group or the other exist. Of course, background information must be considered as well in order to rule out non–brain-injury sources of poor performance (e.g., lack of experience).

*Pattern of performance* consists of studying individual areas of functioning and the relationship among them, rather than studying composite performance. Children with brain impairment, as well as those with certain other problems, tend to have less uniform performance than children in general. In addition, knowing the strengths and weaknesses of each child may make planning more effective.

*Right–left differences* involve comparing sensory and motor performances on one side of the body with the other. Because the body is organized contralaterally, and because the Reitan batteries contain many tasks that directly compare one side of the body to the other, it is possible to make some important inferences. Making inference of this kind ultimately has implications for localization of brain lesions.

Table 8.2. Performance of children with brain damage, with learning disabilities, and without impairments (control) on Halstead-Reitan Neuropsychological Battery Test for Older Children

| | Brain damage | Learning disability | Control |
|---|---|---|---|
| Motor functions | Poor | Mid-range | Good |
| Sensory-perceptual functions | Poor | Mid-range | Good |
| Visual-spatial skills | Poor | Mid-range | Good |
| Attention concentration | Mid-range to poor | Poor | Good |
| Immediate memory | Poor | Mid-range to good | Good |
| Abstraction, reasoning, logical analysis | Poor | Mid-range | Good |

Adapted from Reitan and Wolfson (1992).

For example, the motor strip of the frontal cortex is responsible for motor control; the right side of this area controls left-side body movement, whereas the left side controls right-side body movement. Weakness of the right hand only, as detected by tasks such as grip strength, may thus be used to speculate about dysfunction in a particular location in the brain.

*Pathognomonic signs* relate to the observation of rare signs or symptoms that themselves suggest problems, despite overall performance. For instance, the Aphasia Screening Test's composition of easy items targeted at skills that are especially susceptible to brain injury is an example of how the Reitan batteries attempt to detect clusters of rare but potentially important symptoms.

Clinicians using the Halstead-Reitan or Reitan-Indiana batteries thus have multiple methods of data analysis that allow them to draw inferences about the brain's overall integrity and to locate circumscribed areas of dysfunction. It is especially true of assessment of this type, however, that the examiner must interpret and summarize findings in a coherent, organized fashion if the consumer is to understand their implications. Summary scores alone generally fail to help. By the same token, merely enumerating those skill areas in which the child has impairments and those in which he or she has strengths tends to leave the consumer confused and renders the data less than fully useful. Most well-trained neuropsychological diagnosticians synthesize test findings into a meaningful picture of the child's status and help the consumer by drawing implications from the findings. Of course, each report is expected to reflect the nature of the referral question that led the child to be evaluated initially (see Chapter 2).

Likewise, each test battery is modified to meet the case demands. Most children are administered the WISC–III, either the Reitan-Indiana battery or Halstead-Reitan battery, supplemental neuropsychological tests such as the Grooved Pegboard (a manual dexterity measure) (Matthews & Klove, 1964), and academic achievement and social-emotional measures. The effects of central nervous system dysfunction are so potentially pervasive that a comprehensive, multifaceted battery is often required.

Unfortunately, from a psychometric viewpoint the Reitan-Indiana and the Halstead-Reitan batteries are weak compared to most children's intelligence and achievement tests. There are so few reliability and validity data and the norms are so sparse that it has been contended that the batteries' usefulness derives primarily from the clinical sophistication of the examiner (Sattler, 1988); more recent data call into question the reliabilities of some individual measures, although without questioning the value of the batteries as a whole (Leckliter, Forster,

Klonoff, & Knights, 1992). The batteries have been shown to differentiate children with brain damage from a control group of typical children, with acceptable numbers of misclassifications (Reitan & Davison, 1974). In addition, the test batteries appear generally capable of accurately separating children into those with learning disabilities, brain injury, and typically developing groups (Selz, 1981).

However, the Halstead-Reitan children's battery has been shown to be affected by IQ (Seidenberg, Giordani, Berent, & Boll, 1983), and some have questioned whether it measures as much unique, brain-related performance as has been suggested. For instance, a study conducted by Reitan (1974) found that almost all measures of cognition, academic achievement (i.e., WRAT), and neuropsychological functioning distinguished children with brain injury from typical children, but the WISC–R measure was the most sensitive. Questions also have been raised about the viability of localizing the site of lesions in young children, whose nervous systems are still evolving and for whom functions such as language are not yet firmly localized on one hemisphere of the brain. Some experts have suggested that these batteries not be used to localize damage until further research is completed and that their use with young children be limited (Hynd & Willis, 1988). In practical terms, the Halstead-Reitan Battery takes a long time to administer (generally 4–6 hours or more) and requires extensive materials. The equipment is so extensive and cumbersome that a special neuropsychology lab is often set up to house it and permit efficient administration of the battery. These are, obviously, considerations limiting use of the batteries.

## LURIA-NEBRASKA NEUROPSYCHOLOGICAL BATTERY: CHILDREN'S REVISION

A competitor of the Halstead-Reitan and Reitan-Indiana batteries is the Luria-Nebraska Neuropsychological Battery, first published in 1980 (Golden, Hammeke, & Purisch), and subsequently revised (Golden, 1987) to slightly update and modify its original content. The Luria-Nebraska Neuropsychological Battery: Children's Revision is suitable for children from 8 to 12 years of age, although the battery is virtually identical to the adult version except for a small number of selected areas that are not administered or interpreted.

The Luria-Nebraska battery can be contrasted with the Halstead-Reitan and Reitan-Indiana batteries not only because of its briefer history but also by virtue of its theoretical basis. The Halstead-Reitan and Reitan-Indiana batteries were largely constructed on empirical grounds, with many items originally being investigated, and only those items that discriminated people with brain injury from people without brain injury being retained. Some (Hynd & Snow, 1985) have suggested that the Halstead-Reitan and Reitan-Indiana batteries have been developed with relatively little regard for theory of brain function and dysfunction (although Halstead has published a theoretical position) (Halstead, 1947). In contrast, the clinical tools, practical insights, and theoretical formulations of A.R. Luria are explicitly cited as the beginning points for construction of the Luria-Nebraska battery (Golden, 1981). As is mentioned in Chapter 5, Luria was a famous practitioner and theoretician who assessed literally thousands of individuals with brain injury. Although his work is too complicated to summarize here (see Luria, 1973), a few aspects of his work warrant highlighting.

Luria's contributions are not confined to specific clinical tools; rather, he sought a comprehensive view of how the brain performs psychological functions. Among his conclusions were the following:

1. The three broadest anatomical structures of the brain each perform basic psychological functions: the brain stem, pons, medulla, and thalamus are involved in arousal and filtering of sensory input; the cerebral cortex, including occipital, parietal, and temporal lobes, is involved in receiving, coding, and interpreting sensory input (when involved in organizing and integrating material these brain areas are typically assessed by IQ tests); and the frontal and prefrontal lobes are involved in motor output and, as the child grows, in planning and evaluating complex behavior.
2. Different areas of the brain develop at different times. Arousal functions develop early in the child's history, as do basic (primary) sensory abilities, whereas analysis and interpretation of sensory data, such as judging if two stimuli are the same (secondary) or comparing input from visual and auditory channels (tertiary), develop much later. Some evaluative functions controlled by the prefrontal lobes are not developed until adolescence or later, and therefore should not be assessed by children's tests.
3. Much human behavior can be thought of as consisting of functional systems. Each functional system involves several interacting areas of the brain that are coordinated to produce a specific behavior. No one area of the brain alone is responsible for most behavior emitted by humans (e.g., speech), although various areas do contribute quite specific elements that must be combined to make for action. By investigating which acts an individual cannot perform (e.g., cannot initiate speech, cannot repeat what is said, cannot select pictures of spoken words), and noting common el-

ements (and corresponding brains areas), speculation about the site of brain injury can occur.

4. Investigation of brain dysfunction consequently requires a diagnostician who notes symptoms, performs preliminary tests, generates hypotheses about the nature and location of the problems, and then proceeds to perform additional tests until hypotheses are confirmed or negated. The approach requires a knowledgeable (expert) diagnostician, with many behavioral tests available to him or her and variable periods of time in which to perform the evaluation.

Luria developed an approach to diagnosis that he found to be personally effective. Others, however, took years of training to gain competencies in Luria's techniques. In addition, the American preference for standardization and quantification was inconsistent with Luria's approach. Golden and his colleagues sought to retain the comprehensiveness of Luria's theory and his clinical insights in a simplified, objective test battery that was amenable to empirical research.

In the Children's Revision, the Luria-Nebraska battery consists of 149 items organized into 11 scales (see Table 8.3). Each item is scored with a 0, 1, or 2, denoting normal performance, weak evidence of brain injury, or strong evidence of brain injury, respectively. Items tap abilities ranging from general intelligence and academic skills to more traditionally neuropsychological functions, such as rhythm, tactile discrimination, verbal fluency, and motor control. Because children presumably have yet to fully develop the prefrontal lobes, functions

Table 8.3. Description of Luria-Nebraska Neuropsychological Battery: Children's Revision

| Scale[a] | Abilities assessed |
|---|---|
| Motor Functions | Bilateral motor speed, coordination, construction, verbal control of motor skills |
| Rhythm | Auditory discrimination, perception, verbal/motor imitation |
| Tactile Functions | Tactile sensitivity, awareness, discrimination |
| Visual Functions | Visual recognition, memory, and spatial skills |
| Receptive Speech | Auditory reception and discrimination, language reception and comprehension |
| Expressive Speech | Articulation, fluency, memory, oral formulation, expressive capabilities |
| Writing | Copying, spelling, and writing from dictation |
| Reading | Reading of letters, words, phrases, and sentences |
| Arithmetic | Number recognition and manipulation, arithmetic calculation, and problem solving |
| Memory | Recall of orally and visually presented material |
| Intellectual Processes | Varied cognitive tasks involving language, sequencing, comprehension and judgment |

[a]Spelling and Motor Writing are optional scales.

controlled by these structures are excluded from the Children's Revision but are included in the Adult Battery (for those older than 12). This fact represents the application of Luria's theory to actual use of the Luria-Nebraska battery. The Children's Revision yields T-scores; the higher the T-score, the poorer the child's performance. T-scores are available for each of the 11 scales and are designed to determine if the child surpasses a standard for brain injury, calibrated to consider the child's age. Consistent with Luria's theory, these scales attempt to determine the intactness of various primary, secondary, and tertiary systems in the brain. Summary scales are also available to provide an overall estimate of brain impairment.

Finally, narrow factor scales assess specific neuropsychological functions, but these are generally much less reliable than overall summary scores (Sattler, 1988), which means they must be interpreted cautiously. Although less reliable, factor scores can be examined to permit fine-grained analysis and enable understanding not evident from summary scores. Consider a child with impaired motor performance as revealed by a Motor Functions T-score of 72. Motor Functions is a rather broad summary of motor performance that fails to pinpoint exact problems; examining the narrow factors of motor performance may help. In this hypothetical case it might be found that almost all the child's problems are due to slow response speed. The factor scores on the Luria-Nebraska that measure response speed show impairment: One taps complex motor acts with the hands while being timed (T-score of 81), and one evaluates the time required to draw geometric shapes (T-score of 74). Alternatively, other elements of motor performance, such as the quality of drawing and the ability to perform spatial-based movements (without regard for speed), produced factor scores near average.

Like the Halstead-Reitan and Reitan-Indiana batteries, the Luria-Nebraska battery has been criticized as having a fairly small and poorly defined standardization sample and as having insufficient evidence of reliability. However, the battery does appear to be capable of separating children into groups with and without brain injury with some degree of accuracy. Moreover, the battery appears to assist in the monitoring of brain functioning over time, an important consideration in assessing children with either progressive disease or with continuing improvement after a head trauma (Begali, 1987, 1992).

The Luria-Nebraska has unique advantages and disadvantages. Compared to the Halstead-Reitan batteries, the Luria-Nebraska has two distinctive practical advantages—speed of administration and portability of test materials. In hospital settings, when only a brief time may be permitted for assessment (e.g., when hospital discharge is imminent), the Luria-Nebraska can be quite useful. The kit can be easily transported, and virtually all of the items can be administered in 2–3 hours at bedside (scoring and interpretation, of course, add time to the overall process). Such an evaluation offers a comprehensive, but somewhat brief, look at most of the functional areas that may be affected by neurological involvement. However, the number of items and depth of information that can be gleaned from such an evaluation seems less than that for the Halstead-Reitan batteries.

Although the Halstead-Reitan and Luria-Nebraska batteries have become increasingly popular, their use nonetheless remains confined to a relatively small percentage of all psychologists who work with children. Each battery is long and fairly hard to learn to administer and score; without practice, one has difficulty retaining administration skills. The test batteries and required material, particularly for the Halstead-Reitan, can be quite expensive to acquire. Most psychologists who work with children have not mastered the skills for such testing during their training or if they did, they have not retained these skills after their training was completed. Furthermore, the essential background in neurosciences and first-hand experience with children with neurological disorders are far from universal among psychologists. Even among psychologists who use the batteries, neuropsychological testing may be restricted to quite limited instances, such as when referral questions deal specifically with questions of brain injury. Perhaps the greater significance of these instruments has to do with their impact on theory and conceptualization of children's abilities in general and learning problems in particular.

It has long been speculated that children with learning disabilities who lack obvious signs of brain injury might have nervous systems that are subtly and mildly damaged (i.e., the old and controversial idea of "minimal brain injury"), or might at least have dysfunctions of the nervous system that are understandable from a neuropsychological perspective. Neuropsychological techniques have thus provided a basis for intensified study of learning disabilities. For example, Reitan and his associates have conducted multiple studies describing the differences among children without disabilities, children with learning disabilities, and children with brain injury. Likewise, Luria's work has influenced those who seek a more comprehensive view of intelligence and who intend to devise test instruments that are theory based (i.e., the Kaufman Assessment Battery for Children, discussed in Chapter 5). By conducting neuropsychologically grounded research on teaching children with learning disabilities, it has been suggested that many of the failures of previous theoretical research can be rectified. For instance, the fact that little evidence exists to suggest that matching teaching styles to psychological strengths of children with learning disabilities may be a shortcoming of theory and understanding rather than of the principle of teaching to strength per se. Consequently, although questions remain about the clinical utility of neuropsychological batteries such as the Halstead-Retain battery and the Luria-Nebraska battery, neuropsychological evaluation is probably here to stay as an applied technique and as a source of influence regarding children's abilities. Two concepts rooted in neuropsychology, executive functions and nonverbal learning disabilities (NLD), illustrate the impact that neuropsychological conceptualization is exerting on the understanding of behavior, even when children do not have frank brain impairment. After these two concepts are discussed, the chapter turns to the use of neuropsychological tests with children who clearly do have brain impairment.

## NONVERBAL LEARNING DISABILITY

The very availability of neuropsychological instruments has stimulated empirical research about various aspects of learning and development. This research has prompted theorization, which has led to further research in a synergistic interplay of observation, theory development, further observation, and theory refinement. Such productive research enterprises have occurred even when children without genuine neurological disease or impairment are the focus of investigation. No better example of this scenario exists than the 20-year research efforts of neuropsychologist Byron Rourke from the University of Windsor on NLDs.

Dr. Rourke's research enterprise and his theory is truly extensive, and any effort at brief summarization of it is destined to be inadequate. Nonetheless, early efforts began with children with learning disabilities and followed a basic premise. Children with learning disabilities are extremely heterogeneous; thus, any effort to summarize their psychological attributes by averaging scores across many children is destined to fail. Rourke has argued that it makes more sense to identify differences, even if they are initially simple and superficial differences, and use these to group children more homogeneously before searching for underlying processing impairment. Even using simple groupings based on reading, spelling, and arithmetic scores on the Wide Range Achievement Test, Rourke found obvious differences in psychological profiles of children with learning disabilities. Consider two groups of children with learning disabilities: One has high reading and spelling scores but low arithmetic scores; a second has high arithmetic scores but low reading and spelling scores. Rourke found that language problems (in part reflected by lower WISC Verbal than Performance IQ) characterized the low reading/spelling group; the opposite pattern of nonverbal and visuospatial problems (in part reflected by lower WISC Performance than Verbal IQ) characterized the low arithmetic group. These findings are similar to the emerging data on the neuropsychological bases of learning problems (see Pennington, 1991, for discussion).

This information provided the database necessary for initial hypothesizing about various neuropsychological strengths and deficits that might be associated with each type of learning problem. After copious research, Rourke advanced the idea of NLD and enumerated the neuropsychological, academic, and social/interpersonal strengths and weaknesses associated with it. He also advanced a theory about the development of the various cognitive, academic, and interpersonal skills and the neurological changes that accompany development. In part, his theory depended on the integration of emerging conceptualization about brain functioning, specifically the Goldberg/Costa Model (see Table 8.4). The concept of NLD has remained closely tied to neurology and neuropsychology—neurologist Martha Denckla (1991) defines NLD as "learning disabilities of the right hemisphere" (p. 717). Attempts to find efficient and reliable ways to detect the disorder often rely on neuropsychological tests such as the Tactual Performance Test, Grooved Pegboard, and Trail Making (Harnadek & Rourke, 1994).

In his summary 1989 volume, Rourke described the primary impairments of children with NLD. Tactile perception errors often are found, and these are noted on tests such as the sensory/perceptual items such as found on the Halstead-Reitan battery. Consistent with

Table 8.4. Elements of Goldberg/Costa Model: Hemisphere differences and relationships

The right and left hemispheres of the human brain are not equivalent.

Adequate development of skills performed by the left hemisphere depends, in part, on the prior adequate development of the right hemisphere.

The left hemisphere has relatively more gray matter, and the left has relatively more white matter, which permits communication among various brain regions.

The left hemisphere anatomically is devoted more to performing specific sensory and motor tasks, whereas the right is more devoted to associative tasks such as integrating information from different senses (vision and sound).

Right hemisphere integrity is especially necessary for processing novel information if no preexisting system for organizing or coding that information is available.

Left hemisphere integrity is especially necessary to refine and elaborate applications (and thus to work faster and more efficiently) after a code (e.g., language) is established.

During the course of development, a progressive right hemisphere to left hemisphere shift occurs in the locus of control of cognitive functions.

Summarization of Rourke's (1989) description of the Goldberg/Costa Model.

the presumed relative impairment of the right cerebral hemisphere, errors involving the left side of the body occur more often (sensory pathways are predominantly crossed so that errors involving sensation to the left side of the body imply dysfunction in the right side of the brain), whereas visual perception problems are also present. Poor scores on WISC Performance subtests, such as Picture Completion or Block Design, may indicate impairment with visual detail, visual/spatial relationships, or visual organizational problems. Complex psychomotor impairments further characterize the NLD. These may be noted in the WISC Mazes subtest and in tests that evaluate motor performance first with the dominant side of the body and then the nondominant, such as the Grooved Pegboard Test and the Tactual Performance Test. In these later instances, children with NLD have bilateral problems, with more marked problems tending to occur on the left side of the body. A final primary impairment associated with NLD is difficulty with learning novel material. Children often experience extreme problems with the Category Test because they must learn one rule for solving an ambiguous problem based on examiner feedback (they are told "right" or "wrong" as they venture answers to a series of items; see description of this test later in this chapter).

Inefficiency when confronted with novelty tends to mark children with NLD on initial aspects of the Tactual Performance Test because this task is so unfamiliar and requires learning and adaptation. WISC Performance subtests, too, may be relatively difficult because their format tends to be unfamiliar, and they required greater adaptation than WISC Verbal items (i.e., WISC Verbal items may strike the child as similar to some things done at school, such as answering direct questions from the classroom teacher).

Important social and interpersonal consequences often accompany NLD as well, and some of these are consistent with previously known facts about individuals with right-hemisphere impairment. As a group, children with NLD adapt poorly to novel social situations. The rapid interplay that characterizes much of the communication among children and teenagers may be confusing for them; they are apt to miss social cues and subtle social messages. Even though many of the language functions necessary for school success may not be affected, the social aspects of language may be quite impaired. For example, children with NLD may have poor prosody (emotional tone necessary to impart meaning) as they speak, and their use of language to engage others socially or to make a point (pragmatics of language) may be poor. The clumsy use of language by children with NLD seems similar to adults with frank damage to the right hemisphere who talk a great deal but fail to use language in practical, social ways and who fail to comprehend subtleties such as humor and metaphor (Shields, 1991). Together, these factors may conspire to create extreme social awkwardness. Many children with NLD fail to acquire and maintain friends their own age.

Rourke has also argued that there are predictable academic consequences of NLD. Many children with NLD have graphomotor problems and work slowly, inefficiently, and often with considerable frustration on pencil-and-paper assignments. The amount of such work often must be curtailed or students may need to be allowed to respond orally or via word processor. Although oral reading may not be a problem, reading comprehension is apt to be. This is even more true as reading demands become less rote with passing years and precise inference-making and analysis demands increase. Many science courses also prove difficult for students with NLD.

Even though Rourke's initial research on NLD and the empirical basis for the condition arose from studying children with academic impairments, Rourke contends that children with assorted neurological disorders manifest many, if not most, of the characteristics of NLD. Children with moderate to severe traumatic brain injury (TBI), hydrocephalus, consequences of radiation to treat acute lymphocytic leukemia, congential absence of the corpus callosum, and those who have had removal of the right hemisphere, as well as any condition that involves destruction of the white matter (long myelinated axons of brain neurons), are at risk for symptoms of NLD. The concept of NLD, thus, represents a bridge between neuropsychology and the study of developmental and learning problems.

## EXECUTIVE FUNCTION

Although the psychological processes that are subsumed by the term executive function are hard to define precisely, there is growing recognition that executive functions are an important set of attributes hitherto poorly measured by traditional psychological tests. The professional literature—most of it in the area of neuropsychology—has shown increasing number of investigations of this topic since the early 1990s.

*Executive functions* are a set of interrelated skills; there are not clear boundaries for the concept, and there is not an agreed-upon set of tests to measure it. Still, some things are clear. Rather than measuring individual psychological processes (e.g., visual perception or expressive language), measurement of executive function is concerned with higher-level functions that might be termed "mental control processes," or "meta-cognitive strategies." Tests that purportedly measure executive functions have several elements in common (Denckla, 1994):

1. A delay exists between presentation of the stimulus by the examiner and response by the child.
2. The child makes an internal representation or plan as the basis for responding.
3. Response inhibition is often required; impulsive responding is counterproductive.
4. Efficiency and consistency of responding are tapped and speed of performance is often measured.
5. Solutions to problems require active development of strategies.
6. Strategies may need to be applied flexibly.

Children who possess the capability to perform executive tasks are thus able to use their component psychological skills and abilities in an organized, efficient, and flexible manner. An analogy is an organization directed by an effective chief executive where each unit of the organization performs its component task only when called for, promptly ceases performing when required, and the organization's finished product is manufactured as efficiently as possible given the organization's resources. An individual with effective executive skills performs well, too. Children who possess this capability tend to be adaptive; those without it tend to be nonadaptive regardless of the other competencies they may possess (e.g., large vocabulary, good visual-perceptual development).

There are many tests of executive function, even though few are specifically so labeled. Most originated as part of neuropsychological batteries or at least are used in the context of attempting to measure neuropsychological status. Unfortunately, many of the most interesting executive function measures exist in nonstandardized form or do not yet have established norms that would permit clinical use (e.g., Tower of London). Three standardized techniques for measuring executive function are discussed briefly below.

## Category Test

The Category Test, long used as part of the Halstead-Reitan batteries for both children and adults (in various forms) (Reitan & Wolfson, 1992), was published in shortened version for more general neuropsychological use (Boll, 1993). The test comes in various forms depending on the child's age; the form used for older children is discussed for illustrative purposes. Each subject is exposed to stimuli one at a time. For example, Reitan's test for 9- to 14-year-olds consists of 168 stimuli;

Boll's shortened version for 9- to 16-year-olds consists of 83. Each stimulus consists of geometric shapes (squares, circles, hash marks, Roman numerals, etc.) that the child is allowed to study without time limit. He or she is also provided a response key that consists of the numbers 1, 2, 3, and 4. The child is never told the basis for picking—figuring out how to select the correct answer is the most crucial aspect of the test. He or she is signaled immediately upon responding as to whether each response was correct or incorrect. The child's task is to examine the stimulus and decide which number (1, 2, 3, 4) best matches the stimulus. The test is divided into six subtests and each subtest has a rule for matching, but the child is never informed directly of the rule. For example, Subtest Number 1 may begin with the first stimulus consisting of two circles, the second of three squares, the fourth of two circles. Test confidentiality prohibits revealing the exact basis for selection, but, hypothetically the way to make a correct selection in the first subtest might be on the basis of the total number of elements in the stimulus (hence 2 objects would mean that the respondent should select "2"; 4 objects, select "4").

After all the items from the first subtest are completed, a second, new subtest with a new rule would be presented. For the second subtest, the task may be to count the number of circles, select that number, and disregard the other shapes. There seems to be two critical aspects of the Category Test: 1) The stimuli change with each item of a subtest but the concept remains the same, thus requiring the respondent to use abstraction to respond correctly, and 2) the rules for selecting a correct response change with each new subtest, thus requiring flexibility and developing a new strategy, a demand that often exposes the cognitive problems of those who are perseverative or inflexible. The final subtest, unlike the proceeding 5, required memory. This subtest comprises already-seen items. In this subtest, the child is told that there is not a single concept running throughout, but his or her task is to recall the correct answer from previous trials for that stimulus and make the same selection again.

Not surprising is that individuals with neurological impairment have a particularly hard time with the Category Test. In fact, it was precisely for this reason that the Category Test was developed and included in the Reitan batteries. For example, Reitan and Wolfson (1992) report that typically developing children ages 9–14 who make 31 or fewer errors have "perfectly normal" performance, those with 33–51 have "normal but not excellent" performance, those with 52–64 have "mild to moderate neuropsychological impairment," and those with more than 64 have scores that are "definitely deviant and impaired" (p. 458). If scores on the Category Test alone were used to assign individual children to either groups with brain injury or control groups (a task that is accomplished by summary scores rather than individual tests), then those with brain injury would be misclassified 29% of the time, control 43%. Clearly, this test has a relationship to brain impairment, but diagnosticians could not use scores on it alone to assume brain injury. More clear are the executive aspects of the tests: development of an internal plan, modification of it when necessary, and abstinence from rapid, repetitive responding. Unfortunately, Reitan's version of the Category Test is in need of expanded norms. To the contrary, Boll's version is extremely well developed psychometrically with adequate norms (Russo & Bigler, 1996) and derived scores (T-scores and percentiles are available). Because fewer items are used in each subtest, the child is less challenged to establish and then keep that response set in mind. At an empirical level, early research with Boll's version has shown satisfactory correlations with severity of coma and with psychometric tests among groups of children with brain injuries (Donders, 1996). Which version will be used most often is unclear.

## Wisconsin Card Sorting Test

The Wisconsin Card Sorting Test (Heaton, 1981) is similar to the Category Test in many important ways: Both require problem solving when the examinee is required to respond with limited information; both require the child to develop hypotheses and to adhere to them for a time and then to revise them based on examiner feedback; both require response inhibition and the ability to abandon a previously correct way of responding; and both are nonverbal in nature.

Children take exactly the same form of Wisconsin Card Sorting Test in the same manner as adults. Again, confidentiality forbids disclosing the exact configuration of the test. The following is an approximation: There are four stimulus cards laid before the child; the first contains seven red triangles, the next contains two green squares, and so on with each stimulus card varying on several dimensions. The child is then given a deck of response cards one at a time and told to match them to the stimulus card (see Figure 8.1). No directions are given about how to match—this is the critical element of the Wisconsin Card Sorting Test. Because a card can conceivably be matched in many different ways, the child must select one strategy. If given positive feedback, he or she then, presumably, adheres to that concept when placing subsequent cards. The efficient child must not only generate hypotheses but retain concepts in working memory as feedback is given. Once the correct method of responding has been located, the child must adhere to it if he or she has any chance of continuing to

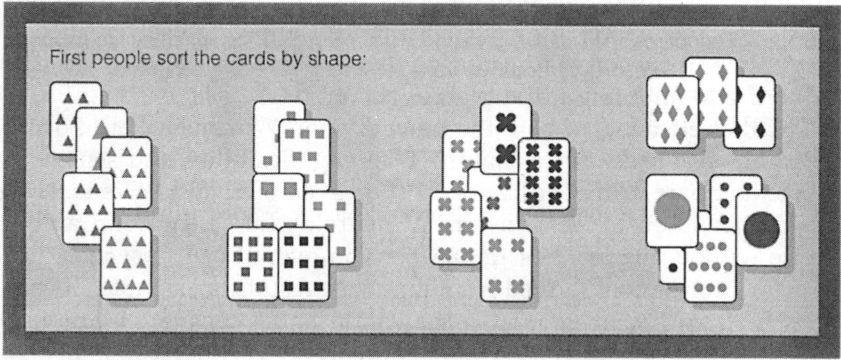


Figure 8.1. Approximation of subjects' first category for card sorting on the Wisconsin Card Sorting Test. (From *Biological Psychology,* by J.W. Kalat. Copyright © 1995, 1992, 1988, 1984, 1981 International Thomson Publishing Inc. By permission of Brooks/Cole Publishing Company, Pacific Grove, CA 93950.)

respond correctly. The strategy must be discarded and substituted with a new one if negative feedback is provided. Eventually, almost all children learn to respond correctly and ultimately master the first concept. (A specified number of correct responses is required to demonstrate concept mastery.) This concept is then substituted with a second concept (e.g., matching to the size of the figures rather than their shape) without notifying the child. He or she must modify responding based on feedback alone. Six concept changes occur during the course of testing. If the child has not mastered all six concepts after reasonable attempts (128 cards), then testing is terminated.

Scores on dimensions such as total number of errors, perseverative errors (those associated with responding to the previously correct concept after it has been replaced by a new concept), and trials necessary to master the first category have been found to discriminate adults with brain injury from control groups (Heaton, 1981), although specificity to lesions in the frontal lobes, the presumed locus of executive functions, is much less ensured (Lezak, 1995). Findings with children are less clear, although evidence in the 1990s suggests that groups of children and adolescents do cluster together in an expected way: Individuals with frontal impairment score worst, those with diffuse impairment somewhat better, and those without neurological impairment better still (Heaton, Chelune, Talley, Kay, & Curtiss, 1993). Previous developmental data have indicated that by age 10 years children's performances approximate those for adults (Chelune & Baer, 1986); current norms seem to imply continuing improvement of the same functions measured by the Wisconsin Card Sorting Test during adolescence (Heaton et al., 1993). The assumed maturation of the frontal lobes is speculated to influence this rise in executive functions. Errors on the Wisconsin Card Sorting Test appear closely related to the notion of executive function, as they concern developing and then adhering to an internalized plan of action.

Other elements of both the Category and Wisconsin Card Sorting Tests are also executive in nature. Planning, flexibility, and sensitivity to feedback are prime requisites for success on these tests. Even among children without a clear history of neurological disease and among those without evidence of impairment on overall neuropsychological scores, information derived from these test results is valuable. Success in school and with general organization and effective execution of everyday life demands a certain allotment of executive capability.

## Verbal Fluency

An executive function task using linguistic rather than predominantly visual material is the verbal fluency task, which comes in several variations. For young children the task involves presentation of a category (e.g., "clothing" items), after which the child is asked to provide as many separate examples as possible within a time limit (e.g., 1 minute). A variation, suitable for older children and adults, is to provide a letter (e.g., "f") with similar requirements to produce as many unique examples as possible before time runs out. The common element of these tasks is the presentation of a rule for responding and the requirement for the person to respond as efficiently as possible within the confines of the rule. Those who develop strategies apparently do better (hence the executive aspect). There are other executive aspects as well, such as sticking to the category, avoiding repetitions, and persisting when responding becomes effortful. Norms for verbal fluency tasks exist for children: The McCarthy Scales of Children's Abilities (McCarthy, 1972) contain a Verbal Fluency subtest; and the Multilingual Aphasia Examination (Benton, Hamsher, & Sivan, 1994) has norms for fluency based on initial letter in a subtest entitled "Controlled Oral Word Association." There is some evidence that these types of tasks converge with other measures of executive function and dissociate from traditional IQ tests (Denckla, 1994)—this type of information offering some support of validity. However, Denckla (1994) has suggested that noting violation of rules (providing examples that do not start with the prescribed letter) or perseveration errors (repeating words from the same category over again or reintroducing words from the prior category) may be more productive. Such a scoring system, which is not now available, would tap into the crux of executive function–poor response inhibition.

## APPLICATION OF NEUROPSYCHOLOGICAL TESTING

Because they have been designed to measure brain–behavior relationships, neuropsychological test batteries are called for in many practical situations. For example, neurologists or neurosurgeons in special medical centers for children, or pediatricians or family practitioners in primary care medical settings, may turn to psychologists to assess children with known or suspected brain impairments, such as brain tumors. With concern about possible brain impairment, the child with head trauma may be seen upon gaining medical stability, and perhaps again as he or she prepares for school reentry, on referral from the treating physiatrist (specialist in physical medicine) or by personnel from the child's school.

### Traumatic Brain Injury

One of the most frequent and most important uses of children's neuropsychological testing is to measure the consequences of head trauma. The issue of measuring this condition takes on special significance with the advent of the TBI category under the new special education guidelines, the Individuals with Disabilities Education Act (*Federal Register,* 1991), implemented in 1991. This legislation stipulates that children with TBI are to be afforded special education services when necessary for their educational progress. With all the advances in medical science, however, one might ask why there is a need for "psychological tests" at all when a head injury has occurred. Can't physicians tell by physical signs alone whether someone's brain has been injured? Isn't it true that unless someone is rendered unconscious brain injury did not take place? Likewise, doesn't a period of coma mean damage has occurred? Wouldn't the nature and extent of damage be evident on CT scan or MRI?

It is beyond the scope of this chapter to cover these issues in depth, but suffice it to say that many myths about TBI have existed in the past and are now giving way to factual knowledge arising from sources such as extremely well-organized and insightfully conceived multicenter research projects. Take the issue of physical condition associated with head trauma and degree of accompanying mental impairment. It is clear that the greater the degree and length of coma, generally the more significant the accompanying impairment (and the worse the long-term prognosis). But this generalization has many exceptions, especially among individuals with apparent mild head trauma. Some individuals with extended coma recover much or nearly all prior functioning. Sometimes adults with brief, or even no, coma may have persistent and clinically significant impairment (Gronwall, 1989). These individuals, even when they appear to have received little physical injury at the time of trauma, may have subtle problems with attention and efficient mental processing. This is true even though their CT and MRI studies of the brain are reported to be normal. The extent to which these findings apply to children is not clear.

Although physical examination and neuroimaging studies (e.g., MRI) have undisputed prominence in basic medical management of patients with head trauma, their shortcomings are obvious in the realms of rehabilitation and education, and, to some extent, they have limitations even regarding establishing prognoses. As patients with head trauma move past the acute phase of care, the determination of whether brain injury has occurred fades as questions about its severity, pervasiveness and pattern, and the constellation of persevered functions arise. Determination of the presence of brain impairment is a minimal accomplishment and alone is of little benefit.

Neuropsychological tests used as comprehensive batteries tap a multitude of discrete functions, which produce a pattern of impairments and strengths. This knowledge, in turn, permits understanding the child's status and allows informed planning to occur. In order to make sense out of psychological test patterns that may accompany head trauma, however, a brief digression into the physical aspects of head trauma is first required.

Consider Figure 8.2, which depicts the head at the time of impact in a closed-head injury. This is the type of injury that might occur if, for example, an unrestrained child were traveling in an automobile that hit a stationary object. It is obvious that damage to brain neurons, supporting cellular structures (e.g., glia cells), and blood vessels can occur the instant that the child's head strikes an object, such as the dash of an automobile. The site of this direct blow and associated damage at that site is called "coup" (meaning "blow"). Many such coup injuries result in damage to the frontal portions of the brain, as these regions of the head are most apt to strike objects in motor vehicle accidents. Especially common are impairments of the frontal lobe, where abnormal signals are frequently found on MRI after moderate to severe closed-head injury (Mendelsohn et al., 1992). In that the frontal and prefrontal lobes are especially involved in executive functions, impairments in these functions have been shown to be associated with such injuries (Levin et al., 1994). It is assumed that the executive / closed-head injury association is mediated by the greater vulnerability of these structured to closed-head injuries. If the coup injury were more prevalent at nonfrontal sites, then it is assumed skills most sub-

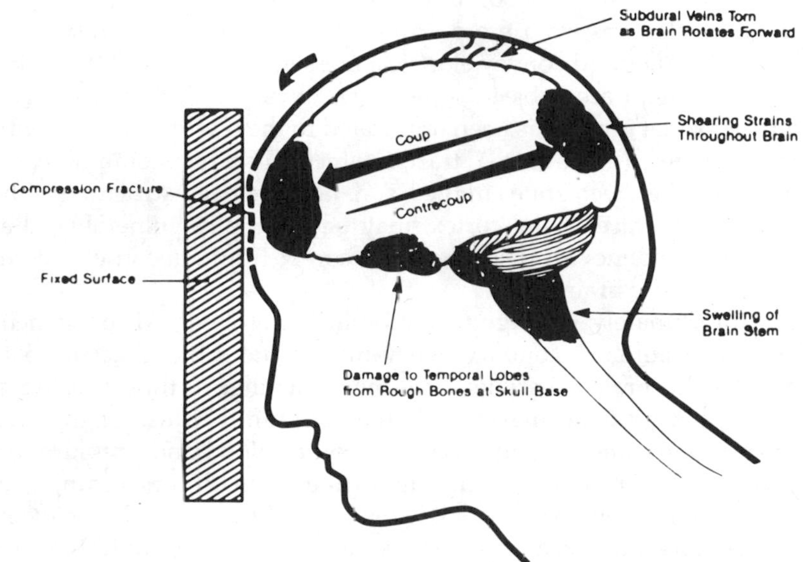


Figure 8.2. Brain damage caused by closed head injury. (From Begali, V. [1987]. *Head injury in children and adolescents: A resource and review for school and allied professionals.* Brandon, VT: Clinical Psychology Publishing Co.; reprinted by permission of John Wiley & Sons.)

sumed by those structures commonly would be reported as impaired (if parietal lobes were especially vulnerable, then sensory impairments would be a common consequence of closed-head injuries).

As Figure 8.2 depicts, other lesions may occur simultaneously with the head trauma; often those directly opposite the coup site experience impact as the brain bounces back from the initial impact, through its surrounding cerebral spinal fluid, and strikes the opposite side of the cranial vault, thus producing damage in "contrecoup" fashion. Specific and focal impairments may thus occur at sites on the other side of the head, far removed from the initial point of impact.

Initial damage may also occur when the brain is bounced over rough surfaces of the cranial vault; temporal and frontal lobes are especially susceptible to this type of damaging phenomenon. Perhaps it comes as somewhat of a surprise that injury of this type can occur even when a direct blow to the head has not occurred. Damage may ensue when rapid deceleration of the head occurs, such as when an automobile hits a fixed object. The abrupt stop may transfer energy throughout the cranium and its contents, causing sufficient agitation of the entire brain above the brain stem to cause bruising and damage. In a similar manner, acceleration / deceleration injuries of all types can produce shearing of the delicate blood vessels surrounding the brain, which may jeopardize blood flow and introduce unwanted blood into the brain. Perhaps even more important, the long axons that extend from cell bodies and convey electrical messages throughout the central nervous system are subject to the same physical sources of damage. Diffuse axonal injury has been implicated to the disruption of essential white matter (myelinated) tracts, which disrupts communication within and between zones in the brain. Because deep structures, those below the surface of the cortex, may be especially vulnerable, there may be a tendency to disconnect the cortex from subcortical centers throughout the brain.

Unfortunately, damage to the brain is not confined to the acute period of trauma. Secondary injury may ensue if blood accumulates between the brain's various coverings (meninges), thus causing an effect like a growing mass inside the cranium. Because of the cranium's strength and rigidity, accumulation of blood and pressure may distort the brain's integrity, causing further damage, or exerting pressure on vital structures located at the base of the brain. These events may produce life-threatening consequences if centers controlling respiration and heartbeat are affected. In addition, swelling and accumulating unnecessary blood may preclude normal circulation and prevent adequate oxygenation and nourishment. Heroic measures, such as neurosurgery, may be required to save the person's life and to minimize additional destruction.

Considering even this simplified account of assault on the brain, it is easy to see why no simple, singular, and absolutely predictable outcome follows traumatic brain injury. In its vast anatomical complexity and staggering functional capability, the brain is too complicated to permit a simple, singular outcome when it is damaged. Not surprising considering the heterogeneity of problems that can arise from TBI, researchers have found that children who have sustained TBI perform more poorly than controls on measures of language (Levin & Eisenberg, 1979a, 1979b), nonverbal and motor skills (Klonoff, Low, & Clark, 1977; Levin & Eisenberg, 1979a, 1979b), memory (Levin et al., 1988), and social-emotional adjustment (Fletcher, Ewing-Cobbs, Miner, Levin, & Eisenberg, 1990). Generalized findings, such as slowed information processing and loss of the potential for new learning, can represent major short-term and long-term consequences for school-age children (Ryan, LaMarche, Barth, & Boll, 1996). Findings from research studies reflect average values, and among children with TBI, many have no impairments whatsoever in language, nonverbal, motor, memory, social-emotional, or any of the other realms typically investigated by neuropsychological assessment, whereas others have severe problems. Of those with focal impairments, many are due to coup and contrecoup factors, others to vascular effects or other pathological processes. In order to conduct a reasonable evaluation of children with TBI, a comprehensive assessment conducted by a trained neuropsycholgist, working alone or in a team, needs to be completed.

Quite specific focal impairments can occur with TBI, and the neuropsychological test battery must be sufficiently comprehensive and detailed to detect these focal impairments. Thus, a typical school-based assessment for learning disabilities that may assess IQ and school achievement will prove insufficient. General intelligence may be perfectly preserved, but the child may have sensory, motor, memory, or language functions that are severely impaired. The comprehensive and exhaustive test batteries used in situations like these may be foreign to those who assess children with exclusively developmental (as opposed to acquired) problems. Children with developmental problems only rarely have severe impairments in discrete areas such as sensory or motor functions with preserved IQ scores. Children with TBI (and other acquired neurological disorders) may have such splinter impairments because they may have sustained focal neurological injuries that can produce such consequences. Table 8.5 list the areas typically measured as part of a neuropsychological test battery. Note the considerable correspondence with Halstead-Reitan and Luria-Nebraska batteries, which are mentioned previously. (Besides the formal Halstead-Reitan and Luria-Nebraska batteries, which can be used in part or in their entirety, psychologists may use individual tests of language, perception, motor speed and dexterity, and complex problem solving. Some of these are discussed elsewhere in this volume [e.g., California Verbal Learning Test, Rey-Osterrieth Complex Figure Test in Chapter 5]. It is beyond the scope of this book to cover the array of supplemental instruments that might be used, however.)

Often, however, focal damage has not occurred, and there are no discrete, isolated areas of impaired functioning observable on neuropsychological testing. This is when neuropsychological tests, because

Table 8.5. Areas typically assessed in neuropsychological evaluation of child with TBI

| |
|---|
| General Cognition and Overall Intellectual Functioning |
| Memory (Immediate and Delayed) |
| Sensory Functioning |
| Motor Functioning |
| Visual Skills and Perceptual Functioning |
| Language Functioning |
| Novel Learning and Problem Solving |
| Executive Functions |
| Academic Skills |
| Emotional, Behavioral, and Personal Adjustment |

they were designed to be sensitive to neurological damage, have special value. Recall that TBI may affect many parts of the brain in mild manner, such as through many small vascular injuries. Also recall that the acceleration/deceleration that accompanies head trauma can hamper communication by impeding impulse transmission among adjacent and widely scattered regions of the brain. Diffuse rather than focal impairment may result. The more dispersed areas of the brain that are involved in a task, and the more intercommunication required for task completion, the greater the likelihood that the task will be performed poorly by someone with TBI (Gentilini, Paolo, & Schoenhuber, 1989).

This poor performance by people with TBI is apparent in data reported by Gulbrandsen (1984) (also summarized by Levin, Ewing-Cobbs, & Fletcher, 1989). Patients who had sustained a head trauma 8 months before testing were compared with a control group (no history of head trauma) on several motor tests. It is important to note that the motor tests differed in complexity and, presumably, in the degree to which diverse regions of the brain would have to be recruited to execute them. Tests ranged in complexity from simple finger tapping, which appears to require mostly integrity of motor centers, to Grooved Pegboard, which requires complex and dexterous motor movements closely integrated with sensory input and vision, to Tactual Performance Test, which requires motor output, sensory input, coordinated with working memory and executive functions, such as planning. Empirical data substantiated that people with TBI have a vulnerability to complex tasks that require concerted organization; indeed, the complex tasks requiring greatest organization among brain areas proved hardest for those with TBI (see Figure 8.3). Whereas neuropsychological tools like the Tactual Performance Test are motor in nature, their value is not limited to detecting focal or isolated motor problems. Like many elements of a neuropsychological battery, the Tactual Performance Test is administered because it is sensitive to overall brain impairment (Reitan & Wolfson, 1992). Batteries comprising tests sensitive to both focal and global brain impairment, thus, have substantial value in determining who has acquired impairment after a head injury, who has not, and what the nature and severity of that impairment is.

This example shows relative differences among neuropsychological motor tests. All of these tests share an advantage over general psychological tests, because they are designed to measure brain functions. Far greater problems arise when diagnosticians attempt to detect brain impairment with tests that were not specifically designed for this purpose in their overall composition, method of score generation, or breadth of content. The use of the wrong instruments seems to

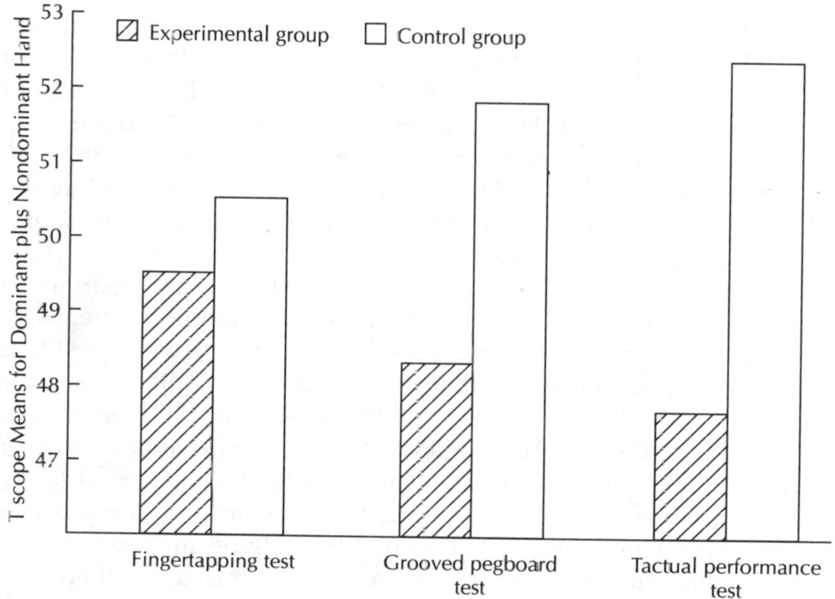


Figure 8.3. Comparison of performance on neuropsychological tests as a function of task complexity in children evaluated four to eight months following mild head injury and in uninjured classmate controls. (From Gulbrandsen, G.B. [1984]. Neuropsychological sequelae of light head injury in older children 6 months after trauma. *Journal of Clinical Neuropsychology, 6*(3), 257–258; reprinted by permission.)

happen most frequently in public schools among diagnosticians unfamiliar with TBI. A typical scenario might involve a child returning to school a few days a week after a head trauma. At this point, questions about capability to resume schoolwork arise, and to check his or her current academic status, an academic achievement test, such as the WRAT–3 or WIAT (see Chapter 6) is administered.

Unfortunately, many of the items on these tests long since have been learned by the mid-elementary years and are thus highly practiced. Well-developed, overlearned skills, in contrast to those that are emergent, may be relatively invulnerable to acute insult (Fletcher, Miner, & Ewing-Cobbs, 1987). Besides, some achievement test tasks require little insight, judgment, perceptual processing, or speed for successful completion. Clinicians are familiar with children who have adequate WRAT reading, spelling, and mathematics scores, yet who have significant neuropsychological impairments after acquiring head injury (Reitan & Wolfson, 1992). In some ways, children with TBI get off easy on tests like this because these instruments put relatively few demands on their potentially compromised brains.

A better, but still imperfect, solution is to add a standardized IQ test like the Wechsler scales to the test battery of the returning student. Greater demands for insight, judgment, perceptual processing, and speed are needed to accomplish these tasks. Logically it would appear that these tests give a better (more complete and sensitive) picture of a child's capability to succeed in school. This supposition is born out by research; the Wechsler IQ scores, particularly Performance IQ scores, have consistently shown to be affected by TBI (see Ryan et al., 1996, for a summary). A still better solution is to rely on tests devised precisely for these purposes—neuropsychological tests used singularly or in organized batteries.

A developmental framework, however, which is as important as the instruments themselves, is crucial in understanding children with TBI. Normal scores on even the most detailed and sensitive test batteries do not guarantee the absence of problems. Unlike adults for whom normal scores auger for positive prognosis, children remain vulnerable even with normal profiles. This is because some aspects of brain development, such as functions mediated by the frontal lobes, have yet to develop among young children. Hence it is not possible to determine whether those skills will ultimately be affected until the child becomes old enough to test in those domains. Furthermore, young children have a great deal of cognitive, motor, perceptual, memory, and executive function development in their futures so their developmental course cannot be fully or accurately forecasted. In considering these points, the statement by Fletcher et al. (1987) seems fitting: "In children, recovery of function is an issue involving not only sparing and restoration of various behaviors, but also the complex issue of how growth and development proceed in an abnormal brain" (p. 289).

The following case studies crystallize some of these points.

## John

John was a healthy 12½-year-old when he was struck by an automobile while in a crosswalk. Reports from the scene suggest that he was thrown approximately 20 feet before landing on his head and chest. He was immediately rendered unconscious and required transport to a trauma center via air ambulance. His Glasgow Coma Score (Teasdale & Jennett, 1974) was 8; he was found to have a subdural hematoma in both frontal lobes and brain swelling, which required emergency neurosurgery and placement of an intracranial pressure monitor. He remained comatose for 3 days and was confused even upon awakening. After another 7 days of medical stabilization, John was transferred to a rehabilitation unit, and physical, occupational, and speech-language therapies were begun. At first, John had so much motor impairment (he could not walk independently), was so confused (his moment-to-moment recall was inconsistent), and had so much linguistic impairment (nonverbal for a short time followed by obviously impaired understanding and expression), that no formal psychological testing was possible. Rapid improvement followed, and approximately 3 weeks after the accident, neuropsychological evaluation was requested to determine John's current functioning and to make suggestions for ongoing treatment.

An abbreviated evaluation was undertaken and even this had to be divided into several settings. Favorably, John was found to have some spared functions. On academic testing using the WRAT–3 he read near average (standard score = 99), he spelled only slightly more poorly (standard score = 91), but he scored extremely poorly on computational arithmetic (standard score = 77). John's WISC–III performance is outlined in Table 8.6. His performance can be summarized as follows: 1) Overall IQ has probably declined from preaccident status, 2) mental speed and efficiency have apparently suffered the most, 3) visual-perceptual and/or motor problems may exist, and 4) auditory attention span as well as skills most closely tied to school appear most preserved.

These hypotheses were confirmed by supplemental neuropsychological evaluation. On the Grooved Pegboard Test, John appeared extremely clumsy: He dropped 2 pegs with his right hand and 2 more with his left; his times of 92 seconds with the right and 99 seconds with the left represent severe motor speed and dexterity problems. Elements of the Halstead-Reitan Battery, Trail Making A and B, were both completed slowly (34 and 69 seconds, respectively), but observations of John's performance during Part B was especially telling. He consistently perseverated on the letter sequence, such as after com-

Table 8.6. John's WISC–III scores after acquiring traumatic brain injury

| **Summary IQ Scores** | **IQ** | **Percentile Rank** |
|---|---|---|
| Verbal | 90 | 25 |
| Performance | 73 | 4 |
| Full Scale | 80 | 9 |
| **Factor Scores** | **Index** | **Percentile Rank** |
| Verbal Processing | 87 | 19 |
| Perceptual Organization | 77 | 6 |
| Freedom from Distractibility | 104 | 61 |
| Processing Speed | 72 | 3 |

**Subtest Scale Scores**

| **Verbal** | | **Performance** | |
|---|---|---|---|
| Information | 9 | Picture Completion | 8 |
| Similarities | 6 | Coding | 4 |
| Arithmetic | 11 | Picture Arrangement | 5 |
| Vocabulary | 6 | Block Design | 5 |
| Comprehension | 9 | Object Assembly | 6 |
| Digit Span | 10 | Symbol Search | 5 |

pleting C he immediately went to the next letter (D) rather than alternating between letters and numbers. Inability to keep two sequences in mind simultaneously and/or to inhibit the impulse to proceed to the next letter were suggestive of executive impairments.

Executive problems appeared on the Category Test, too, where John appeared to become stuck on the easy method of solving the problem and could not alter his responding even with repeated feedback. This error total of 78 shows clear impairment. Moreover, John's initial drawing of Rey-Osterrieth Complex Figure was slightly poor for quality but John used an extremely disorganized and fragmented drawing approach (delayed recall of the figure was also poor).

Formal memory testing using the California Verbal Learning Test–Children's Version found only slight problems with initial registration but the effects of interference between the two lists were obvious. He had much trouble learning list B (presumably because of interference from the previously learned list A) and inordinate difficulty with recall of list A after list B was encountered (presumably because of interference from list B). (See Chapter 5 for discussion of California Verbal Learning Test.) Delayed recall was quite poor but John did substantially better when cues (e.g., tell me all the animals on the list) were provided. This pattern of memory performance is also suggestive that portions of the frontal lobes may be involved and that the ability to generate a strategy to encode and retrieve information, rather than registration capability alone, may be problematic. This supposition, too, would be consistent with the emerging hypothesis of executive problems. The therapy team (speech-language, occupational, and physical therapy) noted subtle language problems (more expressive than receptive) and motor planning and coordination problems. These observations, too, suggest that John probably experienced brain impairment, that its current manifestation was diffuse, and that frontal systems may have experienced the greatest damage resulting in impaired executive functions.

John was discharged from the hospital with the following suggestions:

1. Continuation of rehabilitation therapies (e.g., speech, occupational therapy/physical therapy)
2. Slow reintegration to school, beginning with 2 hours per day, with the expectation that no more than 1 hour of additional instruction would be added each week
3. Reduction of work amounts and relax all timed demands
4. Meeting with resource teacher at the conclusion of each school day as part of TBI program to determine which assignments to attempt

at home, how much time to devote to each and, if necessary, to create a plan for attacking assignments

5. Reduction in memorization demands at school and, if required, use of summary sheets, external aids (e.g., calculator), and reminder sheets posted on desk in lieu of memorization
6. Emphasis on routine at home regarding activities of daily living, such as grooming, and corresponding heightening of the habitual at school
7. Increased emphasis on beginning all school drills with 100% initial success as John was suspected to have less awareness of his own errors (lack ability to self-correct), and he may be unable to overcome initial errors because of his tendency to perseverate
8. Revision of his program each month in a formal meeting and full reevaluation in 6 months, at which time longer-term prognosis should be evident

John's 6-month reevaluation found improved IQ (Full Scale 91) but various and significant neuropsychological impairments that included ongoing evidence of brain dysfunction associated with TBI. His Neuropsychological Deficit Score on the full Halstead-Reitan battery was far beyond the cutoff level and extremely suggestive of ongoing impairment. He continued to receive TBI services that consisted of reduction of work amount and complexity, plus adjustment regarding memory difficulties. At the end of the school year he was still receiving speech and occupational therapy.

## CHILDREN WITH BRAIN TUMORS AND LEUKEMIA

There are few illnesses more frightening to parents and teachers than malignancies, especially those of the brain. Before the advent of sophisticated chemotherapy combined with therapeutic radiation, children with leukemia almost always succumbed to their disease. Although most children with leukemia now survive, treatment often leaves important consequences to the developing nervous system, as is discussed below. Similarly, children with malignancies of the central nervous system (e.g., brain tumors) may now survive through surgery, chemotherapy, radiation therapy, or a combination of these. They, too, may have special learning and developmental problems that eventuate from the treatment that saved their lives. Today, thanks to research efforts, educators and health care professionals understand better the natural progression of problems encountered by these children and how to detect problems should they arise. This knowledge, coupled with the expert use of neuropsychological and associated techniques, can permit the understanding of each child's particular needs and can set the stage for plans to ameliorate problems or, at a minimum, understand and cope with those problems that cannot be ameliorated.

Like TBI, malignancies that affect the central nervous system frequently produce problems that are most fully and accurately evaluated by neuropsychological tests. Children with brain tumors often have circumscribed impairments that are apparent on neuropsychological testing but that are less visible on traditional IQ tests (Archibald et al., 1994). For example, a child with a large tumor that infiltrates the temporal and parietal lobes of the right hemisphere may have a severely confused body image, a distorted sensory perception with the left hand, and a confused interpretation of emotional stimuli; she might or might not have a relatively poor Performance IQ compared to Verbal IQ on the WISC–III. Detailed neuropsychological evaluation would almost certainly detect her problems and gauge their severity. With this information, a neuropsychologist could provide suggestions for her classroom teacher, including ways to minimize the effects of impairments and capitalize on preserved strengths. The same information could help the child's parents, and perhaps, the child herself to plan more reasonably so that potential successes can be attained and potential failures minimized.

Children with leukemia are frequently treated with therapeutic radiation of the brain and spinal cord. This treatment, especially when teamed with chemotherapy, can kill the cancer in the bloodstream and obliterate remnants that may lie dormant in the nervous system. Although effective in destroying the life-threatening cancer cells, this procedure may exact a toll on the child's developing nervous system. Radiation may destroy brain cells (neurons) or supporting structures (glial cells), and these ill effects may not occur immediately. Sometimes cell death follows radiation by several years, and the effects on learning and intelligence may not be apparent until then. As a general rule, radiation treatment earlier in life produces more deleterious effects than later treatment. Most of the same considerations exist for children with malignant brain tumors (Duffner, Cohen, & Parker, 1988; Duffner et al., 1993; Jannoun & Bloom, 1990). Accordingly, physicians are often reluctant to employ radiation treatment in young children except in cases where the procedure has a strong prospect of improving the chances of survival.

Not surprising because radiation of the entire brain and spinal cord (the neuroaxis) may produce cell death at any site, psychological impairments of many types and degrees of intensity can eventuate. General intelligence, language capability, and visual/spatial and motor skills are all at risk. Memory impairments are common (Brouwers

& Poplack, 1990; Mulhern, Wasserman, Fairclough, & Ochs, 1988). Considering the essential role of short-term memory in acquiring information from the world around, it is hardly surprising that problems in this realm can portend many cognitive and information-processing impairments. It is essential that a thorough evaluation of children with leukemia (and other cancers that require radiation of the brain) be conducted and that this evaluation go beyond IQ; this information can sometimes enable the long-term deleterious effects on overall development to be attenuated. Linda's case serves as an example.

## Linda: Special Education Designation as Other Health Impairment

Linda was diagnosed at age 3 years with a tumor defined as a mixed cell glioma (a tumor arising from the supportive glia cells of the brain). Her tumor was located in the areas beneath the cerebral cortex, close to the ventricular system of the brain and the pineal gland. Her neurosurgeon was successful in removing most of the tumor, but chemotherapy and radiation of the brain were also required. She had been a healthy, active child until her disease and treatment. Her hospital team was anxious about her developmental status when she began to seem frustrated in a preschool program.

An evaluation of Linda at age 6 found a WISC–III Full Scale IQ of 80 with accompanying memory problems. Classroom adjustments were made and Linda was able to progress with extra tutoring. No formal special education designation was made then.

By age 8 years her status had deteriorated. Her parents described short-term memory problems and problems with working memory. Not only would Linda fail to remember the last thing to do on a two- or three-direction request, but at times she would even forget what she was doing in the middle of a task. For example, she might be walking to her bedroom intent on getting a game only to stop perplexed and ask her mother what it was she was going to get. Although her teachers were supportive, and even protective, Linda could no longer keep pace with peers. Learning new skills was extremely frustrating for her. Memorization of math facts or spelling words proved impossible. Her oncologist requested a thorough neuropsychological evaluation.

Linda moved with a shuffling gait and some dyscoordination upon entering the evaluation room. She was pleasant, cooperative, and generally well directed. She had only minor signs of frustration, and these were easily overcome with encouragement.

Her scores are outlined in Table 8.7. Linda's overall cognitive status showed continued decline from prior levels and continued to be in the impaired range, with Full Scale IQ in the borderline mentally

Table 8.7. Linda's test scores at age 8 years

**Wechsler Intelligence Scale for Children–III**

| Verbal | | Performance | |
|---|---|---|---|
| Information | 5 | Picture Completion | 6 |
| Similarities | 5 | Coding | 5 |
| Arithmetic | 7 | Picture Arrangement | 5 |
| Vocabulary | 6 | Block Design | 5 |
| Comprehension | 3 | Object Assembly | 2 |
| (Digit Span) | 8 | Symbol Search | 9 |
| Verbal IQ | 73 | | |
| Performance IQ | 68 | | |
| Full Scale IQ | 68 | | |

**Wide Range Assessment of Memory and Learning**

| Subtest | Standard score |
|---|---|
| Picture Memory | 2 |
| Design Memory | 1 |
| Verbal Learning | 3 |
| Story Memory | 5 |
| Memory Screening Index | 47 |

**Wechsler Individual Achievement Test**

| Subtest | Standard score |
|---|---|
| Basic Reading | 82 |
| Spelling | 89 |
| Reading Comprehension | 70 |
| Numerical Operations | 94 |

**Grooved Pegboard Test**

| | |
|---|---|
| Right Hand | 73 seconds |
| Left Hand | 66 seconds |

**Finger Tapping**

| | |
|---|---|
| Right Hand | 29.8 |
| Left Hand | 26.8 |

**Progressive Figures**

55 seconds (1 error)

**Color Form Test**

18 seconds (0 errors)

**Children's Category Test (Boll Version)**

T-score = 42

**Gordon Diagnostic System**

| | | |
|---|---|---|
| Vigilance Task | 2 | Omission errors |
| | 13 | Commission errors |
| Delay Task | 100% | Efficiency Rate |
| | 16 | Total Correct |

handicapped to mentally handicapped range (Full Scale IQ at the second percentile). Her impairments were generally uniform and across the board. She was slow to catch on, had difficulty formulating plans, and tended to work in a trial-and-error manner without much insight.

Her language performance, although generally devoid of conspicuous receptive or expressive problems, was nonetheless reflective of poor conceptual base and poverty of content. Although the overall poor performance could not be dismissed, it was felt that diagnosing mild mental retardation was inappropriate. This was because Linda possessed too many cognitive areas with performance above the threshold for mental retardation. For example, her score on the Category Test was low average, and she showed reasonable ability to catch on to some new tasks and to problem-solve.

Accompanying, and in some ways more debilitating, impairments with short-term memory existed. Her status here was even poorer than it was when assessed 2 years earlier. She showed little ability to remember what she had just seen and only slightly better ability to remember what she had just heard. If she were provided large amounts of information, then it is likely that she would be overwhelmed. Consolidation over time was somewhat better, but it was likely that her functional use of memory in academic and real-life situations would be significantly compromised.

Although by casual observation she did not have attention difficulties, on formal measures that required sustained attention and concentration she had fairly consistent problems. She had only 16 correct responses on Gordon Diagnostic System Delay Task and only 32 of 45 correct detections of target stimuli on the Vigilance Task.

Attention factors may be involved in Linda's inconsistent performance on the Sensory Perceptual Examination (results not included in Table 8.7). She had three extinctions (failure to detect stimuli) on double simultaneous stimulation (i.e., when visual, auditory, or tactile stimulation was provided to both sides of the body simultaneously). However, there was no pattern here indicating impaired sensory reception in the cortex or in the sensory pathways leading to it. Her other sensory scores (two errors with the right hand and three with the left on Tactile Finger Recognition; no errors with the right hand and one with the left on Fingertip Symbol Writing) were only slightly outside of average for a child her age and not strongly indicative of problems with sensory registration and interpretation.

Not surprisingly, motor speed and dexterity on a challenging task such as Grooved Pegboard was poor bilaterally, and somewhat poorer with the right hand. On a simpler measure of motor speed (Finger Tapping) her time was also slightly impaired. Linda also had difficulty with graphomotor (pencil control and speed), and this was reflected in her poor rendering of the Bender Gestalt designs. The quality of her writing on academic tasks was variable and sometimes poor. She would be expected to have difficulty with hands-on tasks at home if not at school.

Fortunately, Linda has acquired reasonably good academic skills considering her cognitive and memory impairment. She performed fairly adequately on word recognition, spelling, and arithmetic computations. However, with higher-level conceptual demands and the requirement to use short-term recall, she struggled with reading comprehension. It is expected, her favorable achievement test scores not withstanding, that she would have enormous difficulty in a classroom setting if novel learning and problem solving were required. One might expect her to become confused with directions, especially if they are presented rapidly.

In summary, Linda was found to have general cognitive impairments that place her at marked disadvantage compared to peers, as well as severe and debilitating problems with short-term memory. Her status on both dimensions was as poor or poorer than was the case 24 months earlier. Additional and mixed neuropsychological impairments that include problems with attention, motor speed, and dexterity would make school success even more difficult. Problems were attributable to the brain tumor and the late effects of radiation and chemotherapy, with the expectation that the effects should plateau considering the time interval since her diagnosis and treatment. It is assumed that Linda would be left with permanent impairments.

Linda's home school district reviewed neuropsychological findings and suggested that she be afforded special education services under the category of "other health impairment." They noted that among the diagnoses from the hospital-based treatment team was "cognitive impairments secondary to neuroaxis radiation."

Far more important than the designation of special education eligibility, the evaluation permitted development of a treatment to help Linda. Among its elements were the following:

1. Linda was placed in a small group and given individual instruction by a special education teacher. The favorable teacher-to-student ratio allowed for clarification of directions, detailed and elaborated explanations of new procedures and concepts, repetition of directions, overlearning, and systematic review. Essential material and skills were distinguished from nonessential and the above-mentioned techniques were applied to essential material whereas nonessential material was either dropped from the curriculum or addressed briefly.
2. An individual education program was developed that ensured that classroom directions were given slowly, in simplified form,

and that Linda's teacher checked with her repeatedly to ensure that she began tasks with proper understanding. Likewise, memory demands within the classroom were reduced. Pencil-and-paper work was reduced and Linda was offered alternative means of responding (e.g., orally) on some tasks that would have proved tedious if completed with pencil and paper. To ensure attention to task, periodic checks for productivity and accuracy were incorporated into her daily schedule. It was expected that as Linda moved through the grades that the increasing complexity of the curriculum would dictate increased accommodations and support.

3. To maximize motivation and maintain a positive self-image, Linda was placed in a program that provided high levels of praise and encouragement. By the same token, her teacher selected her for special duties (e.g., line leader) as a means of providing a niche of perceived competence.
4. An occupational therapy consultation was requested to assist the classroom teacher in modification of instructional activities and to provide guidance to her physical education teacher. Suggestions regarding acceptable and unacceptable playground equipment and activities were put forth by the therapist.
5. Finally, general admonishments were offered to Linda's entire treatment and instructional team at a multidisciplinary meeting: Linda has impairments that are not always apparent on the surface. Even when she tries her best there are many things that she cannot master and much information that she simply cannot remember. Continual adjustments of expectations are called for in dealing with her each day.

## SUMMARY

Neuropsychological tests are concerned with assessing brain functioning through the use of test procedures. By using standardized tests, psychologists can assist neurologists to determine the site of brain injury, help determine if the child has sustained brain injury, monitor the child's progress if brain injury has occurred, and help plan remedial and rehabilitative activities.

Two neuropsychological batteries are suitable for children—the Halstead-Reitan battery (and its variant for younger children, the Reitan-Indiana battery) and the Children's Version of the Luria-Nebraska battery. Both batteries have been criticized on psychometric grounds, but each is capable of distinguishing among groups of children, such as those with known brain injury, those with learning disabilities, and those without disabilities. The ability of these batteries to locate the exact site of lesion in the brain remains much more controversial and less proven, especially for young children. Because neuropsychological test batteries are designed specifically to detect the consequences of brain impairment, they may aid considerably in understanding the needs of children who have traumatic brain injury or a variety of other disorders, such as brain tumors. In addition to clinical utility, neuropsychological procedures have resulted in increasing theory development and have helped spur the development of new test instruments, some of which have wide usage. The concepts of executive function and nonverbal learning disability are examples of neuropsychological conceptualization with applications beyond children with neurological impairment. As time goes on, instruments that have traditionally been confined strictly to neuropsychological applications as well as neuropsychological theorization will probably find widening service.

## Study Questions

1. Identify one or more referral questions for which neuropsychological testing may be more appropriate than traditional testing.
2. Are traditional intelligence tests (e.g., WISC–III) and academic achievement tests (e.g., WRAT–3) typically affected if a child sustains brain injury?
3. List some reasons inferences based on neuropsychological testing of children must be made cautiously.
4. What is the rationale for neuropsychological test batteries' inclusion of tests of motor and sensory functioning?
5. Why might the field of learning disabilities benefit from neuropsychological testing advances?
6. Regarding TBI, what does coma imply, and what relevance might it have for understanding the school performance of a child who has sustained TBI?
7. What differences might occur in the neuropsychological performances of children with leukemia and brain tumors? What might account for these differences?

Chapter Nine

# Special Testing Considerations

## ADHD, Autism, Health Issues, and Children from Minority Groups

Since the last edition of this book was published in 1990, the addition of autism to the federal special education law (PL 101-476, the Individuals with Disabilities Education Act [IDEA] of 1990) has occurred and it has become recognized that attention-deficit/hyperactivity disorder (ADHD) is a condition that often warrants treatment under either IDEA (in the category of "other health impairment") or Section 504 of the Rehabilitation Act of 1973 (Davila & Wodrich, 1994). The need for fair evaluation of students from diverse backgrounds has continued. In response to these factors, psychological tests increasingly have been used to study the psychometric correlates of various conditions on the one hand, and continued scrutiny of tests to ensure fairness for all students has occurred on the other. The consumer of psychological testing will benefit from knowledge in these areas as he or she attempts to understand and help children. This information also further elaborates the empirical and logical aspects of psychological measurement that are espoused throughout this book. It is hoped that this information helps the reader develop a psychological mind-set in thinking about a multitude of learning, developmental, and measurement problems.

## PSYCHOLOGICAL TESTS TO MEASURE SPECIAL DISORDERS AND CONDITIONS

The logic associated with psychological testing has been used to develop tests of general and special abilities. As seen in previous chapters, many commonly used tests, such as IQ or personality tests, can be used across many diagnostic categories. IQ tests for example, are indispensable in establishing the diagnoses of mental retardation and learning disabilities, whereas personality tests help establish the presence of depression, anxiety, or the tendency for a child to act in antisocial ways. IQ tests and personality tests' range of applications can be quite broad.

Some conditions are sufficiently unique, however, to require specialized test instruments to detect them and to measure their severity. Two specific disorders, ADHD and autism, and one broad grouping—other health impairment—are discussed here with an emphasis on the psychological testing techniques that can help the clinician evaluate and understand them.

## ATTENTION-DEFICIT/HYPERACTIVITY DISORDER

Regardless of how the condition is described ("ADD," "attention deficit," "hyperactivity," etc.), the occurrence of ADHD is common. Official estimates of 3% of school-age children are overshadowed by the enormous press coverage and the frequency with which parents and teachers talk about this disorder. At times, it seems as if children with ADHD are present at every turn. Further confounding the problem is the intuitive belief by many parents and teachers that they can recognize the frenzied, chaotic, disorganized, and inefficient behavior that characterizes the disorder well enough to distinguish children with this problem from those without it. Moreover, the issue of ADHD overdiagnosis has so many ardent believers and doubters that personal biases further heighten controversy about the condition and make its accurate diagnosis more difficult for any individual child.

Fortunately, there is an agreed-upon set of diagnostic criteria for ADHD (see Table 9.1); unfortunately, the criteria are sufficiently vague that it is sometimes hard to determine if the condition is present. Ambiguity is made worse because the symptoms necessary for diagnosis are established almost exclusively by parent or teacher report. Notice that the guidelines make no reference to psychological test performance.

ADHD should be established by experienced diagnosticians who recognize that diagnosing ADHD is far more complex than merely reviewing the symptoms and criteria of Table 9.1 and then turning thumbs up or down. The diagnostic process for ADHD is complex, involving a set of interrelated questions to be answered if the process is to be thorough and accurate. Questions to be answered include the following (Wodrich, in preparation):

1. Are sufficient symptoms of restlessness, inattention, and impulsivity present to establish a diagnosis of ADHD?

Table 9.1. DSM-IV diagnostic criteria for ADHD

A. The diagnosis of ADHD should be made when the following criteria of either inattention or hyperactivity-impulsivity are met:

1. A child shows six (or more) of the following symptoms of *inattention* that have persisted for at least 6 months to a degree that is maladaptive and inconsistent with developmental level:
   a. Often fails to give close attention to details or makes careless mistakes in schoolwork, work, or other activities
   b. Often has difficulty sustaining attention in tasks or play activities
   c. Often does not seem to listen when spoken to directly
   d. Often does not follow through on instructions and fails to finish schoolwork, chores, or duties in the workplace (not caused by oppositional behavior or failure to understand instructions)
   e. Often has difficulty organizing tasks and activities
   f. Often avoids, dislikes, or is reluctant to engage in tasks that require sustained mental effort (e.g., schoolwork, homework)
   g. Often loses things necessary for tasks or activities (e.g., toys, school assignments, pencils, books, tools)
   h. Often is easily distracted by extraneous stimuli
   i. Often is forgetful in daily activities

2. A child shows six (or more) of the following symptoms of hyperactivity-impulsivity that have persisted for at least 6 months to a degree that is maladaptive and inconsistent with developmental level:

   Hyperactivity
   a. Often fidgets with hands or feet or squirms in seat
   b. Often leaves seat in classroom or in other situations in which remaining seated is expected
   c. Often runs about or climbs excessively in situations in which it is inappropriate (in adolescents or adults, this symptom may be limited to subjective feelings of restlessness)
   d. Often has difficulty playing or engaging in leisure activities quietly
   e. Often is "on the go" or acts as if "driven by a motor"
   f. Often talks excessively

   Impulsivity
   g. Often blurts out answers before questions have been completed
   h. Often has difficulty awaiting turn
   i. Often interrupts or intrudes on others (e.g., butts into conversations or games)

The diagnosis of ADHD also requires that the following criteria are met:

B. Some hyperactive-impulsive or inattentive symptoms that cause impairment were present before age 7 years.
C. Some impairment from the symptoms is present in two or more settings (e.g., at school [or work] and at home).
D. There is clear evidence of clinically significant impairment in social, academic, or occupational functioning.
E. The symptoms do not occur exclusively during the course of a pervasive developmental disorder, schizophrenia, or other psychotic disorder and are not better accounted for by another mental disorder (e.g., mood disorder, anxiety disorder, dissociative disorder, personality disorder).

Adapted with permission from the *Diagnostic and Statistical Manual of Mental Disorders, Fourth Edition.* Copyright 1994 by American Psychiatric Association; and reprinted from Ernst, M. (1996). Neuroimaging in attention-deficit/hyperactivity disorder. In G.R. Lyon & J.M. Rumsey (Eds.), *Neuroimaging: A window to the foundations of learning and behavior in children* (pp. 95–118). Baltimore: Paul H. Brookes Publishing Co.

ADHD, combined type, should be diagnosed when both criteria A1 and A2 are met for at least 6 months; ADHD, predominantly inattentive type, should be diagnosed when Criterion A1 has been met but Criterion A2 has not been met for at least 6 months; and ADHD, predominantly hyperactive-impulsive type, should be diagnosed when Criterion A2 has been met but Criterion A1 has not been met for at least 6 months.

2. Are there other disorders that would better explain the symptoms that are being reported?
3. Are any of the problems that often co-exist with ADHD (learning disabilities, conduct problems) present in this individual child?
4. Are there other considerations unique to this child that must be considered in establishing a treatment plan?

It is in dealing with the complexity of the evaluation process that ensues from answering these questions that psychological testing techniques can help.

## Single-Dimension ADHD Checklists

The first question, "Are sufficient symptoms of restlessness, inattention, and impulsivity present to establish a diagnosis of ADHD?" can be better addressed if psychological test instruments, in this case, objective rating forms, are used. The advantages of objectivity and quantifiability are outlined in Chapter 1, and their benefit is obvious when incorporated into rating scales for ADHD. Without using rating forms, the diagnostician is left to rely on a child's history as reported by parent or teacher to decide if enough of the ADHD symptoms are present to permit diagnosis. Among the shortcomings of this approach is the necessity to make a yes-or-no decision (present or absent) for each symptom. In contrast, objective questionnaires permit raters to estimate symptom severity along a continuum. For example, the ADHD Rating Scale (DuPaul, 1990) has taken every DSM III-R symptom for ADHD and placed it on a continuum ranging from "not at all," "a little," "pretty much," to "very much." In turn, points are assigned for each rating in a 0, 1, 2, 3 manner, with the higher values assigned to more severe symptom ratings (see Figure 9.1). This procedure permits clearer and more precise notation of child behavior that would be missed in the yes-or-no method.

Equally important is the quantifiably and normed-reference advantages of rating forms. For example, using the DSM-IV system, if 6 Inattention symptoms and 6 Hyperactive-Impulsive symptoms are present (and other stipulations such as age of onset and duration of symptoms can be met), then the ADHD diagnosis can be assigned. This approach is too general to fit both boys and girls and both young children and more mature teens. In point of fact, boys are generally much more active and impulsive than girls; young children generally more so than older. Rating forms like the ADHD Rating Scale handle this problem easily by establishing age- and gender-specific cutoff scores. Thus, in order to denote the most symptomatic 3% of 8-year-old boys, 31 raw score points or more must be evident on the parent-

Rater's Name:______________________________ Child's Age:________________

| | Not at all | Just a little | Pretty much | Very much |
|---|---|---|---|---|
| Often fidgets or squirms in seat | 0 | 1 | 2 | 3 |
| Has difficulty remaining seated | 0 | 1 | 2 | 3 |
| Is easily distracted | 0 | 1 | 2 | 3 |
| Has difficulty awaiting turn in groups | 0 | 1 | 2 | 3 |
| Often blurts out answers to questions | 0 | 1 | 2 | 3 |
| Has difficulty following instructions | 0 | 1 | 2 | 3 |
| Has difficulty sustaining attention to tasks | 0 | 1 | 2 | 3 |
| Often shifts from one uncompleted activity to another | 0 | 1 | 2 | 3 |
| Has difficulty playing quietly | 0 | 1 | 2 | 3 |
| Often talks excessively | 0 | 1 | 2 | 3 |
| Often interrupts or intrudes on others | 0 | 1 | 2 | 3 |
| Often does not seem to listen | 0 | 1 | 2 | 3 |
| Often loses things necessary for tasks | 0 | 1 | 2 | 3 |
| Often engages in physically dangerous activities without considering consequences | 0 | 1 | 2 | 3 |

Figure 9.1. Sample ADHD Rating Scale. (From DuPaul, G.J. [1990]. *The ADHD Rating Scale.* Unpublished manuscript; University of Massachusetts Medical Center, Worchester; reprinted by permission of the author.)

completed ADHD Rating Scale. Owing to the paucity of symptoms for girls generally, a cutoff score of 27 will be needed to identify the most symptomatic 3% of 14-year-old girls. A single-dimension rating scale of ADHD symptoms, like the ADHD Rating Scale, can greatly aid in establishing the presence and severity of ADHD symptoms. Many single dimension rating scales for ADHD symptoms have been developed; most of them have some normative basis, many have been developed empirically by composing a test of items that discriminate children with ADHD from those without. Some venerable instruments, such as the Conners Abbreviated Teacher Questionnaire (Conners, 1973), have been criticized for having too few items (10) or including items that have little to do with the current conception of ADHD (e.g., "temper control problems").

Of course, findings from single-dimension rating forms must also be taken with a grain of salt. Most psychologists recognize that the overall purpose of these scales and the items that compose them are rather transparent. Parents and teacher divine what is being asked and it is easy for them to see how the forms work; personal bias can easily permeate the process. In this regard, parents who would like their child identified as having ADHD (perhaps hoping for a trial on medicine) can simply mark every symptom as "severe." The opposite also holds; desire to avoid an ADHD diagnosis might prompt some parents to mark "absent" for each symptom regardless of the child's actual behavior.

## Multidimensional Rating Forms

Even if he or she were assured that the child is symptomatic for ADHD, the diagnostician's job is far from complete. The second question, "Are there other disorders that would better explain symptoms that are being reported?" demands to be answered. Consider the following example: Harold is an 8-year-old boy who is disruptive in class, irritable, aggressive, and hard to discipline at home. He reportedly is nervous, highstrung, and prone to worry. A single-dimension instrument, such as the ADHD Rating Scale can certainly help the diagnostician determine if ADHD symptoms are present. But what about other possible childhood conditions, such as anxiety, depression, or frank noncompliance and conduct problems? A single measure with items probing only the ADHD facets of behavior may miss other sides of Harold's problems that are equally or even more dominant than his ADHD problems.

Multidimensional instruments, such as the Personality Inventory for Children and Child Behavior Checklist (see Chapter 7), alleviate these problems. In essence, these instruments ask parents and/or teachers to rate the child or teenager on many different dimensions (e.g., ADHD, depression, conduct problems, social skills problems). Some, all, or none of the dimensions can be found to be present at problematic levels. Table 9.2 contains Harold's PIC profile. Note that Harold's parents' responses show elements of both ADHD and depression (in this case, principally irritability and discouragement). Such information can be extremely instructive during treatment plan development. It would be unreasonable to expect Harold's problems to be alleviated with a plan that addresses merely his ADHD symptoms. In fact, even the selection of medication to treat his problem can be influenced by the presence of "co-existing" problems such as depression.

In Harold's case, PIC scores indicate presence of both ADHD and depression. What about less easy to interpret patterns? Assume that the ADHD Rating Scale (single-dimension rating) indicated ADHD symptoms were present. Scores on the PIC, however, showed elevations on the scale that reflects depression but not on the scale that

Table 9.2. Personality Inventory for Children profile for Harold

| Scale | T-score | Clinical range |
|---|---|---|
| Achievement | 57 | Normal |
| Intellectual Screening | 54 | Normal |
| Development | 55 | Normal |
| Somatic Concern | 60 | Normal |
| Depression | 81 | Moderate |
| Family Relations | 57 | Normal |
| Delinquency | 66 | Normal |
| Withdrawal | 55 | Normal |
| Anxiety | 63 | Normal |
| Psychosis | 64 | Normal |
| Hyperactivity | 86 | Severe |
| Social Skills | 57 | Normal |

reflects ADHD. Most diagnosticians, of course, would seek data from other sources, such as observation, interview, and personal history, but one distinctive possibility is that depression (which includes irritability, poor concentration, and discouragement) may be the predominant and perhaps only condition present. In this case, the ADHD rating simply did not reflect reality. Instruments such as the PIC thus can be extremely valuable in directing the clinician to other possibilities that might account for the child's behavior and do so in a manner that is objective and empirical (see Chapter 7). In clinical practice, single-dimension ADHD rating scales can point to the wrong diagnosis.

Unremitting popular press coverage of ADHD coupled with parents' honest desire to determine the cause of their child's failure has swayed many parents to believe that their child, too, must have ADHD. Sometimes parents grasp the ADHD straw hoping it will explain why their child has been so difficult. Thorough assessment, including multidimensions rating forms, are particularly valuable in keeping the process grounded in reality.

## Psychological Test Performance that Indicates ADHD

There are some clear deficiencies in an approach wedded to rating forms and checklists; most obvious is that the information derives from second-hand reports rather than from direct psychological test performance of the child. One might ask, "Aren't patterns on psychological tests such as the Wechsler Intelligence Scale for Children–III capable of detecting children with ADHD?"

Research using earlier versions of the Wechsler Intelligence scale (WISC–R) (Wechsler, 1971) suggested that children with ADHD had relatively greater difficulty on three particular subtests (Arithmetic,

Digit Span, and Coding). Scores from these subtests could be averaged to create a so-called "Freedom from Distractibility" index, and if this index were lower than the child's scores on other sections of the WISC–R, then one might entertain the ADHD hypothesis. Although greeted with some initial enthusiasm as a possible clinically relevant indicator of attention problems, this index was later shown to be too imprecise to add much to the diagnosis of ADHD (Barkley, 1990; Kaufman, 1994; Semrud-Clikeman, Hynd, Lorys, & Lahey, 1993). If the Freedom from Distractibility index alone were used, many children without ADHD would be misidentified as having ADHD and many of those with ADHD would be misclassified as not having it. Still, there is some correlation among scores on subtests such as Arithmetic, Digit Span, Coding, and Symbol Search (a new subtest added to the WISC–III) so that clinicians may scrutinize the scores to determine if they are compatible with the rest of the child's profile. Cautious diagnosticians, however, minimize the importance of Freedom from Distractibility scores on the Wechsler scales as an aid in ADHD diagnosis. Unfortunately, other psychological tests, particularly those that measure executive function (see Chapter 8), have been scrutinized for their ability to detect children with ADHD, without much more success (Barkley & Grodzinsky, 1994). As of the mid-1990s, executive function tests, such as Trail Making or Controlled Oral Word Association (Benton, Hamsher, & Sivan, 1994), may have a limited role in helping diagnosticians understand children's psychological processing and may even shed some light on ADHD itself. No doubt the search for suitable instruments will continue.

## Continuous Performance Task

Unlike other tests that require the child to perform, one type of test, the continuous performance task (CPT), was designed precisely to measure attention and impulse control. Varying in nature and including laboratory versions that present auditory, visual, and haptic material, the CPT requires the examinee to focus attention continuously over an interval of time (e.g., 10 minutes) while occasionally and intermittently performing a task—usually a simple one. One of the few carefully standardized and clinically useful CPT tasks is the Gordon Diagnostic System (Gordon, 1983), which is a computerized system that presents tasks requiring vigilance, concentration, sustained effort, and impulse control. The test's utility is most easily understood if the Vigilance task is described: A display screen (see Figure 9.2) presents single-digit numbers at a one-per-second pace while the child focuses, waiting for a specified number combination (e.g., 2-7), which is to be followed by an immediate lever press. The Gordon System Vigilance

Figure 9.2. Gordon Diagnostic System—Continuous Performance Task. (Photo reproduced with permission of developer, Dr. Michael Gordon.)

task runs for 9 minutes, during which 45 presentations of the target combination (i.e., 2-7) occur. Each child can be appraised for how many of the 45 chances were responded to correctly (or conversely, how many of the 45 chances were missed, so-called "omission errors"), and how many times the lever was pressed incorrectly (e.g., when numbers other than 2-7, for instance, 2-9, had just appeared on the screen), which are referred to as "commission errors."

Norms are available for children from age 4 to 16 years (4- and 5-year-olds perform a simplified task), making the Gordon system one of the few continuous performance tasks to boast a representative and large standardization sample. Scores on both the omissions and commissions dimensions can be categorized as "normal," "borderline," or "abnormal." In addition, the computerized recording system permits detailed data analysis such as the child's performance for the first, second, and third 3-minute time block separately, a valuable aid in detecting problems among children who perform well initially but who lose concentration or become impulsive as time passes. In addition, the Gordon system has two other options—one (the Delay Task) that requires the child to press the lever, wait briefly, then press again, continuously for 8 minutes; and a second (Distraction) that is a variant of Vigilance with a distracting number flashed on either side of the target number. These options may elicit symptoms undetected by Vigilance alone, especially the Delay Task, on which children who act on impulse may show a deficient number of correct to total lever presses (called the Efficiency Ratio).

The Gordon system has competitors among CPT tasks. For example, the Test of Variables of Attention (TOVA) (Greenberg, 1992) presents a single stimulus in either the upper or lower portion of the screen and requires the respondent to move a toggle switch up or down during a 21-minute trial. A similar procedure was developed originally by Keith Conners in the 1970s and has since been marketed more widely (Conners, 1994). Both the TOVA and Conners products are principally software systems that are fitted to the user's own computer. Neither has the durability or portability of the Gordon system. Differences among the various forms of the continuous performance tests not withstanding, any of these techniques may add otherwise unattainable, tangible data about actual child performance when children who are difficult to diagnosis are being evaluated.

### Planning for the Child with ADHD

Besides promoting the establishment of an accurate diagnosis, psychological test data can facilitate the most important issue—development of a workable treatment plan. Consider the situation of a PIC profile where "Hyperactivity" is not the only scale elevated. The diagnostician might consider the following: Hyperactivity and Conduct—implies that discipline techniques and behavior management may be required; Hyperactivity and Achievement—suggests the possibility of school learning problems, which may include the need for special education (after full psychoeducational evaluation); Hyperactivity and Anxiety or Depression—implies that the child may have internalizing problems that require counseling and that the chances of responding well to stimulant medications (e.g., Ritalin) may be reduced; Hyperactivity and Social Skills—implies ADHD symptoms may be interfering with peer relations and that structure in group settings, or development of social skills through a training program may be necessary. As is frequently true, test information can be quite helpful in the hands of a skilled diagnostician, but formulating a treatment plan takes knowledge and expertise rather than merely selecting the proper test battery.

## AUTISM

Autism is a disorder with childhood onset characterized by severe social impairment, communication limitations, and a restricted, and often peculiar, array of interests and activities. Like ADHD, autism is a condition that is identified by the behavior of the child or teenager rather than by performance on psychological tests. This can be seen by reviewing the diagnostic criteria (as outlined in Table 9.3) from DSM-IV, which is probably the most commonly used system for diagnosing autism. Important changes have occurred recently in the understanding of autism, especially regarding the heterogeneity of autistic-like conditions (autism and its associated disorder cumulatively are referred to as pervasive developmental disorders). They are most clearly reflected in the several pervasive developmental disorders listed in the 1994 publication of DSM-IV (see Table 9.4). It should be clear from Table 9.4 that not every child with autistic-like symptoms meets the criteria for autism, although all of these children share

Table 9.3. DSM-IV diagnostic criteria for autism

A. A total of six (or more) items from (1), (2), and (3), with at least two from (1), and one each from (2) and (3):
   1. qualitative impairment in social interaction, as manifested by at least two of the following:
      a. marked impairment in the use of multiple nonverbal behaviors such as eye-to-eye gaze, facial expression, body postures, and gestures to regulate social interaction
      b. failure to develop peer relationships appropriate to developmental level
      c. a lack of spontaneous seeking to share enjoyment, interests, or achievements with other people (e.g., by a lack of showing, bringing, or pointing out objects of interest)
      d. lack of social or emotional reciprocity
   2. qualitative impairments in communication as manifested by at least one of the following:
      a. delay in, or total lack of, the development of spoken language (not accompanied by an attempt to compensate through alternative modes of communication such as gesture or mime)
      b. in individuals with adequate speech, marked impairment in the ability to initiate or sustain a conversation with others
      c. stereotyped and repetitive use of language or idiosyncratic language
      d. lack of varied, spontaneous make-believe play or social imitative play appropriate to developmental level
   3. restricted repetitive and stereotyped patterns of behavior, interests, and activities, as manifested by at least one of the following:
      a. encompassing preoccupation with one or more stereotyped and restricted patterns of interest that is abnormal either in intensity or focus
      b. apparently inflexible adherence to specific, nonfunctional routines or focus
      c. stereotyped and repetitive motor mannerisms (e.g., hand or finger flapping or twisting, or complex whole-body movements)
      d. persistent preoccupation with parts of objects

B. Delays or abnormal functioning in at least one of the following areas, with onset prior to age 3 years: (1) social interaction, (2) language as used in social communication, or (3) symbolic or imaginative play

C. The disturbance is not better accounted for by Rett's Disorder or Childhood Disintegrative Disorder.

Table 9.4. Autism-spectrum disorders

| Condition | Sex | Communication impairments | Social impairments | Stereotyped/ repetitive behavior | Regression of skills |
|---|---|---|---|---|---|
| Autism | M/F | Yes | Yes | Yes | No |
| Rett disorder | F | Yes | Yes | Yes | Yes and decline head growth |
| Childhood disintegrative disorder | M/F | Yes | Yes | Yes | Yes |
| Asperger disorder | M/F | No | Yes | Yes | No |
| Pervasive developmental disorder, not otherwise specified | M/F | Yes | Yes | Yes | No |

some central characteristics. Most of these children have one of the pervasive developmental disorders (if not autism itself), although some have other explanations for their presentation, as discussed below. The diagnosis of autism has taken on enhanced significance since Congress reauthorized IDEA (in 1990) and designated autism as one of the 14 exceptionalities for which children must be provided services.

Even though psychological tests are not crucial to the identification of autism per se, they have value by providing one or more of three sources of information: 1) help confirm the diagnosis by using parent or teacher rating forms (e.g., Childhood Autism Rating Scale), 2) identify co-existing disorders and locate strengths by using tests of cognition and special abilities (e.g., Wechsler intelligence scales, neuropsychological tests), and 3) illuminate the underlying impairments that typify the condition by using tests as research tools.

## Rating Scales for Autism

One of the most commonly used rating scales is the Childhood Autism Rating Scale (CARS) (Schopler, Reichler, & Renner, 1988). This instrument relies upon and is illustrative of the most basic tenets of psychological testing (see Chapter 1): Assessment is enhanced by maximizing objectivity and by converting qualitative information into quantifiable form. Consider the alternative to using a rating form such as CARS: Under these circumstances, a diagnostician would typically rely upon symptoms delineated in a system such as DSM-IV. As a history is collected from the child's parent and teacher, the diagnostician would determine whether each of the enumerated symptoms was present or absent. Ultimately, the diagnostician would have to establish that sufficient symptoms were present to meet the criteria for diagnosis.

In the case of autism, two symptoms of impaired social interaction, one symptom of impaired communication, and one symptom of impaired and stereotyped behavior pattern or interests must be present to meet the DSM-IV criteria. (There are, of course, other tasks required of the diagnostician, such as determining onset of symptoms and ruling out competing diagnostic possibilities, but the verification of symptoms of any disorder is a crucial part of assessment.) The challenge for the diagnostician is to choose whether each symptom is present or absent; he or she is forced to select either "yes" or "no" in a forced-choice, dichotomous manner. There are no options for "gray" areas. Moreover, the descriptors provided in DSM-IV for each symptom are relatively brief ("marked impairment in the use of multiple nonverbal behaviors such as eye-to-eye gaze, facial expression, body postures, and gestures to regulate social interaction" [p. 70]). Therefore, much is required of the diagnostician regarding prior knowledge of autism and its manifestations; one might argue that considerable prior experience in the diagnosis of autism is required to use a system like DSM-IV effectively.

Contrast the DSM-IV diagnostic approach with the use of CARS. CARS has established 15 categories (see Table 9.5) associated with autism, and these are derived from several diagnostic systems (e.g., DSM; National Society for Autistic Children, 1978) thus reflecting a broad consensus of the disorder. Moreover, each category calls for the child to be rated as follows: within normal limits (assigned 1 point),

Table 9.5. Categories of autism on which children are rated using CARS

| |
|---|
| Relating to people |
| Imitation |
| Emotional response |
| Body use |
| Object use |
| Adaptation to change |
| Visual response |
| Listening response |
| Taste, smell, and touch response and use |
| Fear or nervousness |
| Verbal communication |
| Nonverbal communication |
| Activity level |
| Level and consistency of intellectual response |
| General impression |

mildly abnormal (2 points), moderately abnormal (3 points), or severely abnormal (4 points). By observing the child in classroom or play situations or during psychological testing, by interviewing parent or teacher, or by reviewing case history, the diagnostician is able to rate the child in each of the 15 categories. The system even permits gray-area ratings (e.g., 2.5 points). It is important to note that the criteria by which points are to be assigned are detailed in the manual (see Table 9.6) so that there is agreement among diagnosticians. Finally, and critically, each child's scores over the 15 categories are summed and the total value is compared to established cutoff scores. The total value allows each child to be categorized as "non-autistic," "mildly to moderately autistic," or "severely autistic."

Because CARS in quantifiable, it lends itself to the type of reliability and validity studies typically performed for psychological tests. Research has shown that each of the categories of CARS seems to measure a common or related condition (high internal reliability) (Sturmey, Matson, & Sevin, 1992), that scores are reliable over time (test–retest reliability), and that a high degree of agreement exists among raters using CARS (interrater reliability). More important, research also shows that diagnoses established by CARS tend to agree with independent rating of experts who have performed detailed assessment of people for the presence of autism. For example, the test's authors report that when using their cutoff scores, 14.6% of children would be false negatives (assigned a non-autistic classification when they, in fact, did have autism) and 10.7% were false positives (assigned an autistic classification when they did not have autism). The ability

Table 9.6. CARS scoring criteria for "Relating to People Category"

1. *No evidence of difficulty or abnormality in relating to people.* The child's behavior is appropriate for his age. Some shyness, fussiness, or annoyance at being told what to do may be observed, but not to a greater degree than is typical for children of the same age.
2. *Mildly abnormal relationships.* The child may avoid looking the adult in the eye, may avoid the adult or become fussy if interaction is forced, may be excessively shy, may not be as responsive to the adult as a typical child of the same age, or may cling to parents somewhat more than most children of the same age.
3. *Moderately abnormal relationships.* The child shows aloofness (seems unaware of adult) at times. Persistent and forceful attempts are necessary to get the child's attention at times. Minimal contact is initiated by the child; contact may have an impersonal quality.
4. *Severely abnormal relationships.* The child is consistently aloof or unaware of what the adult is doing. He or she almost never responds to the adult or initiates contact with the adult. Only the most persistent attempts to get the child's attention have any effect.

of CARS to make proper classifications like this is vital to its clinical validity.

## Psychological Tests to Identify Intellectual and Adaptive Status

Approximately 75% of children with autism also meet the diagnostic criteria for mental retardation—IQ score below 70 with co-existing delays in adaptive behavior (American Psychiatric Association, 1994). It is sometimes suggested that these individuals do not "truly" have mental retardation because they cannot take tests well because of their autism. Unfortunately, this contention is false for several practical as well as logical reasons. First, children with autism are testable. Experienced examiners, sometimes with the assistance of a parent or familiar teacher, can prompt the child to attend to test material, encourage the child to respond, and motivate the child to persist throughout the testing session. In some instances, unconventional measures, such as the use of primary reinforcers (e.g., cereal bits) are required to promote attention and effort. Poor scores on psychometric tests among children with autism are generally a result of the children's lack of basic skills necessary to respond well on testing (e.g., attention to material, understanding and following directions, comprehension of the task at hand, meaningful interpersonal communication, flexibility, adaptation to novelty). It should also be remembered that IQ or ability test performance alone is insufficient to merit a diagnosis of mental retardation. Parents and/or teachers must confirm via first-hand familiarity with the child's adaptive skills that obvious delays are present. In reality, parents are often shocked to find that their son or daughter scored higher on standardized IQ testing than on adaptive behavior measures that depended entirely on their own descriptions of their child. (See Chapter 4 for a description of adaptive behavior scales.)

Second, it is illogical to contend that children with autism cannot have mental retardation because their "autism" caused them to score poorly on IQ tests. Autism is merely a label used to describe a group of behavioral symptoms. Labels do not cause anything. At the causation level, children who have autism and co-existing mental retardation almost certainly have both problems arising from the same source—that is, impaired brain functioning, the exact origin and pathology being only partially known and understood.

## Psychological Tests Used to Understand the Limitations that Underlie Autism

Goldstein and Minshew (1995) and Goldstein, Minshew, and Siegel (1994) have administered batteries of psychological and neuropsychological tests to groups of individuals with autism with normal or higher intelligence on standardized tests. This so-called "high-functioning" group has particular pertinence in revealing the processes that underlie autism. This is because the high-functioning group's freedom from general cognitive and adaptive delays that characterize most individuals with autism permits clear discernment of any narrow impairments that may characterize the group with autism but be absent in a control group without autism. Somewhat surprising is that the group with autism, as a whole, did not reveal a modality preference for either visual or verbal material (Minshew, Goldstein, & Siegel, 1995). Rather, they tended to do poorly on complex material and well on simple or rote material. For example, in the academic realm, the group with autism tended to perform well on Word Attack on the Woodcock-Johnson or Word Recognition on the Kaufman Test of Educational Achievement (K–TEA) but extremely poorly on reading comprehension subtests from the same instrument (Minshew, Goldstein, Taylor, & Siegel, 1994). Likewise, general memory was adequate but as a group, individuals with autism tended to use higher-order encoding and recall strategies less, such as semantic clustering on the California Verbal Learning Test (see Chapter 5 for discussion of the California Verbal Learning Test) (Minshew & Goldstein, 1993). As a group, individuals with autism were prone to use inefficient judgment and logic in tasks such as "20 Questions." Individuals without autism often zero in on specific objects in this game by asking constraint-seeking questions; that is, questions whose answer allows an entire category of possibilities to be eliminated. Subjects in this study with autism were less apt to use this type of high-level logic to solve the problem (Minshew, Siegel, Goldstein, & Weldy, 1994). Some researchers would contend that these type of problems reflect deficient executive functions (see Chapter 8). Indeed, individuals with autism tend to have unusual difficulty on executive measures such as the Wisconsin Card Sorting Test as well as experimental measures of executive functions and failed to grow in this regard when studied longitudinally (Hughes, Russell, & Robbins, 1994; Ozonoff & McEvoy, 1994); they also are apt to perform with cognitive inflexibility (Ozonoff, Strayer, McMahon, & Filloux, 1994). Nonetheless, the data from Goldstein and colleagues seem to imply more complex and varied impairments than the executive function label alone connotes.

A fascinating alternative explanation of the impairment that may underlie autism comes from work on "theory of mind." Initially reported by British researchers (Baron-Cohen, Leslie, & Frith, 1985, 1986) and subsequently discussed and elaborated upon in the United States (Pennington, 1991), this theory suggests that individuals with autism have unique inability to pass simple false-belief tasks. For example, children with autism might be shown a recognizable container, such as a well-known candy box and asked about its contents. Like most children, they respond that the box contains the expected candy. In the British study they were shown a box of "Smarties," a candy like M&Ms. When shown that in fact the box contained something else, such as a pencil, individuals with autism often seem unable to use this information to predict others' thinking. In point of fact, individuals with autism tend to predict that the next person shown the candy box would also state that it contained a pencil. The individuals with autism had striking difficulty predicting others' false beliefs. Pennington (1991) has argued that failure in the process that "requires representation of another person's underlying mental state" (p. 143) helps explain not only the core symptoms of autism—the social impairments—but also secondary impairments such as the inability to utilize symbolic play as other children do. Researchers continue to investigate whether failure to develop a theory of mind accounts for limitations frequently seen among individuals with autism, such as failure to imitate (Charman & Baron-Cohen, 1994), lack of social interaction that requires insight (Frith, Happe, & Siddons, 1994), and failure on psychometric tests that require social understanding and judgment such as the Wechsler Comprehension subtest (Happe, 1994). In general, these studies suggest that the inability to develop theory of mind is quite prevalent among individuals with autism, that this failure is much less prevalent among children with other disabilities or among individuals matched for mental age, and that this failure may explain many of the disabilities and social peculiarities seen among these individuals.

## DEVELOPMENTAL, PSYCHOLOGICAL, AND SCHOOL PERFORMANCE PROBLEMS ASSOCIATED WITH OTHER HEALTH CONDITIONS

As new diseases arise, as pathological processes that underlie longstanding illness are elucidated, and as researchers examine affected children using psychometric instruments, an explosion of knowledge has resulted at the interface of psychology and medicine. Some of this knowledge has important implications for physicians and other health care professionals, teachers, and parents. This is particularly true because unlike the most common biomedical causes of mental retardation (see Table 4.4), the diseases discussed in this section only inconsistently cause learning or developmental problems, and the severity of the attendant problems varies greatly from child to child.

Some children are affected severely, some only slightly, and some not at all by the very same disorder. Furthermore, these diseases are generally not thought of as neurological or developmental in nature (unlike the conditions such as Down syndrome or fetal alcohol syndrome addressed in Chapter 4), although there may well be neurological aspects of the disease process. For these reasons, learning and developmental problems may not even be considered or, if considered, they may be given minimal import by those caring for the child. Three such conditions, asthma, diabetes, and human immunodeficiency virus (HIV)/acquired immunodeficiency syndrome (AIDS), are discussed here.

## Asthma

It was estimated that more than 1.7 million children under age 18 have asthma and that the rate of prevalence was increasing (Taylor & Newacheck, 1992). Four potential questions have arisen regarding the cognitive development and school learning of children with asthma: 1) Is a specific learning disability associated with asthma? 2) Do these children suffer from the side effects of asthma medication? 3) Are there cognitive consequences of respiratory arrest and hypoxia (lack of oxygen to the brain) that sometimes occur with this illness? and 4) Do the secondary problems associated with the disease, such as school absenteeism, stress, and disruption of physical and social activities alter development or hamper school performance? Each of these questions was addressed by Bruce Bender (1995) at the National Jewish Center for Immunology and Respiratory Medicine in Denver, a major research and treatment center.

Bender reached several conclusions based on his own research and a review of the existing literature. First, neither cognitive delays nor specific learning disability pattern characterize children with asthma more than is true of children without it. Second, most children who have experienced a respiratory arrest as a derivative of asthma do not have permanent damage as a result. Third, effects may accompany the use of medication, but these are quite variable and not always consistent with the supposition of many physicians and parents.

Corticosteroids, historically reserved for significant illness, do seem to be associated with emotional changes (e.g., increased irritability, sadness) and with mildly depressed scores on verbal and visual memory measures for the interval closest to drug administration, but not later. Theophylline, once used as a mainstay of drug treatment, has frequently been supposed to cause attention, memory, and motor control problems. More recent research has suggested that the effects of this medicine may not be as great, that negative effects may either not exist or be extremely subtle, and that individual children respond quite variably. Beta agonists, frequently used in meter dose inhalers, may cause short-lived tremors, but their use does not seem to affect complex perceptual-motor tasks. Antihistamines probably cause drowsiness, but the new generation of antihistamines may eliminate that problem because they do not cross the blood–brain barrier, thus they hypothetically cannot cause central nervous system symptoms such as lethargy.

Regarding the secondary effects of asthma, Bender concluded that there is little evidence that school absenteeism per se causes children with asthma to have educational impairments. Rather, asthma in addition to other risk factors, such as a second chronic illness, poverty, poor self-esteem, or lowered expectations, seems to cause school problems. A multitude of other factors, such as family and personal strength or school success could, apparently, mitigate against negative outcome.

Finally, whereas some case reports and research studies lacking adequate controls suggest that children who experience respiratory arrest and hypoxia may also experience cognitive and neuropsychological effects, other better-controlled studies failed to determine such impairments on average. Individual children, of course, may experience such effects. Detailed neuropsychological evaluations, as discussed in Chapter 8, would seem to be the most appropriate mechanism for detecting these brain-related problems.

## Diabetes Mellitus

Another fairly common childhood disorder is diabetes, which affects approximately 1 in 500 children under age 18 years (Sperling, 1990). Research findings are less positive here than for asthma, a fact that is understandable if the nature of the disorder is considered. Diabetes occurs when the pancreas fails to produce sufficient insulin to permit proper metabolism of glucose. Because the body's major organs depend on this energy source, significant problems can appear in diverse organ systems, including the brain. During the time period of childhood, of course, the brain is undergoing continuing development. Without the capacity to carry reserves of glucose, the brain is dependent on a steady supply in order to function properly.

Two critical questions arise regarding diabetes and cognitive/school performance: What long-term effect does diabetes exert on development; do transient episodes of deficiencies in blood sugar (hypoglycemia) or excesses in blood sugar (ketoacidosis) affect psychological performance? Information on these points was presented in 1995 by Holmes, O'Brien, and Greer.

Regarding the first question, it appears that children with diabetes are at increased risk for delayed cognitive development and that early onset of diabetes and poorly controlled blood sugars are added risk factors (Holmes et al., 1995). For example, children with disease onset before 5 years have IQs on average 10 points lower than those with later onset and are apt to score lower on many types of verbal, visuospatial, memory, motor, and school achievement tasks. As a group they are prone to poorer WISC Performance IQs, in large part due to slow responding; children with later onset are prone to poorer WISC Verbal IQ scores. Children with histories of either hypoglycemia accompanied by seizures or unconsciousness or with episodes of diabetic ketoacidosis had greater risk of learning problems. Furthermore, boys were at even greater risk of learning problems than girls if they experienced hypoglycemia or ketoacidosis.

Regarding the second question, it appears that even minimal levels of hypoglycemia (e.g., 55–65 mg/dl) may affect the performance of children with diabetes. Tests such as Trail Making B (see Chapter 8) that require sustained attention and mental efficiency may be affected not only during, but for an interval time after, hypoglycemia. There is speculation that some children with diabetes may have mild hypoglycemic episodes that are sufficient to affect school performance unless these children are permitted regular and properly placed snacks during the day.

Cognitive problems can be exaggerated by emotional difficulties and by chronic school absenteeism, which may also develop from diabetes. Apparently as a result of such factors, children with diabetes are commonly in need of special education services. In one study, 53% of early onset, 35% of late onset, but only 17% of control group children received services (Hagen et al., 1990).

## HIV/AIDS

HIV can be transmitted from an infected mother to her neonate (so-called vertical transmission), who in turn, can develop AIDS; this is the most common cause of pediatric HIV infection, producing 89% of cases among those younger than 13 years of age (Williams & Williams, 1996). Rarely, children may become infected through mother's milk, by playing with infected needles, or through the more common adult means of transmission: sex, blood transfusion, or intravenous drug usage; these latter factors become increasingly important sources of transmission during the teenage years. Most estimates are assumed to be conservative, but more than 6,000 cases of individuals younger than 19 were identified with AIDS as of December 1994 (Wolters, Brouwers, Moss, & Pizzo, 1995).

Adults with HIV/AIDS may experience any conceivable neuropsychological impairment (e.g., extremely specific memory, perceptual, or motor impairments with general cognition spared). This may occur as direct effects of HIV infection itself or secondary to other infections facilitated by the presence of HIV, or due to strokes or tumors that are more prevalent among individuals with HIV. Later in the disease process, many adults experience dementia characterized by confusion, lack of inhibition, or motor uncoordination as the white matter deep within the brain deteriorates (Lezak, 1995).

The situation is different with children; some, but not all, develop brain involvement. HIV-associated encephalopathy occurs when the virus attacks supporting cells in the brain (rather than neurons), which apparently produce toxins that in turn induce neurological damage. It appears that the antiretroviral agent AZT can diminish the prospect of encephalopathy and diminish or reverse some of the associated cognitive effects (Batshaw & Perret, 1992). Accordingly, researchers have identified four developmental progressions that may occur when an infant is infected with HIV. They are presented in Figure 9.3. (Brouwers, Belman, & Epstein, 1994).

Two groups of children with HIV-associated encephalopathy develop quite inadequately. Children in the poorer developing of these two groups show subnormal development for a period of time followed by obvious deterioration. They lose previously acquired developmental milestones such as sitting and early language skills. Cognitive development is generally impaired on all dimensions. There also may be behavioral peculiarities such as staring, lack of social interest, and even abnormalities that appear autistic-like. A second group of children also fare poorly with delayed initial cognitive, motor, and language development followed by plateauing of development but not regression. These children would, thus, have scores on tests like the Bayley scales that become progressively poorer over time, although they had not actually lost skills. They simply fail to continue to develop.

Favorably, there are also two additional groups with more typical development. One group has static but subnormal developmental progression so that they perform consistently more poorly than age-peers, but they do not either lose previously acquired skills nor do they experience plateauing growth. These children, thus, would show scores on tests like the Bayley scales that are below average (e.g., Mental Developmental Index of 80), but the scores would remain constant across time. Finally, there is a group whose development appears typical through testing even though they have symptoms of HIV disease. It is speculated that some of these children were originally destined to be bright and developmentally precocious; their observed average

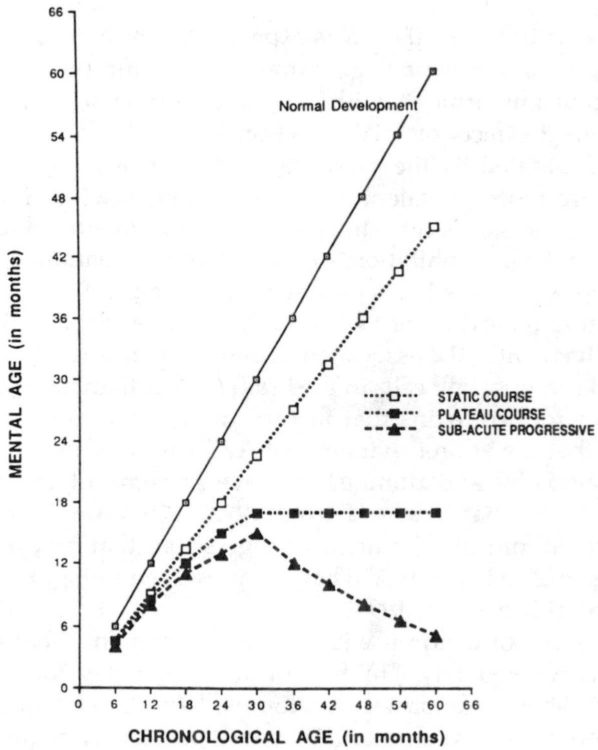


Figure 9.3. Schematic representation of the different courses of encephalopathy in children with HIV infection. (From Brouwers, P., Belman, A.L., & Epstein, L. [1994]. Central nervous system involvement: Manifestations, evaluations, and pathogenesis. In P.A. Pizzo & C.M. Wilfert [Eds.], *Pediatric AIDS: The challenge of HIV infection in infants, children, and adolescents.* Baltimore: Williams & Wilkins. Copyright Philip A. Pizzo, M.D.; represented by permission.)

performance reflects relatively impaired functions due to the adverse effects of HIV on the brain.

Researchers have found other differences between adults and children with HIV. Among children, neural structures appear to have varying degrees of vulnerability based on their timetable for growth. In general, it appears that those portions of the brain undergoing the most rapid growth during the disease's active phase are most threatened. For example, if the disease has failed to progress when primary sensory reception centers are developing, then the psychological functions performed by these centers may not be impaired. In contrast, if the disease is active while centers involved in language are developing, then language functions may be affected. These facts not withstanding, some centers in the brain are especially vulnerable no matter when the disease is most operative. For example, CT scans have consistently shown progressive calcification of brain structures involved in motor movement (basal ganglia). Perhaps because of these timing/developmental issues, certain skills have been affected most consistently among children with HIV. Motor skill problems of many types have been identified among children with HIV. Researchers (Wolters et al., 1995) have found that expressive language has been more vulnerable to disruption than receptive language as measured by standardized tests (Reynell Developmental Language Scales; Reynell, 1977; Clinical Evaluation of Language Fundamentals–Revised; Semel, Wiig, & Secord, 1987). Attention problems have also been documented among children with HIV on measures such as continuous performance tasks (see p. 296) and the WISC "freedom from distractibility" factor. Not surprising is that children affected with HIV have a variety of social/emotional impairment. As a group they have been noted to be more depressed, more autistic acting, more anxious, poorer socially, and to have more conduct problems. Sorting out the causes of these findings is less straightforward than it may appear on the surface. Some behavioral findings are clearly tied to central nervous system impairment in that they correlated with CT brain abnormalities. Furthermore, depressed and autistic-like behavior has been found to diminish when children with HIV-associated encephalopathy are treated with the drug AZT. Even when behavior problems are directly due to brain impairment, HIV may not be the culprit. Many babies born to mothers with HIV are premature, with inadequate nutrition or prenatal care. Many have experienced massive social upheaval that has affected attachment and personal emotional stability. Finally, it can be argued that HIV is disproportionately common among individuals characterized by impulsive, high risk-taking behavior. When impulsivity shows up among their offspring, one plausible explanation is genetic; it has been shown that many personality and/or emotional characteristics are heritable (Plomin, 1989). For any individual child, untangling neurological from environmental and genetic factors is often practically impossible.

## ROLE OF PSYCHOLOGICAL TEST FINDINGS IN CHILDREN WITH HEALTH IMPAIRMENTS

Because psychological and developmental problems associated with health conditions are rare, they may prove confusing. Diagnosticians may not understand the role of psychological testing and thus fail to use this valuable source of information. The consumer of psychological test data is encouraged to keep several points in mind when considering findings for children with health problems.

First, it is essential to remember the distinction between cause and effect. The type of health conditions discussed in this chapter can cause developmental, psychological, and school learning problems, but they do not always do so, and when they do, the effects can be quite varied. The role of assessment, which includes in large part standardized psychological tests, is to determine which effects actually have occurred in an individual child. Thus, a child with diabetes may have some, none, or almost all of the effects established in research studies.

Second, the effects of health problems may be uncommon and not easily detected unless the right tests are used in the right ways. Testing will be most helpful if the diagnostician understands the condition and appreciates which problems might show up and how they may change over time. In the case of diabetes, for example, standardized IQ tests may be insensitive to the problems with alertness and decision making that can occur during episodes of relative hypoglycemia. Likewise, testing a child at optimum times may miss the concentration and decision-making problems that may occur at other less optimum times. The evaluating psychologist must proceed in a logical and inventive way. For children with HIV, as an example, test scores that fall in the average range should not lead one to assume the child will have continued adequate development; by the same token low scores at one point on the Bayley scales do not close the door to better performance later if the child has not had treatment with an antiretroviral agent. Likewise, a test of general cognition, like the WISC–III, may be inadequate to detect typical developmental delays among healthy children, but it may need supplementation with tests of concentration, expressive language, and motor development for a child with HIV.

Third, and consistent with the recognition that psychological test scores are tools useful for answering questions rather than being answers themselves, there must be a legitimate question to be answered via psychological tests to justify their use. Often there is. The most obvious of these is, "Is this child developing normally? If not, what is the scope and severity of any problems?" On the one hand, it is reassuring to parents, educators, and health care professionals to know that a child with asthma, diabetes, or HIV is developing at a typical rate and that his or her disease is not affecting the ability to perform. On the other hand, if a child is not developing adequately, or if there are transient problems secondary to a chronic disease, then determining the nature and severity of the problem is an essential first step. Armed with accurate information about the child's current status, including strengths and weaknesses, a helpful and humane design can be created.

## NONBIASED ASSESSMENT OF MINORITY CHILDREN

Many factors influence the development and use of psychological tests. During the 1980s, the United States became a society with increasing numbers of minority populations who were entering public schools. Educating these children became a pressing need. How to identify fairly the subset of those children from diverse backgrounds who have impairments requiring special services has become, and will continue to be, a crucial issue confronting those who use psychological tests. An overview of issues related to nonbiased assessment of minority children is presented in this chapter.

Is Spanish-speaking Monica's poor academic progress due to limited English language proficiency or limited ability?

Ric, an inner-city student, seems to do very well at home and in his neighborhood, yet is having continued problems with his school work. Is he being lazy? Does he need a special class?

Juan's parents are asking for help. They've been told their son has mental retardation, but they are not sure how this diagnosis was made or if it is accurate.

All of these questions relate to how minority, linguistically different, and culturally different children are assessed. When assessing children, psychologists must not only recognize such differences but also account for them so that accurate testing—free of bias against any one group—occurs. When the influences of language or culture are ignored in the evaluation process, invalid, useless, or potentially damaging data result. When major decisions such as special education enrollment follow from poor data, the result may be not only a disservice to the child but also illegal.

The push for nonbiased assessment can be traced back to several court cases of the 1970s that involved ethnic minority children and special education placements. The main issues in these cases were proper assessment practices for ethnic minority children, such as the use of IQ tests and the role of native language, and overrepresentation of ethnic minority children in programs for children with mental retardation. Not only were standardized tests alleged to be biased, but the school placements that resulted were viewed as inferior and second-rate in educational quality (Reschly, 1982). Moreover, because the number of ethnic minority students in these placements was not proportional to their representation in the general population, there was concern that minority students were not only being overidentified, but actually misdiagnosed.

The controversy arose especially over the types of students being placed in classes for children with mild retardation and how placement decisions were being made (Reschly, 1982). A preponderance of students in classrooms for children labeled educable mentally handicapped were found to be culturally different and minority children, children from impoverished backgrounds, and children who had been segregated. For educational purposes, they were found to have mild mental retardation, but in their respective homes and communities, they were actually quite adaptive. This finding gave rise to the "6-hour retardate" phenomenon, or the child who was only "retarded" for the 6 hours of the school day. This phenomenon was viewed as the result of assessment practices that relied solely on intelligence tests for diagnosing mental retardation. Another significant contributor to the problem was the lack of assessment data on a child's adaptive skills, especially a child's ability to function outside of the school environment. Thus, the adequacy of testing practices, along with the ethnic composition of pupils in special classes, became the focal point for the court cases that were to follow.

Two court cases that focused on the misdiagnosis of bilingual children were *Diana v. Board of Education of California* (1970) and *Guadalupe v. Tempe Elementary District* (1972). In both suits, it was alleged that improper assessment with IQ tests led to overrepresentation, in classes for students labeled educable mentally handicapped, of linguistically different minority children. In the former suit, the courts stipulated that children should be tested in both their native language and English, and that assessment of cognitive functioning must occur primarily with nonverbal tests. Because the children were minority and bilingual, verbal tests (or the contribution of verbal subtests to an overall IQ score) were not considered to yield valid estimates of intellectual functioning. The second case reiterated that testing must use the child's native language, but also went on to add that IQ could not be used as the sole basis for making placement decisions about ethnic minority children. Assessment of other areas, such as adaptive behavior outside of the school environment, was also deemed necessary for making pupil classifications. As is discussed in Chapter 4, the diagnosis of mild mental retardation must be based upon both IQ and adaptive behavior. In both cases, the appropriateness of IQ testing, especially verbal testing with ethnic minority children, was questioned. But, importantly, so was the appropriateness and efficacy of special education placements that resulted from such poor practices.

The aim of both decisions was to improve assessment practices to ensure that factors like language did not lead to misdiagnosis of ethnic minority children.

In a subsequent court case, the focus was more narrowly on the use of IQ tests alone. *Larry P. v. Riles* (1972, 1974, 1979) is one of the longest and most controversial cases to come out of the nonbiased-assessment movement. The basic contention in this suit was, again, overrepresentation of minorities in classes for the educable mentally handicapped and the quality of such programs. The minority population involved, however, was African American children instead of linguistically different children. Although the special education program was identified as a major problem because of educational inferiority, the court instead seemed to zero in on IQ testing, rather than the quality of the programs themselves. This is a situation that Reschly (1982) terms "right problem—wrong solution" (p. 211). Much of the testimony revolved around whether the WISC–R was biased when used with African American children. There was little discussion about whether special class placement was beneficial or harmful to those children who had been identified. Based on the testimony presented, Judge Peckham's decision did indeed find the WISC–R to be biased for African American children. Following completion of the trial in 1979, a permanent injunction was issued throughout the state of California prohibiting IQ testing for African American children who were being considered for educable mentally handicapped programs, unless permission was granted by the court. This ban was later broadened to prohibit all IQ testing with African American children, regardless of potential classification or program, and regardless of whether parental permission had been given for the testing. This decision has not resolved the controversy, however. As of 1990, the *Larry P.* case was being challenged in California by an African American mother who charged that not testing her son may have prevented him from receiving services and thus contributed to discriminatory practice.

Perhaps what is most striking about the sweeping finding of the *Larry P.* case is the fact that, in 1980, a federal judge reached exactly the opposite conclusion in a highly similar case. *Parents in Action on Special Education (PASE) v. Hannon* was brought on behalf of African American children in the Chicago public school system. Like the *Larry P.* case, the focus was on IQ testing—again the WISC–R. In this instance, after inspecting test items, Judge Grady determined that this very same test was not biased against African American children. The same test was under examination, and much of the expert testimony came from the very people involved in the *Larry P.* trial, and yet the opposite conclusion was reached. For psychologists in the Chicago school system, testing of African American children remained an appropriate practice, but for California psychologists, the practice had become inappropriate and potentially illegal.

In the face of such continued challenges and polar decisions, psychologists' standards for correct practice become confused. It makes no sense for a test to be both outlawed and sanctioned at the same time. Is intelligence testing biased, or is it sound, appropriate practice? There is a fallacy in viewing this issue in this framework, however. The problem lies not so much with tests as it does with the uses of tests. The instruments in and of themselves may not be biased, but the way in which they are used can be quite biased and lead to inappropriate decisions (Jensen, 1980). Do psychologists need to stop intelligence testing? The answer is probably not, so long as reasonable safeguards are employed. Many arguments have been advanced against the testing of ethnic minority children; however, all have been cogently addressed (Miller-Jones, 1989; Reschly, 1982; Reynolds, 1982; Sattler, 1988). Some of the more common arguments follow.

1. *The normative base of intelligence tests is inappropriate because minorities are not included in the norming group to a sufficient degree.* This assertion is false because minorities are typically represented in norming samples to the degree that they are present in the general population. So, for instance, if African Americans represent 3% of the population as a whole, then they should represent 3% of the norming group. Among the major intelligence tests (Weschler scales, Stanford-Binet Intelligence Scale: Fourth Edition), this type of procedure was employed in developing norms.

In the past, some researchers, notably Jane Mercer (1979), advocated developing pluralistic norms that could be applied separately to each minority group. Problems with this approach, however, are that the norms may not be particularly relevant, either to the educational environment of the child, or outside the child's immediate geographic area. For instance, a child might appear to have average-range abilities relative to his or her culture. According to general norms, however, the same child might be well below average. Because it is reasonable to expect that schooling would take place in the general culture, this child would be at a severe disadvantage in general classes. And, as noted by Sattler (1988), what norms would be used in the case of a child with a Mexican father and Hungarian mother? Nonetheless, it appears that practicing school psychologists use alternative racial and ethnic norms at least some of the time when identifying children with mental retardation. Thirty-five percent of school psychologists confirmed usage of alternative norms when surveyed about their method of practice (Wodrich & Barry, 1991).

2. *Minority students have inadequate test-taking skills due to a lack of experience with such materials and to not recognizing the achievement nature of testing.* The contention here is that not all minority children ascribe the same meaning to the testing format or to the tasks themselves. Children may not respond to testing demands such as manipulatives, verbalizations, or paper-and-pencil tasks in an expected, standardized fashion. Some children, by virtue of their cultural upbringing, may not be achievement- or competition-oriented, and hence fail to do well. To them, testing might be viewed more as fun than as a challenge to prove themselves. In many Native American cultures, for example, a noncompetitive attitude is valued and encouraged.

Whereas poor test-taking skills might be true of ethnic minority children, it can be equally true of nonminority children as well. The reasons for deficient skills are not necessarily restricted to occurrence in minority children. In any case, such limitations do not automatically rule out testing, however. The responsibility falls on the psychologist to use tests wisely and to state any reservations that may exist about the validity of findings. Additional factors that are important to consider in such cases are the child's background and alternative assessment methods. Because tests measure background as well as ability, test findings must be interpreted in the context of any relevant background information on the child. When poor test-taking skills are the problem, the psychologist must work diligently to keep child motivated and elicit the maximum performance. If formal testing poses a handicap to the child, then informal methods of data collection must also be used. Obviously, the wise psychologist knows that placement or classification decisions are based on all types of information, not just test results.

3. *Most examiners are Caucasian, and they use standard English that results in poor rapport and communication and has detrimental effects on minority children's scores.* The effect of examiner race has been shown to be negligible. A comprehensive review of 25 of 29 available studies with African American children, which included a variety of intelligence tests, grade levels, and geographic areas, was undertaken to examine this issue (Sattler & Gwynne, 1982). The authors found no significant relationship between examiner race and test scores, leading them to conclude that examiner race does not have an adverse effect on African American children's performance. With Hispanic children, a smaller number of studies has been conducted with essentially the same finding.

The contention that standard English negatively affects African American children's IQ scores also appears false. One study in particular found no differences between the Stanford-Binet Intelligence Scale: Form L–M scores for African American children, whether administered in standard English or African American dialect by an African American examiner (Quay, 1974). The general finding is that African American students are equally facile with understanding both English and African American dialect (Sattler, 1988).

4. *Intelligence tests are biased against any minority because they have been developed with a bent toward white, middle-class, Anglo-Saxon experiences.* This has been the preeminent argument against testing ethnic minority children. The central issue here is bias. The courts have traditionally operationalized bias to mean 1) overrepresentation of minority groups in programs and 2) performance differences between groups (Reschly, 1982). Overrepresentation, although seemingly straightforward, can be misunderstood. This was the case in the *Larry P.* trial in 1974. Figures cited were that 30% of students in the school district were African American but 60% of the students attending educable mentally handicapped classes were African American. However, for a 1-year period (1976–1977), only 1% of the total African American student population in the state was actually placed in educable mentally handicapped classes. At first glance, one might think that 60% of African American students were being placed in educable mentally handicapped classes; however, this was not the case. Actually, a much smaller percentage of students was involved. Overrepresentation was used as evidence of bias against African American children in a case quite similar to the *Larry P.* case, *Georgia Conferences of NAACP v. State of Georgia* (1985). In this instance, overrepresentation was struck down as an indicator of bias. The ruling stated that, in and of itself, overrepresentation of African Americans in educable mentally handicapped programs did not constitute discrimination. In other words, simply having greater numbers of minority children in a program is not necessarily due to faulty assessment practices that led to placement, nor does overrepresentation mean that such students are being discriminated against.

An interesting twist may occur if changes in the definition of mental retardation promulgated by AAMR are put into effect. (It is worth noting that these changes were advocated primarily, if not exclusively, by nonpsychologists.) The 1992 revision of the AAMR definition of mental retardation (see Chapter 4), if widely adopted for actual diagnostic purposes, would have potentially dramatic effects on the assessment of minority children. Specifically, the shift of IQ value from 70 to 75 for mental retardation causes the impact. Despite varying beliefs about the fairness of IQ tests, one fact is clear: African American children tend to score about 1 standard deviation (i.e., 15 IQ points on the Wechsler scales) below Caucasian children. This left shift has the possibility of dramatically altering the number of African American children who might be identified as having mental retardation (Matson & Mulick, 1991). This is true almost exclusively among those with minor or mild cognitive impairments. Children with moderate, severe, and profound levels of mental retardation, for example, are almost equally distributed, that is, reflected in the population with disabilities proportionate to the percentage of individuals in the general population. In many ways, these children with more severe impairments have such obvious disabilities that IQ testing helps to confirm the nature and severity of the impairments. This is not so with mild levels of impairment. As discussed in Chapter 4, the use of the 1992 definition of mental retardation would result in many more children of all races being eligible for mental retardation diagnosis based on IQ alone; the proportion of African American children, however, would grow even more disproportionate. This is true because the proportion of African American children with IQ values between 71 and 75 is extremely high compared with Caucasian children. If the 75 value were used alone, 18.4% of African American children would be eligible for mental retardation designation but only 2.62% of Caucasian children would be. This fact seems to be one of the reasons that psychologists and measurement experts have been reluctant to accept the AAMR definition (Gresham, MacMillan, & Siperstein, 1995; Hodapp, 1995; Matson, 1995).

The other method used by the courts for determining bias is examination of performance differences between groups. These differences and test content are statistical definitions of bias, and as such are the most commonly used scientific methods for investigating bias. *Performance differences* between groups simply refers to the difference between the average score of one group and the average score of another group. If Group A receives a lower score than Group B, the test is said to be biased against Group B. This is a mistaken notion of bias, however, contrary to the common meaning of bias: that the test is somehow unfair or disadvantageous to one group. This may not be true, because it illogically assumes all groups of people are equal on the ability or trait being measured. This is what Jensen (1980) has termed the Egalitarian Fallacy. Quite simply, people are not all equally endowed, and it is far more logical to expect differences between groups than it is to expect equal performance. Of course, this is not to say that individuals within a particular group cannot be higher or lower on a score or trait or ability, but viewing the group as one entity is misleading.

The acceptable method of examining group differences is with the statistical procedure of regression. With *regression,* a first (or known) score is used to predict a second (or unknown) score (e.g., IQ predicts academic achievement). There are two parts to determining whether a test is biased: 1) whether the same prediction formula can be used for two different groups, and 2) whether the common formula does not over- or underpredict for either group. If the common prediction formula based on both groups does over- or underestimate the criterion score, then there is bias present. The second definition of bias is that of test content. The usual procedure for determining if items are biased against a minority group is to have a group of experts review items. Reasons for which an item can be found biased include whether minority children have had an opportunity to learn the item, if the scoring is such that a minority child's response would be correct in his or her own culture but is not correct according to the cultural standard chosen by the test maker, and if an item is asked in an unfamiliar way that makes the child unable to respond although he or she may know the answer. Unfortunately, a panel of experts reviewing items, even with guidelines, rarely agrees about which items to keep and which to throw out (Sattler, 1988). A better method for investigating content bias is to use a procedure whereby statistics for every individual item are examined for each group's performance on the item. If a minority group's performance is exceedingly poor on one particular item but relatively better on other items, then the suspicious item probably should be thrown out.

When intelligence tests have been investigated for bias, either by examining predictions for groups or by examining item content, the finding is that generally they are not biased against ethnic minority groups. Studies using tests such as the WISC–R, WISC–III, and Stanford-Binet L–M scale show that a common prediction formula works well for groups of Caucasian, African American, and Hispanic children when predicting expected achievement (Kaufman, 1994; Reynolds, 1982). This means that the tests are equally good predictors that do not over- or underpredict achievement levels for any one group. Similarly, the presence of content bias in intelligence tests has not been uncovered to any meaningful degree. One of the most infamous WISC–R items to be examined for possible bias against African American children is from the Comprehension subtest, which asks the child how to respond if assaulted by a smaller child. The credited response, according to test guidelines, is to show restraint and avoid conflict. The argument has always been that, in an African American culture, this is a disastrous response because African American children need to fight back as part of their survival. When scientifically investigated, however, the item was easier for African American children to get right than it was for Caucasian children (Miele, 1979). This particular item was deemed biased by the judge in the *PASE v. Hannon* case, but again, when scientifically examined, it was passed by 73% of the African American children and 71% of the Caucasian children in Chicago. Findings such as these demonstrate that simple inspection of tests is not sufficient for determining bias. Despite all of the popular notions of bias and arguments set forth against testing ethnic minority children, scientific data using prediction and content analysis do not find intelligence tests to be biased.

Turn away from the many arguments against testing, and focus instead on some of the benefits and positive aspects that testing has to offer ethnic minority children. There are many arguments for testing; chief among them is that testing offers an effective way to assess present functioning (Sattler, 1988). Given that intelligence tests have the same properties across various ethnic groups, they are of significant value in documenting change, progress, and patterns of strengths and weaknesses in children. Rather than being biased, tests represent an objective standard in assessment that is free of examiner prejudice. Because they are not dependent upon educational climates or teachers' whims, tests can, in some cases, help avoid misdiagnosis of ethnic minority students. For example, an African American child whose teacher is convinced that the child cannot learn will not be placed in a classroom for students with mild mental retardation unless there is objective evidence of low IQ and adaptive behavior skills. A second factor in favor of testing is that tests are equally good predictors for Caucasian and minority groups (Neisser et al., 1996), meaning that predictions of future scholastic performance are greatly aided by tests. It might be the case that a minority child's schooling is occurring within the context of mainstream culture; however, it is not realistic to ignore culture as a factor. Individuals do not function in a void or absence of culture; rather, it is how well individuals succeed in the culture around them (Scarr, 1978) that is important. It is the accuracy of prediction that is of importance, not that tests predict the same level of performance for all individuals (Bersoff, 1981).

Third, testing is valuable for both securing and evaluating special services provided in the schools. Without proper evaluation, minority children might be underidentified and might not receive services necessary for them to learn. Whether such programs are effective interventions for ethnic minority children is an issue involving schools, not tests. Accountability of the school system is a factor that cannot be ignored in the overall process of assessment and placement (Miller-Jones, 1989). If programs are truly dead-end, as has been alleged in many court cases, then it would seem that schools are responsible for instituting changes, rather than the tests being the cause of the problem. Tests can show if learning is occurring in such programs or if revisions are necessary. In the case of poor programs, tests are hardly part of the problem, but can be part of the solution.

## SPECIAL CONSIDERATIONS IN TESTING

How have the pros and cons of testing ethnic minority children affected assessment practices for psychologists? What are appropriate standards in light of court cases and research findings? Some have thought the best way to practice nonbiased assessment was to develop "culture-fair" tests. An example of this is the Black Intelligence Test of Cultural Homogeneity (Williams, 1972). The test is based exclusively on African American inner-city culture, and includes African American slang. The Black Intelligence Test, however, is not the way to accomplish nonbiased assessment. Its psychometric properties are poor, and it is not a valid predictor of future scholastic success (Sattler, 1988). Consequently, the test really has no place in cognitive assessment of African American children. Other measures considered to be culture-fair or culture-free are no more successful at closing the gap between scores obtained by various ethnic groups. Minority children are just as likely to perform the same on culture-fair tests as they do on conventional intelligence tests (Sattler, 1988).

Working with conventional tests, however, still requires special considerations for ethnic minority children. Two key considerations for the psychologist are language and cultural differences. Language issues, which must be addressed before a psychologist can construct an appropriate test battery, include the influence of bilingualism, whether language dominance or proficiency exists in English or a native language, whether an interpreter will be necessary to elicit an optimum performance from the child, and whether it will be necessary to test twice (once in each language) to ensure valid results.

Some test makers attempting to make the assessment process easier now offer Spanish translations of intelligence tests. Unfortunately, these tests have some limitations that consumers and psychologists should consider (Wilen & Sweeting, 1986). For instance, most tests use standard Spanish, which does not allow for the many regional and dialectical differences in the Spanish language. Children from two different regions may not use the same Spanish word for a given English word. The converse is also likely to be true; a given Spanish word translates to many different English words, depending on the origin of the child. Simply administering a Spanish-version test is no guarantee that the language factor has been appropriately handled and that better validity will result.

The second key consideration concerns cultural differences. Understanding the nuances and subtleties of a child's culture is particularly important with minority children because several aspects of testing can be affected. For instance, rapport building is always important, but with minority children it is more than a matter of establishing comfort in the testing situation. Effective rapport building is necessary to overcome distrust, communication problems, fear, and hostility—all factors that the ethnic minority child may bring to testing. In order to do this, the psychologist must become familiar with the culture of the child and learn how to adapt testing to meet any differences. Some examples of cultural differences are readily apparent with Native American children (Sattler, 1988). For instance, many Native American children are taught to not make eye contact, as it is a sign of disrespect, and not to offer a firm handshake, as it is a sign of aggression. They also may find direct, personal questioning an affront and are prone to maintaining long silences in a conversation or interview. Cooperation, sharing, and humility may be valued over competition and individual achievements. These cultural characteristics are open to gross misinterpretation, unless understood by the examiner. It would be very easy for the naive psychologist to conclude from his or her evaluation and interactions with a Native American that the child was depressed, unmotivated, and withdrawn. Interpreting the data in the context of culture, however, would yield a much different, more fitting picture of the child. This is but one example of how culture affects both the ease of administration and the validity of testing. Each culture has its own characteristics; it is incumbent upon the psychologist to know how to work within each culture's framework.

Clearly, where cultural influences are concerned, identical scores from children of two different cultures can have very different meanings. Testing ethnic minority children requires more than merely producing numbers; it is the psychologist's job to assimilate test findings with background information and cultural norms. Based on all relevant information, the psychologist then draws appropriate inferences and limitations and interprets the test data accordingly. Remembering that tests do not measure potential so much as they do current functioning, it becomes especially important to use more than numbers when making potentially long-range classification decisions about ethnic minority children.

Although details vary from culture to culture, some general guidelines exist that apply to all ethnic minority children undergoing testing. Evaluations should never be based on a single test or score. A multimethod approach is best for proper assessment of ethnic minority children. This is likely to include several measures of both a formal and informal nature, along with observational data, work samples, and reports from home and school. As mentioned previously, considerable caution should be taken when dealing with linguistically different children and, as much as possible, nonverbal measures should be used when considering general capability. Likewise, placement decisions warrant the same caution, particularly if "educable mentally handicapped" is the placement in question. Ideally, the best use of tests with ethnic minority children is not simply for placement, but to develop strategies that aid learning. Testing information can be used to identify patterns of strength and weakness, modify teaching approaches, make curriculum adjustments, or develop appropriate interventions.

Many of the specific and general guidelines for assessment of ethnic minority children can be traced back to the court cases, *Diana v. Board of Education of California* (1970), *Guadalupe v. Tempe Elementary School District* (1972), and *Larry P. v. W. Riles* (1972). Most obvious are the guidelines dealing with language and the utilization of more than a single IQ score. These federal mandates have become the recognized standard of practice for psychologists. It is wise for consumers to be aware of some of the considerations for testing minority children. Psychological information that does not incorporate the above guidelines or considerations should raise questions and doubts about the validity of results.

## SUMMARY

Psychological tests have a role in helping to identify ADHD. ADHD rating forms can be used to identify characteristics of ADHD as noted by parents or teachers. Personality inventories help not only by objectifying ADHD symptoms but also by determining whether alternative conditions (e.g., anxiety, depression) or co-existing problems (e.g., conduct problems) are present. Despite efforts to use children's test performances to determine ADHD, few instruments, with the exception of continuous performance tasks, appear sufficiently valid and reliable to help. Health-related conditions, asthma, diabetes, and HIV, are also discussed in this chapter with information regarding psychological test findings commonly found among children with these conditions.

Issues of fair assessment of minority group children remains topical. Calls for nonbiased assessment of ethnic minority children resulted largely from court cases in the 1970s that challenged testing practices as biased. The findings were controversial, with the *Larry P.*

case concluding that intelligence tests were biased, whereas the *PASE* case concluded that they were not. There are several arguments against testing ethnic minority children, chief among them the issue of bias, best defined in a statistical sense, as either bias in test content or bias in making predictions for future performance. When such empirical standards are applied to tests, they are generally found not to be biased.

The following practices are suggested when testing children from minority groups: Use a multimethod approach, become familiar with cultural differences, and use caution where mild mental retardation is an assessment question.

## Study Questions

1. By what methods have the courts traditionally recognized bias, and what are the problems associated with such methods?
2. List three arguments in favor of testing children from ethnic minorities.
3. Discuss the use of culture-fair or culture-free tests in the assessment of ethnic minority children.
4. Identify and discuss two appropriate methods for examining bias.
5. Tell why you think intelligence tests are or are not appropriate for use with ethnic minority children.
6. Why might an average score on a test like the Bayley earned by an 18-month-old with HIV have different implications than the same score earned by an 18-month-old without HIV?
7. What problems might arise from the use of tests like the WISC–III to assess the status of a student with diabetes mellitus?
8. Is there a unique learning disability associated with childhood asthma?
9. Is there a pattern on IQ, achievement, or neuropsychological tests that permits accurate diagnosis of ADHD?
10. Which tests are most often used as part of an evaluation of ADHD?

CHAPTER TEN

# Using and Evaluating Test Findings

Throughout this book, the principles and techniques associated with psychological testing are reviewed, and many specific test instruments are presented. How tests are used in the diagnostic process also is examined. As a consumer of psychological testing, however, the nonpsychologist's concern is with the information received back in the form of test findings. This chapter provides guidelines to help the consumer judge test findings.

Although it is important to know instruments and their role in the diagnostic process, the individuals making a referral for psychological testing do not desire to become, nor in fact do they need to become, experts in mental testing. Their goal is to find a professional who can provide usable, understandable, accurate results; these results are the bottom line. Unfortunately, the quality and usefulness of test findings may vary. Some findings seem helpful but may be inaccurate. Others arouse confidence but do not really seem helpful. How is the consumer to separate good findings from bad test findings? There are no easy answers to the question, but several points are worth keeping in mind when evaluating test findings.

## IS THE REFERRAL QUESTION ANSWERED?

That test findings should address the referral question seems obvious. Chapter 2 emphasizes formulating a specific, answerable question. Logically, one would assume that this question gets answered; however, sometimes it does not. Instead, some psychologists give a standard test battery to all children, regardless of the referral question. In these cases, the test findings are often just a listing of scores of the child's performance, rather than a response to the referral question.

A review of referral questions from earlier chapters helps highlight this situation. In Chapter 3, the referral agent asks about the cognitive status of 18-month-old Mark, a near-drowning victim. If Mark had simply been administered a standard test battery, then the findings might list visual-motor development, attention span, and ability to relate to caregivers, but not refer to cognitive functioning. In contrast, a direct statement in response to the referral question might have read as follows: "Cognitively, Mark is functioning in the range of mild mental retardation. His score in this area was 67, compared to an average score of 100. Mark's near-drowning accident appears to have affected primarily his language development. Specifically, his ability to both say words and understand or respond to them is affected, although motor skills are more intact. In this area, Mark's score was 89." With this response, the referral agent has a clear-cut idea of Mark's cognitive functioning after his accident.

Similarly, in Chapter 4, 5-year-old Jimmy's preparedness for kindergarten was questioned. This case, too, needs an explicit statement to address the referral agent's question. For instance, an appropriate answer might be, "Both socially and intellectually, Jimmy is lagging behind peers and may ultimately develop best if placed in a structured preschool program this fall, with the provision to enter kindergarten the subsequent year." The conclusion reached is clear; there is no guessing about whether the referral question has been answered. An inappropriate response might have included simply a description of Jimmy's intellectual functioning, temperament, or fine motor coordination.

With school-based referrals, an explicit answer to a referral question often explains whether a student has an impairment and if that impairment qualifies the child for special program placement. Although teachers do not typically frame their referral questions in terms of placement, such as, "Does the student qualify for a learning disabilities program?", nonetheless, the presence or absence of an impairment needs to be clearly addressed.

Regardless of setting or referral agent, test results need to be understandable in order to be usable. This is often best accomplished by including among test results a diagnostic impression statement or a program eligibility statement. A diagnostic statement may simply be a DSM-IV diagnosis or an educational label. A program eligibility statement might read as follows: "Based on the severe discrepancy among Jason's intellectual functioning and academic achievement, other test results, and background information, he qualifies for a learning disabilities program. He requires services for reading, written language, and math; a full-time program is recommended." By including such statements, findings are made specific, and the referral agent is not left confused or searching for conclusions.

## ARE VARIABLES THAT LIMIT FINDINGS DELINEATED?

There are instances, however, when findings cannot be stated unequivocally. Results are sometimes compromised by factors such as age or something particular to the testing situation. Some of the more common variables that limit what can be said about psychological testing results include the age of the person, effort and motivation put forth, distractibility/hyperactivity, and effects of medication. Whenever such factors exist, their potential effect on the test results should be clearly identified and described in cautionary statements in the written report. Let us return to the example of 18-month-old Mark who was in a near-drowning accident.

Although Mark's cognitive status is clearly addressed in the previous example, this alone would be an insufficient summary. Mark's young age is a variable that necessitates a cautionary statement, such as the following: "Mark's results need to be qualified, however, due to his age. It is likely that he will change significantly through the course of recovery and treatment, as well as through is own maturation. Although mild retardation seems evident now, Mark's status will need close reevaluation as he progresses and matures. A diagnosis of mild retardation is based on post-accident functioning, and is subject to change." With such a statement, the consumer is alerted, clearly and comprehensively, that Mark's findings are not without a limitation. Ideally, findings should document either a clear answer to the referral question or a clear explanation of why the results might be qualified. Findings in which either or both of these aspects are missing should send a caution signal to the consumer.

## INTERPRETATION IS SUPERIOR TO DESCRIPTION

Distinguishing a descriptive report from an interpretive report is sometimes difficult. Nonetheless, the distinction is an important one, for an interpretive report often provides more useful information. A *descriptive report* simply restates, describes, or outlines without interpretation the child's test responses and/or findings. Often, scores or verbatim responses predominate. In contrast, an *interpretive report* may incorporate scores or verbatim responses for illustrative purposes but focuses on summary statements, implications, or interpretation. Generally, the nonpsychologist will struggle less and understand more when reading interpretive rather than descriptive test findings. Below, two examples support this point.

***Why Does Mike Forget What He Reads?*** In Chapter 5, Mike's teacher asks this question and hopes that a psychological evaluation could provide an answer. The following is a *descriptive* summary of Mike's test findings.

> Mike was administered the Wechsler Intelligence Scale for Children–III and the Peabody Individual Achievement Test–Revised. He earned a WISC–III Verbal IQ of 81 at the 10th percentile, a Performance IQ of 100 at the 50th percentile, and a Full Scale IQ of 89 at the 23rd percentile. Mike had the most difficulty on WISC–III subtests requiring word knowledge, verbal conceptualization, and verbal expression of language concepts. Mike did best on tasks requiring spatial ability, and reasoning with and sequencing of nonverbal stimuli, as well as on nonverbal reasoning tasks. His overall intellectual assessment showed him to be in the low average range.
>
> On the Peabody Individual Achievement Test–Revised, Mike earned a Mathematics grade equivalent of 5.3, with a corresponding percentile rank of 47; a Reading Recognition grade equivalent of 6.2, with a corresponding percentile rank of 50; a Reading Comprehension grade equivalent of 3.1, with a percentile rank of 13; a Spelling grade equivalent of 4.9, with a percentile rank of 45; a General Information grade equivalent of 4.2, with a percentile rank of 9; and finally, a Total Test grade equivalent of 3.9, with a 20th percentile rank. Mike does most poorly on reading comprehension and general information tasks. Thus, Mike is achieving below his ability level on reading comprehension tasks. This may be due to a specific learning disability. Mike needs remedial reading drills, particularly in reading comprehension.

Contrast the first, descriptive, summary with the *interpretive* account below.

> Mike was administered the Wechsler Intelligence Scale for Children–Third Edition (WISC–III), where he was found to have adequate nonverbal reasoning skills, as revealed by his Performance IQ of 100. In contrast, he has significant language problems (Verbal IQ = 81). He appears particularly devoid of general knowledge, and his vocabulary is small and unsophisticated. He does not seem to have any of the

> perceptual or memory problems that are often associated with learning disabilities, however.
>
> As might be expected of a child with language problems, Mike is behind academically, particularly on those tasks that require language sophistication. Specifically, although he has an adequate sight vocabulary (immediately recognizable words) and fair phonics skills, he has significant problems understanding what he reads. Mike's reading failure may appear related to recall or memory problems when he is observed at school, but in reality he probably simply fails to comprehend what he reads. This difficulty is often seen among children with language impairments, sometimes simply because they are reading about things not in their speaking vocabulary, or for which they lack background ideas. Until his store of vocabulary words and language concepts increases, Mike should be expected to continue to struggle with reading comprehension. Remedial drills should focus on language concepts, factual information, and general language skill development, as well as remembering and explaining story content after reading.

Although the first summary of Mike's scores is accurate, it actually represents little more than a simplistic recapitulation of test scores. There is no synthesis of information and no real contribution from the psychologist's knowledge of school learning problems. That is, save for the brief mention of remedial reading drills, the first report could have been compiled by a technician who simply administers but does not interpret tests. Many purely descriptive reports barely address the referral question at all.

***Is Joe Depressed?*** A referral question mentioned in Chapter 6 deals with the question of Joe's depression. Compare the first, *descriptive* summary with the second, *interpretive* summary.

> Fifteen-year-old Joe was administered the Thematic Apperception Test (TAT) and the Minnesota Multiphasic Inventory–Adolescent (MMPI–A). The TAT is a series of picture cards, each with an ambiguous social situation, which the respondent is asked to use as the basis for composing a story. Joe composed TAT stories with both adult and child main characters or heroes. The heroes were sometimes sad, enthusiastic, intelligent, frustrated, mixed up, and ambitious. Many of Joe's TAT stories involved family themes. Fathers were often present in Joe's stories, and their interactions with their sons were sometimes filled with conflict, sometimes

> with cooperation. Often the younger heroes in Joe's stories wanted to be like their fathers. Primary defense mechanisms revealed in the stories were projection and denial. Primary conflicts were about self-worth versus inferiority, dependency versus autonomy, and compliance versus opposition. Often the heroes had difficulty resolving conflicts with others. Joe's stories tended to be lengthy, somewhat descriptive, and emitted at a slow pace. Joe was cooperative, but not excited during the evaluation.
>
> After the TAT, Joe was administered the MMPI–A, which consists of true-false items. The MMPI–A yields scores on 10 clinical traits that provide a basis for personality interpretation. Joe earned the highest score on the Depression scale, where his T-score was 75, and his percentile rank was 99. His second highest score was on Hypochondriasis, with a 70 T-score and a 98th percentile rank. His lowest score was on the Mania scale, where he had a T-score of 47. High scores on the Depression scale are believed to often reflect moodiness, self-deprecation, sad feelings, and hopelessness. High scores on the Hypochondriasis scale may reflect individuals who are self-centered, focus a great deal on bodily concerns, and are unwilling or reluctant to accept psychological sources of interpretation for the physical symptoms.

Now contrast an *interpretive* report written about the same child, using the same test data.

> Joe, whose general demeanor and appearance implied sadness, produced both objective and projective test responses suggesting depression. For example, on the TAT, a projective test, Joe consistently produced themes of sadness. The main characters of stories often felt inadequate, frustrated, and pessimistic about their chances for future success. Although Joe was sometimes capable of fantasizing about success, these fantasies quickly gave way to feelings of hopelessness and despair as he began to think about the future. The main characters in his TAT stories almost always ended up frustrated and dejected. Significantly, Joe produced two TAT stories with extremely self-punitive main characters. This implies that Joe may not only be discouraged, but may actively castigate himself, an additional sign of significant depression. Other TAT responses showed the main characters to have poor self-concepts and to view themselves as inferior to their fathers.

> On the MMPI–A, Joe's responses again highlight his depression, but go on to illustrate his severe shyness, oversensitivity, and tendencies toward preoccupation and worry. Joe probably has severe problems with self-confidence and may set unattainable standards for himself that contribute to his frustration and discouragement. All and all, this is probably a depressed child with shyness and oversensitivity problems, who may have difficulty because he cannot achieve his own high standards and because he compares himself negatively with his own father.

As in the case of Mike, the interpretive summary of Joe distills and synthesizes test findings into a concise summary of his current functioning. In contrast, the descriptive summary recounts test data but leaves the implication and meaning of the data largely unaddressed. Often, the reader feels that the descriptive summary is talking about the tests themselves rather than about the child in question, whereas an interpretive summary uses the test information as a vehicle to better understand the child.

Interpretive summaries tend to be better understood and more usable. They also, if they are logical, conservative, and seem accurate, generally indicate that the diagnostician is capable of understanding the child, not just administering tests. Expanding the nonpsychologist's understanding relative to the referral question is the intent of the evaluation.

## ARE TEST FINDINGS WRITTEN IN STANDARD ENGLISH?

Although written psychological reports often deal with difficult topics, they can still be written in understandable, standard English (Sundberg, Tyler, & Taplin, 1973). It often seems that psychologists forget this and instead use an inordinate amount of jargon. The net result is a report that sounds impressive but says nothing (see Table 10.1). Particularly horrid is the long, jargon-filled report. Not only is the report jammed with impressive but incomprehensible words, but it also goes on for pages and pages. This type of report loses even the most conscientious reader. Most psychological information, unless for special purposes or audiences, can be communicated in everyday language, typically in a one-, two-, or three-page report.

## ARE THERE RECOMMENDATIONS FOR PROGRAMMING?

In most instances, the goals of psychological evaluation are to accurately diagnose a problem and to develop a plan that alleviates the

Table 10.1. Jargon and standard English personality descriptions

| Jargon | Standard English |
|---|---|
| Latency-age children exhibit repression as a primary defense mechanism. | Preadolescents often deal with unpleasant thoughts by putting them out of mind. |
| Auditory reception, auditory association, and verbal expression skills seemed unaffected. | Language was unaffected. |
| His vivid childhood introjects and rigid superego made the act impossible. | His strong sense of family values made the act impossible. |
| Development of kinesthetic and vestibular functioning was somewhat attenuated. | The child's sense of movement and balance developed slowly. |
| Blurred generational boundaries and family enmeshment preceded the bulimic episodes. | Binge eating was caused by family overinvolvement in each other's concerns. |

problem. Referral questions often deal with diagnosis and can be answered with a clear diagnostic statement. Developing a plan, however, usually takes the form of programming recommendations, or explicit plans and suggestions to deal with the problem. When information is needed about treatment planning, a series of recommendations needs to be included in the written report. Again, some examples help clarify this point. The parents of 5-year-old Jimmy wanted to know if he was ready for kindergarten, but they also wanted to know how to prepare him for the experience. Detailed suggestions are necessary to help the parents. Some recommendations would be as follows:

1. Jimmy could be better prepared for kindergarten if his attention span were enhanced. Therefore, family games that require concentration, sharing, and give-and-take are suggested. These should occur at least once weekly. When riding in a car, games that require observation, concentration, and remembering, such as keeping track of what has been seen or looking for specific objects, may be of value. At home, stories read by parents with subsequent question-and-answer sessions may also be helpful.
2. Jimmy needs work on developing basic concepts. Preschool developmental books that introduce shape, color, number, letter, and time concepts would be of value. Discussion of these topics at the dinner table or at other family settings also would be appropriate. Television shows such as *Sesame Street* may also help, particularly if an adult reviews concepts with Jimmy afterward.
3. Jimmy would be better prepared for kindergarten if he were more independent. Teaching him simple adaptive skills such as cleaning his room, brushing his teeth, or caring for himself in the bathroom would be of value.

4. Jimmy needs to refine his social skills. Thus, having him play with older children, involving him in structured recreational activities, and exposing him to a preschool program 1 or 2 days a week prior to kindergarten enrollment may aid with this.
5. Under no circumstances would it be beneficial to leave this boy at home, and therefore out of preschool, for another year.

Programming recommendations are especially important when school problems exist, but the child does not qualify for special services. Simply stating that a student does not qualify for a program is of no help to those working with the student. When a student remains in a general classroom, the teacher needs a plan to effectively help him or her. Programming recommendations in schools are generally instructional or behavioral in nature. The following is an example of instructional recommendations for, Eddie, a distractible child with poor attending skills:

1. When Eddie works at his desk, be sure that the surface is free of unnecessary stickers, cards, number lines, or anything that is likely to draw his attention from work.
2. Rather than giving Eddie full-size worksheets, smaller sheets containing less information may be better. For rows of math problems, a line guide will help him focus on one row at a time. Story paragraphs can also be divided, and devices such as headings, underlining, and italics will help Eddie organize his studying.
3. When giving Eddie directions, it is essential that he give eye contact to the speaker and repeat the directions back to ensure his comprehension.
4. Accurate work and attention to task should be immediately rewarded. Rewards might include stickers, 10 minutes of free time, one-to-one time with a staff member, or anything for which Eddie is particularly willing to work.
5. Use of a daily report card is suggested so that Eddie's parents are kept aware of his work productivity and attention to task. Although initially the report card would be used merely to convey information and help keep him aware that his parents are monitoring his school status, later his parents may need to use incentives dispensed at home to help motivate school performance.

Parents and teacher can be directed toward a more extensive and detailed set of suggestions (Wodrich, 1994) if necessary. As might be expected, the detail, logic, and ultimately the usefulness of recommendations vary from psychologist to psychologist. There is nothing inherent in the assessment process itself or psychological tests that indicates which programming recommendations should be developed. That is, tests do not make program recommendations; psychologists do.

## DOUBT TEST FINDINGS THAT DEVIATE FROM ACCEPTED PRACTICE

Psychological testing, as shown in this book's earlier chapters, should be conducted with sound clinical judgment, appreciation of the limitations of mental measurement, and an understanding of research literature. Unfortunately, some practitioners ignore measurement limitations, are unfamiliar with research literature, or lack training and experience with children. When the informed reader encounters test findings that ignore these important points, he or she should be alert. If convinced the practitioner is violating basic principles, exaggerating his or her capabilities, or using unacceptable instruments, then the reader should respond by either requesting an explanation or, if the matter is severe, by directing referrals elsewhere. (A severe infraction might even warrant an ethics complaint.) It is difficult to describe all possible exaggerations or to detail all violations of standard practice. Nonetheless, some examples might be as follows:

1. Claims that unique or newly developed tests can unerringly pinpoint areas of brain dysfunction or diagnose extremely specific learning disabilities that fully account for dyslexia, stuttering, poor handwriting, or inability to do mathematics
2. Claims that clinicians, through years of experience, are able to predict precisely, and virtually without error, specific future outcomes (e.g., claims that suicide potential can be predicted without error)
3. Claims that unestablished tests (often "quick-and-dirty") can diagnose important traits such as intelligence and personality just as accurately as established tests
4. Claims that a diagnostic technique can determine the specific cause of a present condition (This claim often is made without any recognition of the complicated nature of causation.)

Armed with a basic knowledge of mental measurement and with an appreciation of which tests are generally acceptable for various purposes, the nonpsychologist can recognize gross errors in test findings when he or she sees them. That is, understanding the ideas outlined in this book can help the nonpsychologist become an informed consumer of psychological testing. By becoming an informed consumer, the nonpsychologist not only will know when and how to make a referral but can also judge whether the test findings received are acceptable or unacceptable.

## SUMMARY

Judging test findings is, for most consumers, a matter of being able to understand and use the results. What makes findings useful is when the referral question is answered, information is reported in language that avoids jargon, limitations to the results are clearly expressed, and programming recommendations are included for the referral agent. Consumers should be wary of results that do not reflect basic testing practices or that make unfounded claims.

### Study Questions

1. What sort of practices or claims should raise doubts on the part of the consumer?
2. Of what value are descriptive findings and why?
3. What guidelines should be looked for in judging whether test findings are useful?
4. What are variables that typically limit the validity of test results?

# References

Achenbach, T.M. (1986). *Child Behavior Checklist–Direct Observation Form* (Rev. ed.). Burlington, VT: Author.

Achenbach, T.M. (1991a). *Manual for the Child Behavior Checklist/4–18 and 1991 profile.* Burlington: University of Vermont, Department of Psychiatry.

Achenbach, T.M. (1991b). *Manual for the Teacher's Report Form and 1991 profile.* Burlington: University of Vermont, Department of Psychiatry.

Achenbach, T.M. (1991c). *Manual for the Youth Self-Report Form and 1991 profile.* Burlington: University of Vermont, Department of Psychiatry.

Achenbach, T.M. (1991d). *Teacher's Report Form for Ages 5–18.* Burlington, VT: Author.

Achenbach, T.M., & Edelbrock, C. (1983). *Manual for the Child Behavior Checklist and Revised Child Behavior Profile.* Burlington: University of Vermont.

Achenbach, T.M., McConaughy, S.H., & Howell, C.T. (1987). Child/adolescent behavioral and emotional problems: Implications of cross-informant correlations for situational specificity. *Psychological Bulletin, 101,* 213–232.

Adams, W., & Sheslow, D. (1990). *Wide Range Assessment of Memory and Learning* (WRAML). Wilmington, DE: Jastak Associates.

Aiken, L.R. (1982). *Psychological testing and assessment* (4th ed.). Boston: Allyn & Bacon.

Aiken, L.R. (1994). *Psychological testing and assessment* (8th ed.). Needham Heights, MA: Allyn & Bacon.

Akshoomoff, N.A., & Stiles, J. (1995a). Developmental trends in visuospatial analysis and planning: I. Copying a complex figure. *Neuropsychology, 9,* 364–377.

Akshoomoff, N.A., & Stiles, J. (1995b). Developmental trends in visuospatial analysis and planning: II. Memory for a complex figure. *Neuropsychology, 9,* 378–389.

Allen, M.J., & Yen, W.M. (1979). *Introduction to measurement theory.* Monterey, CA: Brooks/Cole.

Als, H., Lester, B.M., Tronick, E., & Brazelton, T.B. (1982). Manual for the Assessment of Pre-term Infants' Behavior (APIB). In H.E. Fitzgerald, B.M. Lester, & M.W. Yogman (Eds.), *Theory and research in behavior prediatrics* (Vol. 1). New York: Plenum.

American Association on Mental Retardation. (1992). *Mental retardation: Definition, classification, and systems of supports* (Special 9th ed.). Washington, DC: Author.

American Psychiatric Association. (1980). *Diagnostic and statistical manual of mental disorders* (DSM-III) (3rd ed.). Washington, DC: Author.

American Psychiatric Association. (1987). *Diagnostic and statistical manual of mental disorders* (DSM-III–R) (3rd ed.–Rev.). Washington, DC: Author.

American Psychiatric Association. (1994). *Diagnostic and statistical manual of mental disorders* (DSM-IV) (4th ed.). Washington, DC: Author.

American Psychological Association. (1985). *Standards for educational and psychological testing.* Washington, DC: Author.

Applebaum, A.S., & Tuma, J.M. (1977). Social class and test performance: Comparative validity of the Peabody with WISC and WISC–R for two socioeconomic groups. *Psychological Reports, 40,* 139–145.

Archer, R.P. (1987). *Using the MMPI with adolescents.* Hillsdale, NJ: Lawrence Erlbaum Associates.

Archer, R.P. (1992). *MMPI–A: Assessing adolescent psychopathology.* Hillsdale, NJ: Lawrence Erlbaum Associates.

Archer, R.P., Stolberg, A.L., Gordon, R.A., & Goldman, W.R. (1986). Parent and child MMPI responses: Characteristics among families with adolescents in inpatient and outpatient settings. *Journal of Abnormal Child Psychology, 14,* 181–190.

Archibald, Y., Lunn, D., Ruttan, M.A., MacDonald, D.R., Maestro, R.F.D., Barr, H.W.K., Pexman, J.H.W., Fisher, B.J., Gaspar, L.E., & Cairncross, J.G. (1994). Cognitive functioning in long-term survivors of high-grade glioma. *Journal of Neurosurgery, 80,* 247–253.

Arter, J.A., & Jenkins, J.R. (1979). Differential-diagnosis-prescriptive teaching: A critical appraisal. *Review of Educational Research, 49,* 517–555.

Bagnato, S.J. (1985). Review of Brigance Diagnostic Inventory of Early Development. In J.V. Mitchell, Jr. (Ed.), *The ninth mental measurement yearbook* (pp. 219–220). Lincoln: University of Nebraska Press.

Bailey, D.B., Jr., Vandiviere, P., Dellinger, J., & Munn, D. (1987). The Battelle Developmental Inventory: Teacher perceptions and implementation data. *Journal of Psychoeducational Assessment, 3,* 217–226.

Ball, E.W., & Blachman, B.A. (1991). Does phoneme awareness training in kindergarten make a difference in early word recognition and developmental spelling? *Reading Research Quarterly, 26,* 49–66.

Barkley, R.A. (1981). Learning disabilities. In E.J. Mash & L.G. Terdal (Eds.), *Behavioral assessment of childhood disorders* (pp. 441–482). New York: Guilford Press.

Barkley, R.A. (1990). *Attention deficit hyperactivity disorder: A handbook for diagnosis and treatment.* New York: Guilford Press.

Barkley, R.A., & Grodzinsky, G.M. (1994). Are tests of frontal lobe functions useful in the diagnosis of attention deficit disorders? *The Clinical Neuropsychologist, 8,* 121–139.

Barnett, D., & Zucker, K. (1985). Best practices in assessment of children's personality. In A. Thomas & J. Grimes (Eds.), *Best practices in school psychology.* Kent, OH: National Association of School Psychologists.

Baron-Cohen, S., Leslie, A.M., & Frith, U. (1985). Does the autistic child have a "theory of mind"? *Cognition, 21,* 37–46.

Baron-Cohen, S., Leslie, A.M., & Frith, U. (1986). Mechanical, behavioral and intentional understanding of picture stories in autistic children. *British Journal of Developmental Psychology, 4,* 113–125.

Bates, J.E. (1987). Temperament in infancy. In J.D. Osofsky (Ed.), *Handbook of infant development* (2nd ed.). New York: John Wiley & Sons.

Batshaw, M.L., & Perret, Y.M. (1992). *Children with disabilities: A medical primer* (3rd ed.). Baltimore: Paul H. Brookes Publishing Co.

Bayley, N. (1933). Mental growth: The first three years. *Genetic Psychology Monographs, 14,* 1–92.

Bayley, N. (1969). *Manual for the Bayley Scales of Infant Development.* New York: The Psychological Corporation.

Bayley, N. (1993). *Bayley Scales of Infant Development* (2nd ed.). San Antonio, TX: The Psychological Corporation.

Beck, F.W., & Black, F.L. (1986). Comparison of PPVT–R and WISC–R in mild/moderate handicapped sample. *Perceptual and Motor Skills, 62,* 891–894.

Beery, K.E. (1982). *Revised administration, scoring, and teaching manual for the Developmental Test of Visual-Motor Integration.* Cleveland, OH: Modern Curriculum Press.

Begali, V. (1987). *Head injury in children and adolescents: A resource and review for school and allied professionals.* Brandon, VT: Clinical Psychology Publishing Co.

Begali, V. (1992). *Head injury in children and adolescents: A resource and review for school and allied professionals* (2nd ed.). Brandon, VT: Clinical Psychology Publishing Co.

Bellak, L. (1947). *A guide to the interpretation of the Thematic Apperception Test.* New York: The Psychological Corporation.

Bellak, L. (1975). *The TAT, CAT, and SAT in clinical use.* New York: Grune & Stratton.

Bellak, L., & Bellak, S.S. (1949). *The Children's Apperception Test.* New York: C.P.S. Company.

Bender, B.G. (1995). Are asthmatic children educationally handicapped? *School Psychology Quarterly, 10,* 274–291.

Bender, L. (1946). *Bender Gestalt Test: Cards and manual of instructions.* New York: American Orthopsychiatric Association.

Benton, A.L. (1987). Mathematical disability and the Gerstmann syndrome. In G. Deloche & X. Seron (Eds.), *Mathematical disabilities: A cognitive neuropsychological perspective* (pp. 111–120). Hillsdale, NJ: Lawrence Erlbaum Associates.

Benton, A.L., Hamsher, K.de.S., & Sivan, A.B. (1994). *Multilingual aphasia examination: Manual of instructions* (3rd ed.). Iowa City, IA: AJA Associates, Inc.

Berk, R.A. (1984). An evaluation of procedures for computing an ability–achievement discrepancy score. *Journal of Learning Disabilities, 17,* 262–266.

Bernstein, J.H., Helmus, A.A., Kammer, B., Prather, P., & Rey-Casserly, C. (1994). *The Rey-Osterrieth complex figure: Administration, scoring, basic interpretation.* Manuscript, Children's Hospital, Neuropsychology Program, Boston.

Bersoff, D.N. (1981). Testing and the law. *American Psychologist, 36,* 1047–1056.

Bigler, E.D., & Ehrfurth, J.W. (1981). The continued inappropriate singular use of the Bender Visual Motor Gestalt Test. *Professional Psychology, 12,* 562–569.

Bloom, A.S., Allard, A.M., Frank, A., Brill, W.J., & Topinka, C.W. (1988). Differential validity of the K–ABC for lower functioning preschool children versus those with higher ability. *American Journal on Mental Retardation, 93,* 273–277.

Bloom, B. (1964). *Stability and change in human characteristics.* New York: John Wiley & Sons.

Blum, G.S. (1950). *The Blacky Pictures: Manual of instructions.* New York: The Psychological Corporation.

Boder, E. (1971). Developmental dyslexia: A diagnostic screening procedure based on three characteristic patterns of reading and spelling. In B. Bateman (Ed.), *Learning disorders* (Vol. 4). Seattle, WA: Special Child Publications.

Boehm, A.E. (1986a). *Boehm Test of Basic Concepts–Preschool Version.* San Antonio, TX: The Psychological Corporation.

Boehm, A.E. (1986b). *Boehm Test of Basic Concepts–Revised.* San Antonio, TX: The Psychological Corporation.

Bolen, L.M., Aichinger, K.S., Hall, C.W., & Webster, R.E. (1995). A comparison of the performance of cognitively disabled children on the WISC–R and WISC–III. *Journal of Clinical Pschology, 51,* 89–94.

Boll, T. (1993). *Children's Category Test manual.* San Antonio, TX: The Psychological Corporation.

Brazelton, T.B. (1984). *Neonatal Behavioral Assessment Scale* (2nd ed.). Philadelphia: J.B. Lippincott.

Brazelton, T.B., Nugent, J.K., & Lester, B.M. (1987). Neonatal Behavioral Assessment Scale. In J.D. Osofsky (Ed.), *Handbook of infant development* (2nd ed.). New York: John Wiley & Sons.

Brigance, A.H. (1978). *BRIGANCE Diagnostic Inventory of Early Development.* Woburn, MA: Curriculum Associates.

Brigance, A.H. (1991). *Revised BRIGANCE Diagnostic Inventory of Early Development (Birth to seven years).* North Billerica, MA: Curriculum Associates, Inc.

Broman, S.H. (1979). Perinatal anoxia and cognitive development in early childhood. In T.M. Field (Ed.), *Infants born at risk: Behavior and development.* Jamaica, NY: Spectrum.

Brouwers, P., Belman, A.L., & Epstein, L. (1994). Central nervous system involvement: Manifestations, evaluation, and pathogenesis. In P.A. Pizzo & C.M. Wilfert (Eds.). *Pediatric AIDS: The challenge of HIV infection in infants, children, and adolescents.* Baltimore: Williams & Wilkins.

Brouwers, P., & Poplack, D. (1990). Memory and learning sequelae in long-term survivors of acute lymphoblastic leukemia: Association with attention deficits. *American Journal of Hematology/Oncology, 12,* 174–181.

Brown, D.T. (1986). Acutarial and automated assessment procedures and approaches. In H.M. Knoff (Ed.), *The assessment of child and adolescent personality.* New York: Guilford Press.

Buck, J.N. (1948). The H-T-P technique: A qualitative and quantative method. *Journal of Clinical Psychology, 4,* 317–396.

Buss, A.H., & Plomin, R.A. (1984). *Temperament: Early developing personality traits.* Hillsdale, NJ: Lawrence Erlbaum Associates.

Butcher, J.N., Dahlstrom, W.G., Graham, J.R., Tellegen, A., & Kaemmer, B. (1989). *Minnesota Multiphasic Personality Inventory–2 (MMPI–2): Manual for administration and scoring.* Minneapolis: University of Minnesota Press.

Butcher, J.N., Williams, C.L., Graham, J.R., Archer, R.P., Tellegen, A., Ben-Porath, Y.S., & Kaemmer, B. (1992). *MMPI–A (Minnesota Personality Inventory–Adolescent): Manual for administration, scoring, and interpretation.* Minneapolis: University of Minnesota Press.

Candler, A.C., Maddux, C.D., & Johnson, D.L. (1986). Relationship of scores on PPVT–R and WISC–R with special education children and youth. *Perceptual and Motor Skills, 62,* 417–418.

Cantwell, D.P. (1972). Psychiatric illness in the families of hyperactive children. *Archives of General Psychiatry, 27,* 414–417.

Carpenter, C.D. (1995). Review of Revised Brigance Diagnostic Inventory of Early Development. In J.C. Conoley & J.C. Impara (Eds.), *The twelfth mental measurement yearbook* (pp. 852–853). Lincoln: University of Nebraska Press.

Chalfant, J.C. (1989). Learning disabilities: Policy issues and promising approaches. *American Psychologist, 44,* 392–398.

Charman, T., & Baron-Cohen, S. (1994). Another look at imitation in autism. *Development & Psychopathology, 6,* 403–413.

Chelune, G.J., & Baer, R.A. (1986). Developmental norms for the Wisconsin Card Sorting Test. *Journal of Clinical and Experimental Neuropsychology, 8,* 219–228.

Chess, S., & Thomas, A. (1977). *Temperament and development.* New York: Brunner/Mazel.

Clarizio, H.F., & McCoy, G.F. (1983). *Behavior disorders in children* (3rd ed.). New York: Harper & Row.

Colligan, R., & Offord, K. (1987). Today's adolescent and the MMPI: Patterns of MMPI responses from normal teenagers of the 1980s. In R.P. Archer (Ed.), *Using the MMPI with adolescents.* Hillsdale, NJ: Lawrence Erlbaum Associates.

Cone, T.E., & Wilson, L.R. (1981). Quantifying a severe discrepancy: A critical analysis. *Learning Disability Quarterly, 4,* 359–371.

Conners, C.K. (1973). Rating scales for use in drug studies with children [Special issue: Pharmacotherapy with children]. *Psychopharmacology Bulletin, 9,* 24–84.

Conners, C.K. (1994). *Conners' Continuous Performance Test.* North Tonawanda, NY: MHS.

Connolly, A.J. (1988). *KeyMath–Revised: Manual.* Circle Pines, MN: American Guidance Service

Covin, T.M. (1977). Relationship of Peabody and WISC–R IQ of candidates for special education. *Psychological Reports, 40,* 189–190.

Cronbach, L.J. (1984). *Essentials of psychological testing* (4th ed.). New York: Harper & Row.

Cronbach, L.J., & Snow, R.E. (1977). *Aptitude and instructional methods.* New York: Irvington.

Cummings, J.A. (1986). Projective drawings. In H.M. Knoff (Ed.), *The assessment of child and adolescent personality.* New York: Guilford Press.

Cummings, J.A. (1995). Review of Woodcock-Johnson Psycho-Educational Battery–Revised. In J.C. Conoley & J.C. Impara (Eds.), *The twelfth mental measurement yearbook* (pp. 1113–1116). Lincoln: University of Nebraska Press.

Das, J.P. (1993). Neurocognitive approach to remediation: The PREP model. *Canadian Journal of School Psychology, 9,* 157–173.

Das, J.P., Kirby, J.R., & Jarman, R.F. (1975). Simultaneous and successive syntheses: An alternative model for cognitive abilities. *Psychological Bulletin, 82,* 87–103.

Das, J.P., Mishra, R., & Pool, J.E. (1995). An experiment on cognitive remediation of word-reading difficulty. *Journal of Learning Disabilities, 28,* 66–79.

Davila, R.R., & Wodrich, D.L. (1994). ADHD and eligibility for special school services. In D.L. Wodrich, *Attention deficit hyperactivity disorder: What every parent wants to know* (pp. 181–194). Baltimore: Paul H. Brookes Publishing Co.

DeBoer, D.L., Kaufman, A.S., & McCarthy, D. (1974, April). *The use of the McCarthy Scales in identification, assessment, and deficit remediation of preschool and primary age children.* Symposium presented at the meeting of the Council for Exceptional Children, New York.

Delis, D.C., Kramer, J.H., Kaplan, E., & Ober, B.A. (1994). *California Verbal Learning Test–Children's Version, manual.* San Antonio, TX: The Psychological Corporation.

Denckla, M.B. (1991). Academic and extracurricular aspects of nonverbal learning disabilities. *Psychiatric Annals, 21,* 717–724.

Denckla, M.B. (1994). Measurement of executive function. In G.R. Lyon (Ed.), *Frames of reference for the assessment of learning disabilities: New views on measurement issues* (pp. 117–142). Baltimore: Paul H. Brookes Publishing Co.

Diana v. Board of Education of California, C-70 37 RFP, District Court for N.D. Cal. (1970).

Donders, J. (1996). Validity of short forms of the intermediate Halstead Category Test in children with traumatic brain injury. *Archives of Clinical Neuropsychology, 11,* 131–137.

Duffner, P.K., Cohen, M., & Parker, M.S. (1988). Prospective intellectual testing in children with brain tumors. *Annals of Neurology, 23,* 575–579.

Duffner, P.K., Horowitz, M.E., Krischer, J.P., Friedman, H.S., Burger, P.C., Cohen, M.E., Sanford, R.A., Mulhern, R.K., James, H.E., Freeman, C.R., Seidel, F.G., & Kun, L.E. (1993). Postoperative chemotherapy and delayed radiation in children less than three years of age with malignant brain tumors. *New England Journal of Medicine, 328,* 1725–1731.

Dumond, R., & Hagberg, C. (1994). Review of the Kaufman Adolescent and Adult Intelligence Test. *Journal of Psychoeducational Assessment, 12,* 190–196.

Dunn, L.M., & Dunn, L.M. (1981). *Peabody Picture Vocabulary Test–Revised.* Circle Pines, MN: American Guidance Service.

Dunn, L.M., & Markwardt, F.C., Jr. (1970). *Peabody Individual Achievement Test.* Circle Pines, MN: American Guidance Service.

DuPaul, G.J. (1990). *The ADHD Rating Scale: Normative data, reliability, and validity.* Unpublished manuscript, University of Massachusetts Medical Center, Worchester.

Education of the Handicapped Act Amendments of 1986, PL 99-457, 20 U.S.C. § 1400 *et seq.*

Elwood, R.W. (1993). Clinical discriminations and neuropsychological tests: An appeal to Bayes' theorem. *The Clinical Neuropsychologist, 7,* 224–233.

Ernst, M. (1996). Neuroimaging in attention-deficit/hyperactivity disorder. In G.R. Lyon & J.M. Rumsey (Eds.), *Neuroimaging: A window to the foundations of learning and behavior in children* (pp. 95–118). Baltimore: Paul H. Brookes Publishing Co.

Eron, L.A. (1950). A normative study of the TAT. *Psychological Monographs, 64* (315).

Esterly, D.L., & Griffin, H.C. (1987). Preschool programs for children with learning disabilities. *Journal of Learning Disabilities, 20,* 571–573.

Estes, G.D., Harris, J., Moers, F., & Wodrich, D.L. (1976). Predictive validity of the Boehm Test of Basic Concepts for achievement in first grade. *Educational and Psychological Measurement, 36,* 1031–1035.

Exner, J.E. (1959). The influence of chromatic and achromatic color in the Rorschach. *Journal of Projective Techniques, 23,* 418–425.

Exner, J.E. (1974). *The Rorschach: A comprehensive system.* New York: John Wiley & Sons.

Exner, J.E., & Weiner, I.B. (1982). *The Rorschach: A comprehensive system: Vol 3. Assessment of children and adolescents.* New York: John Wiley & Sons.

Fawcett, A.J., & Nicolson, R.I. (1994). Naming speed in children with dyslexia. *Journal of Learning Disabilities, 27,* 641–646.

*Federal Register.* (1991). 56 (160), p. 41266.

Felton, R.H. (1993). Effects of instruction on the decoding skills of children with phonological-processing problems. *Journal of Learning Disabilities, 26,* 583–589.

Felton, R.H., & Wood, F.B. (1989). Cognitive deficits in reading disability and attention deficit disorder. *Journal of Learning Disabilities, 22,* 3–13.

Fletcher, J.M., Ewing-Cobbs, L., Miner, M.E., Levin, H.S., & Eisenberg, H.M. (1990). Behavioral changes after closed head injury in children. *Journal of Consulting and Clinical Psychology, 58,* 93–98.

Fletcher, J.M., Miner, M.E., & Ewing-Cobbs, L. (1987). Age and recovery from head injury in children: Developmental issues. In H.S. Levin, J. Grafman, &

H.M. Eisenberg (Eds.), *Neurobehavioral recovery from head injury.* New York: Oxford University Press.

Flynn, J. (1984). The mean IQ of Americans: Massive gains from 1932 to 1978. *Psychological Bulletin, 95,* 29–51.

Fox, H.B., Freedman, S.A., & Klepper, B.R. (1989). *Financing programs for young children with handicaps.* In J.J. Gallagher, P.L. Trohanis, & R.M. Clifford (Eds.), *Policy implementation and PL 99-457: Planning for young children with special needs* (pp. 169–182). Baltimore: Paul H. Brookes Publishing Co.

Francis, P.L., Self, P.A., & Horowitz, F.D. (1987). The behavioral assessment of the neonate: An overview. In J.D. Osofsky (Ed.), *Handbook of infant development* (2nd ed.). New York: John Wiley & Sons.

Freeman, B.J. (1985). Review of Child Behavior Checklist. In J.V. Mitchell, Jr. (Ed.), *The ninth mental measurements yearbook* (pp. 300–301). Lincoln: University of Nebraska Press.

Frith, U., Happe, F., & Siddons, F. (1994). Autism and theory of mind in everyday life. *Social Development, 3,* 108–124.

Gallagher, A., & Frederickson, N. (1995). The Phonological Assessment Battery (PhAB): An initial assessment of its theoretical and practical utility. *Educational & Child Psychology, 12,* 53–67.

Gentilini, M., Paolo, N., & Schoenhuber, R. (1989). Assessment of attention in mild head injury. In H.S. Levin, H.M. Eisenberg, & A.L. Benton (Eds.), *Mild head injury* (pp. 163–175). New York: Oxford University Press.

Georgia Conferences of NAACP v. State of Georgia (11th Cir. 1985).

Gioia, G.A. (1991, February). *Re-analysis of the factor structure of the Wide Range Assessment of Memory and Learning: Implications for clinical interpretation.* Paper presented at the meeting of the International Neuropsychological Society, San Antonio, TX.

Glascoe, F.P. (1995). *A validation study and the psychometric properties of the Brigance screens.* North Billerica, MA: Curriculum Associates.

Goh, D.S., & Youngquist, J.A. (1979). A comparison of the McCarthy Scales of Children's Abilities and the WISC–R. *Journal of Learning Disabilities, 12,* 344–348.

Golden, C. (1981). The Luria-Nebraska Children's Battery: Theory and formulation. In G.W. Hynd & J.E. Obrzut (Eds.), *Neuropsychological assessment and the school-age child: Issues and procedures.* New York: Grune & Stratton.

Golden, C. (1987). *Luria-Nebraska Neuropsychological Battery: Children's Revision.* Los Angeles: Western Psychological Corporation.

Golden, C., Hammeke, T.A., & Purisch, A. (1980). *Manual for the Luria-Nebraska Neuropsychological Battery.* Los Angeles: Western Psychological Corporation.

Goldman, J., L'Engle Stein, C., & Guerry, S. (1983). *Psychological methods of child assessment.* New York: Brunner/Mazel.

Goldstein, G., & Minshew, N. (1995, November). *Neurobiology of high functioning autism.* Paper presented at the National Academy of Neuropsychology annual conference, San Francisco.

Goldstein, G., Minshew, N., & Siegel, D.J. (1994). Age differences in academic achievement in high-functioning autistic individuals. *Journal of Clinical & Experimental Neuropsychology, 16,* 671–680.

Good, R.H., & Salvia, J. (1988). Curriculum bias in published, norm-referenced reading tests: Demonstratable effects. *School Psychology Review, 17,* 51–60.

Goodenough, F.L. (1926). *Measurement of intelligence by drawings.* New York: World Book, Inc.

Goodenough, F.L., & Harris, D.B. (1963). *Goodenough-Harris Drawing Test.* San Antonio, TX: The Psychological Corporation.

Gordon, M. (1983). *The Gordon Diagnostic System.* DeWitt, NY: Gordon Systems, Inc.

Graham, P.J. (1983). Specific medical syndromes. In M. Rutter (Ed.), *Developmental neuropsychiatry.* New York: Guilford Press.

Greenberg, L.M. (1992). *Test of Variables of Attention.* Los Alamitos, CA: Universal Attention Disorders, Inc.

Gresham, F.M., MacMillan, D.L., & Siperstein, G.N. (1995). Critical analysis of the 1992 AAMR definition: Implications for school psychology. *School Psychology Quarterly, 10,* 1–19.

Gronwall, D. (1989). Cumulative and persisting effects of concussion on attention and cognition. In H.S. Levin, H.M. Eisenberg, & A.L. Benton (Eds.), *Mild head injury.* New York: Oxford University Press.

Groshong, C.C. (1987). Assessing oral language comprehension: Are picture-vocabulary tests enough? *Learning Disabilities Focus, 2,* 108–115.

Grossman, H.J. (Ed.). (1983). *Classification in mental retardation.* Washington, DC: American Association on Mental Deficiency.

Guadalupe v. Tempe Elementary School District, 71-435, (D. Ariz. 1972).

Gulbrandsen, G.B. (1984). Neuropsychological sequalae of light head injury in older children 6 months after trauma. *Journal of Clinical Neuropsychology, 6,* 257–268.

Hagen, J.W., Barclay, C.R., Anderson, B.J., Freeman, D.J., Segal, S.S., Brown, G., & Goldstein, G.W. (1990). Intellectual functioning and strategy use in children with insulin-dependent diabetes mellitus. *Child Development, 61,* 1714–1727.

Halstead, W.C. (1947). *Brain and intelligence.* Chicago: University of Chicago Press.

Hammill, D.D. (1985). *Detroit Tests of Learning Aptitude–2.* Austin, TX: PRO-ED.

Hammill, D.D. (1991). *Detroit Tests of Learning Aptitude–Third Edition.* Austin, TX: PRO-ED.

Hannafin, M.J. (1986). Special education assessment. In D.L. Wodrich & J.E. Joy (Eds.), *Multidisciplinary assessment of children with learning disabilities and mental retardation* (pp. 77–108). Baltimore: Paul H. Brookes Publishing Co.

Happe, F. (1994). Wechsler IQ profile and theory of mind in autism: A research note. *Journal of Child Psychology & Allied Disciplines, 35,* 1461–1471.

Harnadek, M.C.S., & Rourke, B.P. (1994). Principal identifying features of the syndrome of nonverbal learning disabilities in children. *Journal of Learning Disabilities, 27,* 144–154.

Harrington, R.G. (1985). Battelle Developmental Inventory. In D.J. Keyser & R.C. Sweetland (Eds.), *Test critiques compendium.* Kansas City, MO: Test Corporation of America.

Harris, D.B. (1963). *Children's drawings as measures of intellectual maturity: A revision and extension of the Goodenough Draw-a-Man Test.* New York: Harcourt, Brace, & World.

Harrison, P.L. (1987). Research with adaptive behavior scales. *Journal of Special Education, 21,* 37–68.

Hart, D.H. (1972). *The Hart Sentence Completion Test for Children.* Unpublished manuscript, Educational Support Systems, Inc., Salt Lake City, UT.

Hart, D.H. (1986). The Sentence Completion Technique. In H.M. Knoff (Ed.), *The assessment of child and adolescent personality* (pp. 245–272). New York: Guilford Press.

Hartje, W. (1987). The effect of spatial disorders on arithmetic skills. In G. Deloche & X. Seron (Eds.), *Mathematical disabilities: A cognitive neuropsychological perspective* (pp. 121–136). Hillsdale, NJ: Lawrence Erlbaum Associates.

Hartlage, L.C., & Telzrow, C.F. (1983). The neuropsychological basis of educational intervention. *Journal of Learning Disabilities, 16,* 521–528.

Hartlage, L.C., & Telzrow, C.F. (1986). *Neuropsychological assessment and intervention with children and adolescents.* Sarasota, FL: Professional Resource Exchange.

Hathaway, S.R., & McKinley, J.C. (1967). *The Minnesota Multiphasic Personality Inventory (MMPI).* New York: The Psychological Corporation.

Haut, J.S., Haut, M.W., & Franzen, M.D. (1992, February) *Assessment of an attentional component of Wide Range Assessment of Memory and Learning (WRAML) subtests.* Paper presented at Meeting of the International Neuropsychological Society, San Diego, CA.

Heaton, R.K. (1981). *A manual for the Wisconsin Card Sorting Test.* Odessa, FL: Psychological Assessment Resources, Inc.

Heaton, R.K., Chelune, G.J., Talley, J.L., Kay, G.G., & Curtiss, G. (1993). *Wisconsin Card Sorting Test: Manual revised and expanded.* Odessa, FL: Psychological Assessment Resources, Inc.

Helmstadter, G.C. (1964). *Principles of psychological measurement.* New York: Appleton-Century-Crofts.

Hertzig, M.E., & Snow, M.E. (1988). The assessment of temperament. In C.J. Kestenbaum & D.T. Williams (Eds.), *Handbook of clinical assessment of children and adolescents* (Vol. 1). New York: New York University Press.

Hetherington, E.M., & Parke, R.D. (1986). *Child psychology: A contemporary viewpoint.* New York: McGraw-Hill.

Hodapp, R.M. (1995). Definitions in mental retardation: Effects on research, practice, and perceptions. *School Psychology Quarterly, 10,* 24–28.

Holcomb, W.R., Hardesty, R.A., Adams, N.A., & Ponder, H.M. (1987). WISC–R types of learning disabilities: A profile analysis with cross-validation. *Journal of Learning Disabilities, 20,* 369–373.

Holmes, C.S., O'Brien, B., & Greer, T. (1995). Cognitive functioning and academic achievement in children with insulin-dependent diabetes mellitus (IDDM). *School Psychology Quarterly, 10,* 329–345.

Horn, J.L., & Cattell, R.B. (1966). Refinement and test of the theory of fluid and crystallized intelligence. *Journal of Educational Psychology, 57,* 253–270.

Horner, T.M. (1980). Test–retest and home-clinic characteristics of the Bayley Scales of Infant Development in nine- and fifteen-month-old infants. *Child Development, 51*, 751–758.

Horner, T.M. (1988). Single versus repeated assessments of infant abilities using the Bayley Scales of Infant Development. *Infant Mental Health Journal, 9*, 209–217.

Horowitz, F.D., & Linn, P.L. (1984). Use of the NBAS in research. In T. Brazelton (Ed.), *Neonatal Behavioral Assessment Scale* (2nd ed.) Philadelphia: J.B. Lippincott.

Hughes, C., Russell, J., & Robbins, T.W. (1994). Evidence of executive dysfunction in autism. *Neuropsychologia, 32*, 477–492.

Hunt, J.M. (1961). *Intelligence and experience.* New York: Ronald Press Company.

Hynd, G., & Snow, J. (1985). Best practices in neuropsychological assessment. In A. Thomas & J. Grimes (Eds.), *Best practices in school psychology.* Kent, OH: National Association of School Psychologists.

Hynd, G.W., & Willis, W.G. (1988). *Pediatric neuropsychology.* Orlando, FL: Grune & Stratton.

Individuals with Disabilities Education Act (IDEA) of 1990, PL 101-476, 20 U.S.C. § 1400 *et. seq.*

Individuals with Disabilities Education Act Amendments of 1991, PL 102-119, 20 U.S.C. § 1400 *et. seq.*

Jannoun, L., & Bloom, H.J.G. (1990). Long-term psychological effects in children treated for intracranial tumors. *International Journal of Radiation Oncology, Biology, Physics, 18*, 747–753.

Jastak, S., & Wilkinson, G.S. (1984). *Administration manual: Wide Range Achievement Test–Revised.* Wilmington, DE: Jastak Associates, Inc.

Jensen, A.R. (1980). *Bias in mental testing.* New York: Macmillan.

Jorm, A.F. (1979). The cognitive and neurological basis of developmental dyslexia: A theoretical framework and review. *Cognition, 7*, 19–33.

Kagan, J. (1989). Temperamental contributes to social behavior. *American Psychologist, 44*(4), 668–675.

Kalat, J.W. (1995). *Biological psychology.* Pacific Grove, CA: Brooks/Cole Publishing.

Kamphaus, R.W., & Pleiss, K.L. (1991). Draw-a-Person techniques: Tests in search of a construct. *Journal of School Psychology, 29*, 395–401.

Kamphaus, R.W., Schmitt, C.S., & Mings, D.R. (1986). Three studies of the validity of the Kaufman Test of Educational Achievement. *Journal of Psychoeducational Assessment, 4*, 299–305.

Kamphaus, R.W., Slotkin, J., & DeVincentis, C. (1990). Clinical assessment of achievement. In C.R. Reynolds & R.W. Kamphaus (Eds.), *Handbook of psychological and educational assessment of children: Intelligence and achievement* (pp. 552–568). New York Guilford Press.

Kaplan, R.M., & Saccuzzo, D.P. (1982). *Psychological testing: Principles, applications, and issues.* Monterey, CA: Brooks/Cole

Kaufman, A.S. (1976). Do normal children have "flat" ability profiles? *Psychology in the Schools, 13,* 284–285.

Kaufman, A.S. (1979). *Intelligent testing with the WISC–R.* New York: John Wiley & Sons.

Kaufman, A.S. (1983). *Kaufman Assessment Battery for Children (K–ABC).* Circle Pines, MN: American Guidance Service.

Kaufman, A.S. (1985). Review of the Woodcock-Johnson Psycho-Educational Battery. In J.V. Mitchell, Jr. (Ed.), *The ninth mental measurement yearbook* (pp. 1762–1765). Lincoln: University of Nebraska Press.

Kaufman, A.S. (1994). *Intelligent testing with the WISC–III.* New York: John Wiley & Sons.

Kaufman, A.S., & Kaufman, N.L. (1977). *Clinical evaluation of young children with the McCarthy Scales.* New York: Grune & Stratton.

Kaufman, A.S., & Kaufman, N.L. (1985). *Manual for the Kaufman Test of Educational Achievement.* Circle Pines, MN: American Guidance Service.

Kaufman, A.S., & Kaufman, N.L. (1990). *Kaufman Brief Intelligence Test: Manual.* Circle Pines, MN: American Guidance Service.

Kaufman, A.S., & Kaufman, N.L. (1993). *Manual for the Kaufman Adolescent and Adult Intelligence Test.* Circle Pines, MN: American Guidance Service.

Kazdin, A. (1989). Developmental psychopathology: Current issues and directions. *American Psychologist, 44*(2), 180–188.

Kelley, M.L. (1985). Review of Child Behavior Checklist. In J.V. Mitchell, Jr. (Ed.), *Ninth mental measurement yearbook.* Lincoln: University of Nebraska Press.

King, J.D. (1995). Review of Gray Oral Reading Tests, Third Edition. In J.C. Conoley & J.C. Impara (Eds.), *The twelfth mental measurement yearbook* (pp. 422–423). Lincoln: University of Nebraska Press.

Kirk, S.A. (1962). *Educating exceptional children.* Boston: Houghton Mifflin.

Kirk, S.A., McCarthy, J.J., & Kirk, W.D. (1968). *Illinois Test of Psycholinguistic Abilities* (Rev. ed.). Urbana: University of Illinois Press.

Klonoff, H., Low, M.D., & Clark, C. (1977). Head injuries in children: A prospective five year follow-up. *Journal of Neurology, Neurosurgery, and Psychiatry, 40,* 1211–1219.

Knoff, H.M. (1986). Identifying and classifying children and adolescents referred for personality assessment: Theories, systems, and issues. In H.M. Knoff (Ed.), *The assessment of child and adolescent personality* (pp. 3–33). New York: Guilford Press.

Koegel, P., & Edgerton, R.B. (1984). Black "six-hour retarded children" as young adults. In R.B. Edgerton (Ed.), *Lives in process: Mildly retarded adults in a large city.* Washington, DC: American Association on Mental Deficiency.

Koppitz, E.M. (1963). *The Bender Gestalt Test for young children.* New York: Grune & Stratton.

Koppitz, E.M. (1968). *Psychological evaluation of children's human figure drawings.* New York: Grune & Stratton.

Koppitz, E.M. (1973). Bender-Gestalt test performance and school achievement: A nine year study. *Psychology in the Schools, 10,* 280–284.

Koppitz, E.M. (1975). *The Bender Gestalt test for young children: Research and application, 1963–1973*. New York: Grune & Stratton.

Krohn, E.J., Lamp, R.E., & Phelps, C.G. (1988). Validity of the K–ABC for a black preschool population. *Psychology in the Schools, 25*, 15–21.

Kuhnert, B.R., Harrison, M.J., Linn, P.L., & Kuhnert, P.M. (1984). Effects of material epidural anesthesia on neonatal behavior. *Anesthesia & Analgesia, 63*, 301–308.

Kundert, D.K. (1995). Review of Gray Oral Reading Test, Third Edition. In J.C. Conoley & J.C. Impara (Eds.), *The twelfth mental measurement yearbook* (pp. 423–425). Lincoln: University of Nebraska Press.

Lachar, D. (1993). Symptom checklists and personality inventories. In T.R. Kratochwill & R.J. Morris (Eds.), *Handbook of psychotherapy for children and adolescents* (pp. 38–57). New York: Allyn & Bacon.

Lachar, D., & Gdowski, C.L. (1979). *Actuarial assessment of child and adolescent personality: An interpretative guide for the Personality Inventory for Children profile*. Los Angeles: Western Psychological Services.

Lachar, D., & Gruber, C.P. (1994). *A manual for the Personality Inventory for Youth (PIY): A self-report companion to the Personality Inventory for Children (PIC)*. Los Angeles: Western Psychological Services.

Lachar, D., Kline, R.B., & Boersma, D.C. (1986). The Personality Inventory for Children: Approaches to actuarial interpretation in clinic and school settings. In H.M. Knoff (Ed.), *The assessment of child and adolescent personality* (pp. 273–308). New York: Guilford Press.

Lambert, N., Nihara, K., & Leland, H. (1993). *AAMR Adaptive Behavior Scale–School* (2nd ed.). Austin, TX: PRO-ED.

Landesman, S., & Ramey, C. (1989). Developmental psychology and mental retardation: Integrating scientific principles with treatment practices. *American Psychologist, 44*, 409–415.

Lanyon, R.I., & Goodstein, L.D. (1982). *Personality assessment*. New York: John Wiley & Sons.

Larry, P. v. Riles, 343 F. Supp. 1306 (N.D. Cal 1972).

Larry, P. et al. v. Wilson Riles et al. United States District Court, Northern District of California, Case No. (71-2270 RFP) (1974, 1979).

Leckliter, I.N., Forster, A.A., Klonoff, H., & Knights, R.M. (1992). A review of reference group data from normal children for the Halstead-Reitan Neuropsychological Test Battery for Older Children. *Clinical Neuropsychologist, 6*, 201–229.

Lee, S.W., & Stefany, E.F. (1995). Review of Woodcock-Johnson Psycho-Educational Battery–Revised. In J.C. Conoley & J.C. Impara (Eds.), *The twelfth mental measurement yearbook* (pp. 1116–1117). Lincoln: University of Nebraska Press.

Lester, B.M. (1984). Data analysis and prediction. In T.B. Brazelton (Ed.), *Neonatal Behavioral Assessment Scale*. Philadelphia: J.B. Lippincott.

Levenson, R.L., Jr., & Zino, T.C., II. (1979). Assessment of cognitive deficiency with the McCarthy Scales and Stanford-Binet: A correlation analysis. *Perceptual & Motor Skills, 48*, 291–295.

Levin, H.S., & Eisenberg, H.M. (1979a). Neuropsychological impairment after head injury in children and adolescents. *Journal of Pediatric Psychology, 4,* 389–402.

Levin, H.S., & Eisenberg, H.M. (1979b). Neuropsychological outcome of closed head injury in children and adolescents. *Child's Brain, 5,* 281–292.

Levin, H.S., Ewing-Cobbs, L., & Fletcher, J.M. (1989). Neurobehavioral outcome of mild head injury in children. In H.S. Levin, H.M. Eisenberg, & A.L. Benton (Eds.), *Mild head injury* (pp. 189–213). New York: Oxford University Press.

Levin, H.S., High, W.M., Ewing-Cobbs, L., Fletcher, J.M., Eisenberg, H.M., Miner, M.E., & Goldstein, F.C. (1988). Memory functioning during the first year after closed head injury in children and adolescents. *Neurosurgery, 22,* 1043–1052.

Levin, H.S., Mendelsohn, D., Lilly, M.A., Fletcher, J.M., Culhane, K.A., Chapman, S.B., Harward, H., Kusnerik, L., Bruce, D., & Eisenberg, H.M. (1994). Tower of London performance in relation to magnetic resonance imaging following closed head injury in children. *Neuropsychology, 8,* 171–179.

Lezak, M.D. (1995). *Neuropsychological assessment* (3rd ed.). New York: Oxford University Press.

Luria, A.R. (1973). *The working brain.* New York: Basic Books.

Lyman, H.B. (1971). *Test scores and what they mean* (2nd ed.). Englewood Cliffs, NJ: Prentice Hall.

Mabry, L. (1995). Review of Wide Range Achievement Test–Third Edition. In J.C. Conoley & J.C. Impara (Eds.), *The twelfth mental measurement yearbook* (pp. 1108–1111). Lincoln: University of Nebraska Press.

Machover, K. (1949). *Personality projection in the drawing of the human figure.* Springfield, IL: Charles C Thomas.

Marks, P., Seeman, W., & Haller, D. (1974). *The actuarial use of the MMPI with adolescents and adults.* Baltimore: Williams & Wilkins.

Markwardt, F.C., Jr. (1989). *Peabody Individual Achievement Test—Revised.* Circle Pines, MN: American Guidance Service.

Matson, J.L. (1995). Comments on Gresham, MacMillan, and Siperstein's paper "Critical analysis of the 1992 AAMR definition: Implications for school psychology." *School Psychology Quarterly, 10,* 20–23.

Matson, J.L., & Mulick, J.A. (1991). *Handbook of mental retardation.* New York: Pergamon Press.

Matthews, C.G., & Klove, H. (1964). *Instruction manual for the Adult Neuropsychology Test Battery.* Madison: University of Wisconsin Medical School.

Mattison, R.E., Lynch, J.C., Kales, H., & Gamble, A.D. (1993). Checklist identification of elementary schoolboys for clinical referral or evaluation for special education. *Behavioral Disorders, 18,* 218–227.

Mayfield, K.L., Forman, S., & Nagle, R.J. (1984). Reliability of the AAMD Adaptive Behavior Scale-Public School Version. *Journal of School Psychology, 22,* 53–61.

McArthur, D.S., & Roberts, G.E. (1982). *Roberts Apperception Test for Children: Manual.* Los Angeles: Western Psychological Services.

McCall, R.B. (1979). The development of intellectual functioning in infancy and the prediction of later IQ. In J.D. Osofsky (Ed.), *Handbook of infant development.* New York: John Wiley & Sons.

McCall, R.B. (1987). Developmental function, individual differences, and the plasticity of intelligence. In J.J. Gallagher & C.T. Ramey (Eds.), *The malleability of children* (pp. 25–35). Baltimore: Paul H. Brookes Publishing Co.

McCall, R.B., Appelbaum, M., & Hogarthy, P.S. (1973). Developmental changes in mental performance. *Monographs of the Society for Research in Child Development, 38*(150).

McCarthy, D.A. (1972). *Manual for the McCarthy Scales of Children's Abilities.* San Antonio, TX: The Psychological Corporation.

McCoy, K.D., Arceneaux, J.M., & Dean, R.S. (1996). Congenital mental retardation. In E.S. Batchelor, Jr., & R.S. Dean (Eds.), *Pediatric neuropsychology: Interfacing assessment and treatment for rehabilitation* (pp. 325–345). Boston: Allyn & Bacon.

McCrowell, K.L., & Nagle, R.J. (1994). Comparability of the WPPSI–R and the S–B:IV among preschool children. *Journal of Psychoeducational Assessment, 12,* 126–134.

McDevitt, S.C. (1976). *A longitudinal assessment of longitudinal stability in temperamental characteristics from infancy to early childhood.* Doctoral dissertation, Temple University, Philadelphia.

McLinden, S.E. (1989). An evaluation of the Battelle Developmental Inventory for determining special education eligibility. *Journal of Psychoeducational Assessment, 1,* 66–73.

Meehl, P.E., & Rosen, A. (1955). Antecedent probability and the efficiency of psychometric signs, patterns, or cutting scores. *Psychological Bulletin, 52,* 194–216.

Mehrens, W.A. (1995). Review of Detroit Tests of Learning Aptitude, Third Edition. In J.C. Conoley & J.C. Impara (Eds.), *The twelfth mental measurement yearbook* (pp. 275–277). Lincoln: University of Nebraska Press.

Mendelsohn, D., Levin, H.S., Bruce, D., Lilly, M., Harward, H., Culhane, K.A., & Eisenberg, H.M. (1992). Late MRI after head injury in children: Relationship to clinical features and outcome. *Child's Nervous System, 8,* 445–452.

Mercer, J.R. (1979). *System of Multicultural Pluralistic Assessment technical manual.* San Antonio, TX: The Psychological Corporation.

Messick, S. (1983). Assessment of children. In P. Mussen (Ed.), *Manual of child psychology* (4th ed.). New York: John Wiley & Sons.

Miele, F. (1979). Cultural bias in the WISC. *Intelligence, 3,* 149–164.

Miller-Jones, D. (1989). Culture and testing. *American Psychologist, 44*(2), 360–366.

Minshew, N.J., & Goldstein, G. (1993). Is autism an amnesic disorder? Evidence from the California Verbal Learning Test. *Neuropsychology, 7,* 209–216.

Minshew, N.J., Goldstein, G., & Siegel, D.J. (1995). Speech language in high-functioning autistic individuals. *Neuropsychology, 9,* 255–261.

Minshew, N.J., Goldstein, G., Taylor, H.G., & Siegel, D.J. (1994). Academic achievement in high functioning autistic individuals. *Journal of Clinical and Experimental Neuropsychology, 16,* 261–270.

Minshew, N.J., Siegel, D.J., Goldstein, G., & Weldy, S. (1994). Verbal problem solving in high functioning autistic individuals. *Archives of Clinical Neuropsychology, 9,* 31–40.

Morgan, C.D., & Murray, H.A. (1935). A method for investigating phantasies: The Thematic Apperception Test. *Archives of Neurology and Psychiatry, 34,* 289–306.

Morgan, R.L., Dawson, B., & Kerby, D. (1992). The performance of preschoolers with speech/language disorders on the McCarthy Scales of Children's Abilities. *Psychology in the Schools, 29,* 11–17.

Morrow, R.S., & Mark, J. (1955). The correlation of intelligence and neurological findings on 22 patients autopsied for brain damage. *Journal of Consulting and Clinical Psychology, 19,* 283–289.

Moscovitch, M. (1992). Memory and working-with-memory: A component process model based on modules and central systems. *Journal of Cognitive Neuroscience, 4,* 257–267.

Mulhern, R.K., Wasserman, A.L., Fairclough, D., & Ochs, J. (1988). Memory function in disease free survivors of childhood onset acute lymphoblastic leukemia given CNS prophylaxis with or without 1800 cGy cranial irradiation. *Journal of Clinical Oncology, 6,* 315–320.

Murray, H.A. (1943). *Manual of Thematic Apperception Test.* Cambridge, MA: Harvard University Press.

Murray, H.A. (1971). *Thematic Apperception Test: Manual.* Cambridge, MA: Harvard University Press.

Naglieri, J.A. (1988). *Draw-a-Person: Quantitative scoring system.* San Antonio, TX: The Psychological Corporation.

Naglieri, J.A., & Jensen, A.R. (1987). Comparison of black-white differences on the WISC–R and K–ABC: Spearman's hypothesis. *Intelligence, 11,* 21–43.

Naglieri, J.A., McNeish, T.J., & Bardos, A.N. (1991). *Draw-a-Person: Screening procedure for emotional disturbance.* Austin, TX: PRO-ED.

National Society for Autistic Children. (1978). National Society for Autistic Children definition of the syndrome of autism. *Journal of Autism and Developmental Disorders, 8,* 162–167.

Neisser, U., Boodoo, G., Bouchard, T.J., Boykin, A.W., Brody, N., Ceci, S.J., Halpern, D.F., Loehlin, J.C., Perloff, R., Sternberg, R.J., & Urbina, S. (1996). Intelligence: Knowns and unknowns. *American Psychologist, 51,* 77–101.

Newborg, J., Stock, J.R., Wnek, L., Guidubaldi, J., & Svinicki, J. (1984). *Battelle Developmental Inventory.* Allen, TX: Developmental Learning Materials (DLM) Teaching Resources.

Newby, R.F., Recht, D.R., & Caldwell, J. (1993). Validation of a clinical method for the diagnosis of two subtypes of dyslexia. *Journal of Psychoeducational Assessment, 11,* 72–83.

Nichols, P.L., & Chen, T.C. (1981). *Minimal brain dysfunction: A prospective study.* Hillsdale, NJ: Lawrence Erlbaum Associates.

Norman-Murch, T., & Bashir, A. (1986). Speech-language assessment. In D.L. Wodrich & J.E. Joy (Eds.), *Multidisciplinary assessment of children with learning disabilities and mental retardation* (pp. 133–160). Baltimore: Paul H. Brookes Publishing Co.

Nunnally, J.C. (1978). *Psychometric theory* (2nd ed.). New York: McGraw-Hill.

Obrzut, A., Nelson, R.B., & Obrzut, J.E. (1987). Construct validity of the Kaufman Assessment Battery for Children with mildly mentally retarded students. *American Journal of Mental Deficiency, 92,* 74–77.

Obrzut, J.E., & Boliek, C.A. (1986). Thematic approaches to personality assessment with children and adolescents. In H.M. Knoff (Ed.), *The assessment of child and adolescent personality* (pp. 173–198). New York: Guilford Press.

Olson, R., Forsberg, H., Wise, B., & Rack, J. (1994). Measurement of word recognition, orthographic, and phonological skills. In G.R. Lyon (Ed.), *Frames of reference for the assessment of learning disabilities: New views on measurement issues* (pp. 243–278). Baltimore: Paul H. Brookes Publishing Co.

Olson, R.K., Wise, B., Conners, F., & Rack, J. (1990). Organization, heritability and remediation of component word recognition and language skills in disabled readers. In T.H. Carr & B.A. Levy (Eds.), *Reading and its development: Component skills approaches* (pp. 261–322). New York: Academic Press.

Olson, R.K., Wise, B., Conners, F., Rack, J., & Fulker, D. (1989). Specific deficits in component reading and language skills: Genetic and environmental influences. *Journal of Learning Disabilities, 22,* 339–348.

Osofsky, J.D. (Ed.). (1987). *Handbook of infant development.* New York: John Wiley & Sons.

Osterrieth, P.A. (1993). Le test de copie d'une figure complexe. [The test to copy a complex figure.] (J. Corwin & F.W. Bylsma, Trans.). *The Clinical Neuropsychologist, 7,* 9–15. (Original work published in *Archives de Psychologie, 30,* 206–356 in 1944).

Ozonoff, S., & McEvoy, R.E. (1994). A longitudinal study of executive function and theory of mind development in autism. *Development & Psychopathology, 6,* 415–431.

Ozonoff, S., Strayer, D.L., McMahon, W.M., & Filloux, F. (1994). Executive function abilities in autism and Tourette syndrome: An information processing approach. *Journal of Child Psychology & Psychiatry & Allied Disciplines, 35,* 1015–1032.

Parents in Action on Special Education v. Hannon, Joseph P. et al. Memorandum Decision No. 74c 3586, (1980). V. S. District Court for the N. D. Ill.

Penfield, D.A. (1995). Review of Revised Brigance Diagnostic Inventory of Early Development. In J.C. Conoley & J.C. Impara (Eds.), *The twelfth mental measurement yearbook* (pp. 853–854). Lincoln: University of Nebraska Press.

Pennington, B.F. (1991). *Diagnosing learning disorders: A neuropsychological approach.* New York: Guilford Press.

Plomin, R. (1989). Environment and genes: Determinants of behavior. *American Psychologist, 44,* 105–111.

Post, K.R., & Mitchell, H.R. (1993). The WISC–III: A reality check. *Journal of School Psychology, 31,* 541–545.

Prasse, D.P. (1983). Legal issues underlying preschool assessment. In K.D. Paget & B.A. Bracken (Eds.), *The psychoeducational assessment of preschool children.* New York: Grune & Stratton.

Prewett, P.N., & Matavich, M.A. (1994). A comparison of referred students' performance on the WISC–III and the Stanford-Binet Intelligence Scale: Fourth Edition. *Journal of Psychoeducational Assessment, 12,* 42–48.

The Psychological Corporation. (1992). *Wechsler Individual Achievement Test: Manual.* San Antonio, TX: Author.

Quay, L.C. (1974). Language dialect, age and intelligence-test performance in disadvantaged black children. *Child Development, 45,* 463–468.

Rack, J.P., & Olson, R.K. (1993). Phonological deficits, IQ, and individual differences in reading disability: Genetic and environmental influences. [Special Issue: Phonological processes and learning disability.] *Developmental Review, 13,* 269–278.

Rack, J.P., Snowling, M.J., & Olson, R.K. (1992). The nonword reading deficit in developmental dyslexia: A review. *Reading Research Quarterly, 27,* 28–53.

Radenich, M.C. (1986). Kaufman Test of Educational Achievement. *Academic Therapy, 21,* 619–622.

Raggio, D.J., Massingale, T.W., & Bass, J.D. (1994). Comparison of Vineland Adaptive Behavior Scales–Survey Form age equivalent and standard score with the Bayley Mental Development Index. *Perceptual & Motor Skills, 79,* 203–206.

Ramey, C.T., Yeates, K.O., & Short, D.J. (1984). The plasticity of intellectual development: Insights from preventive intervention. *Child Development, 55,* 1913–1925.

Reitan, R.M. (1974). Psychological effects of cerebral lesions in children of early school age. In R.M. Reitan & L.A. Davison (Eds.), *Clinical neuropsychology: Current status and applications.* New York: V.H. Winston & Sons.

Reitan, R.M. (1987). *Neuropsychological evaluation of children.* Tucson, AZ: Neuropsychology Press.

Reitan, R.M., & Davison, L.A. (Eds.). (1974). *Clinical neuropsychology: Current status and applications.* Washington, DC: Hemisphere.

Reitan, R.M., & Wolfson, D. (1985). *The Halstead-Reitan Neuropsychological Test Battery.* Tucson, AZ: Neuropsychology Press.

Reitan, R.M., & Wolfson, D. (1987). *The Aphasia Screening Test: Scoring manual for children aged 9 through 14 years.* Tucson, AZ: Reitan Neuropsychology Laboratory.

Reitan, R.M., & Wolfson, D. (1992). *Neuropsychological evaluation of older children.* Tucson, AZ: Neuropsychology Press.

Reschly, D.J. (1982). Assessing mild mental retardation: The influence of adaptive behavior, sociocultural status, and prospects for nonbiased assessment. In C.R. Reynolds & T.B. Gutkin (Eds.), *The handbook of school psychology.* New York: John Wiley & Sons.

Reschly, D.J. (1988). Minority mild mental retardation: Legal issues, research findings, and reform trends. In M. Wang, M. Reynolds, & H. Walberg (Eds.), *Handbook of special education: Research and practice* (Vol. 2, pp. 23–41). Oxford, NY: Pergamon Press.

Reynell, J. (1977). *Reynell Developmental Language Scales.* Windsor: NFER-Nelson.

Reynolds, C.R. (1981). The neuropsychological basis of intelligence. In G.W. Hynd & J.E. Obrzut (Eds.), *Neuropsychological assessment and the school-age child: Issues and procedures* (pp. 87–124). New York: Grune & Stratton.

Reynolds, C.R. (1982). The problem of bias in psychological assessment. In C.R. Reynolds & T.B. Gutkin (Eds.), *The handbook of school psychology.* New York: John Wiley & Sons.

Reynolds, C.R. (1985). Review of Personality Inventory for Children. In J.V. Mitchell, Jr. (Ed.), *Ninth mental measurements yearbook* (pp. 1154–1156). Lincoln: University of Nebraska Press.

Reynolds, C.R., & Kamphaus, R.W. (1992). *Behavior Assessment System for Children: Manual.* Circle Pines, MN: American Guidance Service.

Riccio, C.A. (1992). The WIAT: A critical review. *Child Assessment News, 2(5),* 10–12.

Roberts, C., McCoy, M., Reidy, D., & Crucitti, F. (1993). A comparison of methods of assessing adaptive behaviour in pre-school children with developmental disabilities. *Australia & New Zealand Journal of Developmental Disabilities, 18,* 261–272.

Rosenberger, P. (1986). Neurological assessment. In D.L. Wodrich & J.E. Joy (Eds.), *Multidisciplinary assessment of children with learning disabilities and mental retardation* (pp. 247–280). Baltimore: Paul H. Brookes Publishing Co.

Rotter, J.B. (1950). *Incomplete Sentence Blank: Adult Form.* New York: The Psychological Corporation.

Rotter, J.B., & Rafferty, J.E. (1950). *Manual: The Rotter Incomplete Sentence Blank.* New York: The Psychological Corporation.

Rourke, B.P. (1989). *Nonverbal learning disabilities: The syndrome and the model.* New York: Guilford Press.

Rourke, B.P., & Findlayson, M.A.J. (1978). Neuropsychological significance of variations in patterns of academic performance: Verbal and visual-spatial abilities. *Journal of Abnormal Child Psychology, 6,* 121–133.

Royer, J.M., & Feldman, R.S. (1984). *Educational psychology: Applications and theory.* New York: Alfred A. Knopf.

Russo, A.A., & Bigler, E.D. (1996). Review of The California Verbal Learning Test–Children's Version (CVLT–C) and Children's Category Test (CCT). *Archives of Clinical Neuropsychology, 11,* 171–183.

Rutter, M. (1977). Individual differences. In M. Rutter & L. Hersor (Eds.), *Child psychiatry: Modern approaches.* Oxford: Blackwell Scientific Publishers.

Ryan, T.V., LaMarche, J.A., Barth, J.T., & Boll, T.J. (1996). Neuropsychological consequences and treatment of pediatric head trauma. In E.S. Batchelor, Jr. & R.S. Dean (Eds.), *Pediatric neuropsychology* (pp. 117–137). Newton, MA: Allyn & Bacon.

Saklofske, D.H. (1992). Initial impressions of the WIAT. *Child Assessment News,* 2, 1–8.

Salvia, J., & Ysseldyke, J.E. (1985). *Assessment in special and remedial education* (3rd ed.). Boston: Houghton Mifflin.

Sandler, A.D., Watson, T.E., Footo, M., Levine, M.D., Coleman, W.L., & Hooper, S.R. (1992). Neurodevelopmental study of writing disorders in middle childhood. *Journal of Developmental & Behavioral Pediatrics, 13,* 17–23.

Sattler, J.M. (1988). *Assessment of children.* San Diego, CA: Jerome M. Sattler, Publisher.

Sattler, J.M., & Gwynne, J. (1982). White examiners generally do not impede the intelligence test performance of black children: To debunk a myth. *Journal of Consulting and Clinical Psychology, 50,* 196–208.

Satz, P., Taylor, H.G., Friel, J., & Fletcher, J.M. (1978). Some developmental and predictive precursors of reading disabilities: A six year follow-up. In A.L. Benton & D. Pearl (Eds.), *Dyslexia: An appraisal of current knowledge* (pp. 315–347). New York: Oxford University Press.

Scarr, S. (1978). From evolution to Larry P., or what shall we do about IQ tests? *Intelligence, 2,* 325–342.

Schmidt, K.L. (1994). Review of Detroit Tests of Learning Aptitude–Third Edition. *Journal of Psychoeducational Assessment, 12,* 87–91.

Schock, H.H., & Buck, K. (1995). Review of Bayley Scales of Infant Development–Second Edition. *Child Assessment News, 5*(2), 1, 12.

Schopler, E., Reichler, R.J., & Renner, B.R. (1988). *The Childhood Autism Rating Scale (CARS).* Los Angeles: Western Psychological Services.

Scott, L.H. (1981). Measuring intelligence with the Goodenough-Harris Drawing Test. *Psychological Bulletin, 89,* 483–505.

Seidenberg, M., Giordani, B., Berent, S., & Boll, T.J. (1983). IQ level and performance on the Halstead-Reitan Neuropsychological Tests Battery for Older Children. *Journal of Consulting and Clinical Psychology, 51,* 406–413.

Selz, M. (1981). Halstead-Reitan neuropsychological test batteries for children. In G.W. Hynd & J.E. Obrzut (Eds.), *Neuropsychological assessment and the school-age child: Issues and procedures.* New York: Grune & Stratton.

Semel, E., Wiig, E., & Secord, W. (1987). *Clinical Evaluation of Language Fundamentals–Revised.* San Antonio, TX: The Psychological Corporation.

Semrud-Clikeman, M., Hynd, G.W., Lorys, A.R., & Lahey, B.B. (1993). Differential diagnosis of children with ADHD and ADHD with co-occurring conduct disorder. *School Psychology International, 14,* 361–370.

Seposki, C., Hoffman, J., & Brazelton, T.B. (1986). *The relationship between NBAS profiles, 1-year Bayley and 5-year McCarthy scores.* Paper presented at the International Congress of Infant Studies, Los Angeles.

Shields, J.R. (1991). Semantic-pragmatic disorder: A right hemisphere syndrome? *British Journal of Disorders of Communication, 26,* 383–392.

Shinn, M.R. (Ed.). (1989). *Curriculum-based measurement: Assessing special children.* New York: Guilford Publications.

Silvaroli, N.J. (1986). *Classroom Reading Inventory* (5th ed.). Dubuque, IA: Wm C. Brown.

Silverstein, A.B. (1986). Nonstandard standard scores on the Vineland Adaptive Behavior Scales: A cautionary note. *American Journal of Mental Deficiency, 91,* 1–4.

Sines, J.O. (1985). Review of Roberts Apperception Test for Children. In J.V. Mitchell, Jr. (Ed.), *Ninth mental measurements yearbook* (pp. 1290–1291). Lincoln: University of Nebraska Press.

Slate, J.R. (1994). WISC–III correlations with the WIAT. *Psychology in the Schools, 31,* 278–285.

Smith, B.P., & Gfeller, J.D. (1995, October). *The WISC–III factor structure in a clinical population: Will the real factors please stand up?* Paper presented at the National Association of Neuropsychology, San Francisco.

Snyder, P., Bailey, D.B., & Auer, C. (1994). Preschool eligibility determination for children with known or suspected learning disabilities under IDEA. *Journal of Early Intervention, 18,* 380–390.

Sparrow, S.S., Balla, D.A., & Cicchetti, D.V. (1984). *Vineland Adaptive Behavior Scales.* Circle Pines, MN: American Guidance Service.

Sperling, M.A. (1990). Diabetes mellitus. In S.A. Kaplan (Ed.), *Clinical pediatric endocrinology* (pp. 127–164). Philadelphia: W.B. Saunders.

Squire, L.R. (1987). *Memory and brain.* New York: Oxford University Press.

Stavrou, E., & French, J.L. (1992). The K–ABC and cognitive processing styles in autistic children. *Journal of School Psychology, 30,* 259–267.

Sternberg, R.A. (1984). Kaufman Assessment Battery for Children: An information-processing analysis and critique. *Journal of Special Education, 18,* 269–281.

Stinnett, T.A., Harvey, J.M., & Oehler-Stinnett, J. (1994). Current test usage by practicing school psychologists: A national survey. *Journal of Psychoeducational Assessment, 12,* 331–350.

Stodola, Q., & Stordahl, K. (1967). *Basic educational tests and measurements.* Chicago: Science Research Associates, Inc.

Sturmey, P., Matson, J.L., & Sevin, J.A. (1992). Analysis of the internal consistency of three autism rating scales. *Journal of Autism & Developmental Disorders, 22,* 321–328.

Sundberg, N.D., Tyler, L., & Taplin, J.R. (1973). *Clinical psychology: Expanding horizons* (2nd ed.). Englewood Cliffs, NJ: Prentice Hall.

Taylor, S., Jr. (1982, May 21). Psychological testing of Hinckley said to show long mental illness. *The New York Times,* 7:1.

Taylor, W.R., & Newacheck, P.W. (1992). Impact of childhood asthma on health. *Pediatrics, 90,* 657–662.

Teasdale, G., & Jennett, B. (1974). Assessment of coma and impaired consciousness: A practical scale. *Lancet, 2,* 81–84. The Glasgow Coma Scale.

Terestman, N. (1980). Mood quality and intensity in nursery school children as predictors of behavior disorder. *American Journal of Orthopsychiatry, 50,* 125–138.

Terman, L.M., & Merrill, M.A. (1973). *Stanford-Binet Intelligence Scale: Manual for the third revision Form L–M.* Boston: Houghton Mifflin.

Thomas, A., & Chess, S. (1986). The New York longitudinal study: From infancy to early adult life. In K. Plomin & J. Dunn (Eds.), *The study of temperament: Changes, continuities, and challenges.* Hillsdale, NJ: Lawrence Erlbaum Associates.

Thorndike, R.L., Hagen, E.P., & Sattler, J.M. (1986). *Guide for administering and scoring the Stanford-Binet Intelligence Scale: Fourth Edition.* Chicago: Riverside.

Trohanis, P.L. (1989). An introduction to PL 99-457 and the national policy agenda for serving young children with special needs and their families. In J.J. Gallagher, P.L. Trohanis, & R.M. Clifford (Eds.), *Policy implementation & PL 99-457: Planning for young children with special needs* (pp. 1–17). Baltimore: Paul H. Brookes Publishing Co.

Tuma, J.M. (1985). Review of Personality Inventory for Children. In J.V. Mitchell, Jr. (Ed.), *Ninth mental measurements yearbook* (pp. 1157–1159). Lincoln: University of Nebraska Press.

Vellutino, F.R. (1987). Dyslexia. *Scientific American, 256,* 24–42.

Vellutino, F.R., Scanlon, D.M., & Tanzman, M.S. (1994). Components of reading ability: Issues and problems in operationalizing word identification, phonological coding, and orthographic coding. In G.R. Lyon (Ed.), *Frames of reference for the assessment of learning disabilities: New views on measurement issues* (pp. 279–332). Baltimore: Paul H. Brookes Publishing Co.

Vogel, S.A., & Konrad, D. (1988). Characteristic written expressive language deficits of the learning disabled: Some general and specific intervention strategies. *Journal of Reading, Writing, and Learning Disabilities, 4,* 89–99.

Waber, D.P., & Holmes, J.M. (1985). Assessing children's copy productions of the Rey-Osterrieth complex figure. *Journal of Clinical and Experimental Neuropsychology, 7,* 264–280.

Waber, D.P., & Holmes, J.M. (1986). Assessing children's memory productions of the Rey-Osterrieth complex figure. *Journal of Clinical and Experimental Neuropsychology, 8,* 563–580.

Ward, A.W. (1995). Review of Wide Range Achievement Test–Third Edition. In J.C. Conoley & J.C. Impara (Eds.), *Twelfth mental measurement yearbook* (pp. 1110–1111). Lincoln: University of Nebraska Press.

Watson, R.I. (1968). *The great psychologists: From Aristotle to Freud.* Philadelphia: J.B. Lippincott.

Waugh, R.P. (1975). ITPA: Ballast or bonanza for the school psychologists. *Journal of School Psychology, 13,* 201–208.

Wechsler, D. (1958). *The measurement and appraisal of adult intelligence* (4th ed.). Baltimore: Williams & Wilkins.

Wechsler, D. (1967). *Manual for Wechsler Preschool and Primary Scale of Intelligence.* San Antonio, TX: The Psychological Corporation.

Wechsler, D. (1971). *Wechsler Intelligence Scale for Children–Revised.* San Antonio, TX: The Psychological Corporation.

Wechsler, D. (1974). *Manual for the Wechsler Intelligence Scale for Children–Revised.* San Antonio, TX: The Psychological Corporation.

Wechsler, D. (1989). *Wechsler Preschool and Primary Scale of Intelligence–Revised: Manual.* San Antonio, TX: The Psychological Corporation.

Wechsler, D. (1991). *Wechsler Intelligence Scale for Children: Third Edition: Manual.* San Antonio, TX: The Psychological Corporation.

Weinberg, R.A. (1989). Intelligence and IQ: Landmark issues and great debates. *American Psychologist, 44,* 98–104.

Weiner, I.B. (1986). Assessing children and adolescents with the Rorschach. In H.M. Knoff (Ed.), *The assessment of child and adolescent personality* (pp. 141–171). New York: Guilford Press.

Werner, E.N., & Bayley, N. (1966). The reliability of Bayley's revised scale of mental and motor development during the first year of life. *Child Development, 37,* 39–50.

Whatley, J. (1987). Review of the Battelle Developmental Inventory. In D.J. Keyser & R.C. Sweetland (Eds.), *Test critiques compendium.* Kansas City, MO: Test Corporation of America.

Wiederholt, J.L., & Bryant, B.R. (1986). *Gray Oral Reading Test–Revised.* Austin, TX: PRO-ED.

Wiederholt, J.L., & Bryant, B.R. (1992). *Gray Oral Reading Tests* (3rd ed.). Austin, TX: PRO-ED.

Wilen, D.K., & Sweeting, C.M. (1986). Assessment of limited English proficient Hispanic students. *School Psychology Review, 15*(1), 59–75.

Wilkinson, G.S. (1991). *Wide Range Achievement Test–Third Edition: Manual.* Wilmington, DE: Jastak Associates.

Williams, K.S., & Williams, J.M. (1996). Childhood medical conditions impacting on central nervous system function. In R.S. Dean & E.S. Batchelor, Jr. (Eds.), *Pediatric neuropsychology: Interfacing assessment and treatment for rehabilitation* (pp. 249–268). Boston: Allyn & Bacon.

Williams, R.L. (1972). *The BITCH-100: A culture-specific test.* Paper presented at meeting of the American Psychological Association, Honolulu, HI.

Wilson, J., & Cline, T. (1995). The Naming Speed Test. *Educational & Child Psychology, 12,* 39–45.

Wirt, R.D., Lachar, D., Klinedinst, J.K., & Seat, P.D. (1977). *Multidimensional description of personality: A manual for the Personality Inventory for Children.* Los Angeles: Western Psychological Services.

Witt, J.C. (1988). Review of the Wide Range Achievement Test–Revised. *Journal of Psychoeducational Assessment, 4,* 87–90.

Wodrich, D.L. (1986). The terminology and purposes of assessment. In D.L. Wodrich & J.E. Joy (Eds.), *Multidisciplinary assessment of children with learning disabilities and mental retardation* (pp. 1–30). Baltimore: Paul H. Brookes Publishing Co.

Wodrich, D.L. (1988, August). *Learning disabilities determination: Considerations for measuring achievement.* Paper presented at the annual convention of the American Psychological Association, Atlanta, GA.

Wodrich, D.L. (1994). *Attention deficit hyperactivity disorder: What every parent wants to know.* Baltimore: Paul H. Brookes Publishing Co.

Wodrich, D.L. (in preparation). *ADHD Parent Questionnaire—Manual.*

Wodrich, D.L., & Barry, C.T. (1988, August). *Peabody Individual Achievement Test and Wide Range Achievement Test–Revised as measures of underachievement.* Paper presented at the annual convention of the American Psychological Association, Atlanta, GA.

Wodrich, D.L., & Barry, C.T. (1989, March). *Empirical comparisons of achievement tests: Selecting a suitable battery.* Paper presented at the annual convention of the National Association of School Psychologists, Boston.

Wodrich, D.L., & Barry, C.T. (1991). A survey of school psychologists' practices for identifying mentally retarded students. *Psychology in the Schools, 28,* 165–171.

Wolkind, S., & DeSalis, W. (1982). Infant temperament, maternal mental state and child behavioral problems. *Ciba Foundation Symposium, 84,* 221–239.

Wolters, P.L., Brouwers, P., Moss, H.A., & Pizzo, P.A. (1995). Differential receptive and expressive language functioning of children with symptomatic HIV disease and relation to CT scan brain abnormalities. *Pediatrics, 95,* 112–119.

Woodcock, R.W., & Johnson, M.B. (1989). *Woodcock-Johnson Psycho-Educational Test Battery—Revised.* Allen, TX: DLM.

Worobey, J., & Brazelton, T.B. (1990). Newborn assessment and support of parenting: The Nenonatal Behavioral Assessment Scale. In E.D. Gibbs & D.M. Teti (Eds.), *Interdisciplinary assessment of infants: A guide for early intervention professions* (pp. 33–44). Baltimore: Paul H. Brookes Publishing Co.

Ysseldyke, J., Algozzine, B., Regan, R., & McGue, M. (1981). The influence of test scores and naturally occurring pupil characteristics on psychoeducational decision making with children. *Journal of School Psychology, 19,* 167–177.

# Glossary

This glossary is designed to aid the reader by including unfamiliar terms that may be encountered separately from the main location of their description in the text. It is not a comprehensive list of all the terms used in the book.

**AAMR** Acronym for American Association on Mental Retardation, a group that has developed a definition and diagnostic criteria for mental retardation.

**ADHD** Acronym for attention-deficit/hyperactivity disorder.

**cognitive** Having to do with thinking.

**concurrent validity** The degree to which test scores agree with extra-test criteria or other current test scores; usually reported as a validity coefficient with potential scores ranging from 0 to 1.0.

**construct validity** The extent to which empirical information, such as correlations between test scores and important extra-test criteria, agree with expectations, especially expectations from theory or the "constructs" of theory.

**content validity** The extent to which a test's content (i.e., the items that compose it) measures what the test claims to measure.

**criterion-referenced assessment** Testing that compares students with an objective standard (e.g., percentage of problems correct) rather than with other students.

**derived scores** Test raw scores (usually the number of correct items) that are converted into scores permitting comparison with a norm group.

**DSM** Refers to the *Diagnostic and Statistical Manual of Mental Disorders*; the fourth edition, published in 1994, is known as DSM-IV.

**dyslexia** A reading learning disability.

**executive function** A hypothetical set of superordinate skills that involve planning, judgment, response alteration and inhibition, and, in some cases, speed of responding and attention.

**factor score** Usually refers to a special or supplemental research-based test score that shows how test items intercorrelate (e.g., a speed factor score derived from IQ test items that also happen to require working quickly).

**IDEA** Acronym for Individuals with Disabilities Education Act, the federal law that defines special education services and provides funding.

**IEP** Acronym for individualized education program, a description of the annual, individualized goals for a student in special education and how the goals will be attained.

**LD** Acronym for learning disability, which is one of the categories outlined as meeting eligibility for special education services.

**mean** The arithmetic average.

**motor** Having to do with muscle and body movement.

**neuropsychology** Branch of psychology that studies brain–behavior relationships.

**nonverbal learning disability (NLD)** A concept that includes deficits, perhaps related to right hemisphere dysfunction, that encompass visual/spatial, tactile, sensory, and interpersonal and novel learning.

**norm group** The group of individuals on whom scores are collected for a particular test during its standardization phase; scores that provide the basis for comparison when the test is used in actual practice.

**norm-referenced assessment** A comparison of subjects' performance on a test with that of a norm group's on the same test.

**percentile ranks** Scores simply indicating the percentage of the norm group that would be exceeded by an individual's test score (e.g., a percentile rank of 63 indicates that this person's score exceeds that of 63% of the norm group).

**phonological** Having to do with the aspect of language involving sound.

**predictive validity** The degree to which test scores predict events or other future test scores; usually reported as a validity coefficient with potential scores ranging from 0 to 1.0.

**projective technique** A personality assessment technique that, typically, relies on ambiguous stimulus material and the respondent's presumed tendency to project personal feelings, attitudes, and perceptions into responses.

**psychometrics** Having to do with measurement of psychological characteristics usually through objective, numerical means.

**reliability** The concept of consistency of test scores across time, among test items within a particular test, or between equivalent forms of the same test; usually reported as a statistic (equivalent to a correlation coefficient with values potentially ranging from 0 to 1.0).

**SED** Abbreviation for seriously emotionally disturbed, one of the categories outlined as eligible for special education services.

**semantic** Having to do with the aspect of language involving meaning.

**standard deviation** A statistic that measures the amount of dispersion, or spread of scores, among a group of scores; concept is important in mental testing because test authors use algebraic manipulation to create means and standard deviations of specific sizes when reporting their scores. By using standard deviation as a yardstick, it is possible to determine how far a score falls above or below average (e.g., IQ scores typically have a mean of 100 and standard deviation of 15; T-scores have a mean of 50 and standard deviation of 10—thus scores of 115 and 60 are equivalent).

**standard error of measurement** A statistic that indicates how much difference is likely to occur if a test is repeated. As reliability decreases, the standard error of measurement increases.

**standard score** A precise type of derived score that permits determination of how many standard score units (standard deviations) a particular score is placed above or below the mean of the norm group.

**standardization sample** Same as norm group.

APPENDIX

# Summary of Additional Frequently Used Tests

**Auditory Discrimination Test**
Joseph M. Wepman; Language Research, Chicago
*Type* Special ability (auditory discrimination)
*Ages* 5–8 years
*Uses* Auditory discrimination screening, supplemental learning disability diagnosis
*Psychometric properties* No description of norm group, reliability adequate, little validity data
*Note* To be used and interpreted with great caution

**Balthazar Scales of Adaptive Behavior**
E.E. Balthazar; Consulting Psychologists Press, Palo Alto, CA
*Type* Adaptive behavior scale
*Ages* 5 to adult (institutionalized individuals with severe and profound mental retardation)
*Uses* To assess functional status of children with mental retardation and to determine the effectiveness of interventions
*Psychometric properties* Evidence of adequate inter-rater reliability, but no other empirical evidence of reliability of validity; limited standardization sample
*Note* Although lacking a sophisticated psychometric basis, appears to have content suitable for proposed uses

**Basic Achievement Skills Individual Screener**
The Psychological Corporation; The Psychological Corporation, San Antonio, TX

*Type* Academic achievement
*Ages* First to twelfth grade
*Uses* Screening of academic status
*Psychometric properties* Generally adequate reliability and validity for children younger than high school
*Note* Too few difficult items available to assess the skills of bright high school children

**Behavior Evaluation Scale**
S.B. McCarney, J.E. Leigh, J.A. Cornbleet, and M.T. Jackson; PRO-ED, Austin, TX

*Type* Social-emotional
*Ages* Kindergarten to twelfth grade
*Uses* Screening and documentation of behavioral functioning; provides supplemental data
*Psychometric properties* Small and inadequate normative base, poor reliability, limited validity
*Note* Efficient but limited; not for diagnostic or placement decisions

**Bracken Basic Concept Scale**
Bruce A. Bracken; The Psychological Corporation, San Antonio, TX

*Type* Cognitive ability and school readiness
*Ages* 2 years, 6 months to 8 years
*Uses* Screening for cognitive delays and as measure of school readiness
*Psychometric properties* Well standardized; adequate reliability for Diagnostic Test, but not for Screening Test or individual subtests
*Note* Overall score on the Diagnostic Test is most reliable score

**The Bzoch-League Receptive-Expressive Emergent Language Scale: For the Measurement of Language Skills (REEL)**
Kenneth R. Bzoch and Richard League; Anhinga Press, Tallahassee, FL

*Type* Special ability (language)
*Ages* Birth to 3 years
*Uses* Language component in infant or preschool battery
*Psychometric properties* Small norm group, some reliability evidence, validity uncertain
*Note* Relies on parent report; therefore, interpret cautiously

**The Cattell Infant Intelligence Scale**

Psyche Cattell; The Psychological Corporation, San Antonio, TX

*Type* Intelligence (infant development)

*Ages* 3 months to 3 years

*Uses* Diagnosis of infant delays

*Psychometric properties* Adequate reliability, little predictive validity, dated and unrepresentative normative data

*Note* Less favorable psychometric properties than the Bayley Scales of Infant Development–III

**Children's Apperception Test**

L. Bellak and S.S. Bellak; C.P.S., Co., New York

*Type* Personality (projective)

*Ages* 3–10 years

*Uses* Personality diagnosis

*Psychometric properties* Scoring is generally impressionistic, thus reliability and validity data are unknown

*Note* The cards have stronger stimulus pull than the Thematic Apperception Test

**Columbia Mental Maturity Scale**

Bessie B. Burgemeister, Lucille H. Blum, and Irving Lorge; The Psychological Corporation, San Antonio, TX

*Type* Intelligence (nonverbal)

*Ages* 3 years, 6 months to 10 years

*Uses* Intellectual screening, supplemental intellectual diagnosis for nonverbal or bilingual children

*Psychometric properties* Adequate reliability and some evidence of validity; recent normative sample is good

*Note* Random responding often produces scores above the range for mental retardation

**Conners Parent Rating Scale**

C. Keith Conners; Author, Department of Psychiatry, Children's Hospital National Medical Center, Washington, DC

*Type* Social-emotional assessment

*Ages* 3–17 years

*Uses* Supplementation of other data when conducting thorough evaluation or for screening

*Psychometric properties* Generally adequate evidence of reliability and some evidence of validity

*Note* Some changes between original and revised edition may make for confusion

**Conners Teacher Rating Scale**
C. Keith Conners; Author, Department of Psychiatry, Children's Hospital National Medical Center, Washington, DC

*Type* Social-emotional assessment
*Ages* 4–12 years
*Uses* Assessment of school social and emotional status to supplement other assessment data
*Psychometric properties* Generally adequate evidence of reliability and some evidence of validity
*Note* Several different factor structures and norms available, which may cause confusion

**Developmental Test of Visual-Motor Integration**
K.E. Beery; Modern Curriculum Press, Cleveland, OH

*Type* Special ability (visual perception)
*Ages* 4–13 years
*Uses* Visual-perception screening, supplemental learning disabilities diagnosis
*Psychometric properties* Adequate reliability and validity; norms, ages 2.9–13 years and up
*Note* Nonthreatening measure for use with pre-kindergarten children and early grade school

**Devereaux Behavior Rating Scales—School Form**
Jack A. Naglieri, Paul A. LeBuffe, and Steven I. Pfeiffer; The Psychological Corporation, San Antonio, TX

*Type* Social-emotional rating scale
*Ages* One form 5–12 years, another 13–18 years
*Uses* Assessment of children and adolescents suspected of emotional problems, to help determine eligibility for serious emotional disturbance services
*Psychometric properties* Recent thorough standardizations, carefully developed content validity, factor analysis also used to derive major score dimensions
*Note* Briefer than Devereaux Scale of Psychopathology and is more apt to be used for screening purposes

**Devereaux Scale of Psychopathology**
Jack A. Naglieri, Paul A. LeBuffe, and Steven I. Pfeiffer; The Psychological Corporation, San Antonio, TX

*Type* Social-emotional rating scale
*Ages* One form 5–12 years, another 13–18 years

*Uses* Assessment of children and adolescents suspected of emotional problems, retesting after treatment to determine if improvement has occurred

*Psychometric properties* Recent thorough standardization, carefully developed content validity, factor analysis also used to derive major score dimensions

**Gilmore Oral Reading Test**

John Gilmore and Eunice Gilmore; The Psychological Corporation, San Antonio, TX

*Type* Academic achievement (reading)

*Ages* First to eighth grade

*Uses* Reading diagnosis

*Psychometric properties* Norms and reliability good; good validity for reading accuracy, but less so for comprehension

*Note* Good content, but comprehension scores may be artificially elevated

**The Goldman-Fristoe-Woodcock Test of Auditory Discrimination**

R. Goldman, M. Fristoe, and R.W. Woodcock; American Guidance Service, Circle Pines, MN

*Type* Special ability (auditory discrimination)

*Ages* 4 years to adult

*Uses* Auditory discrimination screening, supplemental learning disability diagnosis

*Psychometric properties* Lacks national norm group; marginal evidence of reliability and validity

*Note* Not without problems, but probably as good or better than the competition

**Hand Test**

Edwin W. Wagner; Western Psychological Services, Los Angeles

*Type* Personality (projective)

*Ages* 6 years to adult

*Uses* Personality diagnosis

*Psychometric properties* Some evidence of inter-rater reliability, but needs more work on validity and standardization

*Note* Some similarities with the Rorschach

**Hiskey-Nebraska Test of Learning Aptitude**
Marshall S. Hiskey; Union College Press, Lincoln, NE
*Type* Intelligence (nonverbal)
*Ages* 3–16 years
*Uses* Intellectual diagnosis of children who are deaf or who have hearing impairments; supplemental diagnosis of bilingual children
*Psychometric properties* Some questions about the norm group; reliability appears adequate; some validity data
*Note* Separate norms for children who are deaf or who can hear help make this a better device than WISC–III Performance IQ for children who are deaf

**Holtzman Inkblot Technique**
Wayne H. Holtzman; The Psychological Corporation, San Antonio, TX
*Type* Personality (projective)
*Ages* 5 years to adult
*Uses* Personality diagnosis
*Psychometric properties* Questionable norm group, adequate reliability, and some validity evidence
*Note* An attempt to bring scientific rigor to a Rorschach-like instrument

**Kohn Social Competence Scale**
M. Kohn; The Psychological Corporation, San Antonio, TX
*Type* Social-emotional
*Ages* 3–6 years
*Uses* Assessing social competence of preschoolers, uses teacher rating
*Psychometric properties* Inadequate reliability, validity appears satisfactory; limited normative data
*Note* Best used as supplemental tool; not for diagnostic purposes

**Leiter International Performance Scale and the Arthur Adaptation**
Russell Leiter and Grace Arthur; C.H. Stoelting Company, Chicago
*Type* Intelligence (nonverbal)
*Ages* 2–18 years
*Uses* Intellectual diagnosis with children who are deaf or bilingual
*Psychometric properties* Inadequately described norm group; some reliability and validity data
*Note* Can be given entirely by pantomime; children who are deaf often score higher on WISC–III Performance IQ

**Marianne Frostig Developmental Test of Visual Perception**
Marianne Frostig; Consulting Psychologists Press, Palo Alto, CA
*Type* Special ability (visual perception)
*Ages* 3–9 years
*Uses* Visual perception screening, supplemental learning disability diagnosis
*Psychometric properties* Limited norm group, some reliability data, little ability to predict important criteria (e.g., reading)
*Note* Derived score reporting method often leads to confusion; little evidence that discrete subareas of visual perception are being measured

**Matrix Analogies Test**
Jack A. Naglieri; The Psychological Corporation, San Antonio, TX
*Type* Special ability (nonverbal reasoning)
*Ages* 5–17 years
*Uses* Screening and as nonverbal supplemental measure
*Psychometric properties* Generally adequate for screening purposes
*Note* Unusually thorough and clear manual for screening test

**Miller Assessment for Preschoolers**
L.J. Miller; The Psychological Corporation, San Antonio, TX
*Type* Special ability (pre-academics)
*Ages* 2.9–5.8 years
*Uses* Screening for possible learning problems in young children
*Psychometric properties* Predictive validity unknown; reliability adequate
*Note* Needs more research data; best for identifying moderate pre-academic problems

**New Sucher-Allred Reading Placement Inventory**
F. Sucher and R.A. Allred; The Economy Company, Oklahoma City, OK
*Type* Reading achievement
*Ages* Primer to ninth grade
*Uses* Provide general overview of children's reading ability
*Psychometric properties* Technical data not reported
*Note* Lack of psychometric properties significant drawback; provides gross level information

**Pictorial Test of Intelligence**
J.L. French; Houghton Mifflin Co., Boston
*Type* Intelligence
*Ages* 3–8 years
*Uses* Intellectual screening, supplemental diagnosis with children who have language impairments or who are bilingual
*Psychometric properties* Adequate for screening, but inferior to the WISC–III and the Stanford-Binet scales
*Note* Apparently seldom used, but appropriate for young children who cannot or will not respond verbally

**Piers-Harris Children's Self-Concept Scale (The Way I Feel About Myself)**
E.V. Piers and D.B. Harris; Western Psychological Services, Los Angeles
*Type* Social-emotional self-report inventory
*Ages* Fourth to twelfth grade
*Uses* Assess self-perceptions; screening aid in social-emotional assessment
*Psychometric properties* Limited standardization sample, adequate evidence of reliability, limited validity
*Note* Authors encourage development of local norms due to limited sample

**Progressive Matrices**
J.C. Raven; Lewis, London
*Type* Intelligence (nonverbal)
*Ages* 5 years to adult
*Uses* Intellectual screening
*Psychometric properties* Recent U.S. norms adequate for screening purposes; reliability and validity generally adequate
*Note* Recent updating of norms makes tests more valuable

**The Quick Test**
R.B. Ammons and C.H. Ammons; Psychological Test Specialists, Missoula, MT
*Type* Special ability (receptive vocabulary)
*Ages* 2 years to adult
*Uses* Language screening, supplemental diagnosis for children with expressive language problems
*Psychometric properties* Dated, unrepresentative norm group; unclear evidence of validity
*Note* Like the PPVT, scores should not be interpreted as intelligence measure

**Scales of Independent Behavior**
R.H. Bruininks, R.W. Woodcock, R.F. Weatherman, and B.K. Hill; DLM Teaching Resources, Allen, TX

*Type* Adaptive behavior scale
*Ages* Birth to adult
*Uses* Fairly in-depth assessment of adaptive behavior
*Psychometric properties* Reliability and validity generally adequate for this type of instrument; standardization is good
*Note* Generally viewed as a very adequate measure of adaptive behavior

**Sequential Assessment of Mathematics Inventories**
F.K. Reisman; The Psychological Corporation, San Antonio, TX

*Type* Academic achievement (mathematics)
*Ages* Kindergarten to eighth grade
*Uses* One component of a comprehensive academic assessment
*Psychometric properties* Mathematic Language strand may have insufficient reliability for primary grade pupils; otherwise psychometric properties are good
*Note* Local schools should judge whether the test has adequate content validity for their uses

**Slingerland Screening Tests for Identifying Children with Specific Language Disability**
Beth Slingerland; Educators Publishing Service, Cambridge, MA

*Type* Special ability (information processing skills)
*Ages* Kindergarten to sixth grade
*Uses* Learning disability screening
*Psychometric properties* No norms, some evidence of validity
*Note* Infrequently used by psychologists

**Slosson Intelligence Test for Children and Adults**
R.L. Slosson; Slosson Educational Publications, New York

*Type* Intelligence
*Ages* 1 month to 27 years
*Uses* Intellectual screening
*Psychometric properties* Content, norms, and research studies show test adequate for screening
*Note* At some ages, almost no nonverbal items; never to be used alone for important clinical decisions

**Southern California Sensory Integration Tests**
A. Jean Ayers; Western Psychological Services, Los Angeles
*Type* Special ability (sensory integration skills)
*Ages* 4–10 years
*Uses* Used primarily by occupational and physical therapists to diagnose underlying neurological problems thought to be associated with learning and perceptual problems
*Psychometric properties* Norm group fairly small and may be unrepresentative; some of the 17 subsets lack reliability; more validity evidence would strengthen
*Note* Greatest danger is overinterpreting small subtest differences and inferring neurological problems for which there is little evidence

**The Test of Early Reading Achievement**
D.K. Reid, W.P. Hresko, and D.D. Hammill; PRO-ED, Austin, TX
*Type* Academic achievement (reading)
*Ages* 3–7.11 years
*Uses* Assess emerging pre-reading skills and possible delays in young children
*Psychometric properties* Satisfactory norming, reliability and validity
*Note* Pre-reading items limited; may be more useful with children already possessing some skills

**Test of Written Language**
Donald D. Hammill and Stephen C. Larsen; PRO-ED, Austin, TX
*Type* Academic achievement (spelling, handwriting, and expressive skills)
*Ages* Third to twelfth grades
*Uses* Measure written language as part of a comprehensive evaluation
*Psychometric properties* Appears to have adequate reliability; some evidence of concurrent validity
*Note* Excellent because it requires actual writing far more than alternative tests

**Token Test for Children**

F.G. DiSimoni; DLM Teaching Resources, Allen, TX

*Type* Special ability (receptive language)

*Ages* 3–12 years, 5 months

*Uses* Supplemental measure as part of comprehensive evaluation and for language screening

*Psychometric properties* Limited standardization sample; marginal evidence of reliability and validity

*Note* Popular among speech-language pathologists

# Index